CW00953650

DUMBARTON OAKS
MEDIEVAL LIBRARY

Daniel Donoghue, General Editor

SONGS ABOUT WOMEN

ROMANOS THE MELODIST

DOML 83

Songs about Women

ROMANOS THE MELODIST

Edited and Translated by

THOMAS ARENTZEN

DUMBARTON OAKS
MEDIEVAL LIBRARY

HARVARD UNIVERSITY PRESS

CAMBRIDGE, MASSACHUSETTS

LONDON, ENGLAND

2024

First Printing

Library of Congress Cataloging-in-Publication Data

Names: Romanus, Melodus, Saint, active 6th century, author. | Arentzen,
   Thomas, 1976– editor, translator. | Romanus, Melodus, Saint, active 6th
   century. Kontakia. Selections (Arentzen) | Romanus, Melodus, Saint,
   active 6th century. Kontakia. Selections (Arentzen). English.

Title: Songs about women / Romanos the Melodist ; edited and translated
   by Thomas Arentzen.

Other titles: Dumbarton Oaks medieval library ; 83.

Description: Cambridge, Massachusetts : Harvard University Press, 2024. |
   Series: Dumbarton Oaks medieval library ; DOML 83 | Includes
   bibliographical references and index. | Facing-page translation with
   Greek on the versos and English on the rectos ; introduction and notes
   in English.

Identifiers: LCCN 2023035206 | ISBN 9780674290938 (cloth)

Subjects: LCSH: Mary, Blessed Virgin, Saint— In literature. | Christian
   poetry, Byzantine—Themes, motives. | Hymns, Greek—Themes,
   motives. | Women in the Bible. | Women in literature.

Classification: LCC BV467.5 .R625 2024 | DDC 264/.23—dc23/
   eng/20231206

LC record available at https://lccn.loc.gov/2023035206

Contents

Introduction   vii

ON FASTING (ADAM AND EVE)   2

ON ABRAHAM'S SACRIFICE   32

ON THE BLESSING OF JACOB   56

ON JOSEPH AND POTIPHAR'S WIFE   80

ON THE PROPHET ELIJAH   118

ON THE BEHEADING OF
THE FORERUNNER   154

ON THE TEN VIRGINS   178

ON THE HARLOT   218

ON THE WOMEN AT THE TOMB   238

ON THE SAMARITAN WOMAN   270

ON THE BLEEDING WOMAN   298

CONTENTS

ON THE NATIVITY OF THE THEOTOKOS   316

ON THE ANNUNCIATION   328

ON THE VIRGIN   352

ON THE NATIVITY
(MARY AND THE MAGI)   366

ON THE NATIVITY
(MARY WITH ADAM AND EVE)   392

ON THE WEDDING AT CANA   414

ON THE WAY TO GOLGOTHA   438

Abbreviations   461
Note on the Texts   463
Notes to the Texts   469
Notes to the Translations   477
Bibliography   529
Index   533

Introduction

Romanos the Melodist

During Emperor Anastasios I's reign (491–518), a young and ambitious man arrived in Constantinople. He called himself "the lowly one" (ὁ ταπεινός). Soon people in the city came to identify him in the same way.[1] He had gone to the capital to offer his musical and poetic talent. As the Christian Church was developing into the dominant religion in the Byzantine Roman Empire, it was in dire need of new songs.

The young man's Christian name was Romanos. Later generations have known him by the epithet ὁ μελῳδός (*melōdos*, "the melodious one" or "the singer"), for he was known as a composer and a performer of sweet songs. Early Christians used the same epithet to describe the biblical poet King David.[2] Nobody could match David's reputation as creator of religious hymns, but as the late antique religion called for an expanding repertoire, new poets started to challenge the psalmist's hegemony with novel genres. Romanos was one of them, and *melōdos*—most often translated in English as "the Melodist"—has clung to this early Byzantine poet-composer. He wrote dramatic songs for the emerging Christian rituals and festivals.

We do not know much about Romanos's biography. Based

on the limited source material, scholars think that he died in the early 560s and thus was born around the 480s. According to a legendary tenth-century source, he grew up in Emesa (modern Ḥomṣ, in Syria) and spent his youth in Berytus (Beirut), where he was ordained a deacon in the cathedral church of the Resurrection. He may have received his education in the same city.[3] Some contemporary poets, like Agathias, had juridical backgrounds, and a training at Berytus's school of law could explain Romanos's poetic use of legal imagery. Ecclesiastically, Berytus depended on Antioch, the epicenter of narrative theologizing. Although Romanos wrote in Greek, Syriac may well have been his first language, for his corpus suggests intimate knowledge of Syriac verse.[4] When he arrived in Constantinople, he settled in a complex known as *ta Kyrou*.

VERSIFYING AROUND *TA KYROU*

Ta Kyrou was a public church. It housed an intellectual environment dedicated to literature and poetry. The fifth-century urban prefect Kyros of Panopolis, who was also a famous poet, had founded the church, and it provided a "venue for the devotions of high-status, learned laymen," under the protection of the Virgin.[5] The Marian shrine, at the current site of the Kalenderhane Mosque, was later called Kyriotissa. For centuries Byzantine literati found inspiration on its grounds, and a confraternity formed around the church. This place came to foster Romanos's poetic vocation.

The Melodist may have been learned, but he was not poetically at home in the classicizing Greek culture embraced by other important Byzantine poets; he wrote in a more popular style than, say, John Geometres (tenth century), who was to enroll in the *ta Kyrou* confraternity centuries later.[6] Despite the occasional inclusion of rare words or poetic constructions, Romanos chiefly drew from everyday language, employing a relatively accessible diction and straightforward syntax. In a style inspired by early Christian preaching and storytelling, he aimed for a broader audience.[7] It would be a mistake, however, to think that the comparative simplicity of form made his poetry unsophisticated. On the contrary, advanced and complex storytelling in a modest and elegant guise distinguishes Romanos's hymns. As so much ancient literature, his words generously echo other stories—not least biblical passages and narratives from early Christian literature—retelling familiar tales, recharacterizing old types, or redramatizing known events. Most of his songs include dramatic dialogues or monologues woven with imagery from ordinary life. Puns and punch lines go hand in hand. Wordplay, irony, rhyming effects, and poetic ambiguities drive his epic storytelling.[8] He sought to engage the whole human register of his listeners by evoking deeply corporeal affects and emotions.[9]

Romanos's verses inscribed themselves in the literary canon of Byzantine religious culture. The enigmatic twelfth-century cento *Christos paschon* consists of quotes, mostly from Euripides, but occasionally also from Romanos. Later poets enthusiastically praised his creative virtuosity and enlisted him in their poetic pantheon. Michael Psellos (1018–ca. 1081) begged the Virgin Mary to grant him an inspiration comparable to the one she had once bestowed upon Romanos:

To Romanos, Lady, your worshipper of old,
you gave a written document to eat;
now fill my cup, O Virgin, to the brim
with the sweet vintage drafts of wisdom.[10]

Psellos's epigram refers to a famous legend about the young poet: one Christmas night, the Mother of God appeared to Romanos and offered him a scroll to eat. Having swallowed it, he brimmed with song, and his Christmas hymn *On the Nativity (Mary and the Magi)* flowed from his lips. Romanos's inspiration, the legend thus claimed, came from heaven, from the most holy Virgin herself.[11]

Once a singer of praises, Romanos himself became an object of sung praise in the Middle Byzantine period.[12] In a short epigram dedicated to Saint Romanos the Melodist, John Geometres wrote:

The fellow chorister of the angels in heaven,
sings the heavenly melodies from the earth as well.[13]

Romanos's melodies may have been angelic and heavenly, as Geometres suggests, but the lyrics told stories that smelled of earth and soil. His dramas are played out in the earthly or subterranean realms. If angels appear, it is because they have strayed into the human world. And were we to call Romanos a theologian, it would have to be a theology of dialogue, a theology of friction, a theology of flesh. With plots and characters, he interpreted divine action in the world, creating lively dramas staged in the audience's imagination, rather than in theaters. As opposed to epigrams, Romanos's pieces were long, strophic songs featuring both didactic and dramatic elements. Future generations were to call them *kontakia*.

Romanos's songs were ritual songs, and he primarily performed them at night, when all visual impressions were dimmed, making the acoustic experience even more intense. People flocked to night vigils *(pannychis)* in late antique Constantinople,[14] where, along with Bible stories and psalms, they might hear stunning poetry, sung in a dramatic way by a professional performer. In one piece, which envisions itself as an instrument of torture for demons, Romanos simultaneously describes and directs the congregation:

> With love of Christ, the faithful people
> have gathered to keep vigil with psalms and songs;
> they hunger for hymns to God.
> So, now that David's psalter has been sung
> and we've been delighted by orderly reading of
>   scriptures,
> let's sing Christ's praises and castigate our enemies![15]

Hymn singing accompanied psalms and scripture reading as the faithful assembled after dusk. And Romanos's compositions featured something both psalter and Bible lacked: an engaging refrain that transformed listeners into singers. This important device flourished in religious song during late antiquity. Romanos brought it to perfection, integrating the refrain words into the narrative of the song; thus he gave the words new gravity, and even new meaning, each time they recurred. So important was the refrain to the Byzantine appreciation for Romanos's legacy that the tenth-century *Souda* encyclopedia defined the word ἀνακλώμενον, "refrain," by citing his works.[16] Refrains enhanced audience participation and made congregations sing.[17]

A century after the *ta Kyrou* church had lost its first great master, there was, in the nearby Oxeia quarter of Constantinople, "a certain man who from tender age used to attend the all-night vigils of the shrine of the Forerunner and who sang the hymns of the lowly Romanos among the saints."[18] Where groups of sick people had gathered to wait for Saint Artemios's nocturnal healing, a cantor sang to them or led them in song. The *Miracles of Saint Artemios* suggests that this singer spent most of his life at the shrine performing these hymns, dressed in fine garments, as part of the "society of all-night celebrants."[19] Romanos made up the bulk of his repertoire. Both the church in *ta Kyrou* and the one in Oxeia, then, housed confraternities that performed kontakia.[20]

While Romanos composed most of the melodies himself, in some form of syllabic style, the musical details of his kontakia are largely unknown to us.[21] What we do know is that later kontakion poets recycled his melodies. No fewer than a hundred of the approximately 740 preserved kontakia from the Byzantine era are written to the tune of his famous *On the Nativity (Mary and the Magi)*.[22]

Poets created kontakia before Romanos and for centuries after. Old and new kontakia were eventually collected in *kontakaria*. These collections remain our most important sources for Romanos's poetry. They organize the kontakia (with very few exceptions) according to the liturgical calendar as it had developed by the Middle Byzantine period. In the sixth century, however, the use of the hymns was not exclusively liturgical.[23] Some of Romanos's songs were composed for unique occasions and rites of passage. *On the Newly Baptized* addresses neophytes, whereas *On Earthquakes and Fires* treats the disasters that struck Constantinople during Justinian's reign, including the Nika riots. One poet wrote a kontakion for the second inauguration of Hagia Sophia in 562. Other early poets composed kontakia for the sick and for the dead. Although modern readers may be prone to consider the kontakion a strictly liturgical genre, written for and performed in church services, these songs served broader purposes in their earliest period. And in the Palae-ologan period, Byzantine emperors would include Roma-nos's *On the Nativity (Mary and the Magi)*—performed by singers from Hagia Sophia and the Church of the Apos-tles—in their palace celebrations.[24] No sources state explic-itly that kontakia were sung during the long religious pro-cessions that were so popular in the imperial city, but we know that other hymns were. It is not difficult to imag-ine that the Melodist's songs, with their engaging refrains, might also have filled the processional air.

Not long after his death, Romanos was considered a saint, and he is still commemorated in the Byzantine rite on Octo-ber 1. One anonymous kontakion, perhaps penned in the *ta Kyrou* district, is written for the celebration of the saintly poet himself. It lauds him as a banquet of fruit to which ev-eryone is welcome, a palm tree that never ceases yielding the dates of sweet song.[25] Yet the hymn also tells us some-thing more puzzling, that Romanos was of the "Hebrew people."[26] Based on these two words, Paul Maas suggested that the Melodist was a converted Jew.[27] No scholarly agree-ment has been reached regarding this issue, but another possibility is that the expression simply points toward Ro-manos's Syrian origin. One may note—although it neither rules out nor proves a Jewish background—that his kon-takia occasionally employ disagreeable and deeply prob-lematic anti-Judaic tropes. Like other groups beyond Byzan-tine orthodoxy, the Jews hardly escape the realm of straw men in his works.[28] Not every aspect of Romanos's writing is worth celebrating.

INTRODUCTION

The Afterlife of the Kontakia

In the centuries after Romanos, kontakion composition flourished in the capital—in the old *ta Kyrou* complex, but also in monasteries like Stoudios. Many wrote pseudepigraphically under the ancient master's name, and the genre remained popular for decades to come, even beyond the capital.[29] Meanwhile, another liturgical rite, a new way of organizing the Christian rituals, developed in Constantinople alongside the old one. These ritual forms, which emerged from Jerusalem, eventually replaced local Constantinopolitan customs. The Palestinian rite came with new religious sensibilities, other manners of singing, and different hymn genres. One such hymn was the *kanon*. For reasons not entirely clear to scholars, the Constantinopolitan churches following the new rite began to sing the prelude and the first stanzas of the kontakia between the sixth and the seventh odes of these kanons, thus including parts of the traditional Constantinopolitan hymns in the morning service *(orthros)* of the new rite.[30] This process secured a long liturgical life for many kontakia, while it gradually threw others into oblivion. And the truncation obscured the narrative and dramatic character of the old hymns. Even in kontakaria, some hymns are transmitted in radically abbreviated versions. The integration of the kontakion genre into the new daily office contributed to a liturgification through which a kontakion came to be thought of as just another short liturgical hymn of a more lyrical form; in the current Byzantine rite the word "kontakion" signifies only the short prelude. As the significance of Constantinople as a Christian liturgical center waned with the Latin conquest in 1204, and finally with the Ottoman one in 1453, the role of the original cathedral rite also waned, and with it the performance of full kontakia.

The *akathistos* hymns represent an exception to this rule. They follow the pattern of the late antique *Akathistos to the Mother of God* and might be called a subgenre of the kontakion. This form has survived, or rather, has been revived, as occasional religious songs still composed and used, not least in Ukraine and Russia.[31]

In the nineteenth century, Jean-Baptiste-François Pitra and later Karl Krumbacher started editing Romanos's hymns. Paul Maas continued the work of establishing a critical text of Romanos's corpus, and Constantine A. Trypanis completed Maas's critical edition *Sancti Romani Melodi cantica* (*Cantica genuina:* Oxford, 1963; *Cantica dubia:* Berlin, 1970). Their edition was immediately followed by José Grosdidier de Matons's French edition in the Sources Chrétiennes series (Paris, 1964–1981) and his monograph *Romanos le Mélode et les origines de la poésie religieuse à Byzance* (Paris, 1977). A renewed fascination with the full kontakion form, which had been almost forgotten for more than half a millennium, bloomed as modern editions became readily available. Romanos was hailed as "Byzantium's Pindar," and his works as "masterpieces of world literature."[32] The twentieth-century poet Odysseas Elytis identified with his sixth-century counterpart and said in his Nobel Lecture (December 8, 1979):

I followed the example of Pindar or of the Byzantine Romanos Melodos who, in each of their odes or canticles, invented a new mode for each occasion. I saw that the determined repetition, at intervals, of certain elements of versification effectively gave to my work that multifaceted and symmetrical substance which was my plan.[33]

As a result of the editors' philological work, the twentieth century developed a newfound interest in various aspects of Romanos's kontakia, from poetics to politics, an interest that has abided into the twenty-first.

The Poetic Form

From the earliest fifth-century experiments, kontakia have included a prelude (προοίμιον or κουκούλιον). This introductory strophe is usually exceptionally tight and elegant. Preceding the other kontakion stanzas (οἶκοι), the prelude presents the refrain and the broader thematic content. Some kontakia come with several preludes, which performers would presumably choose between. The prelude always features a different metrical configuration than the regular stanzas and was sung to a different melody. In the kontakaria, the preludes stand out graphically, and one may assume that they were performed in a more elevated way than the stanzas.[34]

The Melodist signed his songs in acrostics. The initial letters of all the stanzas might read, for instance, "A hymn by the lowly Romanos." This practice allows us to see the various terminology the poet himself used, quite interchangeably it seems, for his poetic forms; the acrostics mention "hymn" (ὕμνος), "praise" (αἶνος), "song" (ᾠδή), "psalm" (ψαλμός), "verses" (ἔπος or ἔπη), and "creation, poetic work" (ποίημα). Despite the confusing diversity, the common denominator is poetry or singing.[35] Kontakia functioned as songs with communal refrains, and the manuscripts assume that they are sung.

Regular end rhyme did not catch on in Greek-speaking Constantinople. Yannai—a Galilean contemporary of Romanos's who wrote Jewish liturgical poetry (*piyyutim*) in Hebrew—started to introduce such rhymes, but Romanos did not follow his lead. Still, he worked zealously with aural effects: occasional rhyme, assonance, and alliteration. Rhythm, moreover, plays a significant role in the structuring of his songs. The variation in syllable quantity, which ancient poetry had used for its prosody, was replaced by syllable quality (stress) in accord with Byzantine vernacular, and the emerging kontakion poetry adopted stress regulation to convey the rhythm (as does modern English verse). Thus the metrics connected the songs to the spoken *koinē* language rather than to the literary style of bygone years. Romanos built on accentual verse forms, such as the Syriac *madrashe* and the earlier Greek kontakia. The Syriac genres featured a somewhat looser meter, which counted the number of syllables but disregarded the regulated play between stressed and unstressed syllables. Whereas early kontakia employed relatively simple stress regulation, Romanos introduced a strict regimen of stressed and unstressed syllables within a complex structure of poetic *kola*.

Kola are the metrical units that make up the kontakion stanzas. Each kolon typically consists of seven or eight syllables. One, two, or sometimes three of these are stressed, depending on what the meter requires, and various kolon types are assembled within one stanza to create complex rhythmic effects. Each stanza (οἶκος) of a particular song (apart from the prelude) follows the pattern of the first stanza;[36] the stanzas are in other words metrically identical and sung to the same melody.[37]

The most common of all prelude patterns, the one from *On the Nativity (Mary and the Magi),* may serve as an example of the metrical complexity:[38]

```
U U — U   — U U      U U U —   U U — U
U U — U   — U U      U U U —   U U — U
— U U   U U U — U      U U U — U
— U U   U U U — U      U U U — U
U U — U      U U — U
U — U — U      U U U — U U —
```

Two different kola constitute the first line, and two kola identical to these appear in the next. Both rhythm and content in these two lines are parallel. The same is true for the shorter lines 3 and 4. The even shorter fifth line builds up to the crescendo of the refrain in the sixth line.

Some refrains are either remarkably short or include a new phrase in every stanza. The latter would make little sense as a refrain repeated by an audience or congregation—especially if, as the *Souda* says, the refrain is "that which is being repeated." I call these instances split refrains; only the last kolon is repeated verbatim, while the penultimate kolon, or clause, features some variation. The soloist may have sung the penultimate, cuing the congregation's choral participation in the last one.

Every kontakion stanza is stretched out between an initial that forms part of the acrostic and a repeated refrain; thus a stanza simultaneously constitutes a complete unit and a fragment of the larger whole. But the whole itself is hardly complete, for there is something episodic and sometimes decentered about these sung stories, even as kolon follows upon kolon. Episodes and stanzas are not always tightly connected nor follow a clear line; inner monologues or imagined speeches seamlessly turn into spoken dialogues, or vice versa, and the narrative flow may culminate in a circle or a spiral, often as part of an interpretational move, a meditational digression spurred by a particular word or phrase, so that the directness of the sung story is broken up for a moment by complex rhetorical ponderings of a more ornate kind, yielding a slowing of the narrative pace. Such dynamics make the songs both simple and elusive at the same time.[39]

Romanos in Translation

The poetry of Romanos's songs emerged from encounters between languages. In Constantinople, as in other late antique metropolises, various tongues filled the streets and marketplaces. The kontakion genre came about at the convergence between the Greek-speaking world and Syriac poetry. As already mentioned, Syriac may have been the language in which Romanos first encountered religious poetry.[40] A good century earlier, Augustine of Hippo had explained that use of hymns in the Church of Milan followed the practices of eastern Churches.[41] The earliest witness we have to Romanos's poetry is in papyri and a parchment fragment from Egypt.[42] Songs and poetry traveled fast and widely. Like translations, they defied borders. Perhaps the songs presented in this volume derive some of their creative energy from the culturally rich world in which the poet found himself. Perhaps his poetry, to rephrase an old definition, is that which appears from translation.[43]

Translation is never neutral territory; a translation conveys the translator's interpretation of the original text. Translations are also done for various purposes. One might translate Romanos's songs for liturgical use, for theological inquiries, or one could create a word-by-word rendering for the student of Greek. I follow none of these strategies. My translations treat the songs as literary works. To the best of my limited abilities, I have wanted to create an English text that transmits some of the poetic freshness, playfulness, and directness that must have contributed to these songs' appeal and the singer's fame.

This ambition requires attention to rhythm, something Romanos's translators have traditionally eschewed. I have not attempted to imitate the intricate metrics of the kontakia; this would restrict the English word choice too much, and, since the melodies are not preserved, we do not know exactly how the accents played with the rhythm of the music. That said, I have tried to render the songs in rhythmical verses, for rhythm and other sonic effects are integral to Romanos's poetry and mark his poetry as song. Rhythmic patterns force poets (as well as translators) into less colloquial and mundane modes of expression some times, and the elegant balance between economic directness and labored artfulness is what gives air to the Melodist's poetics.

Romanos's storytelling explicitly, consciously, and confidently interacts with other forms of literature, cutting from and adding to well-known stories; it is a storytelling that reflects metafictionally and metaleptically on its own narration.[44] The basic plots of almost all the songs in this volume are known from the Bible; whole sentences from scripture and other early Christian sources are occasionally quoted, more or less verbatim. Some of Romanos's compositions might be described as a rewriting of the Bible. Yet what the poet achieves is not a versified Bible as such, but a creative, rich retelling of common religious stories, independent literary expressions of the Christian story world.

I have highlighted the biblical and ritual threads by approximating existing English translations of liturgical and scriptural texts, rather than footnoting all allusions to biblical passages. Such extensive referencing, found in some editions and translations, might give the impression that Romanos has produced a scriptural cento or perhaps a biblical commentary. In spite of the biblical connection, the overall storytelling of these kontakia is original—in tone, in narrative layout, and in interpretation of events. Assembling scriptural and liturgical threads, as well as phrases from older works of Christian literature, and even Homer, the songs add color to their own weave. This resonance with other texts seldom serves to interpret those other texts, however; it emerges from a deeper intertextuality, dyeing the sixth-century poetry in sacred tones. To footnote individual instances would undercut the impression of almost unending reverberations.[45] I thus cite scriptural verses only in cases where a reference may clarify the meaning of a passage or provide context for an otherwise odd translation choice. Biblical references in the Notes to the Translations are to the Septuagint, with the Masoretic numbers (where those differ) in parentheses.

THE SONGS IN THIS BOOK

This volume contains approximately a third of the corpus that MaTr and GdM count as genuine. I have selected songs that include female characters as protagonists, antagonists, or important supporting characters.

Scholars and other modern readers ask questions about gender dynamics in history, and Romanos's kontakia provide a valuable source for such inquiries. His songs offer intriguing perspectives on gendered ideas and ideals in early Christian Byzantium. They also contain, in Rudolph Schork's words, "an impressive parade of heroic—or, better, 'epic' in their piety and their passion—women," and it is worth recognizing their broad register of female characters, often presented as models for Christian life.[46] Admittedly, this striking breadth—from villains to heroines, leaders to followers, saints to sinners, from the exceptionally towering Mother of God to the licentiously lustful Potiphar's wife —may grant us limited insights into the mundane realities of women's lives in Constantinople. The songs represent a male gaze, and literary women rarely behave like physical women anyway.[47] Nevertheless, many of the characters are portrayed with a remarkable psychological depth, combining outstanding boldness with inner struggles of doubt and desires and the sense of being pulled in various directions.[48] With determined faith or faithless determination, bursting with love or wanting in ardor, these women embody the complexities of Christian life. In one kontakion, a torn mother clutches her martyred son in her arms, and the poet exclaims: "The woman could be imagined as a second womb in birth pangs, screaming in torment: . . . 'See how my arms imitate the uterus and how in their old age they sweat!'"[49] Lamentation was a typical task for both literary and corporeal women, but not all turned into new wombs, their twisted maternal flesh transformed into living sources of renewal in their tortured throes. Rebirth is in the details. Romanos's women run freely in and out of stereotype repositories. This mother is birthing her son anew, into his heavenly life.

Sung poetry is intrinsically tied to the communal and ritual life of human societies. What were cultic initiations, wars, or weddings without a breath of song? The kontakion became an important medium for telling stories and interpreting the world of the audience, for expressing joy and remorse, fear and hope, but also for conveying ideology, teaching morals, and crafting a sense of community. Romanos's kontakia, like the *madrashe* of the Syriac-speaking world—some of them in fact performed by women[50]—or the *piyyutim* of the Aramaic and Hebrew realms, emerged in late antiquity as means for modeling religious communities while celebrating or commemorating events in song. They addressed that period's devotional sentiments and existential experiences, that culture's worldviews and values in ritualized settings, and may communicate some of this to us.

Several phenomena that a modern Western mind might interpret as abstracts—time, chastity, fasting—Romanos may portray as anthropomorphic, usually female, presences.[51] While their personal appearance becomes unambiguously evident in visual arts of the late antique period, literature renders it more equivocal, since Greek uses the same pronouns whether they refer to animate or inanimate nouns. In instances where I take Romanos to speak of "Chastity" (Ἁγνεία), for instance, as a person, I have capitalized the word and used the personal pronoun "she" (chastity being female in Greek).

The first four songs in this collection relate stories known from the book of Genesis. The female characters are not protagonists, but Romanos gives them important roles in the ancient narratives of temptation and envy, faithfulness and sacrifice. The middle Byzantine manuscripts assign all these songs to the season of fasting during Lent and Holy Week.

Two kontakia feature prophetic male protagonists but have important female characters. When God sends the zealous prophet Elijah to live with a gentile widow in Zarephath, she is able to awaken his empathy. Herodias and her daughter, however, are instrumental in the beheading of John the Baptist. The manuscripts assign these kontakia to fixed dates devoted to these male saints, but the texts do not refer to a celebration.

The next five hymns relate stories originating from the Christian gospels. They have female protagonists, and the narratives convey various corporeal encounters with Christ. According to the manuscripts, all these songs are to be sung during Holy Week and Easter.

The final section contains songs about the Virgin Mary, or Theotokos (God-bearer, Mother of God) as she is often called in Byzantine Christianity. They seem to be written for Marian feast days or other important celebrations throughout the year.

There are three people without whose impact this volume would not have appeared: Alice-Mary Talbot, who suggested I should undertake the task, Erin Galgay Walsh, who at an early stage enthusiastically cotranslated the lion's share of the kontakia with me, and Derek Krueger, who has keenly read and discussed all my translations. Both Walsh and Krueger have influenced the volume deeply, and their contributions have been invaluable. The same is true for Alexander Alexakis's and Richard Greenfield's priceless editorial comments and support. I would also like to thank Annemarie Weyl Carr, Joshua Robinson, and Christos Simelidis, with whom I shared exciting translation seminars in the Dumbarton Oaks Library, as well as Nicole Eddy, Uffe Holmsgaard Eriksen, Susan Ashbrook Harvey, Christian Høgel, Ingela Nilsson, and David Westberg for helpful discussions and critical comments. I am grateful to Kari Grødum, Nelly Maragkou, and the staff at Metochi Study Centre (Lesbos), who granted peaceful writing weeks in October 2021, and the Bergman Estate on Fårö, which offered the chance to work on these translations in the pregnant silence of Ingmar Bergman's home in May 2022.

The book is dedicated to my beloved children Hedvig, Paul Anders, and Olav Gabriel, who are constantly translating my days into poetry.

Notes

1 For the use of ὁ ταπεινός by Romanos's contemporaries (seventh century), see *Miracles of Saint Artemios* 18, ed. Virgil S. Crisafulli and John W. Nesbitt, *The Miracles of St. Artemios: A Collection of Miracle Stories by an Anonymous Author of Seventh-Century Byzantium* (Leiden, 1997). Georgia Frank suggests that there is a Marian allusion in the epithet, since in the Magnificat (Luke 1:48) Mary sings of her "lowliness"; Georgia Frank, "Singing Mary: The Annunciation and Nativity in Romanos the Melode," in *The Reception of the Mother of God in Byzantium: Marian Narratives in Texts and Images,* ed. Thomas Arentzen and Mary B. Cunningham (Cambridge,

2019), 170–79, at 171. For transgressive gendering of poetic activity in the sixth century, see Steven D. Smith, *Greek Epigram and Byzantine Culture: Gender, Desire, and Denial in the Age of Justinian* (Cambridge, 2019), 25–30.

2 Eusebius of Caesarea writes: "The melodious one says, 'Yonder is the sea [Psalms 104:25].'" Eusebius, *Commentary on the Psalms* (PG 23:1285); my translation. The term eventually becomes a technical term for a poet-composer in Byzantium.

3 For a study and collection of the sources relevant to Romanos's life and career, see José Grosdidier de Matons, *Romanos le Mélode et les origines de la poésie religieuse à Byzance* (Paris, 1977), 159–98, and a summary in Sarah Gador-Whyte, *Theology and Poetry in Early Byzantium: The Kontakia of Romanos the Melodist* (Cambridge, 2017), 7–9. Our information about Romanos's biography stems almost exclusively from the content of his songs and from hagiographical sources postdating his life by at least four centuries.

4 Sebastian P. Brock, "Greek and Syriac in Late Antique Syria," in *Literacy and Power in the Ancient World,* ed. A. K. Bowman and G. Woolf (Cambridge, 1994), 149–60, at 154; for a broader study of interaction, see Sebastian P. Brock, "From Ephrem to Romanos," *Studia Patristica* 20 (1987): 139–51. For more detailed examples, see Manolis Papoutsakis, "The Making of a Syriac Fable: From Ephrem to Romanos," *Le Muséon* 120 (2007): 29–75, and William L. Petersen, *The Diatessaron and Ephrem Syrus as Sources of Romanos the Melodist,* Corpus Scriptorum Christianorum Orientalium 475 (Louvain, 1985).

5 Paul Magdalino, "The Liturgical Poetics of an Elite Religious Confraternity," in *Reading in the Byzantine Empire and Beyond,* ed. T. Shawcross and I. Toth (Cambridge, 2018), 116–32, at 130.

6 Magdalino, "The Liturgical Poetics." For Geometres's style, see John Geometres, *Life of the Virgin Mary,* ed. and trans. Maximos Constas and Christos Simelidis, Dumbarton Oaks Medieval Library 77 (Cambridge, MA, 2023). For a derisive attitude toward ancient Greek culture in Romanos's works, see his *On Pentecost* 17, which does not need to be taken as an expression of personal distaste.

7 K. Mitsakis, *The Language of Romanos the Melodist* (Munich, 1967), especially 171–72.

8 Regarding puns, see Mitsakis, *The Language of Romanos,* 168; regarding irony and performance, see Herbert Hunger, "Romanos Melodos, Dichter,

Prediger, Rhetor—und sein Publikum," *Jahrbuch der Österreichischen Byzantinistik* 34 (1984): 15–42.

9 Derek Krueger, *Liturgical Subjects: Christian Ritual, Biblical Narrative, and the Formation of the Self in Byzantium* (Philadelphia, 2014), 28–66; Andrew Mellas, *Liturgy and the Emotions in Byzantium: Compunction and Hymnody* (Cambridge, 2020), 71–112.

10 Greek text ed. Grosdidier de Matons, *Romanos et les origines,* 190; trans. Magdalino, "The Liturgical Poetics," 126. Magdalino is not convinced that Psellos is the author.

11 Thomas Arentzen, *The Virgin in Song: Mary and the Poetry of Romanos the Melodist* (Philadelphia, 2017), especially 1–6.

12 An earlier poem, attributed variously to a certain Germanos or Anatolios, praises Romanos's poetry as a beautiful and angelic guide toward salvation:

> As the firstfruits of beauty,
> salvation's introduction,
> you appeared, our father Romanos.
> You composed angelic hymnody
> and showed your ways to be God-pleasing.

Sticheron on Saint Romanos, ed. Karl Krumbacher, in *Geschichte der byzantinischen Litteratur: Von Justinian bis zum Ende des oströmischen Reiches (527–1453),* 2nd ed. (Munich, 1897), 668 (my translation).

13 John Geometres, *On Saint Romanos the Melodist* (iambic poem 291), ed. Krumbacher, in *Geschichte,* 668; trans. Christos Simelidis, "Two *Lives of the Virgin:* John Geometres, Euthymios the Athonite, and Maximos the Confessor," *Dumbarton Oaks Papers* 74 (2020): 125–59, at 136n85.

14 Georgia Frank, "Romanos and the Night Vigil in the Sixth Century," in *Byzantine Christianity,* ed. Derek Krueger (Minneapolis, 2006), 59–78; Alexander Lingas, "The Liturgical Place of the Kontakion in Constantinople," in *Liturgy, Architecture and Art of the Byzantine World: Papers of the XVIII International Byzantine Congress (Moscow, 8–15 August 1991) and Other Essays Dedicated to the Memory of Fr. John Meyendorff,* ed. C. C. Akentiev (Saint Petersburg, 1995), 50–57.

15 Romanos, *On the Man Possessed by the Legion of Demons* 1.1–6.

16 "That which is being repeated. As [exemplified] in the honorable

Romanos the Melodist"; English translation by W. Hutton; trans. and Greek text under ἀνακλώμενον at *The Suda On Line*, ed. David White-head, updated June 28, 2015, https://www.cs.uky.edu/-raphael/sol/sol-html/index.html. The more common word for these refrains is ἐφύμνιον.

17 Thomas Arentzen, "Voices Interwoven: Refrains and Vocal Participation in the Kontakia," *Jahrbuch der Österreichischen Byzantinistik* 66 (2016): 1–10; Ophir Münz-Manor and Thomas Arentzen, "Soundscapes of Salvation: Refrains in Christian and Jewish Liturgical Poetry," *Studies in Late Antiquity* 3 (2019): 36–55.

18 *Miracles of Saint Artemios* 18; the translation (slightly modified) is from Crisafulli and Nesbitt, *The Miracles of St. Artemios*, 115–17, at 115.

19 *Miracles of Saint Artemios* 18, trans. Crisafulli and Nesbitt, p. 117. See also Derek Krueger, "The Ninth-Century Kontakarion as Evidence for Festive Practice and the Liturgical Calendar in Sixth- and Seventh-Century Constantinople," in *Towards the Prehistory of the Byzantine Liturgical Year: Festal Homilies and Festal Liturgies in Late Antique Constantinople,* ed. Stefanos Alexopoulos and Harald Buchinger (Münster, forthcoming).

20 Romanos wrote a song to celebrate those who entered a communal life of religious singing. The hymn entitled *On Life in the Monastery* does not describe a particularly ascetic monasticism but an unmarried life devoted to hymns and psalms.

21 Regarding the melodies, however, see Jørgen Raasted, "Zum Melodie des Kontakions Ἡ παρθένος σήμερον," *Cahiers de l'Institut du Moyen-Âge Grec et Latin* 59 (1989): 233–46.

22 Krueger, "The Ninth-Century Kontakarion."

23 While the festal ascription for each work is found in the notes of this book, readers should keep in mind that these designations need not indicate practices in Romanos's own time.

24 Pseudo-Kodinos, *De Officiis,* ed. and trans. Ruth Macrides, J. A. Munitiz, and Dimiter Angelov, *Pseudo-Kodinos and the Constantinopolitan Court: Offices and Ceremonies* (Farnham, Surrey, 2013), 154–55, trans. slightly modified: "After all those of the palace wish 'Many years!' according to their rank . . . the cantors also come and chant the 'Many years' and after this the kontakion 'The Virgin today gives birth to the unworldly one' [that is, *On the Nativity (Mary and the Magi)*] and again the 'Many years.'" See also Jean

B. Pitra, *Analecta sacra spicilegio Solesmensi parata* (Paris, 1876–1891), vol. 1, p. xxi. "Many years!" was (and remains) a common greeting of luck and also a very common song used for birthdays and the like.

25 *On Saint Romanos* 1, ed. Grosdidier de Matons, in *Romanos et les origines,* 168 (my translation):

> The righteous one flourished in the world like a date-palm,
> with the sweet fruit of song, which is eaten insatiably.
> And from his tongue, as the writing says,
> gushed honey and milk, the stuff that scripture suckles.
> He distributed teaching in abundance
> to all the hungry, a food of beauty;
> he possessed an inexhaustible table of grace.
> His sayings sustained not the body but the spirit.
> *Who will praise, with a mouth never silenced,*
> *the godly teaching of the God-orator?*

26 *On Saint Romanos* 2.3.

27 Paul Maas, "Die Chronologie der Hymnen des Romanos," *Byzantinische Zeitschrift* 15, no. 1 (1906): 1–44, at 31; he also takes the third stanza of the anonymous kontakion to mean that Romanos had a high position at the imperial court.

28 Regarding anti-Jewish language in Byzantine hymnography, see Bogdan G. Bucur, "Anti-Jewish Rhetoric in Byzantine Hymnography: Exegetical and Theological Contextualization," *St Vladimir's Theological Quarterly* 61 (2017): 39–60, and George E. Demacopoulos, *Christian Hymns of Violence before and after Herakleios* (forthcoming).

29 Lingas, "The Liturgical Place"; Mary B. Cunningham, "The Reception of Romanos in Middle Byzantine Homiletics and Hymnography," *Dumbarton Oaks Papers* 62 (2008): 251–60.

30 For the liturgical process, see Stig S. Frøyshov, "The Early History of the Hagiopolitan Daily Office in Constantinople: New Perspectives on the Formative Period of the Byzantine Rite," *Dumbarton Oaks Papers* 74 (2020): 1–32.

31 The eighteenth century saw a renewal of *akathistos* composition, especially in Ukraine. See Aleksei Popov, *Pravoslavnye russkie akafisty, izdannye s*

blagosloveniia Sviateishago Sinoda (Kazan, 1903); Per-Arne Bodin, *Eternity and Time: Studies in Russian Literature and the Orthodox Tradition* (Stockholm, 2007), 95–109; Vera Shevzov, "Between 'Popular' and 'Official': *Akafisty* Hymns and Marian Icons in Late Imperial Russia," in *Letters from Heaven: Popular Religion in Russia and Ukraine,* ed. John-Paul Himka and Andriy Zayarnyuk (Toronto, 2016), 251–78.

32 Eva Catafygiotu Topping, "On Earthquakes and Fires: Romanos' Encomium to Justinian," *Byzantinische Zeitschrift* 71, no. 1 (1978): 22–35, at 22; *The Oxford Dictionary of the Christian Church,* ed. F. L. Cross and E. A. Livingstone (Oxford, 2005), under "Romanos, St (*fl. c.* 540)."

33 Available online at https://www.nobelprize.org/prizes/literature/1979/elytis/lecture/.

34 Thomas Arentzen and Derek Krueger, "Romanos in Manuscript: Some Observations on the Patmos Kontakarion," in *Proceedings of the 23rd International Congress of Byzantine Studies, Belgrade, 22–27 August 2016: Round Tables,* ed. Bojana Krsmanović and Ljubomir Milanović (Belgrade, 2016), 648–54.

35 Some scholars have emphasized the kontakia's homiletic aspects—to the degree that *Encyclopaedia Britannica* now defines the word "kontakion" as "a poetic homily, or sermon"; *Encyclopaedia Britannica,* under "Kontakion," last modified July 20, 1998, https://academic.eb.com. This terminology seems to originate with Paul Maas; see his "Das Kontakion," *Byzantinische Zeitschrift* 19 (1910): 285–306 (throughout), and, for instance, MaTr, p. xi.) Although rhetoric and accentual poetry were related fields in late antiquity, and homiletic aspects certainly do show up in Romanos's kontakia, other aspects include drama, narrative, and acclamation. We might also (and perhaps more adequately) label the kontakia "sung dramas" or "epic poetry."

36 In GdM, the pattern stanza is called a *heirmos,* while MaTr reserves this term for the kanon genre.

37 Grosdidier de Matons, *Romanos et les origines,* 119–56. On Romanos in the context of the emerging accentual metrics, see Marc D. Lauxtermann, *The Spring of Rhythm: An Essay on the Political Verse and Other Byzantine Meters* (Vienna, 1999).

38 A stressed syllable is represented by a line (—) and an unstressed by a breve (∪); GdM, vol. 2, p. 46.

39 For more on Romanos's compositional techniques, see Arentzen, *The Virgin in Song,* 14–16.

40 For possible Semitisms in Romanos's kontakia, see MaTr, p. xvi, n. 1; Mitsakis, *The Language of Romanos,* 2–3.

41 Augustine, *Confessions* 9.7.

42 For descriptions, see Krueger, "The Ninth-Century Kontakarion."

43 That poetry is what gets lost in translation is Robert Frost's oft-quoted definition in Cleanth Brooks and Robert Penn Warren, *Conversations on the Craft of Poetry* (New York, 1961), 7.

44 Uffe Holmsgaard Eriksen, "Dramatic Narratives and Recognition in the Kontakia of Romanos the Melodist," in *Storytelling in Byzantium: Narratological Approaches to Byzantine Texts and Images,* ed. Charis Messis, Margaret Mullett, and Ingela Nilsson (Uppsala, 2018), 91–109.

45 Regarding Byzantine reception and intertextuality, see Ingela Nilsson, "Imitation as Spoliation, Reception as Translation: The Art of Transforming Things in Byzantium," in "Spoliation as Translation: Medieval Worlds in the Eastern Mediterranean," ed. Ivana Jevtic and Ingela Nilsson, special issue, *Convivium* 8, supplementum 2 (2021): 20–37.

46 R. J. Schork, *Sacred Song from the Byzantine Pulpit: Romanos the Melodist* (Gainesville, FL, 1995), x.

47 For further reflections on female stock characters and other literary women, see Susan Ashbrook Harvey, *Song and Memory: Biblical Women in Syriac Tradition* (Milwaukee, 2010), 39–45, and Katharine Haynes, *Fashioning the Feminine in the Greek Novel* (London, 2003).

48 See Erin Galgay Walsh, "Sanctifying Boldness: New Testament Women in Narsai, Jacob of Serugh, and Romanos Melodos" (PhD diss., Duke University, 2019); for inner monologue, see Krueger, *Liturgical Subjects,* 44–59.

49 Romanos, *First Kontakion on the Forty Martyrs of Sebasteia* 18; this particular hymn is not included in this volume. It may possibly be pseudepigraphical.

50 Susan Ashbrook Harvey, "Revisiting the Daughters of the Covenant: Women's Choirs and Sacred Song in Ancient Syriac Christianity," *Hugoye* 8, no. 2 (2005): 125–49, and Susan Ashbrook Harvey, "Training the Women's Choir: Ascetic Practice and Liturgical Education in Late Antique Syriac Christianity," in *Wisdom on the Move: Late Antique Traditions in Multicultural Conversation; Essays in Honor of Samuel Rubenson,* ed. Susan Ashbrook Har-

vey, Thomas Arentzen, Henrik Rydell Johnsén, and Andreas Westergren
(Leiden, 2020), 203–23.

51 Damaskinos Olkinuora, "Personification in Byzantine Hymnography:
Kontakia and Canons," in *Personhood in the Byzantine Christian Tradition:
Early, Medieval, and Modern Perspectives,* ed. Alexis Torrance and Symeon
Paschalidis (Abingdon, UK, 2018), 80–99.

SONGS ABOUT WOMEN

Προοίμιον

Σχόλασον, ψυχή μου, ἐν μετανοίᾳ,
ἑνώθητι Χριστῷ κατὰ γνώμην,
βοῶσα ἐν στεναγμοῖς·
"Συγχώρησιν παράσχου μοι
τῶν δεινῶν μου πράξεων,
ἵνα λάβω παρὰ σοῦ, μόνε ἀγαθέ,
τὴν ἄφεσιν καὶ ζωὴν
  —τὴν αἰώνιον."

I

πρός· Τὸ ἰατρεῖον τῆς μετανοίας

Τῆς μακαρίας τυχεῖν ἐλπίδος   δι' ἔργων προσδοκῶμεν
                          καὶ πίστεως, ὅσοι
φυλάττομεν   τὰ τοῦ Κυρίου   καὶ Σωτῆρος διδάγματα·
διὰ τοῦτο τιμῶμεν καὶ στέργομεν
τὸ ἀγγέλοις τίμιον   τῆς νηστείας κατόρθωμα,
ὃ προφῆται τηρήσαντες   μέτοχοι γεγόνασι
τῶν χορῶν τῶν οὐρανίων   οἱ ἐπίγειοι·

ON FASTING (ADAM AND EVE)

in first mode

Prelude

to its own melody

Devote yourself, my soul, to repentance;
join yourself to Christ in mind,
as you cry with sighs,
"Grant me pardon
for my dire deeds,
that I may receive from you, only good one,
forgiveness and life
    —*the eternal one.*"

I

to: The infirmary of repentance

We look for the attainment of blessed hope through works
    and faith,
as we observe the teachings of the Lord and Savior;
for this we honor and cherish
the angelically honored achievement of fasting.
Having kept it, earthly prophets have become members
of the heavenly choirs;

3

ὅπου γε ταύτης   τὴν ἐργασίαν
Χριστὸς οὐκ ἐπῃσχύνθη   ἐκτελέσαι,   ἑκὼν δὲ
                                                  ἐνήστευσεν,
ἡμῖν καθυπογράφων
διὰ ταύτης τὴν ζωὴν
    —τὴν αἰώνιον.

2

Ὅτι μεγάλοι ἐν ἔργοις ἦσαν   Μωσῆς καὶ Ἠλίας, οἱ
                                                  πύρινοι πύργοι,
γινώσκομεν,   ὅτι καὶ πρῶτοι   ἐν προφήταις
                                                  τυγχάνουσι·
πρὸς Θεὸν παρρησίαν ἐκέκτηντο,
ὅτιπερ ἐβούλοντο   προσιέναι καὶ δέεσθαι
καὶ αὐτῷ διαλέγεσθαι   πρόσωπον πρὸς πρόσωπον,
ὃ ὑπάρχει θαυμαστόν τε   καὶ παράδοξον.
Ὅμως καὶ οὕτως   πρὸς τὴν νηστείαν
κατέφευγον σπουδαίως,   διὰ ταύτης   αὐτῷ
                                                  προσαγόμενοι·
Νηστεία οὖν μετ’ ἔργων
ἀποδίδωσι ζωὴν
    —τὴν αἰώνιον.

nor was Christ ashamed
to perform this practice; he gladly fasted.
Through this he signed
our inscription in life
     —the eternal one.

2

We know that Moses and Elijah, those fiery towers, were
     mighty
in works, and they were the first among prophets.
They possessed a boldness before God,
to approach and implore him about whatever they wished
and with him to converse face-to-face,
something that is wondrous and astonishing.
Yet they still zealously took
refuge in fasting and thus drew near to him.
Fasting with works
yields life
     —the eternal one.

3

Ὑπὸ Νηστείας ὡς ὑπὸ ξίφους   οἱ δαίμονες πάντες
                                        ἐλαύνονται, ὅτι
οὐ φέρουσιν   οὐδ᾽ ἐξαρκοῦσι   πρὸς τὴν ταύτης
                                        τερπνότητα·
τρυφητὴν ἀγαπῶσι καὶ μέθυσον,
ἐὰν δὲ θεάσωνται   τῆς Νηστείας τὸ πρόσωπον,
οὔτε στῆναι ἰσχύουσι,   πόρρω δὲ ἐκτρέχουσιν·
ὡς Χριστὸς ἡμᾶς διδάσκει   ὁ Θεὸς ἡμῶν
λέγων· "Τὸ γένος   τὸ τῶν δαιμόνων
νηστείᾳ καὶ δεήσει   ἐκνικᾶται."   Διὸ δεδιδάγμεθα
ὡς δίδωσι Νηστεία
τοῖς ἀνθρώποις ζωὴν
      —τὴν αἰώνιον.

4

Τῆς Σωφροσύνης Ἁγνεία μήτηρ   ὑπάρχει, τῆς Νηστείας
                                        τὸ ἄχραντον κάλλος·
πηγάζει δὲ   φιλοσοφίαν   καὶ παρέχει τὸν στέφανον·
προξενεῖ δὲ ἡμῖν τὸν παράδεισον,
τὴν Πατρῴαν δίδωσιν   οἰκίαν τοῖς νηστεύουσιν,
ἧς ὁ Ἀδὰμ ἀπωλίσθησεν·   εἵλκυσε δὲ θάνατον,
ἀτιμάσας τῆς Νηστείας   τὸ ἀξίωμα·
ταύτης γὰρ τότε   καθυβρισθείσης,
Θεὸς ὁ πάντων Κτίστης   καὶ Δεσπότης   εὐθὺς
                                        ἠγανάκτησε·

6

3

By Fasting, as by a sword, all the demons are chased away;
        they cannot endure
her delight, nor can they withstand it.
They love the voluptuary and the drunkard,
but were they to glimpse the face of Fasting,
they'd have no strength to stand; they'd run
away, as Christ our God teaches us,
saying, "The race of demons is vanquished
by fasting and prayer." Thus we have been taught
that Fasting offers
humans life
        —*the eternal one.*

4

The undefiled beauty of Fasting is Purity, the mother of
        Self-Control.
She gushes with wisdom and offers the garland,
procures paradise for us,
grants to those fasting the house of the Father,
from which Adam slipped. He dragged death in,
dishonoring the dignity of Fasting.
When she was insulted, God, the Creator
and Master of all, was vexed at once,

τοῖς ταύτην δὲ τιμῶσιν
ἀποδίδωσι ζωὴν
    —*τὴν αἰώνιον.*

5

Αὐτὸς γάρ, ὡς μητρὶ φιλοστόργῳ,   Νηστείας ἐντολῇ ὁ
                          Φιλάνθρωπος   πρώην
παρέθετο   ὡς διδασκάλῳ   παραχθέντα τὸν ἄνθρωπον,
ἐν χερσὶν αὐτῆς παραδοὺς τὴν ζωὴν αὐτοῦ·
καὶ εἰ ταύτην ἔστερξε,   μετ' ἀγγέλων ηὐλίζετο·
ἀθετήσας δὲ εὕρετο   πόνους καὶ τὸν θάνατον,
ἀκανθῶν δὲ καὶ τριβόλων   τὴν τραχύτητα
καὶ ἐπιμόχθου   βίου τὴν θλῖψιν.
Εἰ δὲ ἐν παραδείσῳ   ἡ Νηστεία   ὠφέλιμος δείκνυται,
πόσῳ μᾶλλον ἐνταῦθα,
ἵνα σχῶμεν τὴν ζωὴν
    —*τὴν αἰώνιον;*

6

Παντὸς μὲν ξύλου κελεύει φαγεῖν   τὸν ἄνθρωπον Ἀδὰμ
                          τὸν πρωτόπλαστον τότε
ὁ Ὕψιστος   ἐν παραδείσῳ   θεὶς αὐτόν, καθὼς
                                  γέγραπται,
ἀλλ' ἑνὸς ξύλου βρῶσιν ἐκώλυσε·
καὶ αὐτὰ τὰ ῥήματα   τὰ τοῦ Κτίστου φιλάνθρωπα·
"Κατατρύφα," γὰρ ἔλεγε,   "πάντων ὧν κεχάρισμαι,
τῇ τρυφῇ γάρ σου τῇ τούτων   ἀρεσθήσομαι·

but to those who honor her
he yields life
      —the eternal one.

5

The Lover of humanity himself had entrusted the new-
      sprung human
to Fasting's command, an affectionate mother, a teacher,
committing his life into her hands.
And if he loved her, he would dwell with the angels.
But, having rejected her, he found toil and death,
the sharpness of thorns and thistles,
and the affliction of laborious living.
If Fasting revealed herself so helpful in paradise,
how much more here
that we may have life
      —the eternal one?

6

The Most High urged Adam, the first-formed, to eat of
      every tree,
having put him in paradise, as it is written,
but he forbade the eating from one tree.
And these were the Creator's loving words:
"Take delight," he said, "in all I have given you,
for in your delight, I shall be pleased.

ἐὰν φυλάξῃς   τὴν ἐντολήν μου,
φυλάξω σε τρυφῶντα·   διὰ τοῦτο   φθορᾶς ἀνεπίδεκτον
ἡ χάρις μου φρουρεῖ σε
ὡς λαμβάνοντα ζωὴν
          —τὴν αἰώνιον.

7

"Ἐμῶν ῥημάτων ἀνάσχου, Ἀδάμ,   καὶ πρόσχες ἀκριβῶς
                              τῷ προστάγματι τούτῳ·
ἑνὸς γάρ σοι   ἐκ πάντων τούτων   παραγγέλλω
                                        ἀπέχεσθαι·
οὐ κακοῦ μὲν τὴν φύσιν ὑπάρχοντος,
ἀλλὰ σοὶ τὴν κάκωσιν   παραβάντι σκευάζοντος.
Ἡ οὐσία τοῦ ξύλου γὰρ   ἔστι μὲν οὐκ ἄχρηστος,
ἡ δὲ τούτου μετουσία   σοὶ γενήσεται
βλάβης αἰτία·   ἔχει γὰρ τοῦτο
ἀκόνην λογισμῶν ἐγκεκρυμμένην   καὶ γεύσεως
                                        μάχαιραν·
ἂν φάγῃς οὖν ἐκ τούτου,
ἀποβάλλει τὴν ζωὴν
          —τὴν αἰώνιον.

8

"Ἰδού, πρωτόπλαστε, παραγγέλλω   μὴ ἅψῃ ἐκ τοῦ
                              ξύλου οὗ εἶπόν σοι ὅλως·
ἂν ἅψῃ γάρ,   εὐθὺς ὡς κλέπτης   ἐκδοθήσει πρὸς
                                        θάνατον,

If you will keep my commandment,
I will keep you in your delight; and so my grace protects
    you,
impervious to decay,
as you receive life
    —*the eternal one.*

7

"Pay heed to my words, Adam, and careful attention to this
    injunction:
from one of all these I instruct you to abstain;
not that it's harmful by nature,
but if you transgress, it contains harm for you.
The tree's actual being is not without goodness,
but your being a partaker in it
will be a cause of injury for you;
it hides a whetstone of thoughts and a dagger of taste.
Were you to eat from it,
you'd throw away life
    —*the eternal one.*

8

"I instruct you, first-formed one, never to touch the tree I
    spoke of.
If you do, you'll at once, as a thief, be surrendered to death.

οὐχ ὡς ἔχειν αὐτὸ μὴ δυνάμενος,
ἀλλ᾽ ἐπειδὴ ἄπιστος   ἀποβήσῃ καὶ ἄχρηστος·
πρὸς μικρόν σε καὶ εὔκολον   θεῖον νόμον ἤγαγον·
διὰ τοῦτο τὴν τῶν ἄλλων   ἀφθονίαν σοι
ἐδωρησάμην,   ἵν᾽ ὅλων τούτων
ἐν ἀπολαύσει γένῃ,   καὶ θανάτου   μὴ γένῃ ὑπεύθυνος,
ὁ κατ᾽ εἰκόνα ἔχων
καὶ κατέχων ζωὴν
        —τὴν αἰώνιον."

9

Νόμον οὖν θεῖον κρατοῦντές ποτε,   Ἀδάμ τε καὶ ἡ Εὔα
                                    ἐφύλαττον τοῦτον·
ἐτήρει δὲ   ὁρμὰς τὰς τούτων   ὁ φρόνιμος διάβολος
καὶ ἀπάτην σκευάζειν ἐπείγετο,
καὶ ὡς ἐθεάσατο   κρυπτομένους ὡς ἔμφρονας,
προσελθεῖν τῷ ἀνθρώπῳ μὲν   τέως οὐκ ἐθάρρησε·
τὴν δὲ Εὔαν ὁ πανοῦργος   θεασάμενος
παρὰ τὸ δένδρον   μόνην ἑστῶσαν,
ἐντίθησιν εὐθέως   διὰ ταύτης   τοῖς δύο τὸ πρόσκομμα
τοῖς πρότερον λαβοῦσι
διὰ χάριτος ζωὴν
        —τὴν αἰώνιον.

Not that you're unable to have it,
but you'd end up, then, without faith and goodness.
I have led you toward a divine rule
that is both small and simple.
I've bestowed upon you, therefore, the bounty of the
    others,
so you'd enjoy them all and not be subject to death.
You have and you hold,
with the image, life
      —the eternal one."

9

Receiving the divine rule, Adam and Eve observed it,
but the crafty devil noticed their urges
and hastened to prepare deceit;
as he had seen them wisely suppress them,
he hadn't yet dared to approach the man.
But the cunning one, seeing Eve
standing alone next to the tree,
at once, through her, grafted on a stumbling branch for the
    two
who previously through grace
had received life
      —the eternal one.

10

Ὁ πονηρὸς γὰρ πρὸς τὴν γυναῖκα   ὡς φίλος καὶ
                                    συνήθης προσέρχεται δόλῳ,
καὶ πλάττεται   καὶ προκομίζει   τὴν κακοῦργον
                                    ἐρώτησιν·
ὡς συμπάσχων αὐτῇ διαλέγεται·
"Διὰ ποίαν πρόφασιν   ὁ Θεὸς τὸν παράδεισον
ὡς φιλῶν ὑμῖν δέδωκε,   πάντων δὲ ἐκώλυσε
τῶν φυτῶν μεταλαμβάνειν   ὁ φιλότιμος;
Τίνος οὖν χάριν   τοῦ παραδείσου
τὴν οἴκησιν κρατεῖτε,   τῆς δὲ τούτου   τρυφῆς
                                    ἐστερήθητε;
Πῶς δύνασθε οὖν ἔχειν
ἄνευ ταύτης τὴν ζωὴν
    —τὴν αἰώνιον;"

11

Ὑπὸ τῶν λόγων ἀπατηθεῖσα,   ἡ Εὔα πρὸς αὐτὸν
                                    ἀπεκρίνατο ταῦτα·
"Πεπλάνησαι   καὶ οὐ γινώσκεις   τί προσέταξε Κύριος.
Τὸν παράδεισον ὅλον ὡς τράπεζαν
παραχθεῖσι δέδωκεν   ὁ Θεὸς εἰς ἀπόλαυσιν,
ἀλλ' ἑνὸς τὴν μετάληψιν   μόνον διεκώλυσεν,
ἐμποδίου γενομένου   τῇ ζωῇ ἡμῶν,
ὃ χρησιμεύει   τοῖς ἀμφοτέροις

10

With trickery the wicked one approaches the woman as a
    friend or relative
and forges and proffers his harmful questioning.
As if sympathetic, he says:
"On what pretext has God, as though your friend,
given you the garden, while this generous one has forbidden
    you
to partake of all the plants?
For what reason, then, do you occupy the garden
as your home, when you have been deprived of its delight?
Without it, how can you
even have a life
    —*the eternal one?*"

11

Bamboozled by his words, Eve answered him thus: "You are
    misled,
and you do not know what the Lord commanded.
God has given the whole garden
as a table of enjoyment to the ones he produced,
but he's prevented our participation in a single thing,
which is an impediment to our life,
a thing that we both could use,

καὶ ἐκπαιδεύειν οἶδε   τῶν καλῶν τε   καὶ τῶν φαύλων
                                                    τὴν εἴδησιν·
ἐλάβομεν γὰρ ἤδη
ὥσπερ κτῆσιν τὴν ζωὴν
    —τὴν αἰώνιον."

12

Ῥήματι οὖν θανατηφόρῳ   γλυκεῖαν ὁ ἐχθρὸς
                                        συγκατέμιξε γεῦσιν,
σκεπτόμενος   καὶ λέγων ταῦτα   κατ᾽ ἰδίαν ὁ ἔχθιστος·
"Εἰ μὴ δόλῳ κεράσω τὸ βούλημα,
ἂν καταψηφίσωμαι   τοῦ Θεοῦ ἐν τοῖς λόγοις μου,
εὐθέως ὑποπτεύσει με   Εὔα ὡς μισόθεον,
καὶ γενήσομαι πρὸς ταύτην   ἀπαράδεκτος·
οὐδὲ γὰρ οἶδα   τέως τὴν γνώμην
ταύτης· ἐὰν ἰσχύσω   διαστρέψαι,   ἔστιν ὅτι στέργει με·
ἐντέχνως οὖν προσέλθω
τοῖς λαβοῦσι ζωὴν
    —τὴν αἰώνιον."

13

Ὡς δὲ τοιαῦτα διενοήθη,   ὁ ὄφις πρὸς τὴν Εὔαν
                                        ἐφθέγξατο λέγων·
"Συνήδομαι   τῇ ἀφθονίᾳ   τῆς τρυφῆς, ἧς ἐλάβετε·
ἐπαινῶ τοῦ Θεοῦ τὴν ἀλήθειαν,   ὅτι οὐκ ἐψεύσατο
πρὸς ὑμᾶς διηγούμενος
ὡς μεγάλη ἡ δύναμις   τούτου τοῦ φυτοῦ ἐστι·

for it is able to teach us the knowledge of the good and the
    bad,
and we've already received
as our possession life
      —the eternal one."

12

Into his fatal speech the adversary mixed a sweet flavor.
The enemy considered and said to himself,
"Unless I mingle my plan with a trick,
if, with my words, I accuse God,
Eve will at once suspect I'm a god hater,
and I'll be unwelcome to her.
So far, I do not know her thoughts;
if I am able to twist them, she'll find me agreeable.
I must approach craftily
those receivers of life
      —the eternal one."

13

Having entertained such thoughts, the serpent spoke out to
    Eve:
"I rejoice at the abundance of delight you've received!
I applaud the truthfulness of God,
for he wasn't lying when describing to you
how great the power of this plant is.

τῶν καλῶν γὰρ καὶ τῶν φαύλων   γνῶσιν δίδωσι·
μόνος Θεὸς δὲ   διαγινώσκει
διάκρισιν τὴν πάντων·   διὰ τοῦτο   τὴν τούτου
                                                 μετάληψιν
παρήγγειλε μὴ ἔχειν,
ὃ παρέχει ζωὴν
   —τὴν αἰώνιον.

14

"Μὴ γὰρ οὐκ οἶδα ὅτι τὴν κτίσιν   καλὴν ὁ Θεὸς
                                    ἀπειργάσατο πᾶσαν;
Ὁ πάντα οὖν   καλὰ ποιήσας   πῶς φυτεῦσαι ἠνείχετο
παραδείσου εἰς μέσον τὸν θάνατον;
Οὐχ ὑπάρχει πρόσκομμα   τὸ φυτὸν τὸ τῆς γνώσεως·
οὐδὲ γὰρ ἀποθνήσκετε   ἐὰν τοῦτο φάγητε·
ὡς θεοὶ δὲ διὰ τούτου   νῦν γενήσεσθε
ὥσπερ ὁ Κτίστης,   τοῦ διακρίνειν
καλῶν καὶ φαύλων τρόπους·   διὰ τοῦτο   ἐν μέσῳ
                                                 προτέθειται
παντὸς τοῦ παραδείσου,
ὥσπερ ἔχοντα ζωὴν
   —τὴν αἰώνιον."

15

Αὕτη οὖν ἰδοῦσα τὸ δένδρον   ὡς ἔστιν εὐπρεπὲς καὶ
                                    εὐάρεστον Εὔα,
ἐφλέγετο,   καὶ πρὸς τὴν γεῦσιν   ταῖς ἐλπίσιν ἐπείγετο·

It gives knowledge of good and bad,
but God alone discerns
how to judge all things. This is why he instructed you not
to partake of the tree,
which grants life
     —*the eternal one.*

14

"Do I not know that God made the whole creation good?
If he created all good, how could he plant
death in the middle of the garden?
This plant of knowledge will not make you stumble,
and you would not die if you were to eat it.
Through it you'll be like gods,
just like the Creator, discerning the ways
of good and bad. This is why he has placed it in the middle
of the whole garden:
it possesses life
     —*the eternal one.*"

15

Then Eve, who saw how attractive and pleasant the tree
          appeared,
was inflamed, driven by the longing to taste it;

λογισμοῖς ἑαυτὴν συνεκίνησεν·
"Ὁ μηνύσας," λέγουσα,   "οὐκ ἐχθρὸς τοῦ Θεοῦ ἐστιν;
Ποίαν ἔχθραν γὰρ κέκτηται   ὁ ὄφις πρὸς τὸν

Πλάσαντα;
Τὸ φυτὸν δὲ καὶ τῇ θέᾳ   ἐστὶ πάγκαλον·
σπεύσω πρὸς βρῶσιν   θεοποιΐας
καὶ ἀπολαύσω τούτου,   οὗ τὴν θέαν   ὁρῶσα

μαραίνομαι,
καὶ δώσω τῷ ἀνδρί μου,
ἵνα σχῶμεν τὴν ζωὴν
    —τὴν αἰώνιον."

16

Νῦν ἐδέξω θανατηφόρον,   ὦ τάλαινα Εὔα, καὶ ἔφαγες

τούτου·
τί τρέχεις οὖν   συναπολέσαι   καὶ τὸν ἄνδρα τὸν ἴδιον;
Ἀκριβῶς ἑαυτὴν κατεξέτασον,
εἰ ὃ προσεδόκησας   διὰ γεύσεως γέγονας,
εἰ θεὸς εἶ, ὡς ἤλπισας·   γνῶθι τοῦτο πρότερον,
καὶ εἶθ' οὕτως, πρὸς τὴν γεῦσιν   καὶ τὸν ἄνδρα σου,
γύναι, προτρέπου·   μὴ οὖν ποιήσῃς
συγκτήτορα τὸν ἄνδρα   ἀπωλείας·   τί σπεύδεις

νομίζουσα
ὡς βρῶσίς σοι παρέσχεν
ἡ τοῦ ξύλου τὴν ζωὴν
    —τὴν αἰώνιον;

she aroused herself with thoughts:
"Surely the one who reveals this cannot be God's enemy?
What enmity can the serpent hold against his Fashioner?
And the plant is most lovely to look at!
Let me hurry to the god-making food,
and I shall enjoy it; just seeing its appearance is
        breathtaking,
and I'll give it to my man
that we may have life
        —*the eternal one!*"

16

So you took the fatal fruit, wretched Eve, and ate it.
Why do you run to your man and destroy him with you?
Examine yourself thoroughly:
have you, through your tasting, become what you
        expected—
a god—as you hoped? Make sure of that first,
and only then, woman, also invite
your man to taste. Do not make the man
a partner in destruction! Why do you rush, imagining
that eating from the tree
granted you life
        —*the eternal one?*

17

Ὅτε τῷ δένδρῳ ἐπιτερφθεῖσα   ἀπώλετο, οὐ γὰρ
                                          ἀπήλαυσεν Εὔα,
ἐσπούδασε   καὶ ἐπεδίδου   καὶ Ἀδὰμ τοῦ καρποῦ αὐτοῦ·
καὶ ὡς μέγιστον δῶρον προσφέρουσα
οὕτως διεγίνετο·   πρὸς αὐτὸν δὲ ἐφθέγγετο·
"Θησαυρὸν παρετρέχομεν   μέχρι νῦν, ὦ σύζυγε,
καὶ τρυφὴν τὴν μακαρίαν   ἐφοβούμεθα·
νῦν ἔγνων, ἄνερ,   καὶ ἐπειράθην
ὡς ἄκαιρον δειλίαν   ἐκρατοῦμεν·   καὶ γὰρ ἐγὼ ἔφαγον
καὶ ζῶσά σοι παρέστην
καὶ ἐπέχω τὴν ζωὴν
        —τὴν αἰώνιον.

18

"Ὑπάρχει μᾶλλον, ὡς ἔχων πεῖραν,   ὁ λόγος τοῦ
                                          μηνύσαντος βέβαιος ὄντως·
φαγοῦσα γὰρ   οὐκ ἐνεκρώθην,   ὡς Θεὸς
                                          προηγόρευσεν,
ἀλλὰ ζῶσά σοι νῦν παραγέγονα,
καὶ σχηματισμός ἐστι   τοῦ Θεοῦ τὸ παράγγελμα·
εἰ γὰρ ἦν ἀληθέστατον,   ἄρτι σὺ ἐθρήνεις με
ὡς θανοῦσαν καὶ κειμένην   πρὸς τὸν θάνατον.
Δέχου οὖν, ἄνερ,   καὶ κατατρύφα·
προσλάμβανε ἀξίαν   διὰ τούτου   τὴν θείαν καὶ
                                          ἄχραντον·

17

Delighted by the tree, Eve was perishing, for she reaped no
    benefits,
and hurried and gave of its fruit to Adam too.
She behaved as if she was offering
the greatest gift and declared to him,
"My husband, until now we've missed out on a treasure
and been frightened by a blessed delight.
Now I've learned and I have tested
that we've entertained a misplaced cowardice. I have eaten
and am alive beside you
and hold on to life
    —the eternal one.

18

"Yes, the word of the one who told me this is, as I've found,
    truly reliable.
I ate but didn't die, as God had predicted.
Indeed I'm alive here with you.
So, God's precept amounts to a pretense.
If it were really true, you would now be lamenting me
as dead and laid out for burial.
So, take it, husband, and do indulge!
Receive through this your divine and undefiled due!

θεὸς γενήσει ὥσπερ
ὁ παρέχων τὴν ζωὴν
  —τὴν αἰώνιον."

19

Ὁ μὲν οὖν ὄφις, ὡς φθάσας εἶπον,   ἐγγίσαι τῷ Ἀδὰμ
                                  οὐκ ἐθάρρησε τότε,
φοβούμενος   μὴ διαμάρτῃ   τῆς ἐλπίδος ἧς ἔσπευδεν,
ἀλλὰ ἄλλος ἐφάνη δεινότερος
καὶ ὀφιωδέστερος   ὄφις τούτου τοῦ ὄφεως.
Ὃν γὰρ ὄφις οὐκ ἔδακεν,   αὕτη ἐθανάτωσε·
κολακεύουσα γὰρ τότε   τὸν ἰὸν αὐτῆς
τούτῳ ἐμβάλλει,   καὶ ἑαυτήν τε
κἀκεῖνον ἀπορρήσσει,   καὶ σκευάζει   ἀπάτη τῆς
                                        βρώσεως
νεκροὺς ὀφιοπλήκτους
ἀπολέσαντας ζωὴν
  —τὴν αἰώνιον.

20

Ὑπὸ οὖν ταύτης πολιορκεῖται   Ἀδὰμ τῆς ἀπάτης ὁ
                               δείλαιος πρώην·
μιᾷ μὲν γὰρ   πληγῇ τιτρώσκει   διὰ βρώσεως ἅπαντας·
διὰ τοῦτο δὲ οὕτως ὡς ἄτακτος
ἐν τοῖς πόνοις ἅπασιν   ἐπὶ γῆς κατεβέβλητο·
πρὸς νηστείαν γὰρ σύμμετρον   ὄντως καὶ ὠφέλιμον,
μὴ μεθύειν ἀκρασίᾳ,   οὐκ ἠνέσχετο·

You'll be a god,
like he who grants life
    —*the eternal one.*"

19

The serpent, as I said, had not dared to approach Adam;
he feared he would miss the goal he was aiming for,
so another serpent appeared,
more frightening and serpentine than the present serpent,
for she killed the one that the serpent had not bitten.
Sweet-talking with him, she injects her venom
in him and breaks herself and the man
apart and makes them both, with the ruse of food,
serpent-stricken corpses,
losing their life
    —*the eternal one.*

20

Miserable Adam was overcome by the ruse long ago. He
        injured all
by food with just one blow, and so
as a man without constraint he was cast
down upon the earth to all sorts of toil.
He couldn't bear to avoid unrestrained intoxication
for a measured and beneficial fast.

χριστιανῶν δὲ   πάντα τὰ γένη
νηστείᾳ προσεθίζειν   καὶ ἐρίζειν   ἀγγέλοις ἐπείγονται,
ἐλπίζοντα ἐντεῦθεν
προσλαμβάνειν τὴν ζωὴν
    —τὴν αἰώνιον.

21

Μεγάλη ἐστὶν ἡ νηστεία   πρὸς ἣν ὁ Ἀδὰμ ἐκεκλήρωτο
                                                        πρώην·
ἐν μόνοις γὰρ   φυτοῖς ὑπῆρχεν   ἡ τροφὴ τῷ γεννήτορι·
ἀκρατὴς δὲ καὶ οὗτος ἐγένετο.
Νῦν παντοδαπής ἐστι   τῶν βρωμάτων ἀπόλαυσις·
τῶν ἰχθύων τὰ ἥδιστα,   ὄρνεις καὶ τετράποδα,
τῶν φυτῶν καὶ τῶν σπερμάτων   τὰ ποικίλματα,
αἱ μαγγανεῖαι   αἱ τῶν τρυφώντων,
τῶν τραπεζῶν ἡ χάρις   ἡ κινοῦσα   ἡμᾶς πρὸς τὴν
                                                        ὄρεξιν
τὴν τῆς γαστριμαργίας,
ἀφαιροῦσα δὲ ζωὴν
    —τὴν αἰώνιον.

22

Νῦν ταῦτα λέγων, μὴ ἐρεθίσω   πολλοὺς πρὸς
                                        γυμνασίαν παμφάγον, ὦ φίλοι·
μὴ δείξω δὲ   τοῦ πρωτοπλάστου   λιχνοτέρους ἐν
                                                        βρώμασι·
τὸν γὰρ ζῆλον ἡμῶν, ὦ πιστότατοι,

ON FASTING (ADAM AND EVE)

But all generations of Christians are striving
to train themselves in fasting and thus rival the angels,
hoping in this
to obtain life
  —the eternal one.

Great indeed is the fast to which Adam was formerly
   appointed.
Plants alone were our father's food,
but even he became self-indulgent.
These days all sorts of fare is enjoyed:
the delicious fish, fowl, and quadrupeds,
the garnish of plants and seeds,
the enticements of gourmands,
the charm of tables, that which arouses in us
gluttonous appetites
and deprives us of life
  —the eternal one.

Saying this, friends, I'm not trying to promote ravenous
   practices,
nor to portray you as greedier for food than the first-formed
   one.
What I have proclaimed is our zeal,

περὶ τὴν ἐγκράτειαν τὴν μεγίστην ἐκήρυξα·
λειτουργεῖν γὰρ ἐπείγεσθε, τὴν νηστείαν στέργοντες,
ἐτησίως νῦν δεκάτας τῷ Θεῷ ἡμῶν,
ὥσπερ Ἑβραῖοι ἐκ τῶν χρημάτων
προσέφερον Κυρίῳ τὰς δεκάτας, τῷ τύπῳ
        σημαίνοντες
τὴν μέλλουσαν νηστείαν,
δι᾽ ἧς ἔχομεν ζωὴν
 —τὴν αἰώνιον.

23

Ὁ ἀριθμὸς οὖν ἐν τῇ νηστείᾳ δηλούσθω ὁ τῆς
        δεκατώσεως, φίλοι·
ἑπτὰ μὲν γὰρ αἱ ἑβδομάδες τῆς νηστείας ὑπάρχουσιν·
αἱ δὲ πέντε ἡμέραι ὑπόψηφοι
ἐφ᾽ ἑκάστῃ δείκνυνται ἑβδομάδι νηστεύσιμοι,
ὡς ὑπάρχειν τριάκοντα πέντε ἃς νηστεύομεν,
καὶ νυχθήμερον πρὸς τούτοις τὸ τοῦ Σαββάτου
τοῦ σωτηρίου ἔχομεν Πάθους·
τριάκοντα ἓξ οὖν ἡμέραι πᾶσαι καὶ ἥμισυ γίνονται,
δεκάτωσις τοῦ ἔτους,
δι᾽ ἧς κτώμεθα ζωὴν
 —τὴν αἰώνιον.

most faithful ones, for the greatest self-control.
With a love for fasting, strive now to serve
God with your yearly tithes,
just as the Hebrews offered the Lord
tithes from their goods and indicated with their example
the fasts to come,
through which we have life
     —the eternal one.

23

Let the sum, my friends, of the tithing, then, be clarified in
    the fasting:
seven are the weeks of which the fast consists;
five are the days that are reckoned
as belonging to the fast each week,
which equals thirty-five days when we're fasting,
and to these we add the night
and day of the Passion's saving Saturday.
It adds up to thirty-six days and a half, a tenth of the year,
through which we
may gain life
     —the eternal one.

24

Σῶτερ τοῦ κόσμου, σὲ προσκυνοῦντες   λατρείαν
                    λογικήν σοι προσφέρομεν ταύτην·
φιλάνθρωπε   καὶ ἐλεῆμον,   σὺ τοὺς πάντας ἐλέησον·
καὶ ἐσθίοντες γὰρ καὶ νηστεύοντες,
πάντες σὲ δοξάζομεν   τὸν τοὺς πάντας ῥυόμενον
ἐκ τῆς πλάνης οὓς ἔπλασας·   σὺ γὰρ εἶ ὁ Θεὸς ἡμῶν,
εἰ καὶ ἄνθρωπος ἐγένου,   ὡς ἠθέλησας,
ἐκ τῆς παρθένου   καὶ παναγίας
Μαρίας τῆς ἀχράντου   Θεοτόκου·   διὸ σοὶ
                                προσπίπτομεν·
πρεσβείαις τῆς μητρός σου,
δὸς τοῖς δούλοις σου ζωὴν
    —τὴν αἰώνιον.

24

Savior of the world, with prostrations we offer you our
        spiritual worship.
Benevolent and merciful one, have mercy on everyone.
Whether we eat or fast,
we all glorify you, who deliver everyone
whom you formed from error. You are our God,
although you also became human,
as you willed it, from Mary, the all-holy virgin,
the immaculate Mother of God, and so we fall down before
        you.
By your mother's intercessions,
give your servants life
        —*the eternal one.*

Προοίμιον

ἰδιόμελον

Ὡς καθαρὰν θυσίαν   καὶ ἄμωμον προσφορὰν
ἀναιμωτὶ ἐδέξω   τὸν ἄκακον Ἰσαὰκ
ἐκ πατρὸς προσαγόμενον   ὑπὲρ υἱῶν ἀγαπώντων σε·
τῆς γὰρ φιλίας   θριαμβεύσας τὴν γνώμην,
τῆς ἀτεκνίας   τὸν πρεσβύτην ἐρρύσω,   φιλάνθρωπε,
ὁ δοτὴρ τῶν ἀγαθῶν   καὶ Σωτὴρ τῶν ψυχῶν ἡμῶν.

α

ἰδιόμελον

Εἰς ὄρος ἀναβαίνοντα   σὲ τὸν πρεσβύτην   ὁ νέος ἐγὼ
ζηλῶσαι θέλω   καὶ ναρκοῦσί μου πόδες·
εἰ γὰρ καὶ τὸ πνεῦμα πρόθυμον,   ἡ σὰρξ ἀσθενής·
ὢ ψυχή μου,   θάρρησον θεωροῦσα
τὸν Ἀβραὰμ νῦν γῆρας ἀποθέμενον   καὶ νεάζοντα·
οὐ ἔκαμνον πόδες,   ἀλλ᾿ ἠνδρίζετο γνώμη·
ἠγνόει τὸν τόπον   καὶ ἀπήει τῷ τρόπῳ
ὁδηγοῦντος αὐτὸν τοῦ καλέσαντος,
ὅτι μόνος ἀγαθὸς   ὁ Σωτὴρ τῶν ψυχῶν ἡμῶν.

ON ABRAHAM'S SACRIFICE

in first plagal mode

Prelude

to its own melody

As a pure sacrifice you received the innocent
Isaac without bloodshed, an offering without blemish,
presented by the father, for the sons who love you.
When you let your affectionate inclination triumph,
you delivered the elder from childlessness, benevolent one,
the giver of good and Savior of our souls.

I

to its own melody

You ascend the mountain, and I, a youngster, aspire to
    follow
you who are older, yet my feet are turning stiff.
While the spirit is willing, the flesh is weak.
My soul, take courage when you witness
Abraham lay aside his age, growing young!
His feet were weary, but his mind was brave;
he didn't know where, but he followed the way
of his guide, the one who was calling him,
for but one is good, the Savior of our souls.

2

Ἰσχὺς οὖν ἦν ἡ πίστις σου,   ὅθεν ὁ πόθος   πολὺς ἦν ὁ
                                                            σὸς
τοῦ ἐκτελέσαι   τοῦ καλοῦντος τὴν βουλήν.
Τί δέ σοι ὁ καλῶν προσέταξεν,   ἀκούσωμεν·
"Λάβε παῖδα   τὸν ἐκ τῶν σῶν λαγόνων,
ὅνπερ ἐν γήρει ἔσχες παραμύθιον,   καὶ σφάξον μοι."
Ὦ πόσης ὑπῆρχε   τούτῳ λύπης τὸ ῥῆμα·
οὐκ εἶπε γὰρ "παῖδα"   καὶ ἠρκέσθη τῷ λόγῳ,
ἀλλὰ ἠρέθιζε σπλάγχνα γέροντος,
ὅτι μόνος ἀγαθὸς   ὁ Σωτὴρ τῶν ψυχῶν ἡμῶν.

3

Σκληρὸν μὲν τὸ πρόσταγμα·   σὺ δὲ πρὸς
                                    τοῦτο,   πρεσβύτα, ὀξύς·
τοῦ γὰρ παιδός σοι   ποθεινότερος Θεός·
διὸ πρὸς τὸ ῥηθὲν ἀμφίβολος   οὐ γέγονας.
Πῶς οὐκ εἶπας·   "Διὰ τί με πατέρα
καὶ οὐ φονέα τέκνου προσηγόρευσας,   ὦ Δέσποτα;
Ὃ γίνομαι λέγε,   ὃ γέγονα μὴ κάλει.
Καιρὸν γὰρ ὀλίγον   ὠνομάσθην γενέτης,
εἰς αἰῶνα δὲ σφαγεὺς γόνου κηρύττομαι,
ὅτι μόνος ἀγαθὸς   ὁ Σωτὴρ τῶν ψυχῶν ἡμῶν;

2

Your strength was your faith, and thus you were filled with
    intense desire
to fulfill the will of the one who called you.
Let us hear what he who was calling commanded:
"Take the child, the one from your loins,
your old-age consolation, and sacrifice him for me!"
Oh, what pain contained in these words!
He did not just say "child," letting that suffice,
but, upsetting the old man's heart,
that but one is good, the Savior of our souls!

3

The command was tough, but you, old man, were sharp and
    swift.
God was more precious to you than your child,
so you weren't hesitant about what you heard.
How could you not ask, "Why did you address me
as father, my Master, not as killer of my child?
Call me what I'll be and not what I was.
For a short while I was known as parent,
but forever I'll be called an offspring slayer,
since but one is good, the Savior of our souls?

4

"Τί ἄρα οἱ ὁρῶντές με   σφάττοντα τέκνον   λογίσονται
                                                   νῦν;

Μανέντα, οἴμοι,   ἢ ἐκστάντα τῶν φρενῶν;
Καὶ λῆρόν μου τὸ γῆρας δόξωσιν   οἱ ἀκούοντες.
Πῶς χερσὶ δὲ   ταῖς ἰδίαις ὀλέσω
οὓ τοῖς δακτύλοις ἤλπιζον κλεισθῆναί μου   τὰ βλέφαρα;
Ὃν ἔλυσα σπαργάνων   —πῶς δεσμήσας φονεύσω;
Ὃν βλέπων σκιρτῶντα,   σὲ εὐλόγουν τὸν δόντα·
οὐ γέγονα τροφεύς, σφαγεὺς οὐ γίνομαι,
ὅτι μόνος ἀγαθὸς   ὁ Σωτὴρ τῶν ψυχῶν ἡμῶν.

5

"Ὅταν μὲν τῷ κάλλει σου   βλέψω, ὦ
                                      τέκνον,   πληροῦμαι χαρᾶς·
ὅταν δὲ πάλιν   τοῦ Δεσπότου ἀκούσω,
ὁ γέλως μου εἰς πένθος τρέπεται   καὶ δάκρυα.
Οἴμοι, σπλάγχνον,   τὴν ψελλίζουσαν γλῶσσαν
ἄφωνον δείξει χεὶρ τοῦ σὲ γεννήσαντος   ἡ σφάζουσα·
τὰ δὲ βλέφαρά σου   οὐ καμμύσει ἡ Σάρρα·
τὰ ῥοδίζοντα χείλη   νῦν ἀδόνητα δείξω
ὅτι πρόσταγμα τελῶ τοῦ δώσαντος,
ὅτι μόνος ἀγαθὸς   ὁ Σωτὴρ τῶν ψυχῶν ἡμῶν.

4

"What will those who see me slaying a child think?
That I'm mad, alas, or have lost my mind?
Demented old age, those who hear will assume.
How can I destroy with my own two hands
the one whose fingers I hoped would close my eyelids?
I undid his swaddling bands—how, then, do I bind and slay
    him?
When I saw him leaping, I blessed you as the giver.
I cannot just slaughter the one I nurtured,
since but one is good, the Savior of our souls!

5

"Whenever I look at your beauty, my child, I am filled with
    joy;
when I listen, conversely, to the words of the Master,
my laughter turns to sorrow and tears.
Alas, my dear one, your prattling tongue
will be silenced by your begetter's slaying hand.
Sarah will not close your eyelids.
Your rosy lips will quiver no more,
as I accomplish what the giver decreed,
that but one is good, the Savior of our souls!

6

"Ναρκῶσαν τὴν χεῖρά μου   καὶ δεδοικῶσαν   τὸ ξίφος
                                                              κρατεῖν
τίς κραταιώσει   καὶ διδάξει φονεύειν
οὐ μόσχους σου, οὓς ἔθος ἔσχηκεν,   ἀλλὰ τέκνον μου;
Τίς ὠμὸν δὲ   καὶ ἀνοίκτειρον δείξει
τὸν εὐσπλαγχνίας χάριν εἰσδεξάμενον   τοὺς ἅπαντας;
Ὁ πρώην ἀγνώστους   δεξάμενος καὶ θρέψας,
σὲ τὸν κληρονόμον   σὸς πατὴρ πῶς ὀλέσω;
Τίς ἀκούσεται κἀμὲ οὐ φεύξεται
ὅτι μόνος ἀγαθὸς   ὁ Σωτὴρ τῶν ψυχῶν ἡμῶν;

7

"Ἀκούσει τοὺς λόγους σου   πάντας ἡ Σάρρα,   ὢ
                                                              Δέσποτά μου,
καὶ τὴν βουλήν σου   ταύτην γνοῦσά μοι λέξει·
Εἰ αὐτὸς ὁ διδοὺς ἐλάμβανε,   τί παρέσχηκε;
Σύ, πρεσβῦτα,   τὸν ἐμὸν ἔα πρός με,
καὶ ὅταν θελήσῃ τοῦτον ὁ καλέσας σε,   δηλώσῃ μοι·
ὁ πρώην δι᾽ ἀγγέλου   τόκον τούτου σημάνας,
τὸν φόνον μοι αὖθις   ὡς ἂν θέλῃ, δηλώσῃ·
οὐ πιστεύω σοι τὸ τέκνον, οὐ δώσω σοι,
ὅτι μόνος ἀγαθὸς   ὁ Σωτὴρ τῶν ψυχῶν ἡμῶν.

6

"If my hand is stiff and if it dreads holding the sword,
who shall brace it and teach it to kill
not your customary calves, but my child?
Who shall prove me cruel and pitiless,
when I've welcomed everyone out of compassion?
Once I received and provided for strangers,
how can I, your own father, destroy you, my heir?
Who won't flee from me when they hear
that but one is good, the Savior of our souls?

7

"Sarah is going to hear all the words you speak, my Master.
When she learns of your plan, she will say to me,
'If the giver takes his gift, what has he offered?
Just leave what's mine, old man, to me!
And the one who called you can let me know when he wants
    him.
The one who through an angel once signaled his birth,
may make known to me now what he wishes about the
    killing!
You I don't trust with the child and won't grant
that but one is good, the Savior of our souls!

8

"'Βραχὺν καιρὸν ζήσουσα,   τούτῳ συζήσω·   μετὰ τὸ
                                                                      θανεῖν,
ἐὰν θελήσῃς,   τοῦτο δρᾶσον ἐν αὐτῷ·
μὴ λείπῃ με καὶ λύπῃ κτείνῃ με,   σοῦ αἰτέομαι.
Μόλις τούτου   ἐπετύχομεν, ἄνερ,
καὶ παρ' ἐλπίδας παῖδα ἐκ κοιλίας μου   ἐκτησάμεθα·
εἰ οὖν πρώην τυχόντες   ἀποτύχωμεν ἄρτι,
ἢ τάχα κυῆσαι,   θηλαῖς θρέψαι ὀφείλω,
καὶ ἀκμάσαντα δοῦναι τῷ δώσαντι;
ὅτι μόνος ἀγαθὸς   ὁ Σωτὴρ τῶν ψυχῶν ἡμῶν.

9

"'Ῥοπὴν ἐμοῦ ἀπόστηθι·   τοῦτον ἀγκάλαις   λαμβάνω
                                                                      ἐγὼ
πόνον γαστρός μου·   κορεσθῆναι γὰρ ζητῶ·
εἰ χρῄζει θυσιῶν ὁ καλέσας σε,   λάβῃ πρόβατον.
Οἴμοι, τέκνον   Ἰσαάκ, εἰ κατίδω
σοῦ ἐπὶ γῆς τὸ αἷμα ἐκχυνόμενον . . .   μὴ γένοιτο·
φονεύσει με πρώτην,   εἶθ' οὕτως σε φονεύσει—
πρὸ σοῦ τὴν τεκοῦσαν,   μετ' αὐτὴν σὲ τὸν τόκον·
μὴ κατίδω σου σφαγήν, καὶ ἀπόλωμαι·
ὅτι μόνος ἀγαθὸς   ὁ Σωτὴρ τῶν ψυχῶν ἡμῶν.

8

"'I've a short while to live; I will spend it with him. After my
        death,
if you so wish, carry it out on him.
Don't leave me, I beg you, don't let sorrow kill me.
We were barely able to have him, husband,
but beyond our hopes came a child from my womb.
If given to us once, should we give it up now?
Or should I bear a child and nurse with my breasts,
and when he's in bloom give him back to the giver,
since but one is good, the Savior of our souls?

9

"'Stay away from me for a moment! I am taking him, the
        labor of my womb,
in my own arms. I want my fill of him!
If he who called you needs sacrifices, let him take a sheep!
Alas, my child Isaac, if I should witness
your blood pouring forth on the ground . . . God forbid!
He must kill me first to kill you next—
your mother before you, and then her offspring.
May I not witness your slaughter and die,
since but one is good, the Savior of our souls!

10

"Ἀγγέλου σημάναντος   ἄκαιρον τόκον   ἐγέλασα πρίν,
καὶ νῦν τὸ ῥῆμα   ἰδοῦσα πρᾶγμα, ἐχάρην·
ἀλλ' ἤδη ἡ χαρὰ εἰς δάκρυα   τάχα τρέπεται·
σύ μου φάος,   σὺ αὐγὴ ἐμῶν βλεφάρων·
σὲ ὥσπερ ἄστρον βλέπουσα λαμπρύνομαι,   ὦ τέκνον
μου·
σὺ τῆς ἐμῆς κοιλίας   καρπὸς ὥριμος ὤφθης·
σὺ βότρυς περκάζων   ἀκμασάσης ἀμπέλου·
οὐ σβέσει σε πατήρ, οὐ τέμνει σε·
ὅτι μόνος ἀγαθὸς   ὁ Σωτὴρ τῶν ψυχῶν ἡμῶν.

11

"Ἀκμάσας γενήσει μου   στήριγμα γήρους,   ὦ
σπλάγχνον ἐμόν,
τὰ σὰ δὲ τέκνα   βακτηρία πολιᾶς·
κατίδω σῆς ὀσφύος ἔκγονα   καὶ οὕτω θνήξομαι·
σὺ δὲ κόρας   τὰς ἐμὰς ἀποκλείσεις,
σὺ σὺν τοῖς τέκνοις κόλποις παραπέμψεις με   τῶν
πατέρων μου,
σὺ κλίνης μου πρῶτος   πορευόμενος κλαύσεις·
ἐγὼ δέ σου θνῆσιν   οὐδαμῶς μὴ θρηνήσω
ὀλετῆρα σὸν πατέρα ἀκούσασα·
ὅτι μόνος ἀγαθὸς   ὁ Σωτὴρ τῶν ψυχῶν ἡμῶν.'

IO

"'Once, when the angel had signaled the untimely birth, I
      laughed,
yet knowing the word as deed, I rejoiced.
But perhaps the joy is now turning to tears.
You, my radiance, are the light of my eyes!
You I see as a star, my child, and so I shine.
You appeared as the ripe fruit of my womb.
You are the dark cluster of a vine in its prime.
Your father won't quench you nor cut you down,
since but one is good, the Savior of our souls!

II

"'When you've reached your prime, you will be my support
      in old age, my dear heart,
and your children a walking cane when I'm gray!
I shall see the brood of your loins, and so die.
You will cover my pupils; you and your children
will surrender me to the bosom of my fathers!
You will be first to come wailing by my bed.
I will not ever lament your death,
having heard from your destroyer father
that but one is good, the Savior of our souls!'

12

"Μὴ τουτοισὶ τοῖς ῥήμασι   γύναι, χρωμένη,   ὀργίσῃς
                                                    Θεόν·
ἀλλότριόν τι   οὐκ αἰτεῖται παρ' ἡμῶν·
ὃ πρώην γὰρ αὐτὸς δεδώρηται,   τοῦτο λήψεται.
Μὴ σπιλώσῃς   τὸ ὁλοκαύτωμα θρήνοις
μηδὲ δακρύσῃς· μῶμον ἐπιθήσεις γὰρ   τῇ θυσίᾳ μου·
Θεὸς αὐτὸν θέλει,   καὶ τίς τοῦτον ἐπέχει;
Καὶ κόλποις σοῖς ὄντα   θανατῶσαι ἰσχύει·
τὴν οὖν πρόθεσιν δεῖξόν σου πέμψασα
ὅτι μόνος ἀγαθὸς   ὁ Σωτὴρ τῶν ψυχῶν ἡμῶν.

13

"Ῥαντίσω τοῖς δάκρυσι   πᾶσαν τὴν γαῖαν,   καὶ σὺ σὺν
                                                    ἐμοί,
ἀλλ' οὖν ἐκ τούτου   κέρδος ἡμῖν οὐκ ἔσται·
ὅταν γάρ τι Θεὸς βεβούλευται,   τίς ἀνθίσταται;
Ἤ, δοκεῖς σύ,   μόνος σὸς πέλει γόνος;
Τέκνον ἐμὸν δὲ οὗτος οὐχ ὑπάρχει νῦν   ὃν ἐγέννησα;"
"Σπορεὺς αὐτοῦ πέλεις   καὶ σφαγεὺς τούτου μέλλεις;"
"Ὁ τοῦτο προστάξας,   γύναι, πάντων δεσπόζει,
δῶρον εὔκαιρον ἡμῶν ἐξαιτήσας με,
ὅτι μόνος ἀγαθὸς   ὁ Σωτὴρ τῶν ψυχῶν ἡμῶν."

12

"Wife, you should not anger God by using such words!
He does not ask for another's property.
He will merely take what he has formerly given.
Do not defile the holocaust with mourning,
do not weep! You are spoiling my sacrifice.
God wants him; who can hold him back?
He has the power to take a life, even from your bosom,
so show your resolve by your gift,
since but one is good, the Savior of our souls!

13

"I could sprinkle the whole earth with my tears, and you
    with me,
but this will be of no use to us,
for when God has decided, who can oppose?
Or do you think he is your child only?
Is he not my son, the one I begot?"
"You're the boy's sower, and you'll be his slayer?"
"The one who decreed this, rules over all, wife,
and has demanded I surrender our precious gift,
for but one is good, the Savior of our souls!"

14

Ὡς ἤκουσε τὰ ῥήματα   τοῦ ὁμοζύγου,   ἡ Σάρρα
                                                    φησίν·
"Εἰ εἰς ζωήν σε   θέλει, ζῆσαι προστάξει·
ἀθάνατος ὑπάρχων Κύριος,   οὐ μὴ κτείνῃ σε·
νῦν αὐχήσω,   σὲ προσάξασα δῶρον
ἐκ κοιλίας μου τῷ δωρησαμένῳ σοι   μακαρίζομαι.
Πορεύου οὖν, τέκνον,   καὶ γίνου Θεῷ θῦμα,
σὺν τῷ σῷ γενέτῃ,   φονευτῇ δέ σου μᾶλλον·
πιστεύω δέ, γονεὺς σφαγεὺς οὐ γίνεται,
ὅτι μόνος ἀγαθὸς   ὁ Σωτὴρ τῶν ψυχῶν ἡμῶν.

15

"Μητέρα λιμπάνων με,   εὕρῃς πατέρα   τὸν πάντων
                                                    Θεόν·
αὐτὸς σφαγέντα   ἀναδείξει μοι ζῶντα,
εἰ καὶ μὴ τῷ παρόντι, δείξει μοι   ἐν τῷ μέλλοντι·
ἄσπασαί με,   Ἰσαάκ, τὴν τεκοῦσαν
καὶ τῶν ὠδίνων μήπω ἀπολαύσασαν,   καὶ ἀποτρέχετε."
Τοιαῦτα ἦν ἄρα   ἅπερ ἔφη Σάρρα·
ὁ πρέσβυς δὲ πάντως   εἶπεν ἄλλ᾽ ὑπὲρ ταῦτα,
ἀλλ᾽ οὐκ ἔστερξαν ὑπὲρ τὸν Κύριον,
ὅτι μόνος ἀγαθὸς   ὁ Σωτὴρ τῶν ψυχῶν ἡμῶν.

14

When she had heard her spouse's words, Sarah said to Isaac:
"If he wants you alive, he'll decree that you live.
The Lord is immortal, he will not kill you.
So I shall boast: having offered you as a gift
from my womb to the giver, I'll call myself blessed!
Go, then, child, be a sacrifice to God
together with your father, or rather your killer.
But I believe a father cannot be a murderer,
that but one is good, the Savior of our souls!

15

"When you leave me, your mother, may you find a father,
    the God of all.
He will show me the slain one alive again,
if not in the present, then in the time to come.
Embrace me, Isaac, the one who bore you
but never profited from her pangs. Be off, both of you!"
Something like this Sarah must have uttered,
and the old man certainly said more than that,
yet they did not love more than the Lord,
for but one is good, the Savior of our souls!

16

Αὐτὸς ὁ γεννήσας γὰρ   σχίδακας τέκνῳ   ἐπέθηκεν,
καὶ ὤμοις φέρει   οἷς ἐτίθετο ὁ παῖς·
ἐνταῦθα πᾶς πιστὸς νοείτω μοι   τὸ μυστήριον.
Ἤλυθαν δὲ   οὗπερ ἦσαν κληθέντες,
καὶ ὡς προβλέπων ἔφησε τὰ μέλλοντα   ὁ πιστότατος,
"Καθίσατε," λέγων   τοῖς συνοῦσιν, "ἐνταῦθα·
ἐγὼ δὲ σὺν τέκνῳ   πορευθεὶς ἀναστρέψω."
Καὶ τὰ ῥήματα ἐφάνη πράγματα,
ὅτι μόνος ἀγαθὸς   ὁ Σωτὴρ τῶν ψυχῶν ἡμῶν.

17

Νευρώσας ναρκήσαντας   πόδας τῇ πίστει   καὶ τὴν
                                                                           δεξιὰν
ὁπλίσας ξίφει,   πρῶτον εἶχεν Ἰσαάκ,
ἀλλ᾽ εὗρε πειρασμὸν τὰ ῥήματα   τοῦ παιδός· φησίν·
"Φράσον, πάτερ,   τίς ὁ σφάττεσθαι μέλλων;
Ἔχω τὰ ξύλα, πῦρ σὺ καὶ τὴν μάχαιραν·   ποῦ τὸ
                                                                           πρόβατον;"
Ὦ σπλάγχνον γενέτου·   πρὸς τοὺς λόγους τοῦ τέκνου
τίς τότε ὑπάρχων   ἀπηνὴς οὐκ ἐκάμφθη;
Καὶ οὐκ ἔκαμψε λαλῶν, ἀλλ᾽ ἤγγρισεν,
ὅτι μόνος ἀγαθὸς   ὁ Σωτὴρ τῶν ψυχῶν ἡμῶν.

16

On his own child the father himself laid the firewood,
and the boy carried on his shoulder what he was to be
    placed upon.
Ponder with me this mystery, all here who have faith!
They reached the place to which they were called,
and the most faithful one foretold to his men,
as if prescient, what would happen: "Stay right here!
And I, having gone ahead with the child, shall return."
And these, his words, became deeds,
that but one is good, the Savior of our souls.

17

He braced his stiffened feet and equipped his right hand
with a sword. At first he kept up with Isaac,
but he ran into trouble when the boy said:
"Tell me, father, what will be sacrificed?
I've wood, you fire and knife, but where's the lamb?"
Ah, the father's heart! Who could be so hard,
not to be moved to pity by his child's words?
Still it didn't shake his resolve but upset him,
since but one is good, the Savior of our souls.

18

"Ὁ πρώην καλέσας με   ὄψεται, τέκνον,   εἰ θέλει
                                                σφαγήν·
ἡμεῖς δὲ τούτῳ   ὑπουργήσωμεν," φησίν.
"Ὦ πάτερ, κατ᾽ ἐμοῦ τὴν μάχαιραν   ἠκόνησας;
Βλέπω τύμβον   τὸν βωμόν, ὦ γενέτα·
σὲ δὲ δεσμοῦντα ἅμα καὶ φονεύοντα   ἐνοπτρίζομαι·
εἰ τοίνυν ὃ βλέπω   ἀληθῶς ὁρῶ, λέγε·
μὴ ἄκοντα σφάξῃς,   ἵν᾽ εὐπρόσδεκτον εὕρῃς
τὴν θυσίαν σου, ἐμὲ τὸ τέκνον σου,
ὅτι μόνος ἀγαθὸς   ὁ Σωτὴρ τῶν ψυχῶν ἡμῶν;"

19

Υἱοῦ μὲν τὰ ῥήματα   τότε παρίδε   πιστὸς Ἀβραάμ,
καὶ τῆς θυσίας   ἣν ἐργάτης ἰσχυρός,
καὶ πόδας σὺν χερσὶν ἐδέσμησεν   ὃν ἐγέννησε,
"Πρῶτον," λέγων,   "δήσω, εἶτα φονεύσω,
μήποτε τούτου σκίρτημα κωλύσῃ μου   τὸ ὅρμημα."
Χειρὶ λαβὼν ξίφος   εἰς σφαγήν, ἐπεσχέθη,
οὐ τέκνου σκιρτῶντος,   τοῦ Θεοῦ δὲ καλοῦντος
καὶ σημαίνοντος αὐτοῦ τὰ μέλλοντα,
ὅτι μόνος ἀγαθὸς   ὁ Σωτὴρ τῶν ψυχῶν ἡμῶν.

20

Ὑψόθεν ἐπέβλεψεν   ὁ ἐπιβλέπων   ἀβύσσους Θεός,
καὶ τῷ δικαίῳ   ἀνεβόησε φωνήν·

18

"It will be apparent, my child, if the one who called me
     wants a sacrifice.
Let us, you and me, assist him," he replied.
"Father, did you hone the knife for me?
I see a grave in the altar, father,
and glimpse, as in a mirror, you binding and slaying.
Tell me if I'm seeing truly what I'm imagining.
Surely you cannot slay an unwilling victim,
me your child, as an acceptable sacrifice,
since but one is good, the Savior of our souls?"

19

But faithful Abraham now disregarded his son's words;
he devoted his strength to the labor of sacrifice,
and he bound the feet and hands of his offspring.
"First, I'll bind," he says, "then slay,
so no jerking leap may hinder my thrust."
With the sword in his hand to kill, he was stopped,
not by the leaping child, but by God calling out
and signaling what was to come,
that but one is good, the Savior of our souls.

20

The God who watches over abysmal depths watched from
     on high,
and his voice cried aloud to the righteous one, "Abraham,

"Ἀβραάμ, Ἀβραάμ, πιστότατε,   στεῖλον χεῖρά σου·
γνῶναι θέλων   σὲ ὁ μὴ ἀγνοήσας
σὲ πρὸ τοῦ πλάσαι, τὴν πίστιν σου νῦν εὗρον   ἥνπερ
                                        μέλλουσι
βλέπειν οἱ τῆς ἀληθείας   θερμοὶ ἐρασταί μου
ἐπ' ἐσχάτων τῶν αἰώνων,   ὅτι μέλλει ὁ υἱός μου
εἰς τὸ ὄνομα ἐμὸν δοξάζεσθαι,
ὁ δοτὴρ τῶν ἀγαθῶν   καὶ Σωτὴρ τῶν ψυχῶν ὑμῶν.

21

"Μὴ κτείνῃς τὸν παῖδά σου·   νῦν γάρ σε
                            ἔγνων   φοβούμενόν με·
τοῦ υἱοῦ σου   οὐκ ἐφείσω δι' ἐμέ,
ὅντινα λαβὼν ἀπότρεχε   καθὼς προεῖπας."
Ταῦτ' ἀκούων   Ἀβραὰμ ἔφη τότε·
"Μή τινα μῶμον εὗρες ἐν θυσίᾳ μου   καὶ ἐπέσχες με;
Μή τι παρερρύη   ἐν λόγῳ ἢ ἐν ἔργῳ;
ἢ δόλος ἐν τῷ στόματί μου;   Ὡς καρδίας ἐτάζων,
σὺ καθάρισον καὶ σφάξαι πρόσταξον,
ὁ δοτὴρ τῶν ἀγαθῶν   καὶ Σωτὴρ τῶν ψυχῶν ἡμῶν."

22

"Νῦν στεῖλον τὴν χεῖρά σου·   εὗρον ὡς θέλω   σὴν
                                    πίστιν ἁγνήν,
διὸ καὶ ἐν σοὶ   προσκιάζω τὰ ἐμά·
ἐμὸν γὰρ εἶ σαφῶς ἐκτύπωμα,   ναί, δίκαιε·
θέλεις γνῶναι   ἐκ τῶν σῶν τὰ μετὰ σέ;

most faithful Abraham, stay your hand!
I wanted to know you, who were not unknown to me
before I formed you, and I've found your faith, upon which
    my ardent
lovers of truth will gaze
in the final ages. For my own son
is going to be glorified in my name,
as giver of good and Savior of your souls.

21

"Do not kill your boy! I know now that you fear me.
For my sake you did not withhold your son.
Take him and hurry off as you foretold!"
Upon hearing this, Abraham spoke,
"Did you find a blemish in my sacrifice and stop me?
Was it something I neglected, in word or deed,
some deceit in my mouth? You search the heart;
now, cleanse it and command it to slay,
as giver of good and Savior of our souls."

22

"Stay your hand now! I found your faith pure, as I wished,
and so in you I can sketch my own patterns;
indeed, righteous one, you clearly bear my imprint.
Do you wish to know what of yours follows after you?

Τούτου γὰρ χάριν ἔνθα σε ἀνήγαγον,   τοῦ δεῖξαί σοι.
Ὥσπερ οὖν οὐκ ἐφείσω   δι᾽ ἐμὲ τοῦ υἱοῦ σου,
κἀγὼ διὰ πάντας   οὐ φείσομαι τοῦ υἱοῦ μου·
ὑπὲρ κόσμου δὲ σφαγῆναι δίδωμι,
ὁ δοτὴρ τῶν ἀγαθῶν   καὶ Σωτὴρ τῶν ψυχῶν ὑμῶν.

23

"Οὕτως δ᾽ ὡς ἐβάσταξε   ξύλα τοῖς ὤμοις   ὁ σὸς Ἰσαάκ,
ἐπ᾽ ὤμων φέρει   ὁ ἐμὸς υἱὸς τὸν σταυρόν·
ὁ πόθος ὁ πολύς σοι ἔδειξε   καὶ τὰ μέλλοντα.
Βλέψον ἄρτι   καὶ κριὸν τὸν ἐν ξύλῳ·
πόθεν κρατεῖται βλέπων καταμάνθανε   τὸ μυστήριον·
τοῖς κέρασιν τοῦτον   τὰ δεσμὰ περιέχει,
τὰ κέρατα χεῖρας   τοῦ υἱοῦ μου σημαίνει·
καὶ σφάξον μοι, καὶ σὸν υἱὸν φυλάττω σοι,
ὁ δοτὴρ τῶν ἀγαθῶν   καὶ Σωτὴρ τῶν ψυχῶν ὑμῶν."

24

Σφαγὴν οὐ δεχόμενον   βλέπουσα Σάρρα   σὺν τῷ
                                                          Ἀβραάμ,
χορεύει πάλιν   δεξαμένη Ἰσαάκ·
"Ὁ δείξας σε ἐμοί, ὦ τέκνον μου,   λάβῃ πνεῦμά μου."
Ταύτην ἡμῖν   τὴν χαρὰν σὺ παράσχου,
ὁ ἐπὶ ξύλου χεῖρας ὥσπερ κέρατα   δεσμηθεὶς δι᾽ ἡμᾶς·
ἡμῶν ἱκεσίας   κενὰς μὴ ἀποστρέψῃς,
δι᾽ οὓς ἐσταυρώθης   ἐν θυμῷ σου μὴ κτείνῃς·
τούτων πρέσβευε καὶ σύ, πάτερ, τυχεῖν ἡμᾶς,
ὁ δοτὴρ τῶν ἀγαθῶν   καὶ Σωτὴρ τῶν ψυχῶν ἡμῶν.

That is what I brought you up here to show you:
as you did not withhold your son for my sake,
I shall not withhold my son for the sake of all.
I give him to be slain for the world,
as giver of good and Savior of your souls.

23

"In a similar way to how your Isaac's shoulders carried the
    wood,
so my son bears the cross on his.
And your great ardor has revealed what will come:
just look there, the ram in a tree!
Grasp the mystery when you see how it's held!
By its horns it is held in bonds;
these horns signify my son's hands.
Slaughter it for me, and I'll protect your son,
as giver of good and Savior of your souls."

24

When Sarah sees her son with Abraham, unbound by
    sacrifice,
she holds on to Isaac and dances with bliss again:
"He who's shown you to me, child, may take my spirit!"
Grant us such joy, you who were bound
on the tree for us by the hands as by horns.
Do not leave our prayers unanswered,
do not slay in your anger those for whom you were
    crucified!
And you, our father, pray for these things to benefit us,
the giver of good and Savior of our souls.

Προοίμιον

Τὸν Ἠσαῦ μισήσας   ὡς ἄσωτον
καὶ Ἰακὼβ ἀγαπήσας   ὡς δίκαιον,
τὴν εὐλογίαν ἐξ ἐκείνου   εἰς τοῦτον μετήγαγες·
ἀλλ' ὡς τῷ πράῳ τῇ συμβουλίᾳ τῆς μητρός,
ταῖς ἱκεσίαις τῆς ἀχράντου σου μητρός,
Χριστὲ ὁ Θεός,
ἐξ οὐρανοῦ εὐλογίαν παράσχου ἡμῖν.

I

πρός· Τὸν πρὸ ἡλίου ἥλιον

Τὸν διὰ τῆς ὑπακοῆς   σώσαντα γένος ἀνθρώπων,
πατήσαντα τὸν ὄφιν   καὶ φωτίσαντα τὸν κόσμον
καὶ ἐκ τῆς παρθένου   τεχθέντα ἀγεωργήτως,
τὸν τῆς κατάρας   ἀπαλλάξαντα κτίσιν ἅπασαν,
τὸν τοὺς παραβάντας   ῥήξαντα ἀγγέλους
καὶ παραπεσόντα   χειρὶ ἐγείραντα Ἀδὰμ
ὑμνήσωμεν, δοξάσωμεν.
Γνῶμεν τί   ἔδρασεν   ἡμῖν τὸ πτῶμα

ON THE BLESSING OF JACOB

in fourth plagal mode

Prelude

to its own melody

You hated Esau as prodigal
and loved Jacob as righteous,
so you passed the blessing from the former to the latter.
As you did for the gentle one through his mother's counsel,
so, through your undefiled mother's supplications,
Christ our God,
grant unto us a blessing from heaven.

I

to: The maidens with perfume

The one who through obedience saved the human race,
trampled the snake and enlightened the world,
and was born from a virgin never tilled,
who released the whole creation from the curse,
who overthrew the offending angels
and raised the fallen Adam by his hand,
let us praise and glorify him!
Let us learn what it accomplished for us,

τῆς παραβάσεως   ἐν τῇ παρακοῇ,
καθὼς καὶ ἡ βίβλος   τῆς κτίσεως λέγει
τοῦ πρωτοπλάστου   τὴν ἀθεσίαν·
ὅθεν σπεύσωμεν ἅπαντες
καὶ κράξωμεν   τῷ Θεῷ ἡμῶν·
"Ἐξ οὐρανοῦ εὐλογίαν παράσχου ἡμῖν."

2

Οἱ τῶν μελλόντων τύποι οὖν   σύγγονοι δύο ὑπῆρχον,
τεχθέντες ἐκ Ῥεβέκκας   Ἰσαὰκ τῷ πατριάρχῃ·
τὸν Ἠσαῦ δὲ τότε   καλέσας ἔφη ὁ πρέσβυς·
"Πορεύου, τέκνον,   ἐν ἀγρῷ σπουδῇ καὶ ἀγώνισαι·
λάβε σου τὸ τόξον   καὶ τὴν φαρέτραν·
θήρευσόν μοι θήραν   καὶ σπεῦσον ἀρέσαι πατρί,
καὶ ἔνεγκέ μοι ἔδεσμα,
ὅπως σου   δέξωμαι   τὴν προθυμίαν,
καὶ εὐλογήσω σε   πρὶν τελευτῆσαί με·
ἀνάστηθι, δεῖξον   τὴν διάθεσίν σου,
καὶ πλήρωσόν μου   ἐπιθυμίαν·
ὁρῶν γάρ σου τὴν ἅπασαν
προαίρεσιν,   τῷ Θεῷ κράζω·
'Ἐξ οὐρανοῦ εὐλογίαν παράσχου ἡμῖν.'"

3

Ὑπέστησεν ὁ γηραιὸς   τὸν ἐκ τῶν σπλάγχνων τεχθέντα,
καὶ τρέχειν κατεπείχθη   ὁ Ἠσαῦ τότε εἰς θήραν·
ἡ δὲ μήτηρ τούτου   πρὸς Ἰακὼβ ἀνεβόα·

the fall as he stepped into disobedience,
as the book of creation also relates,
the faithlessness of the first-formed human.
Let us eagerly, then,
all cry to our God,
"Grant unto us a blessing from heaven!"

2

The two siblings were figures of future events,
borne by Rebecca to Isaac the patriarch.
The old man once called for Esau and said,
"Go out in the fields, child, and compete fiercely!
Take your bow and your quiver.
Hunt game for me! Hurry to please your father,
and bring me meat,
so I may enjoy your goodwill
and give you my blessing before I pass.
Get up and show your affection
and satisfy my craving!
Seeing your full commitment,
I'll cry to God,
'Grant unto us a blessing from heaven!'"

3

The elder supported the one who came from his loins,
and Esau hastened to run to the hunt.
His mother, then, called out to Jacob,

"Σπούδασον φθάσαι   εἰς τὴν ποίμνην καὶ ἀγωνίσασθαι·
ἤκουσα λαλοῦντος   τοῦ σοῦ γενέτου
πρὸς τὸν ἀδελφόν σου·   'Θήρευσόν μοι θήραν, ὦ παῖ,
καὶ ἔνεγκέ μοι ἔδεσμα·
καὶ φαγὼν   καὶ εὐφρανθεὶς   σὲ εὐλογήσω·
πρὸ τοῦ ἐμὲ θανεῖν   συντόμως πείσθητι.'
Καθώς σοι οὖν εἶπον·   Πορεύθητι, λάβε
ἀπὸ τῆς ποίμνης   δύο ἐρίφους.
Ποιήσω τῷ γενέτῃ σου
τὸ ἔδεσμα,   ἵν' εὐξάμενος
ἐξ οὐρανοῦ εὐλογίαν παράσχῃ ἡμῖν."

4

Ταῦτα ἀκούσας Ἰακὼβ   πρὸς τὴν τεκοῦσαν ἐβόα·
"Πῶς φθάσω εἰς τὴν ποίμνην   καὶ κομίσω τοὺς ἐρίφους;
Ὁ Ἠσαῦ, ὦ μῆτερ,   ἀνὴρ δασὺς φύσει ἐστίν·
ἐγὼ δὲ πάλιν   ὡς ἀνὴρ λεῖος ἐπαισχύνομαι·
μήπως ὁ πατήρ μου   ἐμὲ γνωρίσῃ
καὶ ὑπὸ αἰσχύνης   ὡς καταφρονήσας αὐτοῦ
ἀπέναντι γενήσομαι·
ἐπάξω δὲ   ἐμαυτῷ   μᾶλλον κατάραν,
καὶ οὐκ εὐλογήσει με,   ἀλλ' ἀπολέσει με.
Ὦ μῆτερ, πτοοῦμαι   τὸ τόλμημα πάνυ,
τοῦ ἀδελφοῦ μου   καὶ τὴν μανίαν·
σιγήσομαι οὖν καὶ εὔξομαι
τῷ Πλάσαντι   κράζων· Εὔσπλαγχνε,
ἐξ οὐρανοῦ εὐλογίαν παράσχου ἡμῖν.'"

"Hurry to the flock and join the contest!
I heard your father saying to your brother,
'Go, my boy, hunt game for me,
and bring me meat!
When I'm full and content, I'll give you my blessing.
Obey me now, before I die!'
As I said to you, go take
two kids from the flock.
I'll prepare for your father
the meat so he'll pray and
grant unto us a blessing from heaven!"

4

When Jacob heard this, he exclaimed to her, "How
can I go to the flock and fetch those kids?
By nature Esau is a hairy man,
while I, mother, being a smooth-skinned man,
am worried that my father will recognize me
and I shall be put to shame before him
as one who has mocked him;
so instead I'll bring a curse on myself,
and he will not bless but destroy me!
Mother, I'm utterly terrified of my brother's
ruthlessness and fury.
I'll be quiet and pray to the Fashioner,
crying, 'Compassionate one,
grant unto us a blessing from heaven!'"

5

"Ἄκουσον λόγων τῶν ἐμῶν   καὶ μὴ δειλία, ὦ τέκνον,"
ἡ μήτηρ ἀνεβόα   κολακεύουσα τὸν νέον·
"νῦν ἐπάκουσόν μου   καὶ δεῖξον ὡς ἀγαπᾷς με·
ἡ σὴ κατάρα   ἐπ' ἐμὲ γενήσεται, τέκνον μου·
μόνον τῇ βουλῇ μου   παράσχου χάριν
ὡς ἐνετειλάμην,   καὶ δύο ἐρίφους καλοὺς
καὶ ἁπαλούς μοι κόμισον."
Ὁ δὲ παῖς   πορευθεὶς   ἤγαγε ταύτῃ
δύο ἐρίφια,   καὶ τὰ ἐδέσματα
ἐποίησε τάχος   καθὼς καὶ ἐφίλει
ὁ πατὴρ τούτου,   τῇ προθυμίᾳ
ἀγαπῶσα· τὸ τέκνον δὲ
προσηύχετο·   "Σύ, φιλάνθρωπε,
ἐξ οὐρανοῦ εὐλογίαν παράσχου ἡμῖν."

6

Περιεπτύξατο στολὴν   τοῦ πρεσβυτέρου συγγόνου
ὁ νεανίσκος τότε,   ὡς διδάσκει τὸ Βιβλίον·
τὰ δὲ δάση πάλιν   τὰ τῶν ἐρίφων λαμβάνει
καὶ περισφίγγει   τῷ τραχήλῳ σὺν τοῖς βραχίοσι
μέχρι καὶ τῶν ὤμων   καὶ τῶν δακτύλων·
ἦρε δὲ τοὺς ἄρτους   καὶ τὰ ἐδέσματα ὁμοῦ
καὶ τρέχειν κατεπείγετο.
Ἔνδον δὲ   εἰσελθών,   τῷ γηραλέῳ
εὐθὺς ἐβόησεν·   "Ὦ πάτερ, κέλευσον,

5

"Heed my words, child, and have no fear,"
replied the mother as she coaxed the youngster.
"Obey me now, and show me how you love me!
Your curse, my boy, shall be upon me.
Just grant me this favor according to my wish,
as I instructed, and fetch me two kids,
choice and tender!"
The boy went and brought her two kids,
and she quickly prepared
dishes of meat as his father liked it;
she loved his goodwill.
But the child was praying,
"You, who are benevolent,
grant unto us a blessing from heaven!"

6

The youth then wrapped himself in the garment
of his older sibling, as the Bible teaches.
He took the fleece of the kids, moreover,
and bound them around his neck and his arms,
all the way from his shoulders to his fingers.
He picked up the loaves and dishes of meat
and ran off in haste.
As soon as he entered, he exclaimed to the old one,
"Father, here is your son at your service,

ἰδοὺ ὁ υἱός σου   ὁ Ἡσαῦ ὁ πρῶτος·
ἐγὼ λαλῶ σοι,   ἐπάκουσόν μου·
ἐδέσματά σοι ἤγαγον,
ὡς ἔφης μοι,   καὶ αἰτοῦμαί σε·
ἐξ οὐρανοῦ εὐλογίαν παράσχου μοι."

7

Εἶπεν δὲ τότε Ἰσαὰκ   τῷ υἱῷ αὐτοῦ· "Τέκνον,
ταχὺ ὑπήκουσάς μου   καὶ τὴν θήρα ἐκομίσω."
Ὁ δὲ νέος πάλιν   πρὸς τὸν γενέτην ἐβόα·
"Τοῦτο ὑπάρχει   ὅπερ ὁ Θεός σοι ἀπέστειλεν,
ὅστις θωρακίσας   ἐπὶ τὴν θήραν
ὥσπερ πρὸς ἀρνίον   ἐν τῷ πεδίῳ μοι ὀφθεὶς
παρέσχε μοι τὴν δύναμιν.
Καὶ λοιπὸν   ἔφθασα   ὥσπερ εἰς μάνδραν,
καὶ κομισάμενος   τὸ θῦμα ἤγαγον,
γενέτα, ὡς εἶπας   ἐπλήρωσα ἔργον
ἵνα μετάσχω   τῆς εὐλογίας·
τὴν χάριν οὖν, ἣν πρότερον
ὑπέσχου μοι   ἐκπληρώσας νῦν,
ἐξ οὐρανοῦ εὐλογίαν παράσχου μοι."

8

Ἰσαὰκ γνοὺς τὸν υἱὸν   τάχος ἐλθόντα τῆς θήρας,
τὸν νοῦν αὐτοῦ ταράξας,   ἐλογίζετο τοιαῦτα·
"Τίς ὁ δρόμος οὗτος;   τίς ἡ σπουδὴ ἡ τοσαύτη;
Ὁ λογισμός μου   περιβάλλει με πρὸς ἐνθύμησιν·

Esau, your first. It is I who speak to you;
pay attention to me!
I brought you meat
as you told me, and I urge you,
grant unto me a blessing from heaven!"

7

Isaac then said to his son: "Child,
you obeyed me quickly and fetched the game."
The youngster in turn told his begetter,
"This is what God, the one who equipped me
for the hunt, has sent you;
when it appeared like a lamb in the plain,
it gave me strength.
And so I came, as though into a sheepfold,
and having caught the victim, I left.
Father, as you asked, I completed the task
to share in the blessing.
Conferring the grace
that you promised me before,
grant unto me a blessing from heaven!"

8

Seeing how soon his son had returned from the hunt
troubled Isaac's mind, and he wondered,
"What is this race? What's the rush?
My thoughts make me worry.

μή τις ἄρα τέχνη   γέγονεν αὕτη;
μή τις μετὰ δόλου   ἁρπάσαι ἦλθεν ἀπ' ἐμοῦ
τὴν δωρεὰν τοῦ τέκνου μου;
Μᾶλλον δὲ   Κύριος,   πληρῶσαι θέλων
ἐπιθυμίαν μου,   αὐτὸς συνήργησε,
καὶ ὅπερ ἐζήτει   εὗρεν ὁ υἱός μου,
διὸ καὶ ἦλθεν   εὐθυδρομήσας,
μισθὸν λαβὼν τὸ χάρισμα
τοῦ πέμψαντος,   ὃν αἰτήσομαι·
ἐξ οὐρανοῦ εὐλογίαν παράσχου ἡμῖν."

9

"Νῦν ἔγγισόν μοι, τέκνον μου,   καὶ ψηλαφήσω σε τάχος·
εἰ πέλεις ὁ Ἠσαῦ σὺ   ὁ πρωτότοκός μου, δεῖξον."
Ψηλαφῶν δὲ τοῦτον,   ὁ Ἰσαὰκ ἐνθυμεῖται·
"Ἡ μὲν φωνὴ νῦν   Ἰακὼβ ἠχεῖ εἰς τὰ ὦτά μου,
χεῖρες τοῦ Ἠσαῦ δὲ   τοῦ υἱοῦ μου."
"Δεῦρο οὖν, ὦ σπλάγχνον,   καὶ καταφίλησον ἐμέ,
καὶ ἔνεγκε τὸ ἔδεσμα."
Καὶ φαγὼν   Ἰσαάκ,   καταφιλήσας
τὸν υἱὸν αὐτοῦ,   ὠσφράνθη τῆς στολῆς
τῆς τούτου καὶ εἶπεν·   "Ἰδοὺ τοῦ υἱοῦ μου
ὡς ἀγροῦ πλήρης   ὀσμὴ ὑπάρχει,
ἀγροῦ οὗπερ ηὐλόγησεν
ὁ Κύριος·   εἰσακούσας μου,
ἐξ οὐρανοῦ εὐλογίαν παρέσχεν ἡμῖν."

Isn't it some kind of hoax?
Isn't it someone who has come deceitfully
to snatch my child's gift?
No, it must be the Lord who himself was involved,
as he wanted to satisfy my craving,
and what he sought, my son found,
so he ran directly
to receive the reward
of the sender, whom I ask,
grant unto us a blessing from heaven!"

9

"Come near now, child, and I'll feel you briefly.
If you are indeed Esau, my firstborn, prove it!"
As he was feeling him, Isaac wondered,
"The voice of Jacob resounds in my ears,
while the hands are Esau's, my son's."
"Come, my dear one, give me a kiss
and bring me the meat!"
After he had eaten, Isaac kissed
his son and smelled his
garment and said, "Ah, my son's
smell is that of a rich field,
a field that the Lord
has blessed; he heard me and
granted to us a blessing from heaven!"

10

Ὅτε εὐλόγησε σαφῶς   τὸν Ἰακὼβ ὁ γενέτης,
κατήχησε τὸν παῖδα   ταῖς εὐχαῖς αὐτοῦ ὁ γέρων
λέγων· "Ὁ Θεός μου   σὲ εὐλογήσει ἐν κόσμῳ
σίτῳ καὶ οἴνῳ,   καὶ τὰ ἔθνη πάντα δουλεύσει σοι·
προσκυνήσουσί σοι   ἄρχοντες πάντες·
κύριος δὲ πάλιν   γίνου καὶ τοῦ σοῦ ἀδελφοῦ.
Ὁ σὲ δὲ καταρώμενος
λήψεται   τὴν ἀράν,   ὁ δὲ εὐλογῶν σε
εὐλογηθήσεται   τῇ θείᾳ χάριτι."
Τοιαῦτα ἀκούσας,   ἐξῆλθεν ὁ νέος
εὐλογημένος,   ὑμνῶν τὸν Κτίστην,
βοῶν· "Δίκαιος Κύριος,
φιλάνθρωπος·   ὡς γὰρ εὔσπλαγχνος,
ἐξ οὐρανοῦ εὐλογίαν παρέσχεν ἡμῖν."

11

Ὑπὸ τοῦ πόθου τὸν υἱὸν   ὁ γηραλέος εὐλόγει,
Χριστὸν τὸν πάντων Κτίστην   ἐντυπῶν ταῖς εὐλογίαις.
Ἰακὼβ δὲ τότε   πρὸς τὴν τεκοῦσαν ἐκτρέχει,
λέγων πρὸς ταύτην·   "Ἰδού, εὐλογίαν ἀπέλαβον,
παρὰ τοῦ πατρός μου   ἔλαβον χάριν."
Τότε προσεπλάκη   τῷ νέῳ ἡ μήτηρ αὐτοῦ
καὶ κλαίειν κατεπείγετο,
λέγουσα·   "Εἷς ἐστιν   ὁ τοῖς ἁγίοις
παρέχων σύνεσιν·   αὐτὸς ἐλεύσεται

68

10

When the father had clearly blessed Jacob,
the elder instructed the boy with his prayers.
He said, "My God will bless you in the world
with grain and wine. And all nations shall serve you,
all rulers bow down to you.
Be lord, then, over your brother.
Whoever curses you
shall receive the curse; whoever blesses you
shall also be blessed with divine grace."
After he had heard this, the blessed youth
departed and, praising the Creator, he cried,
"Just and benevolent Lord,
being compassionate you have
granted to us a blessing from heaven!"

11

With desire the old one blessed his son,
sketching Christ, the Creator of all, in his blessings.
Jacob then runs over to his mother,
saying, "Look, I obtained a blessing;
I received grace from my father."
His mother then embraced the youth
and was driven to tears.
"He is One," she said, "who grants
discernment to the holy ones. He will come

σαρκὶ ἐν τῷ κόσμῳ   ἐκ ῥίζης βλαστοῦ σου,
Πατρὸς τοὺς κόλπους   μὴ καταλείψας.
Αὐτὸν οὖν δυσωπήσωμεν
τὸν εὔσπλαγχνον   καὶ φιλάνθρωπον·
Ἐξ οὐρανοῦ εὐλογίαν παράσχου ἡμῖν.'"

12

Ῥήματα καὶ ὁ Ἰσαὰκ   εὐχαριστίας ἐκπέμπειν
οὐδόλως ἐνεδίδου,   ἕως ὅτε ἐπληρώθη
ἡ ψυχὴ ἡ τούτου   χαρᾶς μεγάλης, καὶ λέγει
πρὸς τὴν Ῥεβέκκαν·   "Νῦν Θεὸς ἡμᾶς ἐπεσκέψατο,
καὶ ἐκ τῶν ὑψίστων   τὴν γῆν ἐπεῖδεν,
ὅπως τοῖς ἁγίοις   τὴν εὐλογίαν τὴν αὐτοῦ
δωρήσηται ὡς Κύριος·
παῖδας δὲ   εἰς τιμὴν   ἡμῖν παρέσχε,
καὶ χάριν δίδωσι   τὴν ἐκ τοῦ Πνεύματος
ἐκχέων πλουσίως,   ὅτε εὐδοκήσει
τὸ γένος σῶσαι   ἐνανθρωπήσας·
νυνὶ γὰρ προετύπωσε
τὰ μέλλοντα   ἐν τῇ χάριτι·
ἐξ οὐρανοῦ εὐλογίαν παρέχει ἡμῖν."

13

Ὡς οὖν ἐλάλει Ἰσαὰκ   τῇ ὁμοζύγῳ τοιαῦτα,
Ἡσαῦ ὁ γόνος τούτων   ἐκ τῆς θήρας ἐπανῆλθε,
καὶ αὐτὸς ἐποίει   ἐδέσματα τῷ γενέτῃ·
προσήνεγκε δὲ   τῷ πατρὶ αὐτοῦ πρὸς μετάληψιν,

in flesh to the world, from the shoot of your root,
without abandoning the bosom of the Father.
So let us implore him,
the compassionate and benevolent one,
'*Grant unto us a blessing from heaven!*'"

12

Isaac did not cease from uttering words
of thanksgiving, as this great joy
had filled his soul.
He said to Rebecca, "Now God has cared for us;
from the highest he's watched over the earth,
so that as Lord he may give his blessing
to the holy ones.
He has honored us with children,
and he gives us the grace that abundantly pours
forth from the Spirit when it pleases him
to take human form and save the race.
What he'll do in the future,
he has gracefully prefigured;
grant unto us a blessing from heaven."

13

As Isaac was saying these things to his wife,
their son Esau returned from his hunt,
and he also prepared meat for his father.
He offered it to him for him to eat

λέγων· "Ὦ γενέτα,   ἐπάκουσόν μου,
καὶ ἀπὸ τῆς θήρας   εὐφράνθητι τοῦ σοῦ υἱοῦ,
δι' ἧς καὶ εὐλογήσεις με."
Εἶπε δὲ Ἰσαὰκ   τότε ὁ πρέσβυς
πρὸς τὸν υἱὸν αὐτοῦ·   "Τίς εἶ σύ, δήλωσον."
Ὁ δὲ ἀπεκρίθη·   "Ἐγώ εἰμι," λέγων,
"Ἠσαῦ, γενέτα,   ὁ υἱός σου,
πρωτότοκός σου πέφυκα
ἐκ σπλάγχνων σου·   ἀλλὰ δέομαι
ἐξ οὐρανοῦ εὐλογίαν παράσχου μοι."

14

Μετὰ τοὺς λόγους τοῦ παιδὸς   καὶ τὰς αὐτοῦ ἱκεσίας,
ἐξέστη ὁ πρεσβύτης   σφόδρα ἔκστασιν μεγάλην,
λέγων· "Τίς οὖν ἐστιν   ὁ εἰσενέγκας μοι θήραν,
καὶ ἀπὸ πάντων   εὐφρανθεὶς ἐκεῖνον εὐλόγησα,
καὶ εὐλογημένος   ἐστὶν ἐν πᾶσι;
Πρὸ τοῦ γάρ σε φθάσαι   ἐκ τοῦ ἀγροῦ εἰς τὴν σκηνὴν,
ἐδέσματά μοι ἤγαγεν."
Ὅτε δὲ   ἤκουσε   τούτους τοὺς λόγους,
Ἠσαῦ ἐβόησεν   ὀδυνηρὰν φωνήν,
κραυγάζων καὶ λέγων·   "Εὐλόγησον σπεύσας
κἀμέ, ὦ πάτερ,   ὥσπερ ἐκεῖνον,
κἀμοὶ ἀξίως δώρησαι
τὴν χάριν σου,   καὶ ὁ Ὕψιστος
ἐξ οὐρανοῦ εὐλογίαν παράσχῃ ἡμῖν."

and said, "My father, listen to me,
let this game from your son's hunt make you happy,
and bless me for it!"
Then Isaac, the elder, exclaimed to his son,
"Who are you—explain!"
He replied and said, "Father, I am
Esau, your son,
the firstborn of your loins.
And I am begging,
grant unto me a blessing from heaven!"

14

With the boy's words and entreaties the old one
was shaken with great agitation:
"Who was he, then, that brought me game,
whom I blessed, pleased by everything,
and who is blessed in every way?
Before you came into the tent from the field,
he served me meat."
When Esau heard his father's words,
he cried out in a tormented voice,
shouting and exclaiming, "Hurry up and bless
me too, like him, father;
I too am worthy
of your grace; may the Highest
grant unto us a blessing from heaven!"

15

Ἀκούσας ταῦτα Ἰσαὰκ   τοὺς λόγους τούτους ἐβόα·
"Ἐλθὼν ὁ ἀδελφός σου   Ἰακὼβ πρὶν μετὰ δόλου
ὑπεδέξατό σου   τὴν εὐλογίαν ἐκεῖνος.
Τί οὖν ποιήσω;   Πῶς εἰς τοῦτό σοι ὑπακούσομαι;"
Ὁ Ἡσαῦ δὲ ἔφη   πρὸς τὸν γενέτην·
"Ὄντως καὶ δικαίως   ἐκλήθη οὗτος Ἰακὼβ
τῷ λόγῳ καὶ τῷ πράγματι·
ἤδη γὰρ   δεύτερον   ἐπτέρνισέ με·
τὰ πρωτοτόκια   αὐτὸς ἀφεῖλέ μου,
καὶ νῦν, καθὼς ἔγνων,   καὶ τὴν εὐλογίαν
αὐτὸς ἐδέξατο τοῦ πατρός μου·
ἐστέρησέ με δεύτερον
ἐκ μήτρας μου·   ἀλλὰ δέομαι
ἐξ οὐρανοῦ εὐλογίαν παράσχου μοι."

16

Νενικημένος Ἰσαὰκ   τοῖς σπλάγχνοις καὶ ἡττημένος,
πρὸς τὸν Ἡσαῦ ἐβόα   λέγων· "Ἄκουσον, ὦ τέκνον·
εἰ τῷ ἀδελφῷ σου   τὴν ἐξουσίαν παρέσχον,
σίτῳ καὶ οἴνῳ   εἰ τὸν οἶκον τούτου ἐπλήρωσα,
σοὶ νῦν τί ποιήσω,   τέκνον, εἰπέ μοι."
Πάλιν ἀπεκρίθη   Ἡσαῦ τῷ γενέτῃ αὐτοῦ,
καὶ κλαίων οὕτως ἔλεγε·
"Μία γὰρ   μόνη σοι   ἔστιν εὐλογία;
Ἐξ ἧς κατέλιπας   κἀμὲ εὐλόγησον."

15

When Isaac heard this, he cried out with these words:
"Your brother Jacob came deceitfully before,
and he thus received the blessing that was yours.
What can I do? How shall I give what you ask?"
Esau said to his father,
"Truly and rightly in word and in deed
was he called Jacob.
It's the second time that he's supplanted me.
He divested me once of my birthright, and now,
as I have learned, he has even taken for himself
my father's blessing.
He's deprived me twice
since the womb, but I'm begging,
grant unto me a blessing from heaven!"

16

Overcome by emotions and defeated, Isaac
cried out to Esau, "Listen, my child,
if I have granted your brother authority
and filled his house with grain and wine,
tell me, what then can I do for you, child?"
Esau answered his father again
and said, while weeping,
"Do you have only one blessing?
From what you have left, bless me too!"

Τότε κατενύγη   Ἰσαὰκ ὁ γενέτης
καὶ ἀνεβόα   μετὰ δακρύων·
"Εὐλογῶν εὐλογήσει σε
ὡς βούλεται   ὁ φιλάνθρωπος·
ἐξ οὐρανοῦ εὐλογίαν παρέχει ἡμῖν."

17

Ὅτε ἐπαύσατο θρηνῶν,   ὁ γηραλέος ἐκτείνει
τὴν χεῖρα καὶ ηὐλόγει   τὸν Ἠσαῦ, τοιαῦτα λέγων·
"Ἰδοὺ ἐκ τῆς δρόσου   τῶν ὑψωμάτων σοι ἔσται,
καὶ ἐκ τῆς γαίας   τῆς πιότητος ἡ κατοίκησις,
καὶ ἐν τῇ μαχαίρᾳ   τῇ σῇ τραφήσει,
καὶ τῷ ἀδελφῷ σου   προθύμως δουλεύσεις ἀεί,
καὶ ἔσει εὐφραινόμενος.
Ἐὰν γὰρ   τὸν ζυγὸν   τὸν τῆς δουλείας
αὐτοῦ μὴ καθέλῃς   ἐκ τοῦ τραχήλου σου,
ἐν πάσῃ εἰρήνῃ   πορεύσει ἐν κόσμῳ,
ὅτι ἐκλέλοιπεν ἡ ὀργή σου·
πληρώσει σου τὰ αἰτήματα
ὁ Κύριος,   καὶ ὡς βούλεται
ἐξ οὐρανοῦ εὐλογίαν παράσχῃ σοι."

18

Ὑπὸ τοῦ φθόνου ὁ Ἠσαῦ   τῷ Ἰακὼβ ἐνεκότει,
καὶ κτεῖναι ἐνενόει   τοῦτον μετὰ τὸ θανῆναι
τὸν αὐτοῦ γενέτην,   καὶ ἔλεγεν ἐν καρδίᾳ·
"Νῦν ἐγγισάτω   ἡ ἀσθένεια τοῦ γενέτου μου,

76

Isaac the father was heartbroken now,
and he cried out with tears,
"The benevolent one who blesses
will bless you as he wishes,
granting to us a blessing from heaven!"

17

When he had stopped lamenting, the old one stretched out
    his hand
and blessed Esau with these words: "Behold,
your portion shall be of the dew from the heights
and your dwelling out of the fatness of the earth,
and by the sword you shall feed your own,
and you shall always eagerly serve your brother,
and you shall be happy.
If you avoid breaking the yoke
of his servitude from your neck,
you will walk in peace throughout the world,
since your anger has waned.
The Lord will fulfill
your requests, as he wishes,
granting to you a blessing from heaven!"

18

Out of envy Esau bore a grudge against Jacob,
and he planned to kill him after the death
of his father, and so he said in his heart,
"Let my father soon grow weak now,

καὶ μετὰ τὸ θνῆξαι   τοῦτον εὐθέως
τότε εὐκαιρίας   λαβόμενος, κτείνω ἐγὼ
τὸν πτερνιστήν μου σύγγονον."
Ἀλλ' εὐθὺς   ὁ Θεὸς   ὁ προγινώσκων
τὰ ἐνθυμήματα,   Ἡσαῦ τὰ ῥήματα
μητρὶ ἀμφοτέρων   γνωρίσας, σοφίζει
αὐτὴν ἐμφρόνως   σκεδάσαι ταῦτα.
Αὐτὸν οὖν δυσωπήσωμεν
τὸν εὔσπλαγχνον·   "Σύ, φιλάνθρωπε,
ἐξ οὐρανοῦ εὐλογίαν παράσχου ἡμῖν."

19

Ὑμεῖς οὖν ταῦτα ἀκριβῶς   κατανοήσατε, φίλοι·
τὰ πάντα γὰρ ἐν τύπῳ   προερρέθη καὶ ἐγράφη.
Ὁ Ἡσαῦ μὲν τύπος   τῶν Ἰουδαίων ὑπάρχει·
Χριστιανῶν δὲ   Ἰακὼβ εἰκόνα προέφερεν,
ὃς τὴν εὐλογίαν   τὴν τοῦ συγγόνου
ἔλαβεν ἀξίως   τῇ συμβουλίᾳ τῆς μητρός,
τὴν χάριν προσημάνας μοι.
Τύπος δὲ   τοῦ Χριστοῦ   τῆς Ἐκκλησίας
καὶ ἡ Ῥεβέκκα μοι   σαφῶς προδέδεικται·
καθάπερ γὰρ αὕτη   καὶ ἡ Ἐκκλησία
υἱοὺς προσάγει   Πατρὶ τῶν ὅλων,
ἐν ᾗ συναθροιζόμενοι
κραυγάζωμεν   τῷ Θεῷ ἡμῶν·
"Ἐξ οὐρανοῦ εὐλογίαν παράσχου ἡμῖν."

and directly after he has died,
seizing the moment, I shall kill
my sibling who supplanted me."
But immediately God, who knows in advance
every intention, revealed Esau's thoughts
to the mother of them both and prudently gave her
the wisdom to disperse them.
So let us implore the compassionate one,
"You, benevolent one,
grant unto us a blessing from heaven!"

19

Now, you, my friends, consider this carefully;
all is already told and sketched in outline:
While Esau is a sketch of the Jews,
Jacob presented an image of the Christians,
who received his brother's blessing
worthily through his mother's counsel,
presaging grace to me.
And Rebecca is clearly presented to me
as a sketch of the Church of Christ.
Just like her, the Church too
brings her sons to the Father of all.
Assembled in her,
let us cry to our God,
"*Grant unto us a blessing from heaven!*"

ἦχος πλάγιος δ´

Προοίμιον 1

πρός· Χαίρετε

Οἱ τὸ στάδιον τῶν νηστειῶν   πανσόφως διανύσαντες
καὶ τὴν ἔναρξιν τοῦ πάθους τοῦ Κυρίου   ἐν πόθῳ
                                    ποιούμενοι,
δεῦτε, πάντες ἀδελφοί,   τὴν τοῦ σώφρονος ἁγνείαν
Ἰωσὴφ σπουδῇ ζηλώσωμεν·
τῆς δὲ συκῆς τὴν ἀκαρπίαν φοβηθέντες,   τῶν παθῶν
                                    ξηράνωμεν
δι᾽ ἐλεημοσύνης τὴν ἡδύτητα,
ἵνα καὶ τὴν ἔγερσιν   εὐθύμως προφθάσαντες,
ὡς μύρα κομισώμεθα   ἐξ ὕψους τὴν συγχώρησιν,
ὅτι πάντα ἐφορᾷ   τὸ ἀκοίμητον ὄμμα.

Προοίμιον 2

πρός· Οὐ παυόμεθα

Τοὺς τὸ πάθος σου πεφθακότας   καὶ τὴν ἔγερσιν
προσκυνῆσαι ἀξίωσον, Σωτήρ,   τὸ ἀκοίμητον ὄμμα.

ON JOSEPH AND POTIPHAR'S WIFE

in fourth plagal mode

Prelude 1

to: Hail

With the course of fasting so wisely completed,
and longing for the beginning of the Lord's passion,
come, all brothers and sisters, let us zealously aim
for the chastity of the self-controlled Joseph!
Alarmed by the fig tree's fruitlessness, let us dry up the
     sweetness
of our passions through charity,
so that, when we arrive at the resurrection with cheer,
we may win, like fragrant oil, approval from above,
for the sleepless eye watches over all.

Prelude 2

to: We do not cease

Consider those who have arrived at your passion
worthy also to venerate your resurrection, Savior, *the sleepless*
    eye.

Προοίμιον 3

ἰδιόμελον

Ἀκολασία τὸν νέον ἐξαπατᾷ πρὸς ἡδύτητα,
ἡ Ἁγνεία ἀνδρείαν συνεισάγει τῷ σώφρονι·
δι' ὧν ὤφθη ὁ δίκαιος Ἰωσὴφ ἐν Αἰγύπτῳ,
δεδοικὼς μὴ ἁμαρτῆσαι,
ὅτι πάντα ἐφορᾷ   τὸ ἀκοίμητον ὄμμα.

Προοίμιον 4

πρός· Τῇ ὑπερμάχῳ στρατηγῷ

Τὸν ὀδυρμὸν τοῦ Ἰακὼβ   νῦν θεωρήσωμεν,
τῶν ἀδελφῶν τὴν δολερὰν   γνώμην μισήσωμεν,
Ἰωσὴφ δὲ τὸν δίκαιον ζηλώσωμεν·
σωφροσύνην γὰρ φυλάξας ἀθόλωτον,
ἐκ παντοίων οὖν κινδύνων ἠλευθέρωται,
ὅτι πάντα ἐφορᾷ   τὸ ἀκοίμητον ὄμμα.

Ι

πρός· Ἄγγελος πρωτοστάτης

Ἔχοντες βασιλέα   οὐρανῶν βασιλείαν
διδοῦντα τοῖς αὑτοῦ στρατιώταις,
ἐνδυσώμεθα τὴν ἀρετήν,   πανοπλίαν οὖσαν
τῶν ψυχῶν ἄτρωτον,
ἵνα καὶ πολεμήσωμεν   ὡς ἔμφρονες τὴν Ἁμαρτίαν.

Prelude 3

to its own melody

Licentiousness lures the young man to sweetness.
Chastity brings courage to the self-controlled.
Thus the righteous Joseph in Egypt
could be seen to be afraid to sin,
for the sleepless eye watches over all.

Prelude 4

to: To you, our leader in battle

Let us pay heed to Jacob's lament
and hate the deceitful mindset of the brothers,
that we might rival the righteous Joseph!
Preserving his self-control unsullied,
Joseph was freed from all sorts of dangers,
for the sleepless eye watches over all.

I

to: A prince of the angels

Since we have a king who grants the kingdom
of heaven to his soldiers,
let us put on virtue, the impenetrable full
armor of souls,
and as right-minded ones, go to war against Sin.

Τίνα δὲ τὴν ἀρετὴν νοῶμεν;   Φιλοσοφίαν ὁρῶμεν
                                                ταύτην·
τέχνη γάρ ἐστι τῶν τεχνῶν, ὡς ἀκούομεν,
τῶν ἐπιστημῶν ἐπιστήμη τυγχάνουσα·
δι' αὐτῆς, ὡς διὰ κλίμακος,   χειραγωγεῖται ψυχὴ
καὶ πρὸς ὕψος ἀναφέρεται   τῆς οὐρανίου ζωῆς·
φρόνησιν καὶ ἀνδρείαν   τοὺς ἀνθρώπους διδάσκει,
ἔτι δὲ σωφροσύνην   καὶ τὴν δικαιοσύνην.
Τούτοις ἡμεῖς   τοῖς ὅπλοις στοιχήσωμεν,
καὶ τοῦ Χριστοῦ   τὴν χάριν αἰτήσωμεν·
δίδωσι γὰρ   τοῖς αὐτὸν ἀγαπῶσι
τὴν κατ' ἐχθρῶν   ἀναδήσασθαι νίκην,
ὅτι πάντα ἐφορᾷ   τὸ ἀκοίμητον ὄμμα.

2

Ἵνα μάθωμεν πάντες   τὴν ὑπέρλαμπρον δόξαν,
ἣν ἔχει ἀρετὴ καὶ παρέχει,
τὴν ὑπόθεσιν τοῦ Ἰωσὴφ   ἐνεγκεῖν εἰς μέσον,
εἰ δοκεῖ, σπεύσωμεν,
καὶ βίον φιλοσώφρονα   κτησώμεθα δι' ἐγκρατείας.
Οὗτος πραθεὶς διὰ πάθος φθόνου   δοῦλος παθῶν
                                                ούδαμῶς εὑρέθη·
εἶχε γὰρ τὸν νοῦν ὡς σοφὸν αὐτοκράτορα
καὶ τῶν φιλοσάρκων παθῶν ἐκυρίευσε·
διὰ τοῦτο οὐκ ἐσείετο   κολακείαις γυναικός,
ἀλλὰ ταύτης ἀπεσείετο   τὰς θωπείας ἀνδρικῶς·
ἔπεμπε μὲν ἐκείνη   ὡς ἀνέμους τοὺς λόγους,

What, then, is virtue? Let us see it as philosophy,
for it is the art of arts, so we hear;
in fact, it's the science of sciences.
By it the soul is led, as by a ladder,
and lifted to the height of heavenly life.
It teaches humans prudence and courage,
self-control and righteousness too.
Let's array in battle with these very weapons,
and let us entreat for Christ's favor;
indeed, he grants those who love him
to be crowned with victory against the enemies,
for the sleepless eye watches over all.

2

So we all may learn of the splendid glory
that virtue possesses and passes on,
let us quickly introduce in our midst, if I may,
the subject of Joseph,
to acquire through self-restraint a virtue-loving life!
He who was sold with the passion of envy never turned into
  a slave of the passions;
for he had his mind as a wise master,
and thus took charge of the flesh-loving passions,
so he was not shaken by a woman's flatteries,
but shook her caresses off in a manly way.
Like wind, she was letting loose her words

ἵνα τῆς Σωφροσύνης   καταβάλῃ τὸν οἶκον·
καὶ ὡς βροχὴν   τὴν μέθην κατέχεε
καὶ ποταμοὺς   χρημάτων προσέφερε·
νέος δὲ ὤν,   Ἰωσὴφ ὁ γενναῖος
ἦν ἑστηκὼς   ἐπὶ πέτρας ἀσείστου,
ὅτι πάντα ἐφορᾷ   τὸ ἀκοίμητον ὄμμα.

3

Σῶμα μὲν ἐδουλώθη,   τὸ δὲ φρόνημα εἶχεν
ἀδούλωτον ὁ σώφρων ἐκεῖνος·
ὁ κατ' ὄναρ φανεὶς βασιλεὺς   νῦν καθάπερ δοῦλος
ὠνητὸς γέγονεν·
ἀλλ' ὅμως καὶ κρατούμενος,   ἐκράτησε τῶν
                                    κρατησάντων·
ὑπὸ δεσπότου μὲν ἐτιμᾶτο,   ὑπὸ δεσποίνης δὲ ἐποθεῖτο·
ἦν μὲν ἀγαθὴ τοῦ δεσπότου ἡ εὔνοια,
ἄχρηστος δὲ λίαν ἡ ταύτης διάνοια·
ἔστεργε διὰ σεμνότητα   ὁ ἀνὴρ τὸν Ἰωσήφ,
ἔθελγε διὰ φαυλότητα   ἡ γυνὴ τὸν εὐγενῆ·
ἔτερπε μὲν ἐκεῖνον   ἡ ὀρθότης τοῦ τρόπου,
ἔτρωσε δὲ ἐκείνην   ὡραιότης προσώπου·
οὗτος αὐτῷ   τὸν οἶκον παρέδωκεν,
αὕτη αἰσχρῶς   τὸ σῶμα προδέδωκεν·
ὅπερ ἰδὼν   Ἰωσὴφ ἀπεστράφη,
τὴν φοβερὰν   ἐνθυμούμενος κρίσιν,
ὅτι πάντα ἐφορᾷ   τὸ ἀκοίμητον ὄμμα.

to bring down the house of Self-Control,
and like rain she spewed her drunkenness out,
and she offered rivers of riches.
Although he was young, the noble Joseph
was standing firm on unshakable rock,
for the sleepless eye watches over all.

3

With a body enslaved, this self-controlled man
had an unenslaved mind.
He who appeared as a king in a dream
had been bought as a slave,
but although ruled, he would rule those ruling him.
Esteemed by his master, he was wanted by his mistress.
Whereas the master's affection was worthy,
the wife's intention was quite worthless.
The man cherished Joseph for his dignity;
the woman charmed the wellborn one with frivolity.
His upright ways delighted the former;
his beautiful face, then, wounded the latter.
He entrusted his house to the slave;
she surrendered her body to disgrace.
And seeing this, Joseph turned away,
bearing in mind the terrible judgment,
for the sleepless eye watches over all.

4

Τῶν πραγμάτων τὴν τάξιν   ἡ παράνομος πρᾶξις
ἀπέστρεφε πρὸς τὸ ἐναντίον·
ὁ μὲν δοῦλος ἐκράτει παθῶν,   ὡς δεσπότης πάσης
ἡδονῆς τέλειος·
ἡ δέσποινα δὲ γέγονεν   ἀνδράποδον τῆς Ἁμαρτίας.
Πᾶς γὰρ ὁ πράττων τὴν ἁμαρτίαν   δοῦλος ὑπάρχει τῆς
                                                                                Ἁμαρτίας,
πάντα μὲν τὰ ἄλλα ὡς ὄναρ ἡγούμενος,
πρὸς δὲ τὸ ποθούμενον ὅλως ἑλκόμενος,
ὥσπερ ἔπαθεν ἡ δέσποινα   τοῦ δικαίου Ἰωσὴφ
πρὸς ἐκείνην τὴν ἐπέραστον   εὐμορφίαν τοῦ παιδός.
Βλέπουσα γὰρ τὸν νέον   ὀφθαλμοῖς ἀκολάστοις,
βέλεσιν ἀοράτοις   τὴν ψυχὴν ἐκολάσθη·
ὅσον αὐτὸς   τῷ κάλλει ἐξέλαμπε,
ταύτης ὁ νοῦς   τοσοῦτον ἐξέλειπεν·
αὕτη πυρσὸν   ἡδονῆς προετίθει,
οὗτος δὲ πῦρ   ἄσβεστον ἀντετίθει,
ὅτι πάντα ἐφορᾷ   τὸ ἀκοίμητον ὄμμα.

5

Ὅλην τῆς Αἰγυπτίας   τὴν καρδίαν συνεῖχεν
ἡ τῆς ἐπιθυμίας μανία,
καὶ πληγεῖσα κρυφίαν πληγήν,   ὑπεδέχετο μὲν
τὰ πικρὰ φάρμακα,
γλυκέα δὲ ἐνόμιζε   τὰ τραύματα, ὡς μαινομένη·

4

Her lawless behavior inverted the order
of the matter entirely:
the slave was indeed in control of his passions,
as a perfect master of every pleasure,
while the mistress became a bondswoman to Sin,
for everyone who sins is a slave to Sin
and is led to regard all else as a dream,
wholly attracted to the object of desire.
So the mistress of Joseph was under the sway
of that righteous boy's handsome physique.
When she gazed at the youngster with licentious eyes,
invisible arrows tortured her soul.
The more the boy shone with beauty,
the more the mistress's mind was darkened.
She proposed the flame of pleasure;
he opposed with unquenchable fire,
for the sleepless eye watches over all.

5

The frenzy of lust seized the Egyptian
woman's heart entirely;
smitten with an unseen blow, she took
such bitter potions
but, frenzied, considered the wounds sweet.

δι' ὀφθαλμῶν δεχομένη βέλη   ἀπὸ τῆς σώφρονος
                                                βελοθήκης
καὶ τὴν ἑαυτῆς ἀσωτίαν τιτρώσκουσα,
τέρψιν ὑπενόει τὴν τρῶσιν ἡ τάλαινα.
Ὁ μὲν πόθος ὁ ἀκόλαστος   ἐπολιόρκει τὸν νοῦν,
τὸ δὲ πάθος οὐκ ἡδύνατο   φανερῶσαι τὸ αὐτῆς·
αὕτη γὰρ καὶ παρόντος   Ἰωσὴφ ὠδυνᾶτο,
πάλιν δὲ καὶ ἀπόντος   ἀνεφλέγετο πλέον·
λόγοις αὐτὸν   χρηστοῖς ἐκολάκευε,
πεῖραν αὐτοῦ   λαβεῖν κατασπεύδουσα·
ὁ δὲ σεμνὸς   Ἰωσὴφ παρῃτεῖτο
τῆς γυναικὸς   τὴν ἀθέμιτον πρᾶξιν,
ὅτι πάντα ἐφορᾷ   τὸ ἀκοίμητον ὄμμα.

6

Νυμφοστόλος μοιχείας   ὁ Διάβολος ἦλθεν,
ἵνα τῇ Αἰγυπτίᾳ συμπράξῃ·
καὶ "Ἀνδρίζου, ὦ γύναι," φησίν,   "ὡς ἀρχαῖον οὖσα
καὶ στερρὸν ἄγκιστρον·
ἑτοίμασον τὸ δέλεαρ   καὶ θήρευσον τὸν νεανίαν.
Τοὺς μὲν πλοκάμους τῆς κεφαλῆς σου   πλέξον ὡς
                                                δίκτυα κατὰ τούτου·
τὴν δὲ τοῦ προσώπου μορφὴν κατακάλλυνον,
πᾶσι ῥοδοχρόοις κοσμοῦσα σοφίσμασι·
φαίδρυνόν σου καὶ τὸν τράχηλον   τοῖς χρυσοπλόκοις
                                                δεσμοῖς·
ἐπὶ πᾶσιν ἀμφιάσθητι   πολυτίμητον στολήν·

Pierced through her eyes by arrows from his self-controlled
    quiver,
which wounded her debauched self, the miserable
woman awaited the wounding as delight.
Unbridled desire was attacking her mind,
but she was unable to show her passion.
She suffered indeed in Joseph's presence
but was even more inflamed in his absence.
The woman enticed him with flattering words,
so eager to have her way with him,
but the dignified Joseph repulsed
the woman's illicit behavior,
for the sleepless eye watches over all.

6

As a bridal attendant in adultery, the Devil
entered now to assist the Egyptian.
"Man up, woman," he said, "like an old
and stiff fishhook!
Prepare the bait and catch the youth;
plait the locks on your head, and trap him in that net!
Adorn your face, embellish your looks
with every kind of rosy cunning!
Brighten your neck with gold-braided chains;
drape yourself, finally, in a luxurious robe!

μύροις ἄλειψαι πλείστοις,   ἐκθηλύνουσι νέους·
πρόκεινται γὰρ ἀγῶνες   ἰσχυροὶ καὶ γενναῖοι·
οὗτος μὲν σοὶ   ἁγνείαν ἀντέστησε,
σὺ δὲ αὐτῷ   λαγνείαν ἀντίστησον·
μὴ νικηθῇς   καὶ καταγελασθῶμεν·
λέξει γὰρ σοί·   'Οὐ ποιήσω ὃ θέλεις,
ὅτι πάντα ἐφορᾷ   τὸ ἀκοίμητον ὄμμα.'"

7

Ἴδεν ἄσεμνον ὄψιν   ὁ σεμνὸς νεανίας,
καὶ μᾶλλον ἐβδελύξατο ταύτην·
ἐθεώρει μορφὴν ἱλαράν,   ἀλλ' ἐνόει γνώμην
δολερὰν ἔσωθεν,
καὶ σπεύσας ταύτην ἔφυγεν   ὡς ἔχιδναν ἐγκεκρυμμένην·
ὅθεν μὴ φέρουσα ἡ ἀθλία   τὴν περιφρόνησιν τοῦ
                                           γενναίου,
πᾶσαν τὴν αἰδῶ τῆς καρδίας ἀπέρριψε
καὶ τὴν ἑαυτῆς ἀσωτίαν ἐγύμνωσε.
Πρῶτον μὲν γὰρ ἐθεράπευσε   διὰ μέσης γυναικός,
καὶ αὐτὴ δὲ μετεπέμπετο   καὶ ὡμίλει μετ' αὐτοῦ·
γλῶσσαν εἶχεν ὀξεῖαν   ὑπὲρ μάχαιραν οὖσαν
καὶ διὰ τῆς τῶν λόγων   ἡδονῆς ἀναιροῦσαν·
τέχναις αὐτὸν   πολλαῖς ἐγοήτευεν,
ἀλλὰ τὸν νοῦν   αὐτοῦ οὐ παρέτρεψεν·
ἔλεγε γάρ·   "Οὐ ποιήσω τὸ μύσος,
ἔχων ἀεὶ   πρὸς τὰ φαῦλα τὸ μῖσος,
ὅτι πάντα ἐφορᾷ   τὸ ἀκοίμητον ὄμμα."

Douse yourself with perfume; it softens the young!
Fierce and intense battles lie ahead.
If he has fought you with chastity,
you should fight him with lechery.
You mustn't be beaten, or we'll be mocked
and he'll say 'I won't do what you want,
for the sleepless eye watches over all.'"

7

The dignified youth saw the undignified spectacle
and was rather appalled.
He looked at her smart appearance but discerned
the underlying intention of deceit,
and he fled from her quickly, as from a hidden viper.
Unable to bear the nobleman's disdain, the miserable
    woman
tossed aside all her heart's modesty
and stripped down to her debauchery.
She flattered him first through another woman,
and then she personally summoned him to chat.
Hers was a tongue sharper than a knife;
by pleasurable words she would lift it to strike.
With various ploys she would beguile him,
but she could not lead his mind astray.
He'd say, "I won't do the filthy deed;
I've always abhorred what is base,
for the sleepless eye watches over all."

8

Ὦ μανίας ἐσχάτης   γυναικὸς ἀκολάστου
ἐπὶ τοῦ Ἰωσὴφ ἐκφλεχθείσης·
ἐπειδὴ γὰρ κατεῖδεν αὐτὸν   ταῖς αὐτῆς θωπείαις
οὐδαμῶς εἴκοντα,
μὴ πάθεσι νεότητος   ἡττώμενον, ἐβόα τούτῳ·
"Δοῦλος ἐμὸς ὠνητὸς ὑπάρχεις,   πέπρασαί μοι, ἵνα μοι
                                                    δουλεύῃς·
ὅλου σε δεσπότην τοῦ οἴκου πεποίηκα,
γενοῦ δὲ κἀμοῦ τῆς κυρίας σου κύριος·
οὐ λογίζομαι ὑβρίζεσθαι   καταβαίνουσα πρὸς σέ·
δεσποτείας καὶ δουλείας γὰρ   οὐκ ἔστι διαφορά·
ἕνα πάντων πατέρα   τὸν Ἀδὰμ ἐδιδάχθην,
μίαν πάντων μητέρα   τὴν ἀρχέγονον Εὔαν·
πάντες ἐσμὲν   ἀλλήλων ὁμότιμοι,
ὡς τῆς αὐτῆς   μετέχοντες φύσεως·
μὴ φοβηθῇς   ὡς ἀθέμιτα πράττων,
μηδὲ πεισθῇς   τοῖς λαλοῦσί σοι ταῦτα,
ὅτι πάντα ἐφορᾷ   τὸ ἀκοίμητον ὄμμα.

9

"Σοῦ τοὺς τρόπους ὁρῶσα   κοσμουμένους ἐν πᾶσι,
τῶν ἄλλων προτιμῶ σε συνδούλων·
ἐν τοῖς ὄμμασι γὰρ τὴν αἰδῶ,   ἐν τοῖς χείλεσι δὲ
τὴν πειθὼ κέκτησαι,
καὶ πᾶσαν ἔχεις αἴσθησιν   εὐσχήμονα, καθάπερ θέλω.

8

How wildly the frenzy of an unbridled woman
burned for Joseph!
When she saw that he did not at all succumb
to her cajoling and was not overcome
by the passions of youth, she burst out to him,
"You are my own bought slave, sold to me to serve me;
I've made you lord of my whole house;
become now also the master of your mistress!
I find no affront in descending to you;
being in charge and being enslaved are not so different.
All have one father in Adam, I'm told;
all have one primal mother in Eve.
All of us are equal in honor,
since we all share the same nature.
Don't be afraid of behaving badly,
don't be persuaded by those who are saying
that the sleepless eye watches over all.

9

"Seeing your manners, in all ways refined,
I prefer you over your fellow slaves.
In your eyes is modesty, and upon your lips
you hold persuasion.
You show forth, as I wish, every graceful feature.

Δεῦρο, ἐπάκουσον τῆς φωνῆς μου,   ἵνα σοι δείξω τὴν
                                              πρόθεσίν μου·
πλείστων γὰρ καλῶν σε ἐμπλήσω πεισθέντα μοι
καὶ δωροδοκίαις πλουσίαις ἀμείψομαι·
καὶ γὰρ πλεῖόν σε παράθωμαι   τῷ συμβίῳ τῷ ἐμῷ,
καὶ γενέσθαι σε ἐλεύθερον   κατασπεύσω παρ' αὐτοῦ·
δοῦλος γὰρ οὐ κληθήσῃ,   συγκαθεύδων δεσποίνῃ·
ἐὰν δὲ μὴ πεισθῇς μοι,   κινδυνεύσεις δικαίως·
σὲ γὰρ πικροῖς   δεσμοῖς παραδίδωμι,
καὶ πονηρῷ   θανάτῳ ἐκδίδωμι·
μὴ οὖν σαυτὸν   ἀδικῆσαι θελήσῃς·
οὐ γὰρ ἔστιν   ἀληθὲς ὃ νομίζεις,
ὅτι πάντα ἐφορᾷ   τὸ ἀκοίμητον ὄμμα."

                              10

Ἡ γυνὴ μὲν τοιαῦτα·   ἀλλ' οὐκ ἴσχυσεν ὅλως
σαλεῦσαι τὸν ἀσάλευτον πύργον·
οὐκ ἐνύσταξε ταῖς κολακείαις,   ἀλλὰ μᾶλλον εἶχε
λογισμὸν ἄγρυπνον
καὶ ἄσυλον ἐφύλαττε   τὸ καύχημα τῆς Σωφροσύνης.
Ἔνθεν καὶ ἔνθεν περισκοπήσας,   ταύτην ἑώρα τὴν
                                              μαινομένην·
πάντας γὰρ τοὺς ἄλλους τοῦ οἴκου ἐξέπεμψε,
μόνη δὲ πρὸς μόνον τοιαῦτα ἐφθέγγετο·
"Ἕως πότε σου ἀνέξομαι   παρακούοντος ἐμοί;
νῦν καιρὸς τοῦ ἀπολαῦσαί με   τῆς ποθουμένης εὐνῆς·
οὐ γὰρ ἔστιν ἐνταῦθα   οὐδὲ εἷς τῶν τοῦ οἴκου,

Come, heed my voice; I'll lay bare my intention:
when you give in to me, I'll satisfy you lavishly
with lovely things; I'll repay you with ample gifts.
I'll also commend you to my husband
and urge that he will set you free.
You won't be called slave when you are sleeping with your
      mistress.
If you don't give in to me, you're in serious trouble;
I'll hand you over to bitter bonds,
I'll give you up to dreadful death.
Do not will such harm for yourself;
it's not true what you are thinking,
that the sleepless eye watches over all."

10

The woman said this, but could not at all
shake his unshakable tower.
He was not lulled by her sweet talk,
but instead kept a vigilant mind,
and preserved intact the pride of Self-Control.
Looking round here and there, he saw only the frenzied
      woman,
for she had sent everyone out of the house.
Alone with him, she said something like this:
"How long shall I endure that you disobey me?
Now is my chance to enjoy the desired bed,
for there is nobody here, none from the household,

καὶ οὐδὲν ἐμποδίζει   τοῦ γενέσθαι ὃ λέγω."
Βέλη πυρὸς   αὐτῷ κατηκόντιζεν,
ἀλλ' οὐδαμῶς   αὐτὸν κατεφλόγιζεν·
ἔσωθεν γὰρ   σωφροσύνην πηγάζων,
τὰς πονηρὰς   ἔσβεσεν ὁμιλίας,
ὅτι πάντα ἐφορᾷ   τὸ ἀκοίμητον ὄμμα.

II

Φθεγγομένης τοιαῦτα   τῆς μαινάδος ἐκείνης
καὶ καταθωπευούσης τὸν νέον,
εἰς τὰ σκάμματα τῶν πειρασμῶν   Ἰωσὴφ ὁ μέγας
ἀθλητὴς ἔρχεται,
πολύμορφον ἀντίπαλον   βουλόμενος ἀντιπαλαῖσαι·
καὶ βραβευταὶ συνεισῆλθον δύο   καὶ παρειστήκεισαν
                                        ἀμφοτέροις·
τῷ μὲν Ἰωσὴφ ἡ Ἁγνεία συνίστατο,
τῇ δὲ γυναικὶ ἡ Λαγνεία προΐστατο·
μέσον τούτων ἠγωνίζετο   ὁ φιλοσώφρων ἀνήρ,
πρὸς αὐτὸν ἀντηγωνίζετο   ἡ δολιόφρων γυνή·
ἔθελγε μὲν ἐκείνη   πρὸς μοιχείαν καλοῦσα,
ἤθελε δὲ νικῆσαι   τὴν αἰσχρὰν ὁ γενναῖος·
τῷ Ἰωσὴφ   συνέπραττον ἄγγελοι,
τῇ γυναικὶ   συνέτρεχον δαίμονες·
ἄνωθεν δὲ   θεωρῶν ὁ Δεσπότης,
τὸν νικητὴν   ἔστεφε τοῖς ἐπαίνοις,
ὅτι πάντα ἐφορᾷ   τὸ ἀκοίμητον ὄμμα.

and nothing prevents what I propose from happening!"
She was shooting fiery arrows at him,
but still she could not set him ablaze.
With self-control flowing freely inside him,
he quenched the wicked exhortations,
for the sleepless eye watches over all.

II

With the frenzied woman uttering such things
and fawning over the youth,
the great contender, Joseph, enters
into the ring of temptations
ready to wrestle his shape-shifting foe.
Two coaches entered together, and they took one side each:
Chastity stood with Joseph,
while Lechery directed the woman.
Battling in the middle was the man who loved self-control,
and struggling against him, the crafty-minded woman.
While she was beguiling, inviting adultery,
the noble man aimed to conquer the shameful one.
Angels assisted Joseph;
demons supported the woman;
the Master observed from on high
and crowned the victor with praises,
for the sleepless eye watches over all.

12

Ῥήματα σωφροσύνης   Ἰωσὴφ ἀπεκρίθη
πρὸς τὴν παραφρονοῦσαν βοήσας·
"Σὸς μὲν δοῦλός εἰμι ὠνητός,   διὰ φθόνον τοῦτο
πεπονθὼς ἄδικον,
κἂν πέπραμαι δὲ σώματι,   ἐλεύθερός εἰμι τῇ γνώμῃ.
Τὴν γὰρ εὐγένειαν τὴν τῶν τρόπων   χάρτης καὶ μέλαν
                                        οὐκ οἶδε βλάπτειν,
ὥσπερ ἡ ἀχλὺς τὸν ἀέρα σκοτίζουσα
τὴν ἡλιακὴν οὐκ ἀμβλύνει λαμπρότητα·
ὡς γὰρ νέφος ἀπελαύνεται   ὑπ' ἀνέμου διωχθέν,
τοῦ ἡλίου δὲ μετέπειτα   καταλάμπουσιν αὐγαί,
οὕτω καὶ ἡ δουλεία   παρελεύσεται αὕτη
καὶ ἡ ἐλευθερία   ἡ ἐμὴ ἀναλάμψει.
Πᾶσα ἡ γῆ   Αἰγύπτου δουλεύσει μοι
τῷ ἡδοναῖς   αἰσχραῖς μὴ δουλεύοντι·
τοῦτο γάρ μοι   προεμήνυσε πάλαι
ὁ προειδὼς   τὰ ἐσόμενα Μόνος,
ὅτι πάντα ἐφορᾷ   τὸ ἀκοίμητον ὄμμα."

13

Ὡς ἀκήκοε ταῦτα   προσλαλοῦντος τοῦ νέου,
καὶ πάλιν κολακεύειν πειρᾶται
καὶ τοιαῦτά φησι πρὸς αὐτόν· "Ὅτι δούλου τρόπους
οὐδαμῶς κέκτησαι,

12

Joseph replied with words of self-control,
exclaiming to the deranged woman,
"I, your purchased slave, endure this injustice
because of envy;
although sold in body, I am free in my will.
Paper and ink can never mar nobility of manners;
just as mist dimming the air
does not weaken the sun's splendor.
As when a cloud lifts, chased by the wind
and afterward the sunshine radiates,
so this enslavement will also pass,
and my freedom shine out anew.
The whole of Egypt will be enslaved to me,
whom shameful pleasures cannot enslave.
This was told me once by the only
One who foresees what will come,
for the sleepless eye watches over all."

13

Having heard the youth asserting these things,
she once again tries to flatter
and says something like this: "That you by no means
have the manners of a slave,

δι' ἔργων τοῦτο ἔμαθον,   καὶ πέπεισμαι καὶ μαρτυρῶ σοι·
καὶ γὰρ τὴν πρέπουσαν ἐλευθέρῳ   σὺ ἐξετέλεσας
                                                    λειτουργίαν·
γέγονας ἐν πᾶσι τοῖς ἔργοις σου ἄμεμπτος
καὶ πρὸς τοὺς συνδούλους τοὺς σοὺς ἀκακούργητος·
ὅθεν φαίνει καταγόμενος   ἐκ γονέων εὐγενῶν·
διὰ τοῦτο καὶ ἐλήλυθας   εἰς τὰς χεῖρας τὰς ἐμὰς
ἵνα γένωμαι πλείστων   ἀγαθῶν ἀρχηγός σοι,
καὶ ἡ χώρα Αἰγύπτου   δι' ἐμοῦ σοι δουλεύσῃ·
μόνον ἐμὲ   τὴν νῦν σου δεσπόζουσαν
καὶ τὴν πρὸς σὲ   στοργὴν διασῴζουσαν
δέξαι λοιπὸν   εἰς κοινὴν εὐφροσύνην,
καὶ μὴ πτοοῦ,   λογιζόμενος πάλιν
ὅτι πάντα ἐφορᾷ   τὸ ἀκοίμητον ὄμμα."

14

Μετὰ τούτους τοὺς λόγους   Ἰωσὴφ ἀντιλέγει
πρὸς τὴν ἀσελγεστάτην ἐκείνην·
"Ἀληθὲς μὲν ὃ λέγεις ἐστίν,   ὅτι ῥίζης εἰμὶ
ἀγαθῆς βλάστημα·
ὡς ἄλογον δὲ βλέπω σε   καὶ φεύγω σου τὴν συνουσίαν.
Ὅταν γάρ τις λογισμὸν οὐκ ἔχῃ   τὸν χαλινοῦντα αὐτοῦ
                                                    τὸν βίον,
δίκην ἀλογίστων κτηνῶν περιφέρεται,
καὶ εἰς ἀπρεπεῖς ἡδονὰς καταφέρεται·
διὰ τοῦτο οὐκ ἀνέχομαι   τῶν φιλοσάρκων παθῶν,
ἀλλὰ τούτων τὰ σκιρτήματα   δι' ἐγκρατείας κρατῶ·

I learned from your deeds; I'm convinced and can
    witness it.
You've performed duties befitting a free man.
In all your deeds you've been impeccable,
and you've been guileless toward fellow slaves.
You clearly descend from noble parents,
and thus you have also come into my hands,
so I'll be your source of the finest things,
and the land of Egypt your slave through me.
Take me now and me only
in shared delight, me, your mistress,
the one who harbors affection for you,
and don't be afraid, thinking once more
that the sleepless eye watches over all!"

14

After these words, Joseph spoke up
against that most wanton woman:
"It is true what you say, that I am a shoot
of a fine root,
but you I see as a mindless animal and flee from this union.
When someone's devoid of a rational mind to bridle his life,
he wanders about just like stray herds.
and he sinks in indecent pleasures on his way.
For this reason I can't bear the flesh-loving passions,
but control their restiveness with self-restraint.

μέχρι νῦν καθαρεύων   ἀπὸ μύσους τοιούτου,
ἄρτι διὰ μοιχείας   οὐ ῥυπῶ μου τὸ σῶμα·
ἔστι μὲν γὰρ   βαρὺ καὶ ἀθέμιτον
γάμον ἀνδρὸς   συλῆσαι ἀλλότριον·
μεῖζον δέ μοι   καταφαίνεται κρῖμα,
εἰ τὴν εὐνὴν   τοῦ δεσπότου ὑβρίσω,
ὅτι πάντα ἐφορᾷ   τὸ ἀκοίμητον ὄμμα."

15

"Ἄκουσον, νεανίσκε,"   ἡ γυνὴ ἀπεκρίθη
πρὸς τὸν τῆς σωφροσύνης ἐργάτην·
"ὁ δεσπότης, ὡς οἶδας, ὁ σὸς   καταπείθεταί μου
τῇ βουλῇ πάντοτε
καὶ δύναμαι κακῶσαί σε   καὶ πάλιν παραθέσθαι τούτῳ·
ἔχει ἐν σοὶ ἀγαθὰς ἐλπίδας   ἐκ τῆς προλήψεως τῆς
                                        προτέρας·
στέργει καὶ ἐμέ, ὡς ἀεὶ σωφρονήσασαν·
μέχρι γὰρ τοῦ νῦν ἀκατάγνωστος ἔμεινα.
Τοῦ δεσπότου οὖν, ὡς εἴρηκα,   πεποιθότος ἐφ' ἡμῖν,
οὐδενὸς δὲ τὸ πραττόμενον   θεωροῦντος ἐπὶ γῆς,
τί ὀκνεῖς πειθαρχῆσαι   τῇ ἐμῇ παρακλήσει,
ἧς οὐκ ἂν ἠξιώθης   μετὰ σὰς παρακλήσεις;
Τοῖχοι ἡμᾶς   παντόθεν καλύπτουσι,
ἄνωθεν δὲ   ἡ στέγη ἐφήπλωται·
μὴ οὖν φοβοῦ   οὐ οὐκ ἔστι σοι φόβος,
μηδὲ πτοοῦ,   ἐνθυμούμενος πάλιν
ὅτι πάντα ἐφορᾷ   τὸ ἀκοίμητον ὄμμα."

Until now I've been clean from such pollution;
I still won't defile my body with adultery.
While it is a brutal, unlawful act
to plunder another man's marriage,
the crime seems even worse to me
if I prance about in the bed of my master,
for the sleepless eye watches over all."

15

"Listen, young man," replied the woman
to the one behaving with self-control,
"your master, as you know, always complies
with the will of his wife,
so I'm able to harm you but also commend you.
He has held high hopes for you since he first considered
      you.
He loves me too, for my steady self-control;
to this very day I've remained irreproachable.
With the master, as I've said, trusting in us,
and no one on earth observing the act,
why do you hesitate to obey my request
for what you'd be unworthy yourself to request?
Walls conceal us on all sides,
and up above the roof spreads out.
So do not fear where there's no cause for fear!
Don't be afraid, nor consider once more
that the sleepless eye watches over all!"

16

Νουθετῆσαι σπουδάζων   τὴν ἀθλίαν ἐκείνην,
ὁ σώφρων Ἰωσὴφ ἀπεκρίθη·
"Μὴ συμβούλευέ μοι πονηρά,   ὡς ἡ Εὔα πάλαι
τῷ Ἀδάμ—ἄπαγε·
τοῦ ξύλου γὰρ οὐ γεύσομαι   τοῦ θάνατόν μοι
                                        προξενοῦντος.
Ἔχω παράδεισον τὴν ἁγνείαν   πᾶσαν βλαστάνουσαν
                                        εὐωδίαν·
τί γὰρ τῆς ἁγνείας ἐστὶ θαυμαστότερον,
ἣν οἱ κατορθοῦντες ὡς ἄγγελοι λάμπουσι;
Κἂν τὴν πρᾶξιν οὐ μὴ ἴδωσιν   οἱ οἰκοῦντες σὺν ἡμῖν,
ὅτι ἄνθρωποι ὑπάρχουσιν   μὴ ὁρῶντες τὰ κρυπτά,
ἀλλὰ τὸ συνειδός μου   τὸν κατήγορον ἔχω·
εἴ γε πρᾶξαι τολμήσω   τὸ παράνομον ἔργον,
εἰ καὶ μηδεὶς   ἐλέγξει μοιχεύσαντα,
ἔχω κριτὴν   ἐλέγχου μὴ χρῄζοντα,
ὅνπερ ἀεὶ   ἐνθυμούμενος φρίττω
καὶ τὰς αἰσχρὰς   ἡδονὰς ἀποφεύγω,
ὅτι πάντα ἐφορᾷ   τὸ ἀκοίμητον ὄμμα.

17

"Ὅταν σοὶ δὲ πιστεύσω   ὅτι τοῖχοι παντόθεν
καλύπτουσιν ἡμᾶς πλημμελοῦντας,
καὶ οὐ βλέπει οὐδεὶς ἐπὶ γῆς   ὅπερ θέλεις πρᾶξαι
σὺν ἐμοὶ ἄδικον,

16

Eager to admonish the wretched woman,
the self-controlled Joseph replied:
"Don't give me wicked advice, as Eve once did
to Adam—leave me alone!
I shall not taste of the tree that produces death for me.
My paradise is chastity, which sprouts with every fragrance!
What is indeed more wonderful than chastity,
as those who attain it shine like angels?
And even if people who live in this house do not see the act,
because they are humans who can't see what's hidden,
I still have my conscience as my accuser.
If I dared to do the unlawful deed,
even if no one could prove my adultery,
I have a judge who needs no proof,
and considering him, I always shudder
and flee from the shameful pleasures,
for the sleepless eye watches over all.

17

"If I were to believe you that the walls on all sides
conceal our offenses,
that no one on earth observes the wicked act you desire
to perform with me, woman,

τὸν βλέποντα τὰ κρύφια   ποῦ φύγωμεν, εἰπέ μοι, γύναι;
Κἂν γὰρ οὐ πάρεστιν ὁ ἀνήρ σου,   ἀλλ᾽ οὐκ ἀπέστη νῦν
                                                    ὁ κριτής μου·
κἂν οὐκ ἐφορᾷ με τῆς κλίνης ὁ κύριος,
ἀλλὰ ἐφορᾷ με ὁ κρίνων τὰ κρύφια.
Πῶς οὖν λάθω τὸν ἐτάζοντα   τὰς καρδίας καὶ νεφρούς;
Καὶ αὐτὸς δὲ κινηθήσεται   κατ᾽ ἐμοῦ ὁ οὐρανός·
μάτην τοίχοις θαρροῦμεν   τοῖς μηδὲν ὠφελοῦσιν·
στέγη ἐπουρανία   τὴν μοιχείαν οὐ σκέπει·
πάντα γυμνὰ   ὑπάρχει καὶ πρόδηλα
τῷ τὰ κρυπτὰ   γινώσκοντι πταίσματα·
ὅθεν ἐγὼ   οὐκ ἀνέχομαι πρᾶξαι
τὸ πονηρὸν   ἐναντίον Κυρίου,
ὅτι πάντα ἐφορᾷ   τὸ ἀκοίμητον ὄμμα.”

18

Ὑπὸ τούτων τῶν λόγων   ἡ μαινὰς ἐκκαυθεῖσα
τῷ σώφρονι ἐπέρχεται ἄφνω,
καὶ τὸν τούτου χιτῶνα κρατεῖ   καὶ βιαίως σύρει
τὸν σεμνόν, λέγουσα·
“Ἐπάκουσόν μου, φίλτατε,   καὶ δεῦρο, συνομίλησόν
                                                    μοι.”
Ἔνθεν καθεῖλκεν ἡ Αἰγυπτία,   πάλιν ἡ Χάρις ἀνθεῖλκε
                                                    τοῦτον·
αὕτη μὲν ἐβόα· “Ἐμοὶ συγκοιμήθητι”·
ἄνωθεν δ᾽ ἡ Χάρις· “Ἐμοὶ συγγρηγόρησον.”
Μετ᾽ ἐκείνης ὁ Διάβολος   ἠγωνίζετο πικρῶς,

where might we flee the one who can see what is hidden?
    Tell me!
Your husband may not be present, but my judge has still not
    left.
The lord of the bed may not watch me,
but the one who judges what's hidden watches.
How may I escape the examiner of minds and hearts?
Heaven itself will be moved down against me.
In vain would we trust walls that won't help;
the heavenly roof doesn't cover adultery.
All is bare and plain to see
for the one who knows the hidden faults;
thus I myself cannot bear to do
wicked deeds before the Lord,
for the sleepless eye watches over all."

18

Inflamed by these words, the frenzied woman
throws herself suddenly at the self-controlled man.
She grasps his tunic and violently tugs
the honorable man.
"Heed me, darling, and come," she said, "and have sex with
    me!"
On one side, she was pulling him down, on the other, Grace
    was pulling him up.
The former cried out, "Sleep with me!"
Then Grace from above, "Stay awake with me!"
Alongside the woman the Devil intensely

καὶ χερσὶ σφοδρῶς κατέσφιγγε τὸν γενναῖον ἀθλητήν·
πάλιν ἡ Σωφροσύνη ἐκινεῖτο πρὸς πάλην,
λῦσαι ἐπειγομένη τὰ κρατήματα τούτων·
ἔλεγε δέ· "Ραγῇ τὸ ἱμάτιον,
καὶ μὴ φθαρῇ τὸ σῶμα τοῦ σώφρονος·
λήψεται γὰρ παρὰ τοῦ ἀθλοθέτου,
ὡς νικητής, ἔνδυμα ἀφθαρσίας,
ὅτι πάντα ἐφορᾷ τὸ ἀκοίμητον ὄμμα."

19

Ἔχει στέφανον μέγαν Ἰωσὴφ ὡς ἀθλήσας
ὑπὲρ τῆς Σωφροσύνης νομίμως·
τὴν γὰρ ταύτης φυλάττων στοργήν, ἀπεδύθη μᾶλλον
τὴν στολὴν ἔξωθεν,
καὶ δόξαν ἐνεδύσατο παράδοξον ὁ στεφανίτης·
τούτῳ ἐπῆλθεν ἡ Αἰγυπτία ὥσπερ ἀμπέλῳ δεινὴ
                                                    ἀλώπηξ,
ὅλον μὲν τὸν βότρυν τρυγῆσαι ἐλπίζουσα,
μόνα δὲ τὰ φύλλα εὑρέθη κατέχουσα.
Ἄνω ἄγγελοι συνέχαιρον τῷ δικαίῳ Ἰωσήφ,
κάτω δαίμονες συνέκλαιον τῇ ἀδίκῳ γυναικί·
οὗτος μὲν ἐγυμνώθη τῆς ἰδίας ἐσθῆτος,
ἵνα πάσας τηρήσῃ ἀβλαβεῖς τὰς αἰσθήσεις·
ἡ δὲ μαινὰς αἰσχύνην ἐνδύεται
καὶ τὴν αἰδῶ ἀσέμνως ἐκδύεται·
ὁ δὲ σοφὸς κατ' ἀξίαν τιμᾶται
ὡς ἐκφυγὼν Ἁμαρτίαν μεγάλην,
ὅτι πάντα ἐφορᾷ τὸ ἀκοίμητον ὄμμα.

struggled, seizing the noble contender with violent hands.
Self-Control also entered the battle,
striving to loosen the others' grips.
"Let his clothes be torn asunder," the latter said,
"but let his body not be violated!
This self-controlled man will receive, as victor,
imperishable garments from the prize-giving judge,
for the sleepless eye watches over all."

19

Having competed as a professional athlete for Self-Control,
Joseph wins a great crown.
Defending his love for her, the crowned man was stripped
of his outer robe,
but was dressed in wondrous glory instead.
The Egyptian woman attacked him as a wily fox a vine,
hoping to grab the whole cluster of grapes,
but ended up grasping nothing but leaves.
Above, the angels were celebrating with the righteous
    Joseph;
below, the demons shared the unrighteous woman's
    weeping.
He was stripped bare of his own clothing,
so he might keep all his senses intact;
she, the frenzied one, put on shame
and without dignity threw off her modesty.
The wise man is esteemed according to his worth
since he has escaped great Sin herself,
for the sleepless eye watches over all.

20

Πῶς ἀξίως ὑμνήσω   πολυύμνητον ἄνδρα
τὸν κρείττονα παντὸς ἐγκωμίου;
Ὅτι σκάφος ἐδείχθη στερρόν,   καὶ ἀγρίαν ζάλην
ἡδονῶν ἔφυγε
καὶ εἰς λιμένα εὔδιον   προσώρμισε τῆς Σωφροσύνης·
οὗτος καὶ κάμινον κατεπάτει   ἔνδον τοῦ οἴκου
                                                    ἀναπτομένην·
πνεῦμα γὰρ τῆς δρόσου ἑλκύσας τῆς ἄνωθεν,
παμφάγον πυρὸς δυναστείαν κατέσβεσε.
Τοῦτό ἐστι τὸ παγκράτιον   τοῦ μεγάλου Ἰωσήφ,
τοῦτό ἐστι τὸ ἐγκώμιον   τοῦ γενναίου ἀθλητοῦ·
ὅπερ τότε ἐπράχθη   ἐν οἰκίσκῳ λαθραίως
ᾄδεται ἐν τῷ κόσμῳ   καθ᾽ ἑκάστην ἡμέραν·
τὰ γὰρ καλὰ   οὐδέποτε σβέννυται,
κἂν πειρασμοὶ   πολλοὶ περικλύζουσι·
ῥύεται γὰρ   ἀπὸ τούτων ἁπάντων
ὁ Λυτρωτὴς   τῶν αὐτοῦ θεραπόντων,
ὅτι πάντα ἐφορᾷ   τὸ ἀκοίμητον ὄμμα.

21

Οἱ συναίμονες πρώην   ἐπεβούλευσαν τούτῳ
διὰ τὴν βασιλείαν φθονοῦντες·
καὶ ὁρμήσαντες κτεῖναι αὐτόν,   ἐν τῇ γνώμῃ μόνον
τὸ κακὸν ἔστησαν,
εἰς ἔργον δὲ οὐκ ἤγαγον   τὴν ἄδικον σφαγὴν ἐκείνην,

20

How can I worthily laud a man
so widely applauded, superior to any praise?
He proved to be a steady boat;
he escaped from the wild surge of pleasures,
and anchored in the calm harbor of Self-Control.
He even trampled on the furnace that was lit inside the
      house;
having drawn a breath of dew from above,
he quenched the fire's voracious power.
This is the *pankration* of the great Joseph.
This is the panegyric for the noble contender.
What once came to pass in the secrecy of a room
is extolled each day throughout the world.
The beauties of life are never extinguished,
even if myriad temptations engulf them.
The Redeemer rescues from all of this
everyone who serves him devotedly,
for the sleepless eye watches over all.

21

Previously his kindred plotted against him,
envious of his sovereignty.
They were about to kill him, yet only in their minds
did they perform the evil deed,
not carrying that unjust slaughter to completion.

αἵματι βάψαντες τὸν χιτῶνα,   ἀλλ᾽ οὐχὶ βλάπτοντες τὸν
                                               φοροῦντα·
ζῶντα γὰρ αὐτὸν ὁ Θεὸς διεφύλαξεν,
εἰ καὶ ὁ πατὴρ ὡς θανέντα ὠδύρετο·
αὕτη πάλιν ἐπολέμησε   τῷ χιτῶνι μοιχαλίς,
τὴν ψυχὴν δὲ οὐ κατέτρωσε   τοῦ γενναίου στρατηγοῦ·
ἦν γὰρ ἐνδεδυμένος   ἀσφαλῆ πανοπλίαν
πάσας τὰς ἑλεπόλεις   τῶν παθῶν καταργοῦσαν.
Τοῦτον, πιστοί,   μιμεῖσθαι σπουδάσωμεν,
ὅτι καὶ νῦν   ἡμῖν ἐπανίσταται
τῶν σαρκικῶν   ἡδονῶν ἡ ἀπάτη,
ἀλλὰ μηδεὶς   ὑπὸ ταύτης ἡττάσθω,
ὅτι πάντα ἐφορᾷ   τὸ ἀκοίμητον ὄμμα.

22

Στέμμα κέκτηται θεῖον   καὶ ἀοίδιμον νίκην
ὁ μέγας τῶν παθῶν αὐτοκράτωρ,
καὶ δικαίως τὴν μνήμην αὐτοῦ   πανταχοῦ τιμῶσιν
οἱ πιστοὶ πάντοτε,
ὅτι οὐκ ἐκυρίευσε   τοῦ σώματος ἡ Ἁμαρτία·
τῆς γυναικὸς γὰρ τῆς ἀκολάστου   λόγοις καὶ ἔργοις
                                               κολακευούσης
πᾶσαν μὲν ὑπόσχεσιν ἔρριψεν ἄθεσμον,
θάνατον δὲ μᾶλλον ἠγάπησεν ἔνδεσμον.
Τί δὲ πράξω ὁ ταλαίπωρος   καὶ κατάκριτος ἐγώ,
ὅτι πάντοτε συνέχει με   τῆς Ἁμαρτίας ἡ χείρ;
Ὥσπερ ἡ Αἰγυπτία   Ἰωσὴφ ἐπιβαίνει,

They dipped the tunic in blood but did not injure the
    wearer.
God was keeping the young man alive,
even as his father mourned him as dead.
Now, then, this adulteress waged war on his tunic,
but in no way wounded the noble general's soul,
for he had put on a secure suit of armor
which rendered impotent all the passions' bombardments.
Let us hasten, faithful ones, to emulate this man,
for the treachery of fleshly pleasures
is rising up against us even now.
But let no one be conquered by it,
for the sleepless eye watches over all!

22

The grand champion has secured against the passions
a divine garland and a victory hailed in song,
and rightly the faithful always and everywhere
honor his memory,
since Sin did not control his body.
The licentious woman was flattering him with words and
    deeds,
but he cast aside every disgraceful promise,
and he had greater fondness for death in chains.
What, then, can I do, miserable and condemned,
when Sin's hand always holds me tight?
As the Egyptian woman jumps on Joseph,

οὕτως ἕλκει με αὕτη   πρὸς ἀτόπους ἔννοιας·
ἀλλὰ βοῶ   πρὸς σέ, Παντοδύναμε·
"Ῥῦσαι κἀμέ,   Χριστέ, τυραννούμενον,
ἵνα σωθῶ   διὰ τῆς Θεοτόκου,
ὡς Ἰωσὴφ   ὁ πιστός σου θεράπων,
ὅτι πάντα ἐφορᾷ   τὸ ἀκοίμητον ὄμμα."

so she pulls me toward indecent thoughts,
but I call out to you, the Almighty one:
"Christ, rescue me too, who am enslaved to a tyrant,
that I may be saved by the Mother of God,
just like Joseph, your faithful servant,
for the sleepless eye watches over all."

Προοίμιον

Προφῆτα καὶ προόπτα   τῶν μεγαλουργιῶν τοῦ Θεοῦ
                                                                    ἡμῶν,
Ἠλία μεγαλώνυμε,   ὁ τῷ φθέγματί σου   στήσας τὰ
                                                        ὑδατόρρυτα νέφη,
πρέσβευε ὑπὲρ ἡμῶν
τὸν μόνον φιλάνθρωπον.

I

Τὴν πολλὴν τῶν ἀνθρώπων ἀνομίαν,   τοῦ Θεοῦ δὲ
                                                        πολλὴν φιλανθρωπίαν
θεασάμενος   ὁ προφήτης ἐταράττετο   Ἠλίας
                                                                θυμούμενος,
καὶ λόγους ἀσπλαγχνίας   πρὸς τὸν εὔσπλαγχνον
                                                                    ἐκίνησεν·
"Ὀργίσθητι," βοήσας,   "ἐπὶ τοὺς σὲ ἀθετήσαντας   νῦν,
                                                        Κριτὰ δικαιότατε."
Ἀλλὰ τὰ σπλάγχνα τοῦ ἀγαθοῦ   οὐδὲ ὅλως παρεκίνησε
πρὸς τὸ τιμωρήσασθαι   τοὺς αὐτὸν ἀθετήσαντας·

ON THE PROPHET ELIJAH

Prelude

to its own melody

Greatly famed Elijah, prophet and diviner
of our God's great deeds, who checked the rain-gushing
    clouds with your voice,
intercede for us before
the one who is benevolent.

I

to its own melody

The scope of humans' lawlessness and that of God's
    benevolence
the prophet Elijah saw and was stirred to anger; he hurled
heartless words to the kindhearted one:
"Let out your wrath," he cried, "upon those who've rejected
    you, Judge most just!"
But he did not provoke the good one's heart
to punish in the least those who reject him;

ἀεὶ γὰρ τὴν μετάνοιαν   τῶν πάντων ἀναμένει
ὁ μόνος φιλάνθρωπος.

2

Ὅτε πᾶσαν τὴν γῆν ἐν ἀσεβείαις   ἐθεάσατο τότε ὁ
                                        προφήτης,
τὸν δὲ Ὕψιστον   οὐδὲ ὅλως ὀργιζόμενον,   ἀλλὰ
                                        ἀνεχόμενον,
κινεῖται πρὸς μανίαν   καὶ μαρτύρεται τὸν εὔσπλαγχνον·
"Ἐγὼ καταυθεντήσω   καὶ κολάσω τὴν ἀσέβειαν   τῶν
                                        παροργιζόντων σε·
τῆς γὰρ πολλῆς σου ἀνοχῆς   οὗτοι πάντες
                                        κατεφρόνησαν
καὶ οὐκ ἐλογίσαντο   σὲ πατέρα τὸν εὔσπλαγχνον·
αὐτὸς δέ, ὡς φιλότεκνος,   οἰκτείρεις τοὺς υἱούς σου,
ὁ μόνος φιλάνθρωπος.

3

"Νῦν δικάσω ἐγὼ ὑπὲρ τοῦ Κτίστου,   ἀσεβεῖς δὲ τῆς
                                        γῆς ἐξολοθρεύσω
καὶ ψηφίσομαι   τιμωρίαν, ἀλλὰ δέδοικα   τὴν θείαν
                                        χρηστότητα·
ὀλίγοις γὰρ δακρύοις   δυσωπεῖται ὁ φιλάνθρωπος.
Τί οὖν νῦν ἐννοήσω   πρὸς τοσαύτην ἀγαθότητα   καὶ
                                        στήσω τὸν ἔλεον;
Τὴν ψῆφον ὅρκῳ βεβαιῶν,   ἵνα τοῦτον δυσωπούμενος

he always awaits the repentance of all,
the one who is benevolent.

2

When the prophet saw the whole earth in godless impiety
and the Most High not angered at all, but forbearing,
he was moved to rage and objection toward the kindhearted
    one:
"I'll take charge and chasten the impiety of those who
    provoke your anger!
They've all scorned your great forbearance
and not considered you a kindhearted father,
yet you, who love your children, have compassion on your
    sons,
as the one who is benevolent.

3

"So I'll rather judge, instead of the Creator, and eradicate
    the impious
from the earth and declare their punishment, but I fear
    divine kindness.
By a few tears the benevolent one is persuaded.
What can I think up against such goodness to stop the
    mercy?
By oath I'm endorsing the verdict, so that, persuaded by it,

μὴ λύσῃ ὁ δίκαιος   τὴν τοιαύτην ἀπόφασιν,
ἀλλὰ καὶ βεβαιώσῃ μου   τὴν κρίσιν ὡς δυνάστης
ὁ μόνος φιλάνθρωπος."

4

Προτερεύει τῆς κρίσεως ὁ ὅρκος   καὶ προοίμιον ἦν τῶν
ψηφισθέντων·
ἀλλ' εἰ βούλεσθε,   πρὸς τὴν Βίβλον ἀναδράμωμεν   καὶ
γνῶμεν τὰ ῥήματα.
Φησὶ γὰρ ὁ προφήτης   ὀργιζόμενος, ὡς γέγραπται·
"Ζῇ Κύριος, οὐ δρόσος   οὐδὲ ὄμβρος κατελεύσεται   εἰ
μὴ διὰ τοῦ λόγου μου."
Ἀλλὰ εὐθέως ὁ Βασιλεὺς   τῷ Ἠλίᾳ ἀπεκρίνατο·
"Ἂν ἴδω μετάνοιαν   καὶ πηγάζοντα δάκρυα,
μὴ χορηγεῖν οὐ δύναμαι   τὰ σπλάγχνα τοῖς ἀνθρώποις
ὁ μόνος φιλάνθρωπος."

5

Ῥητορεύει εὐθέως ὁ προφήτης   καὶ προβάλλει τὸ
δίκαιον τοῦ ὅρκου·
"Κατὰ σοῦ," φησίν,   "τοῦ Θεοῦ τῶν ὅλων,
ὤμοσα   πανάγιε Δέσποτα,
τοὺς ὄμβρους μὴ δοθῆναι   εἰ μὴ πάλιν διὰ λόγου μου·
ἡνίκα γὰρ κατίδω   τὸν λαὸν μεταμελούμενον,   ἐγὼ
ἱκετεύσω σε.
Οὐκ ἔστι τοίνυν ἐν τῇ σῇ   ἐξουσίᾳ, δικαιότατε,

the just one will not annul the sentence,
but rather as ruler endorse my judgment,
the one who is benevolent."

4

An oath precedes the judgment, a preamble to the verdict's
    pronouncement.
Let's return, though, if you will, to the Bible and study the
    passages!
The angry prophet says, as is written,
"As the Lord lives, no dew nor rain shall fall, except by my
    word."
But the King answered Elijah immediately:
"When I see repentance and flowing tears,
I'm unable to withhold my affection for humanity,
as the one who is benevolent."

5

The prophet speaks up at once and points to the oath's
    lawfulness:
"By you, God of all," he says, "I swore, all-holy Master,
that no rain shall be granted, except at my word.
Whenever I see the people with remorse, I'll appeal to you,
but it's not now within your authority, most just,

κωλῦσαι τὴν κόλασιν   ἐκ τοῦ ὅρκου οὗ τέθεικα
ὃν φύλαξον καὶ σφράγισον,   συστέλλων σου τὰ
σπλάγχνα,
ὁ μόνος φιλάνθρωπος."

6

Ὁ λιμὸς οὖν τὴν γῆν ἐπολιόρκει,   κατεφθείροντο δὲ οἱ
ἐνοικοῦντες
ὀδυρόμενοι   καὶ τὰς χεῖρας ἀνατείνοντες   πρὸς τὸν
Πανοικτίρμονα.
Συνείχετο δὲ τούτοις   ὁ Δεσπότης ἑκατέρωθεν·
τὰ σπλάγχνα μὲν ἀνοίγων   τοῖς αὐτὸν
καθικετεύουσι   καὶ σπεύδων πρὸς τὸν ἔλεον,
τὸν δὲ προφήτην ἐρυθριῶν   καὶ τὸν ὅρκον ὅνπερ
ὤμοσε,
τοὺς ὄμβρους οὐ δίδωσιν,   ἀλλ᾽ ἐσκεύασε πρόφασιν
συνέχουσαν καὶ θλίβουσαν   ψυχὴν τὴν τοῦ προφήτου
ὁ μόνος φιλάνθρωπος.

7

Φυσιούμενον βλέπων ὁ Δεσπότης   κατὰ τῶν ὁμοφύλων
τὸν Θεσβίτην,
ἐδικαίωσε   τῷ λιμῷ συντιμωρήσασθαι   τοῖς ἄλλοις τὸν
δίκαιον,
ἵνα τῇ ἀτροφίᾳ   πιεζόμενος βουλεύσηται
περὶ τῆς ἐνωμότου   ἀποφάσεως φιλάνθρωπα   καὶ
παύσῃ τὴν κόλασιν·

to deny the punishment I've ordained with an oath;
respect it and seal it, contain your compassion,
the one who is benevolent."

6

So famine plagued the earth. Its inhabitants, in their
    terrible plight,
lamented and raised their hands toward the all-merciful
    Lord.
He was pressed on either side:
while he opened his heart to those who implored him and
    hastened toward pity,
he blushed before the prophet and the oath he had sworn,
so he provided conditions that pressed and squeezed
the prophet's soul, but he didn't grant rain,
the one who is benevolent.

7

The Lord, who saw the Tishbite puffed up against his own
    people,
thought it right that the righteous one be punished by the
    famine along with them,
and, tormented by starvation, he might decide
with benevolence about the oath-bound sentence and halt
    the punishment;

ἔστι γὰρ ὄντως φοβερὸν   τῆς γαστρὸς τὸ ἀπαραίτητον,
καὶ ἕκαστον ἔμψυχον   λογικόν τε καὶ ἄλογον
σοφίᾳ τῆς θεότητος   διὰ τροφῆς φυλάττει
ὁ μόνος φιλάνθρωπος.

8

Ἡ γαστὴρ μὲν τὴν Φύσιν συνηγόρει   καὶ τοὺς νόμους
                                    τῆς Φύσεως λαβοῦσα
ἐπετίθετο   τῷ πρεσβύτῃ μεθοδεύουσα   τὸ
                                    μεταβουλεύσασθαι·
αὐτὸς δὲ ὥσπερ λίθος   ἀναίσθητος ἐνίστατο
τὸν ζῆλον κεκτημένος   ἀντὶ πάσης ἑστιάσεως   καὶ
                                    τούτῳ ἀρκούμενος·
ὃν θεωρήσας ὁ Κριτὴς   ἐπεκούφισε λιμώττοντι
τῷ φίλῳ τὴν ἔνδειαν,   οὐχ ἡγούμενος δίκαιον
σὺν ἀδίκοις καὶ ἀνόμοις   τὸν δίκαιον λιμώττειν
ὁ μόνος φιλάνθρωπος.

9

Τὴν τροφὴν οὖν αὐτῷ ὁ Πανοικτίρμων   μετὰ πάσης
                                    σοφίας εὐτρεπίζει·
τοῖς γὰρ κόραξι τοῖς ἀσπλάγχνοις ἐγκελεύεται   τροφὴν
                                    χορηγεῖν αὐτῷ·
κοράκων δὲ τὸ γένος   εὐσπλαγχνίας ἐστὶν ἄμοιρον,
τροφὴν μὴ χορηγοῦντα   νεοσσοῖς ὡς τέκνοις
                    πώποτε,   ἀλλ' ἄνωθεν τρέφονται.
Ἐπειδὴ τοίνυν καὶ αὐτὸς   μισοτέκνου ἀνελάβετο

for truly terrible is the stomach's implacability,
but every living being, rational and irrational,
is preserved with food by the divine wisdom of
the one who is benevolent.

8

His stomach was pleading alongside Nature and tenaciously
    tried
by the laws of Nature to change the old man's mind.
But he was unmoved, like an unfeeling stone,
and lived on zeal instead of meals, content with that.
When the Judge saw this, not reckoning it right
for the righteous to starve with the unrighteous and lawless,
he relieved his starving friend of his hunger,
the one who is benevolent.

9

Food is what the All-Merciful prepares with unreserved
    wisdom;
he orders the heartless ravens to provide the man with
    food.
The ravens' race has no kindheartedness,
not providing their nestlings like nurslings with food; they
    are fed from above.
So with God thus adopting the manners and mind

καὶ τρόπους καὶ ἔννοιαν, μισοτέκνοις ἐχρήσατο
πρὸς τοῦτον ὡς μισάνθρωπον τοῖς κόραξι πανσόφως
ὁ μόνος φιλάνθρωπος.

10

"Ἡ πολλή σου," φησίν, "φιλοθεΐα," ὁ Θεὸς τῷ Ἠλίᾳ
                                        διελέχθη,
"μὴ μισάνθρωπον ἐπενέγκῃ σοι διάθεσιν· ἀλλ᾽ ὅρα
                                    τοὺς κόρακας·
οἱ γὰρ πρὸς τοὺς ἰδίους νεοσσοὺς ἀεὶ μισότεκνοι
αἰφνίδιον, ὡς βλέπεις, περὶ σέ εἰσι φιλότιμοι καὶ νῦν
                                    μεταβέβληνται·
τῆς εὐσπλαγχνίας τῆς ἐμῆς ὑπηρέται ἀνεδείχθησαν
τροφήν σοι κομίζοντες· ὡς ὁρῶ δέ, οὐ δύναμαι
τὴν φύσιν ἐκβιάζεσθαι τὴν σὴν πρὸς τοὺς ἀνθρώπους,
ὁ μόνος φιλάνθρωπος.

11

"Νῦν αἰδεῖσθαι ὀφείλεις, ὦ προφῆτα, καὶ μιμεῖσθαι
                                        ἀλόγων εὐπειθίαν·
πῶς τὰ ἄσπλαγχνα αἰδεσθέντα με τὸν
                    εὔσπλαγχνον εὐθὺς μετεβλήθησαν·
τιμῶ σου τὴν φιλίαν καὶ οὐ λύω τὴν ἀπόφασιν·
οὐ δύναμαι δὲ φέρειν ὀδυρμὸν καὶ θλῖψιν
                    πάνδημον ἀνθρώπων ὧν ἔπλασα·
τῶν δὲ νηπίων τὴν κραυγὴν πῶς ἐνέγκω καὶ τὰ δάκρυα,

128

of a child-hating raven, in relation to this man-hater
the child-haters were wisely used by him,
the one who is benevolent.

10

"Let your great love for what's godly," says God conversing
    with Elijah,
"not impose upon you a misanthropic attitude, but look at
    the ravens:
always hating their own nestlings,
they're now suddenly generous to you, as you see, and have
    changed.
By bringing you food they are shown to be
servants of my kindheartedness. Your disposition toward
    humanity
cannot, I see, be driven out by me,
the one who is benevolent.

11

"Now, you ought to respect, my prophet, and imitate the
    compliance of the animals,
how the heartless were changed at once to respect my
    tender heart.
I honor your friendship and won't annul your sentence,
but can't bear the ubiquitous wailing and affliction of the
    humans whom I formed.
How can I bear the infants' tears,

κτηνῶν δὲ τὸν ἄσημον   μυκηθμὸν ἐπερχόμενον;
Ἐγὼ γὰρ τούτοις ἅπασιν   ὡς Πλάστης συμπαθήσω
ὁ μόνος φιλάνθρωπος."

12

Ἠγριοῦτο ἐν τούτοις ὁ προφήτης·   ἀπεκρίθη τότε τῷ
                                                Δεσπότῃ·
"Μηδὲ κόρακας   ὑπηρέτας πρὸς τὸ θρέψαι
                                με   προτρέψῃ, ὦ Δέσποτα·
λιμῷ διαφθαρῆναι   ἐπιλέξομαι, πανάγιε,
καὶ μόνον ἀσεβοῦντας   τιμωρήσομαι, καὶ ἔσται
                                μοι   μεγάλη ἀνάπαυσις·
συναπολέσθαι οὐκ ὀκνῶ   πᾶσι τοῖς ἀπαρνουμένοις σε·
μὴ οὖν οἰκτειρήσῃς με,   μὴ λιμώττοντος φείσῃ μου,
καὶ μόνον ἐξολόθρευσον   τῆς γῆς τοὺς ἀσεβοῦντας,
ὁ μόνος φιλάνθρωπος."

13

Λόγους τούτους ὡς ἤκουσεν ὁ Κτίστης,   μεθιστᾷ τὸν
                                προφήτην ἐκ τοῦ τόπου
ἐντειλάμενος   πετεινοῖς μὴ χορηγεῖν αὐτῷ   τροφὴν ὡς
                                τὸ πρότερον,
καὶ πέμπει ἐν Σαρέφθοις   πρὸς τὴν χήραν τὸν
                                λιμώττοντα,
εἰπὼν ὡς "Ἐντελοῦμαι   γυναικὶ τοῦ διαθρέψαι
                σε,"   σοφὰ βουλευόμενος.

the resounding, inarticulate cattle lowing?
I feel for them all, for I gave them form,
the one who is benevolent."

12

This provoked the prophet's wild temper, and he answered
      the Master,
"You shouldn't even urge your servant ravens to feed me;
I prefer, all-holy one, to waste away in hunger.
I'll just punish the impious; that's my great relief.
I'm not afraid to be destroyed along with all who deny you.
Don't pity me; don't spare me from starving!
But just eradicate the impious from the earth,
as the one who is benevolent."

13

When the Maker heard these words, he removed the
      prophet from that place
and commanded the birds not to provide him with food as
      before;
he drove the famished one to the widow in Zarephath,
made wise plans, and said, "I'm commanding a woman to
      sustain you."

Ἦν γὰρ καὶ χήρα καὶ ἐθνικὴ   ἡ γυνὴ πρὸς ἣν
                                        ἀπέσταλτο
καὶ τέκνων ἀντείχετο,   ἵν᾽ ἀκούων ὁ δίκαιος
τῆς ἐθνικῆς τὸ ὄνομα   βοήσῃ· "Δὸς τοὺς ὄμβρους,
ὁ μόνος φιλάνθρωπος."

14

Ἰουδαίοις ἀθέμιτον ὑπῆρχε   συνεσθίειν ποτὲ τοῖς
                                        ἀλλοέθνοις·
διὰ τοῦτο οὖν   τὸν Ἠλίαν πρὸς ἀλλόφυλον   γυναῖκα
                                        ὡδήγησεν,
ἵνα τὴν παρ᾽ ἐκείνης   βδελυττόμενος ἑστίασιν
εὐθὺς περὶ τῶν ὄμβρων   δυσωπήσῃ τὸν
                                  φιλάνθρωπον·   ἀλλ᾽ οὐκ ἐλογίσατο
τὴν πρὸς τὰ ἔθνη ἀποφυγήν,   ἀλλὰ τρέχει πρὸς τὸ
                                        γύναιον,
τροφὴν ἀπαιτῶν αὐτὴν   μετὰ πάσης τραχύτητος·
"᾽Εμοί," φησίν, "προσέταξεν   εἰσπρᾶξαί σε, ὦ γύναι,
ὁ μόνος φιλάνθρωπος."

15

Ἀλλὰ ταῦτα ἀκούσασα ἡ χήρα   ἐν σπουδῇ τῷ προφήτῃ
                                        ἀπεκρίθη
ὡς "Οὐκ ἔστι μοι   ἐγκρυφίας, ἀλλ᾽ ἢ ἄλευρον   δρακός,
                                        ὅπερ βούλομαι
ποιῆσαι εἰσελθοῦσα,   ἵνα φάγω σὺν τοῖς τέκνοις μου·

The woman he was sent to was both widowed and gentile
and was caring for children, so that, when he heard her
    gentile name,
he might cry, "Grant rainstorms,
as the one who is benevolent!"

14

It was forbidden for Jews then to eat with people of other
    nations,
which is why he led Elijah to a woman of another tribe,
so that, repelled by eating at her place,
he'd immediately pray the benevolent one for rain. He
    didn't consider
avoiding the gentiles, but ran to the woman
and with brutal harshness demanded food:
"I require it from you, as requested by him,
the one who is benevolent!"

15

But when the widow heard this, she swiftly answered the
    prophet,
"I have nothing baked, just a handful of meal, which I
    intend
to prepare to eat with my children when I go inside.

οὐδὲν δὲ τῆς δρακός μοι   πλέον τι περιλείπεται   ἢ
                                        μόνος ὁ θάνατος."
Πρὸς δὲ τῆς χήρας τὴν φωνὴν   ἐκινεῖτο καὶ συνέπασχε
διαλογιζόμενος   ὡς "Ἐμοῦ πλέον τήκεται
καὶ τῷ λιμῷ ἐκθλίβεται   ἡ χήρα, εἰ μὴ φθάσει
ὁ μόνος φιλάνθρωπος.

16

"Νῦν στενά μοι," φησί, "τὰ τοῦ γυναίου·   κἂν πεινῶ γὰρ
                                        ἐγώ, ὑπάρχω μόνος,
μετὰ τέκνων δὲ   ἐκλιμώττει ἡ χηρεύουσα   πρὸς ἣν
                                        παραγέγονα.
Μὴ γένωμαι ὁ ξένος   τοῦ θανάτου ταύτης πρόξενος,
μηδὲ τῇ ξενοδόχῳ   τεκνοκτόνος λογισθήσομαι,   ἀλλ᾽
                                        ἐλῶ νῦν πρὸς ἔλεον·
πρὸς πάντας ἔσχον ἀπαθῶς,   πρὸς δὲ ταύτην
                                        μεταβάλλομαι·
ἐκθήσω τὴν φύσιν μου   οἰκτιρμοῖς συναγάλλεσθαι·
οἰκτίρμων γὰρ καθέστηκεν   ὁ αἴτιος τῶν πάντων,
ὁ μόνος φιλάνθρωπος."

17

Ὁ προφήτης τῇ χήρᾳ ἀπεκρίθη·   "Δρὰξ μέν ἐστιν
                                        ἀλεύρου σοι, ὡς ἔφης·
οὐκ ἐκλείψει σοι   ἡ ὑδρία, ὁ καμψάκης δὲ   τὸ ἔλαιον
                                        βλύσει σοι."
Καὶ λόγοις μὲν Ἡλίας   εὐλογίαν ἐχαρίσατο,

This handful is all that I have left, apart from death."
The widow's voice moved him to compassion,
and he thought, "She is wasting away more than I,
succumbing to hunger, unless he comes soon,
the one who is benevolent!

16

"The woman's situation troubles me," he says, "and
      although I'm hungry, I'm alone.
The widow to whom I have come is starving with her
      children.
May I, a stranger, not be her death's arranger!
And may I not be thought a child killer by my hostess—I'm
      aiming at mercy now.
I stayed callous to everyone; toward her I am changing.
I'll leave my nature outside and compassionately rejoice
      with them,
for the cause of all is himself compassionate,
the one who is benevolent!"

17

The prophet answered the widow: "You've a handful of
      meal, as you said.
The jar will not be emptied, and the cruse will flow with oil
      for you."
While Elijah with words offered the blessing,

ὁ Κτίστης δὲ εὐθέως   ὡς φιλότιμος καὶ
                    εὔσπλαγχνος   τὸ ἔργον ἐπήγαγε·
τοῦ μὲν προφήτου τὸν σκοπὸν   ἐκπληρῶν, φησίν, ὁ
                                              πάνσοφος,
τὸ δὲ ἀληθέστερον   τῆς καλλίστης προφάσεως
δραξάμενος, χαρίζεται   τὸ ἄφθονον τῇ χήρᾳ
ὁ μόνος φιλάνθρωπος.

18

Ῥήμασι Θεὸς προφήτου ἐπεκάμφθη   καὶ τροφὴν
                        παρεῖχε τούτῳ καὶ τῇ χήρᾳ·
ὁ Ἠλίας δὲ   οὐδὲ ὅλως ἐσπλαγχνίζετο,   ἀλλ' ἔμενεν
                                              ἄκαμπτος.
Ὁ εὔσπλαγχνος δὲ βλέπων   τὸν λαὸν διαφθειρόμενον
καὶ τοῦτον ἀπειθοῦντα,   ἐφ' ἑτέραν τέχνην
                    πάνσοφον   μετῆλθεν ὡς δίκαιος.
Τὸν γὰρ τῆς χήρας υἱὸν   τελευτήσαντα ἀπέδειξεν,
ἵνα κἂν τὰ δάκρυα   καὶ τὴν ἄλλην περίστασιν
τῆς χήρας θεασάμενος   βοήσῃ· "Δὸς τοὺς ὄμβρους,
ὁ μόνος φιλάνθρωπος."

19

Ὡς οὖν εἶδεν ἡ χήρα νεκρωθέντα   τὸν υἱόν, ἐπανέστη
                                        τῷ προφήτῃ·
"Εἴθε," λέγουσα,   "τῷ λιμῷ προαπετέθνηκα   πρὶν ἤ σε
                                        θεάσωμαι·
συνέφερε γὰρ πάλαι   τελευτῆσαί με λιμώττουσαν

the Creator, generous and kind, immediately brought it to
      pass.
The all-wise one, it says, fulfilled the prophet's intention;
but, more precisely, he seized on this as an excellent excuse
and abundance was offered to the widow by him,
the one who is benevolent.

18

Yielding to his words, God gave Elijah and the widow food,
but, not yet fully compassionate, the prophet remained
      unyielding.
When he saw the people wasting away
and Elijah disobeying, the compassionate one, being just,
      took up another clever ruse:
he rendered the widow's son dead,
so that seeing her tears and her other misfortune,
Elijah would cry, "Grant rainstorms,
as the one who is benevolent!"

19

When she saw her son dead, the widow turned on the
      prophet:
"Would that I'd died of hunger," she said, "before I saw you!
It would be better if I'd starved to death already

καὶ μὴ τὸν υἱόν μου   θεωρεῖν με νεκρὸν κείμενον   ἐν
τῇ παρουσίᾳ σου.
Οὐχ οὗτοί εἰσιν οἱ μισθοὶ   τῆς καλλίστης δεξιώσεως;
Ὑπῆρχον γὰρ εὔτεκνος   πρὶν ἐλθεῖν σε, ὦ ἄνθρωπε·
ἐλθὼν δὲ ἀτεκνίαν μοι   παρέσχες ὀνομάσας
τὸν μόνον φιλάνθρωπον."

20

Μάλα μὲν ἐκρατεῖτο ὑπὸ χήρας   ὁ κρατήσας νεφῶν τε
καὶ τῶν ὄμβρων
καὶ συνείχετο   ὑπὸ μίας ὁ τοὺς ἅπαντας   συνέχων διὰ
ῥήματος·
γυνὴ δὲ παναθλία,   πάσης ἄμοιρος δυνάμεως,
τὸν λόγῳ καὶ δυνάμει   οὐρανοὺς κρατεῖν
νομίζοντα   κρατεῖ ὡς κατάδικον,
καὶ συμπλακεῖσα μανικῶς   ὡς φονέα εἰς κριτήριον
καθεῖλκε κραυγάζουσα·   "Δός μοι γόνον ὃν ἔκτεινας·
οὐ χρῄζω τοῦ ἀλεύρου σου·   μὴ θρέψῃ με νομίζων
τὸν μόνον φιλάνθρωπον.

21

"Ἄρτους ἐν τῇ γαστρί μου κατασπείρας   τὸν καρπὸν
τῆς γαστρός μου καὶ τὸν κλάδον
ἐξερρίζωσας,   καὶ πωλεῖς μοι ὑπερτίμια   τὰ δῶρα τὰ
βρώσιμα·
ψυχὴν ἀντὶ ἀλεύρου   καὶ ἐλαίου ἐμεθόδευσας·

and not seen my son lying as a corpse in your presence.
Is this the reward for my finest hospitality?
I was happy with my children before you arrived, sir;
you've come and made me childless, mentioning the
       name of
the one who is benevolent."

20

The man who withheld clouds and rain was held back by a
       widow.
The one who captured all with his words was captured by
       this one;
a woman so wretched, without any power,
holds as a criminal the man who thinks by word and power
       he can hold the heavens,
and madly grabs and drags him like a murderer
to court, screaming, "Give me the child you killed!
I don't need your meal. Don't feed me and think yourself
the one who is benevolent!

21

"By sowing bread in my belly, you've uprooted the fruit and
       the shoot
of my belly, and you're selling me these overpriced gifts as
       food!
For oil and meal you exacted a soul.

ἐγὼ δὲ δυσωπῶ σε   ἀνατρέψαι τὸ συνάλλαγμα   καὶ
                                        δοῦναι ὃ ἔλαβες·
ἢ τοῖς θανάτοις τοῦ λαοῦ   οὐκ ἠρκέσθης, ἀλλ᾽
                                        ἐσπούδασας
τοῦ οἴκου μου ἅψασθαι;   Τὴν ψυχὴν τοῦ παιδίου μου
ἀπόλυσον καὶ κόμισον   ψυχήν μου ἀντ᾽ ἐκείνης,
καὶ γενοῦ φιλάνθρωπος.”

22

Νυγεὶς τούτοις ὡς κέντροις ὁ Ἠλίας,   αἰσχυνόμενος
                                        κράζουσαν τὴν χήραν
ὑποπτεύουσαν   ὡς αὐτὸς ἐξεβιάσατο   ψυχὴν τοῦ υἱοῦ
                                        αὐτῆς,
καὶ θέλων ταύτην πεῖσαι   διὰ λόγων οὐκ ἠδύνατο·
εἰδὼς ὡς ἠπιστεῖτο   παρ᾽ αὐτῆς
                        ἀπολογούμενος,   ἐθρήνει γὰρ ἄπαυστα.
Ἀλλ᾽ ἀτενίσας εἰς οὐρανούς·   “Οἴμοι, Κύριε,” ἐβόησεν,
“ὁ μάρτυς ὁ ἄμεμπτος   τῆς λαβούσης με σύνοικον,
σὺ ταύτην παρεκίνησας   ἀπαιτεῖν με τὸ τέκνον,
ὁ μόνος φιλάνθρωπος.

23

“Οὐ πιστεύω, Σωτὴρ παντοδύναμε,”   τῷ Θεῷ ὁ
                                        προφήτης ἀνεβόα,
“ὡς ὁ θάνατος   τῷ παιδίῳ ἐκ τῆς φύσεως,   ὡς πᾶσι,
                                        συμβέβηκεν·
ἀλλ᾽ ἔστι τοῦτο τέχνη   τῆς σοφίας σου, ἀναμάρτητε,

I beg you, please, undo the deal and return what you've
     taken.
Weren't the deaths of your people enough,
but you had to mess with my household too?
Release the child's soul; take mine for his,
and then you'll be benevolent!"

22

Pricked by her charges as by stings, Elijah felt ashamed
before the crying widow who suspected he had forced out
     her son's soul,
and he wished to convince her, but couldn't with words.
He saw her disbelief when he made his defense; she
     wouldn't stop wailing.
So he gazed toward heaven: "Alas, Lord," he shouted,
"the woman hosted me, but was led to beseech me
for her child by you, her blameless witness,
the one who is benevolent!

23

"I do not believe, Savior almighty," the prophet bellowed to
     God,
"that death naturally befell the child, as it does all people,
but this is the work of your wisdom, sinless one,

καὶ πάντως μηχανᾶσαι   κατ᾽ ἐμοῦ ἀνάγκην
                    εὔσπλαγχνον,   ἵνα ὅταν αἰτήσω σε
ὅτι ῾Τῆς χήρας τὸν υἱὸν   νεκρωθέντα ἐξανάστησον,᾽
εὐθὺς ἀντιφθέγξῃ μοι·   ῾Τὸν υἱόν μου τὸν Ἰσραὴλ
ἐλέησον θλιβόμενον   καὶ πάντα τὸν λαόν μου,
ὁ μόνος φιλάνθρωπος.᾽᾽᾽

24

Σῶσαι θέλων τὴν γῆν ὁ Πανοικτίρμων   τῷ Ἠλίᾳ
                    εὐθέως ἀπεκρίθη·
῾῾Νῦν τοὺς λόγους μου   ἐνωτίζου φανερώτερον   καὶ
                    ἄκουέ μου λέγοντος.
Ὠδίνω καὶ σπουδάζω   πρὸς τὴν λύσιν τῆς κολάσεως,
ἐπείγομαι τοῦ δοῦναι   πᾶσι τὴν τροφὴν λιμώττουσιν·
                    ὑπάρχω γὰρ εὔσπλαγχνος·
τοὺς τῶν δακρύων ὀχετοὺς   βλέπων, ὡς πατὴρ
                    συγκάμπτομαι,
οἰκτείρω ἐκλείποντας   ὑπὸ πείνης καὶ θλίψεως·
ἁμαρτωλοὺς γὰρ βούλομαι   τοῦ σῴζειν μετανοίᾳ,
ὁ μόνος φιλάνθρωπος.

25

῾῾Ἄκουε οὖν, προφῆτα, παρρησίᾳ·   καὶ γὰρ πάνυ εἰδέναι
                    σε σπουδάζω·
ὡς χειρόγραφον   εὐσπλαγχνίας με κατέχουσιν   οἱ
                    ἄνθρωποι ἅπαντες,
ἐν ᾧπερ συνεθέμην   ὡς οὐ βούλομαι τὸν θάνατον

and you are clearly devising a compassionate penalty for
    me, so that when I beg you,
'Raise up the widow's dead son!'
you'll echo me at once, 'Have mercy on my son,
the tormented Israel, and all my people,
the one who is benevolent!'"

24

Wanting to save the earth, the All-Merciful immediately
    replied
to Elijah, "Listen more clearly to my words, and hear what
    I'm saying:
I'm longing and I'm eager to undo the punishment.
I'm striving to give all the famished food, for I am
    compassionate.
As a father, I'm moved, seeing streams of tears;
I feel with those suffering from hunger and torments;
I want to save the sinful with a change of heart,
as the one who is benevolent!

25

"So, prophet, listen well; I really want you to learn:
humans all hold on to me as a guarantee of compassion,
by which I've vouched that I don't wish to see

ἰδεῖν τῶν πλημμελούντων, ἀλλὰ μᾶλλον τὴν ζωὴν
                        αὐτῶν. Μὴ οὖν ἀποδείξῃς με
ὡς ψευδολόγον παρ' αὐτοῖς ἀλλὰ δέξαι μου τὴν
                            αἴτησιν—
πρεσβείαν προσφέρω σοι· σὲ γὰρ μόνα τὰ δάκρυα
τῆς χήρας συνετάραξαν, ἐγὼ δὲ περὶ πάντας
ὑπάρχω φιλάνθρωπος."

26

Νοῦν καὶ φρένα τοῖς λόγοις τοῦ Ὑψίστου ὁ Ἠλίας
                         ὑπέθηκε καὶ ὦτα,
καὶ ὑπέταξε τὴν ψυχὴν καὶ ἐκαλλώπισεν αὐτὴν ἐν
                         τοῖς ῥήμασι,
καὶ εἶπε· "Γενηθήτω τὸ θέλημά σου, Δέσποτα·
παράσχου καὶ τοὺς ὄμβρους καὶ ζωὴν τῷ τελευτήσαντι,
                         καὶ ζώωσον τὰ σύμπαντα·
ζωὴ ὑπάρχων ὁ Θεὸς καὶ ἀνάστασις καὶ λύτρωσις,
παράσχου τὴν χάριν σου τοῖς ἀνθρώποις καὶ κτήνεσιν·
αὐτὸς γὰρ μόνος δύνασαι τὰ πάντα περισῴζειν,
ὁ μόνος φιλάνθρωπος."

27

Εὐθὺς ταῦτα εἰπόντος τοῦ προφήτου, ἀπεκρίθη πρὸς
                         τοῦτον ὁ οἰκτίρμων·
"Τὴν προαίρεσιν ἐδεξάμην καὶ ἐπήνεσα, καὶ σπεύδω
                         τιμῆσαί σε.
Ἐγὼ ὑπὲρ ἐκείνων παρὰ σοῦ τὴν χάριν ἔλαβον,

wrongdoers' death but their life instead. Don't make me out
    to be
a liar in front of them, but accept my request—
I offer to negotiate. You were only upset
by the widow's tears, but I am for all,
the one who is benevolent!"

26

Elijah subjected his mind and thought and ears as well
to the Most High's speech and subdued his soul and
    adorned it with words,
and said, "Your will be done, Master!
Grant both rain and life to the deceased, and quicken all
    things!
God who is life, resurrection and redemption,
grant your grace to humans and beasts!
Only you can rescue all,
the one who is benevolent!"

27

When the prophet had said this, the merciful one answered
    at once:
"I am in receipt of your commitment and approve it; I'll
    hasten to honor you.
I've obtained from you grace pertaining to them,

γενοῦ δὲ σὺ μεσίτης   καὶ χορήγησον τὴν χάριν
                                            μου· οὐδὲ γὰρ ἀνέχομαι
καταλλαγῆναι χωρὶς σοῦ, ἀλλὰ βάδισαι καὶ μήνυσον
τῶν ὄμβρων τὸ χάρισμα, ἵνα πάντες κραυγάσωσιν
ὅτι ὁ πρώην ἄσπλαγχνος ἐφάνη νῦν ἐξαίφνης
πρὸς πάντας φιλάνθρωπος.᾽

28

"῞Υπαγε οὖν ταχέως, ὦ προφῆτα,   καὶ ὀφθεὶς Ἀχαὰβ
                                            εὐαγγελίζου,
καὶ ἐντέλλομαι   ταῖς νεφέλαις καὶ ποτίσουσι   τὴν γῆν
                                            ἐν τοῖς ὕδασι·
τὴν τούτων χορηγίαν   σὺ ἀπόφηναι, ὦ φίλε μου·
ἐγὼ δὲ ὑπογράψω   ταῖς τοιαύταις ἀποφάσεσι,   τιμῶν
                                            σου τὸ εὔγνωμον."
Ἀκούσας ταῦτα παρευθὺ   προσεκύνησε τὸν ῞Υψιστον,
βοῶν τῷ Οἰκτίρμονι· "Πολυέλεον οἶδά σε·
γινώσκω ὡς μακρόθυμος   ὑπάρχεις, ὁ Θεός μου,
ὁ μόνος φιλάνθρωπος."

29

Φοβηθεὶς οὖν τὸ πρόσταγμα ἐκτρέχει   πρὸς τὸν Ἀχαὰβ
                                            ὁ προφήτης
καὶ εὐαγγέλια   πρὸς ἐκεῖνον ἀποφθέγγεται   ὡς εἶπεν ὁ
                                            εὔσπλαγχνος.
Εὐθὺς δὲ αἱ νεφέλαι   τῇ προστάξει τοῦ Ποιήσαντος

so become an arbitrator and dispense my grace, for I
    couldn't bear
to settle this without you. So, go and show
the favor of the downpours, so all may shout
that he who was heartless has suddenly appeared
to all as most benevolent!

28

"Go quickly, prophet, and present yourself to Ahab with the
    tidings,
and I shall command the clouds, and they'll quench the
    earth's thirst
with their water. My friend, you announce the subvention,
and I'll sign the decrees, honoring your goodwill."
Having heard this, he fell down at once before the Most
    High,
crying to the Compassionate: "As plenteous in mercy
and patient I know you; you are, my God,
the one who is benevolent!"

29

Awestruck by his orders, the prophet ran off toward Ahab
to declare the good tidings to him as the compassionate one
    had said.
At once the clouds, pregnant with water,

ἐγκύμονες ὑδάτων   τὸν ἀέρα ἐπενήξαντο,   τοὺς
                                    ὄμβρους πηγάζουσαι·
ἠγαλλιάσατο δὲ ἡ γῆ   καὶ ἐδόξαζε τὸν Κύριον·
τὸν παῖδα μὲν ἔλαβεν   ἀναστάντα τὸ γύναιον·
σὺν πᾶσιν ἐπευφραίνετο   ἡ γῆ καὶ ἀνευφήμει
τὸν μόνον φιλάνθρωπον.

30

Ἤδη χρόνου τοσούτου προϊόντος   τῶν ἀνθρώπων ἑώρα
                                    τὴν κακίαν
καὶ ἐμελέτησε   βαρυτέραν ἀποφήνασθαι   Ἠλίας τὴν
                                    κόλασιν.
Ἰδὼν δὲ ὁ οἰκτίρμων   τῷ προφήτῃ ἀπεκρίνατο·
"Τὸν ζῆλον ὅνπερ ἔχεις   πρὸς τὸ δίκαιον
                        ἐπίσταμαι,   καὶ οἶδα τὴν πρόθεσιν·
ἀλλὰ συμπάσχω ἁμαρτωλοῖς   ὅταν ἄμετρα κολάζωνται·
ὀργίζει ὡς ἄμεμπτος   καὶ οὐ δύνῃ ἀνέχεσθαι;
Ἐγὼ δὲ οὐκ ἀνέχομαι   οὐδένα ἀπολέσθαι
ὡς μόνος φιλάνθρωπος."

31

Μετὰ ταῦτα δὲ βλέπων ὁ Δεσπότης   ὡς ἀπότομος
                                    οὗτος πρὸς ἀνθρώπους,
προὐνοήσατο   τοῦ γένους, καὶ ἐχώρισεν   Ἠλίαν τῆς
                                    γῆς αὐτῶν,
"Χωρίζου," λέγων, "φίλε,   τῆς ἀνθρώπων κατοικήσεως·

at the Maker's command, swam on the air, gushing
  downpours.
The earth was glad and glorified the Lord.
The woman received her child resurrected.
With everyone, the earth rejoiced and praised
the one who is benevolent.

30

After some time had passed, seeing the humans'
  wickedness,
Elijah contemplated rendering an even harsher
  punishment.
The merciful one was aware and responded to the prophet:
"I note the zeal you show for justice, and I see your intent,
but I suffer with the sinners when they're punished without
  measure.
Are you angered and can't bear it because you are
  blameless?
I cannot bear it if anyone is lost,
as the one who is benevolent."

31

After that, when the Lord saw how relentless Elijah was
  toward people,
he provided for the human race and removed him from
  their earth and said,
"Remove yourself, friend, from where humanity lives!

ἐγὼ δὲ πρὸς ἀνθρώπους   ὡς οἰκτίρμων
               καταβήσομαι,   γενόμενος ἄνθρωπος.
Ἀνέρχου τοίνυν ἀπὸ τῆς γῆς   ὡς ἐνέγκαι μὴ δυνάμενος
ἀνθρώπων τὰ πταίσματα·   ἀλλ' ἐγὼ ὁ οὐράνιος
ἁμαρτωλοῖς συνέσομαι   καὶ ῥύσομαι πταισμάτων,
ὁ μόνος φιλάνθρωπος.

32

"Εἰ οὐ δύνῃ, ὡς εἶπον, ὦ προφῆτα,   συνοικεῖν τοῖς
                       ἀνθρώποις πλημμελοῦσι,
δεῦρο μέτελθε   καὶ κατοίκει ἀναμάρτητα   χωρία
                           γηθόμενος·
ἐγὼ δὲ καταβαίνω   ὁ τὸ πρόβατον δυνάμενος
τὸ ἐκπεπλανημένον   ἐν τοῖς ὤμοις περιφέρεσθαι   καὶ
                        κράζειν τοῖς πταίουσι·
Δρομαῖοι πάντες ἁμαρτωλοί,   δεῦτε πρός με,
                      ἀναπαύεσθε·
ἐγὼ γὰρ ἐλήλυθα,   οὐ κολάσαι οὓς ἔπλασα,
ἀλλὰ τοὺς ἁμαρτήσαντας   ἁρπάσαι ἀσεβείας,
ὁ μόνος φιλάνθρωπος.'"

33

Ἰδοὺ τύπος Ἡλίας τῶν μελλόντων   ἐν τῷ ὕψει
                       στελλόμενος ἐδείχθη.
Ὁ Θεσβίτης γὰρ   ἀνελήφθη ἐπὶ ἅρματος   πυρός,
                       καθὼς γέγραπται·
Χριστὸς δὲ ἀνελήφθη   ἐν νεφέλαις καὶ δυνάμεσι.

But I am willing to descend among humans and with
  compassion become human.
Ascend, then, from the earth, since you cannot endure
human wrongs. But I who am heavenly
shall live with sinners and deliver them from wrongs,
as the one who is benevolent.

32

"Prophet, if you cannot live, as I said, with people who err,
cross over to here, settle in the sinless regions, and be
  happy!
And I will descend with the strength to carry
upon my shoulders the sheep gone astray and call to those
  lost,
'Run, all you sinners, come to me and find rest,
for I have not come to punish those I've made,
but to seize the sinful from impiety I'm here,
the one who is benevolent.'"

33

And see, being summoned on high, Elijah was shown to
  prefigure what was coming,
for the Tishbite was lifted in a chariot of fire, as it's written.
Christ was lifted in clouds and powers.

Ἀλλ' οὗτος Ἐλισσαίῳ   μηλωτὴν ἐξ ὕψους ἔπεμψεν· ὁ
                                        Χριστὸς δὲ κατέπεμψε
τοῖς ἀποστόλοις τοῖς ἑαυτοῦ   τὸν Παράκλητον καὶ ἅγιον
ὃν πάντες ἐλάβομεν   οἱ τὸ βάπτισμα ἔχοντες,
δι' οὗ ἁγιαζόμεθα,   ὡς πάντας ἐκδιδάσκει
ὁ μόνος φιλάνθρωπος.

The former sent Elisha a mantle from on high, while Christ
    sent down
to his own apostles the Comforter, the holy one,
whom all have received who share in baptism,
through which we are hallowed, as he teaches us all,
the one who is benevolent.

ἦχος πλ. α΄

Προοίμιον 1

ἰδιόμελον

Πρέπει σοι, Πρόδρομε, ἔπαινος ἄξιος,
ὅτι τῆς αἰωνίας ζωῆς ὕπερ ἀπέθανες
ὡς μισήσας τὴν
πρόσκαιρον.

Προοίμιον 2

ἰδιόμελον

Ἡ τοῦ Προδρόμου ἔνδοξος ἀποτομὴ οἰκονομία γέγονέ
τις θεϊκή,
ἵνα καὶ τοῖς ἐν Ἅιδῃ τοῦ Σωτῆρος κηρύξῃ τὴν ἔλευσιν·
θρηνείτω οὖν Ἡρωδιὰς ἄνομον φόνον αἰτήσασα·
οὐμενοῦν γὰρ τὸν τοῦ Θεοῦ ζῶντα αἰῶνα ἠγάπησεν,
ἀλλ᾽ ἐπίπλαστον,
πρόσκαιρον.

ON THE BEHEADING OF
THE FORERUNNER

in first plagal mode

Prelude 1

to its own melody

Worthy praise befits you, Forerunner,
as you died for the sake of eternal life,
while despising what is
    just fleeting.

Prelude 2

to its own melody

The glorious beheading of the Forerunner was a divine
    arrangement,
so that even to those in Hades he might proclaim the
    Savior's coming.
Lament, then, Herodias, who demanded lawless murder!
Indeed she did not love the living age of God,
but one that is feigned
    and fleeting.

I

ἰδιόμελον

Τὰ γενέσια τὰ τοῦ Ἡρώδου   πᾶσιν ἐφάνησαν ἀνόσια,
ὅτε ἐν μέσῳ τῶν τρυφώντων   ἡ κεφαλὴ ἡ τοῦ
νηστεύοντος
παρετέθη ὥσπερ ἔδεσμα·
τῇ χαρᾷ συνήφθη λύπη,   καὶ τῷ γέλωτι
ἐκράθη   πικρὸς ὀδυρμός,
ὅτι τὴν κάραν   τοῦ βαπτιστοῦ πίναξ φέρων
ἐπὶ τῶν πάντων εἰσῆλθεν,   ὡς εἶπεν ἡ παῖς·
καὶ διὰ στρῆνον   θρῆνος ἐπέπεσε πᾶσι
τοῖς ἀριστήσασι τότε   σὺν τῷ βασιλεῖ·
οὐ γὰρ ἔτερψεν ἐκείνους   οὔτε Ἡρώδην αὐτόν·
φησὶ γὰρ ἐλυπήθη   λύπην οὐκ ἀληθινήν,
ἀλλ' ἐπίπλαστον,
πρόσκαιρον.

2

Οὐκ ἀνέμεινε γὰρ ὁ Ἡρώδης   οὔτε ἐχρόνισε
λυπούμενος·
ἀλλ' ὥσπερ ἤδη μελετήσας   τὸ ἀσεβὲς εὐθὺς ἐποίησεν,
ἵνα τέρψῃ ἣν ἐμοίχευσεν·
ἡ μοιχὰς γάρ, οὐχ ἡ κόρη   ἀποκόψαι τὸν τῆς
στείρας   ἐζήτει καρπόν·
ἥτις καὶ τάχα   πρὸ τῆς τομῆς τὴν ἰδίαν
γνώμην ἐδήλου τῇ κόρῃ   βοῶσα αὐτῇ·
"Δεῦρό μοι, τέκνον,   συναίνεσον τῇ μητρί σου·

I

to its own melody

Herod's birthday celebration appeared monstrous to all,
when in the banqueters' midst the head of the one who
      fasted
was served up as meat.
Grief was added to the joy and the laughter mixed with
      bitter wailing,
as the platter carrying the baptizer's head
was brought before all, as the girl had requested.
And, through their wantonness, sadness assailed
all who were dining together with the king;
it delighted neither them nor Herod himself.
It says that he grieved, yet not a true grief
but one that is feigned
      and fleeting.

2

Herod neither mournfully waited nor delayed;
as if he'd already planned it, he instantly did his godless
      deed
in order to delight his partner in adultery.
The adulteress, not her daughter, was seeking to cut off the
      fruit of the barren one.
She probably also disclosed her own will
to her daughter before the cleaving, exclaiming:
"Come to me, child, and stand by your mother!

λόγον γὰρ κρύφιον ἔχω   γυμνῶσαι πρὸς σέ·
φανερῶ σοι τὴν βουλήν μου·   ἐπιθυμῶ ἀνελεῖν
τὸν υἱὸν Ζαχαρίου·   ἔδωκε γάρ μοι πληγὴν
αἰωνίαν, οὐ
　　　πρόσκαιρον."

3

Ὑπακούσασα δὲ ἡ παιδίσκη   τοῦ παρανόμου
　　　　　　　　　　　　μελετήματος
ἔφριξεν, ἔκραξεν· "Ὦ μῆτερ,   ὦ τί δεινόν ἐστι τὸ πάθος
　　　　　　　　　　　　σου·
ἄφες τοῦτο ἀνιάτρευτον·
ἂν γὰρ θέλης θεραπεῦσαι   χαλεπώτερον τὸ
　　　　　　　　　　τραῦμα   ποιεῖς σεαυτῇ·
κοίμησον ἔνδον   τῶν λογισμῶν σου τὸ ῥῆμα,
μήποτε γένηται πτῶμα   τῷ γένει ἡμῶν·
οὔτε γὰρ μόνη   τὸν ἐξ αὐτοῦ μόρον δέχῃ,
ἀλλὰ κἀγὼ καὶ Ἡρώδης   καὶ οἱ ἐξ ἡμῶν·
ἐὰν θάνῃ Ἰωάννης,   γέγονε πάντα νεκρά,
καὶ ἐτάφημεν ζῶντες   μνήμην λείψαντες κακήν,
αἰωνίαν, οὐ
　　　πρόσκαιρον."

4

"Τί ἐγένετο σοί, ὦ παιδίσκη;   Τί σοι συμβέβηκεν
　　　　　　　　　　　　αἰφνίδιον;
Πόθεν ἐφείσω Ἰωάννου   καὶ τῆς μητρὸς ὑπερηγάπησας

I've a secret idea to reveal to you,
I'll let on what I plan: I want to do away with
Zechariah's son, for he gave me a wound,
one eternal and not
    just fleeting."

3

When the girl had listened to the illicit plan,
she trembled, screamed: "Oh, mother, how terrible is your
    passion!
Dismiss this incurable impulse!
You will make it more painful for yourself if you try to
    remedy the injury.
Put your thought to sleep inside your mind,
so it never lands as a corpse in our family.
Not only will it offer its doom to you,
but to Herod and me, and our progenies too.
If John is killed, everything dies,
and we're buried alive, leaving a disgraceful memory,
one eternal and not
    so fleeting."

4

"What's happened to you, girl, what's struck you so
    suddenly?
Where did your care for John come from? Do you love
    more dearly than your mother

τὸν μισοῦντα τὴν ζωὴν ἡμῶν;
Ἀγνοεῖς πολλάκις, τέκνον,   ἃ ὑπέθετο Ἡρώδῃ   ἕνεκεν
ἐμοῦ,
'Οὐκ ἔξεστί σοι,'   λέγων, 'ἔχειν τὴν γυναῖκα
Φιλίππου τοῦ ἀδελφοῦ σου·   ἀπόθου αὐτήν·
θέλω οὖν ἤδη   τὴν ἄκαιρον παρρησίαν
τοῦ τολμηροῦ ἀποκόψαι,   ἂν εὕρω καιρόν·
ἀφελῶ αὐτοῦ τὴν γλῶτταν,   μᾶλλον δὲ τὴν κεφαλήν,
καὶ λοιπὸν οὐ λυποῦμαι   ἔχουσα ἐν ἀσφαλεῖ
τὴν ζωήν μου τὴν
πρόσκαιρον."

5

"Ἀσεβοῦμεν, μῆτερ, οὐκ εἰς ἄλλους,   ἀλλ' εἰς ἡμᾶς καὶ
τὴν ζωὴν ἡμῶν,
ὥσπερ Ἰεζάβελ τὸν Ἠλίαν   ὀλέσαι θέλουσα τὸν δίκαιον
ἑαυτὴν μᾶλλον ἀπώλεσεν·
Ὁ Ἠλίας μὲν ἐντόνως,   Ἰωάννης δὲ ἐννόμως   ἤλεγξεν
ἡμᾶς·
ὁ ἐρημίτης   σὺν αὐστηρότητι εἶπεν
ὡς παραινῶν τῷ Ἡρώδῃ·   'Οὐκ ἔξεστι σοί'·
ὁ δὲ Θεσβίτης   μετὰ πραΰτητος εἶρξε
τοῦ Ἀχαὰβ τὰς νεφέλας·   οὐκ ἔβρεξε γάρ·
διὰ τοῦτο, δέσποινά μου,   θάψον τὸ σκέμμα σου νῦν
καὶ τὸ σκάμμα νεκρώσῃς,   μὴ ποιήσῃς ὡς ἀεὶ
τὴν αἰσχύνην τὴν
πρόσκαιρον."

the man who hates our life?
Perhaps you don't know, child, how he admonished
Herod about me: 'It is not lawful for you,'
he said, 'to have your brother Philip's wife. Reject her!'
That's why I want to cut off his inopportune
boldness at once, if I can find an opportunity.
I'll get rid of his tongue, or rather his head,
so I won't be grieving, when I have secured
my life, which is
    so fleeting."

5

"We're doing wrong, mother, not to the others, but to
    ourselves and our lives,
just as Jezebel, who wanted to destroy the righteous Elijah,
caused her own destruction instead.
Elijah eagerly, as John legally, corrected us.
The hermit harshly declared,
exhorting Herod, 'It is not lawful for you.'
The Tishbite gently withheld
the clouds from Ahab; it was not raining on him.
So then, my lady, bury your scheme,
kill your wiles, so you don't make eternal
any shame which is
    just fleeting."

6

"Παρ' ἐμοῦ διδάσκου, ἀνοσία,   μὴ ἐπιχείρου νουθετῆσαί
                                                            με·
ὅταν γὰρ πάντα μάθῃς, πληροῖς,   τὰ νῦν ἐπιλανθάνει σε·
οὐ νοεῖς, οὐδὲ γὰρ δύνασαι·
ἂν γὰρ οὗτος ὁ βαπτίζων   ἐπιμείνῃ με ὑβρίζων   καὶ
                                                            φαίνηται ζῶν,
ἕκαστος αἴρει   τὴν πρὸς ἐμὲ παρρησίαν,
καί, ἅπερ θέλει, ὡς θέλει   λέγει κατ' ἐμοῦ
ὡς τῆς τυχούσης,   οὐχὶ δὲ βασιλευούσης,
ὡς γυναικὸς ἰδιώτου   καὶ οὐ σεβαστοῦ·
ἀλλ' ἡσύχασον, παιδίσκη·   πλέον γὰρ σοῦ καὶ πολλῶν
τὸ συμφέρον γινώσκω·   οἶδα κτήσασθαι τιμὴν
αἰωνίαν, οὐ
        πρόσκαιρον."

7

"Ἐρωτῶ σε, μῆτερ, τὸ τοιοῦτον   πότε βουλεύει
                                                            τελεσθῆναί σοι;
Ἐν τῷ φωτὶ ἢ ἐν τῷ σκότει;   Τὸ ἀσεβὲς γάρ σου
                                                            ἐνθύμημα
τῆς νυκτός ἐστιν ἐπάξιον·
διὰ τίνος οὖν τελεῖται;   Τίς μὴ ναρκήσει
                                        φονεῦσαι   προφήτην Χριστοῦ;"
"Σὺ ὡς θυγάτηρ   συνέρχου τῇ σε τεκούσῃ

6

"Learn from me, irreverent girl, don't attempt to lecture
   me;
when you've grasped it all, you'll fill in what you're missing
   now.
You don't understand, nor are you able to.
If this baptizer does persist in insulting me, and is seen
   alive,
everyone will assume such boldness toward me
and say as he wishes what he wishes against me,
as if I were an ordinary woman, not a royal one,
a common man's wife, not an august one's.
No, girl, be quiet! More than you and many others
I know what works, what yields an esteem
that's eternal and not
         just fleeting."

7

"Let me ask you, mother, when do you plan to do this deed?
In daylight or in darkness? Your wicked thought
is worthy of the night.
How will it be done? Who won't shrink from murdering
   Christ's prophet?"
"You, as my daughter, must help the one who bore you

τοῦ ἀνελεῖν τὸν ἐχθρόν μου   καὶ γένῃ μοι χείρ"·
"Δέομαι, μῆτερ,   μὴ δι' ἐμοῦ τῆς ἀθλίας
δέξεται γῆ τὸ ἀθῷον   αἷμα τοῦ σοφοῦ·
ὡς ἐσφάγη Ζαχαρίας,   νῦν Ἰωάννης τμηθῇ·
κἀγὼ μὴ ὑπουργήσω,   μήπως λήψωμαι πληγὴν
αἰωνίαν, οὐ
        πρόσκαιρον."

8

"Ἰωάννης σοι προετιμήθη,   ὦ παναθλία καὶ ταλαίπωρε,
τῆς βαστασάσης σε κοιλίας;   Ὁ βαπτιστὴς
                        ἀναγκαιότερος
κατεφάνη τῇ ἀνοίᾳ σου;
Οὐκ αἰδεῖσαι τοὺς μαστούς μου,   οἳ ἐποίησαν τροφήν
                        σοι;   Ὡς εἴθοις γε μή·
τί γὰρ ἐζήτουν   κατ' ἐμαυτῆς ἀναθρέψαι
τὴν διὰ τῆς ἀπειθείας   ἐχθραίνουσάν με;
Τί δὲ ἠπείχθην   τῷ βασιλεῖ συναφθῆναι
διὰ τὸ περισωθῆναι   τὴν θλίβουσάν με;
Διὰ τί δὲ προλυποῦμαι;   Γένηται ῥῆμα ἐμόν·
καὶ ὃ θέλω τελεῖται·   καὶ μὴ θέλουσα ποιεῖς
τὴν βουλήν μου τὴν
        πρόσκαιρον.

get rid of my enemy and give me a hand!"
"I beg you, mother, don't let the earth receive,
through wretched me, the innocent blood of the wise man!
As Zechariah was slain, now John will be butchered.
But I can't assist, or I'll receive a wound,
one eternal and not
     just fleeting."

8

"Is John more valuable to you, you wretched and miserable
     girl,
than the womb that carried you? Does the baptizer seem
     dearer
to the folly of your mind?
Don't you respect my breasts, which provided you
     nourishment? I wish they hadn't!
Why was I striving to nurture by myself
the one who has turned against me in defiance?
Why was I eager to ally with the king
for her, who's causing me trouble, to be safe?
But why do I worry in advance? Let my plot be
     accomplished,
and my will be done! Though unwilling, you'll fulfill
what I've planned, which is
     just fleeting.

9

"Νῦν οὖν ἡσυχάσω καὶ μὴ δείξω   τῇ παγκακούργῳ ἃ
βουλεύομαι·
μήποτε σκέψηται καὶ εὕρη   τοῦ ἐνθυμίου μου ἀναίρεσιν
ἡ τεχθεῖσά μου εἰς κόλασιν."
Τῶν τοιούτων ἐσκεμμένων   καὶ πολλάκις
εἰρημένων   ὑπὸ τῆς μητρὸς
ἡ μὲν θυγάτηρ   ἐν ἡσυχίᾳ διῆγεν,
ἡ δὲ τεκοῦσα ἐνήχει   τότε τῷ ἀνδρὶ
λέγουσα· "Ἄνερ,   τῶν γενεσίων σου ὥρα·
ποίησον ἡμῖν ἡμέραν   φαιδρᾶς ἑορτῆς·
εὐφρανθῶμεν ἐν τῷ γήρει·   τὴν γὰρ νεότητά μου
λαβὼν ὁ ἀδελφός σου   περιέσυρε κακῶς
εἰς τὸν βίον τὸν
πρόσκαιρον."

10

Ὁ Ἡρώδης οὖν ὑπὸ τῶν λόγων   τῆς ἐπιβούλου
βουκολούμενος
μέγα ἐκραύγασε βοήσας   καὶ ὡς ἀσύνετος ἐν γέλωτι
τὴν φωνὴν αὐτοῦ ἀνύψωσε·
"Κοινωνέ μου," λέγων, "γύναι,   καὶ ἐν τούτῳ χάριν
ἔχω   τῷ φίλτρῳ τῷ σῷ·
ἂν οὖν τελέσω   τῶν γενεσίων τὴν ὥραν,
σὺ τί προσάγεις μοι δῶρον   ἄξιον ἐμοῦ;"
"Τί σοι προσάξω;   Δούλην ἐμαυτήν, καὶ πάλιν

9

"But now I'll be quiet, not expose my intensions to that
    wickedest girl,
so she who was born as punishment for me doesn't search
    and find a way
to thwart my plan."
While such things were thought and perhaps even uttered
by the mother, her daughter kept silent,
but the former spoke in her husband's ear,
"Husband, it is time for your birthday party.
Make the day a brilliant feast for us!
Let's enjoy ourselves in our old age,
for your brother snatched my youth and cruelly paraded it
    around
in this life, which is
    so fleeting."

10

And Herod then, beguiled by the insidious woman's words,
let forth a loud roar and, like a laughing fool,
he raised his voice and said,
"My partner, my wife, I'm grateful for the love you show me
    with this!
If I am going to celebrate my birthday,
what present will you give that is worthy of me?"
"What shall I give you? Myself as your servant! And I'll even

τὴν ἐξ ἐμοῦ παραστήσω   ὀρχήστριάν σοι,
τὴν εὐφραίνουσάν σε πάνυ,   καὶ φαιδρυνῶ ἀληθῶς
τὴν τῆς γενέσεως ἡμέραν,   ἣν ποιήσεις, βασιλεῦ,
διὰ τέρψιν τὴν
     πρόσκαιρον."

II

Ὑπεβλήθη οὖν τῷ παρανόμῳ   τῆς πονηρᾶς αὐτοῦ
                               γενέσεως
ἡ τρισκατάρατος ἡμέρα,   ἣν καὶ αὐτὸς κατηράσατο
ὁ Ἰὼβ οὕτω φθεγξάμενος
ἢ ὡς εἶπε Ζαχαρίας·   "Ἡ ἡμέρα ἔσται ἐκείνη   σκότος
                               καὶ οὐ φῶς"·
κἂν γὰρ ἐρρέθη   τοῦτο περὶ τῆς ἡμέρας,
ὅτε τὸ Φῶς τῶν ἐν σκότει   ἦν ἐν τῷ σταυρῷ,
ὅμως ἁρμόττει   τῇ τοῦ Ἡρώδου ἡμέρᾳ,
ὅτι ἐν ταύτῃ ἐκτάνθη   φίλος τοῦ Φωτός·
καὶ ὁ κτείνας μὲν οὐκ ἔστιν,   ὁ δὲ κτανθεὶς καί ἐστι
καὶ λαλεῖ μετὰ θνῆσιν   ἕλκων πάντας πρὸς ζωὴν
τὴν ἀεὶ καὶ οὐ
     πρόσκαιρον.

12

Ῥίψας ταῦτα πάντα ὁ Ἡρώδης   τῶν ἑαυτοῦ λοιπὸν
                               ἐγένετο,
καὶ τῆς ἡμέρας συμφθασάσης   τῶν γενεσίων, καθὼς
                               γέγραπται,
ἐν αὐτῇ δεῖπνον ἐποίησε

168

present my very own dancing girl for you,
heaping delights upon you. I'll truly
brighten your birthday, which you'll celebrate, my king,
with the bliss that is
    so fleeting!"

II

This thrice-accursed day of his wicked birth
was subjected to the lawless man, a day
Job even cursed like this,
and said, as Zechariah: "That day shall be darkness, not
    light!"
And if this was said of the day when the Light
of those in darkness was on the cross,
it is still fitting for Herod's day;
for the friend of the Light was killed on that day.
Now the killer is no longer, but the killed one is,
and he speaks after death, drawing everyone to a life
that's eternal and not
    just fleeting.

12

Herod disregarded all this and returned to his own matters.
The date of his birthday arrived, as is written,
and on this day, he gave a banquet

μεγιστᾶσι καὶ τοῖς φίλοις,   χιλιάρχοις καὶ
                              συμβούλοις   πᾶσιν ὁμαδόν·
τοῦ δὲ ἀρίστου   μετὰ χαρᾶς τελουμένου
καὶ ἐσθιόντων ἡδέως   τῶν ἀριστητῶν,
ἄφνω ἐτράπη   ἡ τράπεζα εἰς παγίδα,
καὶ ἐγενήθη τὸ βρῶμα   σκάνδαλον αὐτοῖς,
ἐπειδὴ τὴν κεκρυμμένην   παγίδα τοῦ βαπτιστοῦ
οὐ συνέτριψαν αὐτήν,   ἀλλ᾽ ἠνέσχοντο ὁρᾶν
διὰ τέρψιν τὴν
       πρόσκαιρον.

                    13

Ὡς οὖν εἶδε πάντας μεθυσθέντας   Ἡρωδιὰς ἡ
                                 πολυμήχανος,
ἥνπερ ἐζήτει εὐκαιρίαν   εὑροῦσα, εἶπεν ἐν ψυχῇ αὑτῆς·
"Ἴδε, ὥρα ἦν ἐθήρευον·
νῦν τελεῖται ὅπερ ἤθελον,   καὶ φονεύεται ὁ
                           λέγων   μοιχάδα ἐμέ·
δεῦρο οὖν, τέκνον,   προσάξω σὲ τῇ ἡμέρᾳ
δῶρον καλὸν ὑπότασσον   Ἡρώδην ἡμῖν·
εἴσελθε, τέκνον,   χαρίτωσον τῷ ποδί σου
τὸν βασιλέα καὶ πάντας   τοὺς φίλους αὐτοῦ·
μεταστρέφῃς τὴν καρδίαν   τοῦ Σεβαστοῦ πρὸς ἡμᾶς
ὡς στρεβλὸν τόξον ἄρτι·   κερδανοῦμεν τιμὴν
αἰωνίαν, οὐ
       πρόσκαιρον."

                    170

for his courtiers and friends, officers and counselors,
    everyone together.
As the meal was joyfully progressing
and the guests were eating with pleasure,
suddenly the table turned into a trap,
and the food a scandalous snare for them.
Facing unawares the baptizer's hidden
trap, they didn't shatter it but delighted in watching
for the bliss that is
    so fleeting!

13

When she saw that all were drunk, the conniving Herodias
    had found
the opportunity she'd sought and said to herself, "Look, it's
    the moment
I have been hunting for!
My wish is coming true, and the man who calls me
    adulteress will be killed.
Come now, my child, I'll present you today
as a lovely gift to make Herod submit to us!
Come here, my child, and entice with your feet
the king and all his friends as well!
You'll turn the heart of His Majesty toward us,
like a twisted bow. We'll gain our honor,
that's eternal and not
    just fleeting."

14

Μετεποίησεν ἡ ἀνοσία   τοῖς λόγοις τούτοις τὸ κοράσιον,
καὶ κοσμηθὲν ἐπὶ τὸ πρᾶγμα   τὸ ἀναιδὲς περιεβάλλετο
ἀτιμίαν ὡς ἱμάτιον·
οἱ δὲ φίλοι τοῦ Ἡρώδου   τὸ μὲν κάλλος τῆς
                                        παιδίσκης   ἤνεσαν πολύ,
τῆς δὲ τεκούσης   τὴν ἀδιάτρεπτον γνώμην
καὶ τὸν σκοπὸν ἐννοοῦντες   εἶπαν ἐν κρυφῇ·
"Βλέπετε γνώμην   Ἡρωδιάδος τῆς πόρνης,
πῶς καὶ ἣν ἔτεκε θέλει   δεῖξαι κατ' αὐτήν;
Οὐκ ἠρκέσθη τῇ ἰδίᾳ   ἀναισχυντίᾳ αὐτῆς,
ἀλλὰ καὶ τὴν ἐκ σπλάγχνων   ἔχρανεν ἐπὶ ἡμῶν
διὰ τέρψιν τὴν
        πρόσκαιρον.

15

"Ἀψευδὴς ὁ λόγος τῆς Σοφίας·   Τέκνα μοιχῶν ἔσται
                                        ἀτέλεστα,
καὶ παρανόμου κοίτης σπέρμα   ἀφανισθήσεται εἰς
                                        τέλεον·
ὥσπερ τοῦτο τὸ κοράσιον,
ὃ πρὸς ὥραν μὲν ἠσχύνθη,   μετ' ὀλίγον δὲ
                                        πολλάκις   χεῖρόν τι ποιεῖ."
Τούτων δὲ πάντων   οὐ φανερῶς λεγομένων,
ἦλθε κατόπιν τῶν λόγων   ἔργα πονηρά·
ἡ γὰρ παιδίσκη   ὀρχησαμένη ἐν μέσῳ

14

The wicked woman's words changed the girl's mind,
and, all adorned for the shameless deed, she draped herself
in her dishonor worn as a dress.
As Herod's friends lavished praise on the youngster's
    beauty,
they pondered the mother's headstrong will
and intentions, and spoke among themselves:
"Do you see the harlot Herodias's determination,
how she tries to present her child like herself?
Her own shamelessness did not suffice;
even her dearest she's smeared for us,
to have bliss that is
    so fleeting!

15

"Wisdom does not lie: 'Children of adulterers will not come
    to maturity,
and offspring of an unlawful union will perish in the end.'
Just like this girl for now
has a sense of shame, but soon will do something much
    worse."
None of these words was spoken in the open,
but wicked deeds followed the words.
Dancing in their midst, the girl filled

τῶν ἀριστώντων τὸ στόμα   ἔπλησε κραυγῶν·
"Βασιλεῦ," φησίν, "Ἡρώδη,   ὡς ἐκ μελέτης ἐστὶν
ἡ ὀρχήστρια αὕτη·   πάνυ ἔχει ἐν ψυχῇ
τὴν πορείαν τὴν
    πρόσκαιρον."

16

Νικηθεὶς ὁ ἄναξ τοῖς ἐπαίνοις   τῶν εὐφημούντων τὸ
                                            κοράσιον
ὤμοσε τότε ἐπὶ πάντων·   "Ὃ ἂν αἰτήσῃ με, παρέχω σοι
ὑπὲρ ταύτης τῆς ὀρχήσεως."
Ἡ δὲ παῖς ἐξῆλθε   καί φησι πρὸς τὴν
                            τεκοῦσαν·   "Αἰτήσομαι τί;"
"Αἴτησον, τέκνον,   τὴν κεφαλὴν Ἰωάννου
τοῦ βαπτιστοῦ, ὅτι ταύτης   μόνης ὑστερῶ."
"Οἴμοι, τεκοῦσα,   εἴθε ἐτμήθην τοὺς πόδας
καὶ μὴ ἐξέδραμον πρός σε   μαθεῖν παρὰ σοῦ·
εἴθε πάλιν ἐφιμώθην   καὶ μὴ ἠρώτησά σε
ἃ οὐκ ἔδει·   εἴθε ἤσκησα σιγὴν
αἰωνίαν οὐ
    πρόσκαιρον."

17

Οὕτως ἔδει λέξαι τὴν παιδίσκην·   ὅμως οὐδὲν τούτων
                                            ἐφθέγξατο·
ἦν γὰρ ἐκ γῆς ἀκανθηφόρου,   ῥίζης κακῆς πικρὸν
                                            ζιζάνιον,

the mouths of the dining guests with shouts:
"King Herod," they said, "how well trained she seems.
This dancing girl has clearly got it in her,
all the moves that are
    so fleeting!"

16

The ruler, won over by these admiring praises for the
    maiden,
vowed in front of all, "Whatever you ask me, I will grant
    you,
on account of this dancing."
So the girl went out and said to her mother: "What should I
    ask for?"
"Ask, my child, for the baptist's head,
for that is the only thing I lack."
"Alas, mother! I wish my feet had been cut off,
so I couldn't run out to you and let you teach me!
And I wish I'd been muzzled, and had not asked you
what I did not need to! I wish I'd practiced silence
that's eternal and not
    just fleeting!"

17

That's what she should have said, but she spoke nothing of
    the sort.
She came from an earth that grew thorns, a bitter weed
    from a wicked root,

νόσον ἔχουσα θανάσιμον·
ἧς γευσάμενος Ἡρώδης   οὐκ ἀπέπτυσεν, ἀλλ᾽
                                    ἔσχεν   ἔνδον ἑαυτοῦ·
ὅθεν μὴ πέμψας   τοῦτο ἠρεύξατο φόνον
καὶ τὴν τοῦ θείου Προδρόμου   ἤμεσε τομὴν
πόνον γεννῶσαν   τῷ ἐκτελέσαντι φόνον
καὶ τὴν τομὴν τοῖς τιμῶσι   νέμουσαν τιμήν·
ἠφανίσθη γὰρ ὁ κτείνας,   οἱ δὲ τιμῶντες πιστοὶ
εἰσὶν ἔτι καὶ ζῶσι   ποριζόμενοι ζωὴν
αἰωνίαν, οὐ
        πρόσκαιρον.

18

Υἱὲ τοῦ ὄντως ἱερέως,   τέκνον τῆς στείρας καὶ
                                            προφήτιδος,
θρέμμα ἐρήμου, Ἰωάννη,   ὅτι νηστείας σου ἐμνήσθημεν,
δὸς ἰσχὺν ἵνα νηστεύσωμεν·
γενηθῶμεν μιμηταί σου,   κἂν εἰς τοῦτο ὃ
                                        ἰσχύει   ἕκαστος ἡμῶν·
οὐ γὰρ δεσπόζει   τινὸς ἡμῶν ἡ κοιλία,
ἀλλὰ ἡμεῖς τῆς κοιλίας   κρατοῦμεν ἀεὶ
κατὰ τὸν Παῦλον·   "Τὰ βρώματα τῇ κοιλίᾳ
καὶ ἡ κοιλία τοῖς βρώμασιν"·   ἡμεῖς δὲ Χριστοῦ
τοῦ νηστεύσαντος βουλήσει   καὶ ἀφελόντος ἡμῶν
τὴν πεῖναν τὴν ἀρχαίαν,   ἣν ἐπείνασεν Ἀδὰμ
διὰ τέρψιν τὴν
        πρόσκαιρον.

causing a deadly illness.
Tasting it, Herod did not spit it out but held it within;
by not expelling it he was belching murder
and vomited the chop for the godly Forerunner.
It gave pain to the man who performed the murder
but honor to those who honor the beheading.
The killer perished, while the faithful who honor
are still present and live, gaining a life
that's eternal and not
     just fleeting.

18

Son of a true priest, child of a barren mother and
     prophetess,
John, nursling of the desert, give us strength when we
     remember
your fasting, that we may fast!
May we become your imitators, if only as much as each has
     strength!
The stomach should not be ruling us,
but we should always be in charge of our stomach.
According to Paul, "Food is for the stomach
and the stomach is for food." We belong to Christ,
who fasted voluntarily and detached us from
the ancient hunger that Adam felt,
for the bliss that is
     so fleeting!

ἦχος δ΄

Προοίμιον 1

πρός· Ὁ ὑψωθεὶς ἐν τῷ σταυρῷ

Τὸν νυμφίον, ἀδελφοί,   ἀγαπήσωμεν,
τὰς λαμπάδας ἑαυτῶν   εὐτρεπίσωμεν,
ἐν ἀρεταῖς ἐκλάμποντες   καὶ πίστει ὀρθῇ,
ἵνα ὡς αἱ φρόνιμοι,   τοῦ Κυρίου ἐλθόντος,
ἕτοιμοι εἰσέλθωμεν   σὺν αὐτῷ ἐν τῷ γάμῳ·
ὁ γὰρ οἰκτίρμων   δῶρον ὡς Θεὸς
πᾶσι παρέχει
τὸν ἄφθαρτον στέφανον.

Προοίμιον 2

ἰδιόμελον

Ὁ νυμφίος τῆς σωτηρίας,   ἡ ἐλπὶς τῶν σε
                                    ἀνυμνούντων,   Χριστὲ ὁ Θεός,
δώρησαι ἡμῖν   τοῖς αἰτοῦσί σε
ἄσπιλον εὑρεῖν   ἐν τῷ γάμῳ σου,
ὡς αἱ παρθένοι,
τὸν ἄφθαρτον στέφανον.

ON THE TEN VIRGINS

in fourth mode

Prelude 1

to: You who were lifted up on the cross

Let us love, brothers and sisters,
the bridegroom and prepare our lamps
to shine with virtues and true faith,
so that when Christ comes, we are ready to enter
into the marriage with him like the wise virgins,
for he bestows, as compassionate God,
a gift upon each,
the imperishable wreath.

Prelude 2

to its own melody

Groom of salvation, the hope of those who celebrate you,
    Christ our God,
grant to us, as to the virgins,
what we beg for: to find, unfading
there at your wedding,
the imperishable wreath.

Προοίμιον 3

πρός· Ὁ ὑψωθεὶς ἐν τῷ σταυρῷ

Ἐν τῇ δευτέρᾳ σου, Χριστέ,   παρουσίᾳ,
ὅταν καθήσῃς, ὁ Θεός,   ἐπὶ θρόνου
τοῦ φοβεροῦ σου, Δέσποτα   φιλάνθρωπε,
δέομαι μὴ καταισχύνῃς με   κατενώπιον πάντων·
ἄνοιξον τὰς θύρας μοι   τοῦ νυμφῶνος, οἰκτῖρμον,
ὡς ταῖς φρονίμοις   τότε γυναιξίν,
πᾶσιν παρέχων
τὸν ἄφθαρτον στέφανον.

Προοίμιον 4

πρός· Ἐπεφάνης σήμερον

Τὰς φρονίμους μίμησαι,   ψυχή, παρθένους,
καὶ αὐτῶν ζηλώσασα   τὴν ἐλεήμονα στοργήν,
ἐν μετανοίᾳ νῦν κραύγαζε·
"Πᾶσι παράσχου,
Χριστέ, στέφος ἄφθαρτον!"

Προοίμιον 5

πρός· Ἐπεφάνης σήμερον

Ὁ νυμφὼν ηὐτρέπισται,   ψυχὴ ἀθλία·
ἕως πότε πάθεσιν   ἐκδαπανᾶς σου τὴν ζωὴν
καὶ οὐκ ἐργάζει τοῦ δέξασθαι
ὡς αἱ παρθένοι
τὸν ἄφθαρτον στέφανον;

Prelude 3

to: You who were lifted up on the cross

When at your second coming, Christ,
you sit as God on your fearsome throne,
I implore you not to expose my shame
in everyone's presence, benevolent Master.
Open the doors of the bridechamber for me;
as upon the wise women, compassionate one,
bestow upon all
the imperishable wreath!

Prelude 4

to: Today you have appeared

Imitate the wise virgins, my soul,
and emulate the merciful love they showed,
as you cry in repentance,
"Bestow upon all,
Christ, a wreath imperishable!"

Prelude 5

to: Today you have appeared

The bridechamber is ready, my wretched soul;
how long will you spend your life among passions
and not, like the virgins,
strive to receive
the imperishable wreath?

Προοίμιον 6

πρός· Ὁ ὑψωθεὶς ἐν τῷ σταυρῷ

Νῦν ὁ καιρὸς τῶν ἀρετῶν   ἐπεφάνη
καὶ ἐπὶ θύραις ὁ Κριτής·   μὴ στυγνάσωμεν,
ἀλλὰ δεῦτε, νηστεύοντες   προσάξωμεν
δάκρυα, κατάνυξιν   καὶ ἐλεημοσύνην,
κράζοντες· "Ἡμάρτομεν   ὑπὲρ ψάμμον θαλάσσης·
ἀλλ' ἄνες πᾶσιν,   πάντων Ποιητά,
ἵνα καὶ σχῶμεν
τὸν ἄφθαρτον στέφανον."

I

πρός· Τῇ Γαλιλαίᾳ τῶν ἐθνῶν

Τῆς ἱερᾶς παραβολῆς   τῆς τοῦ εὐαγγελίου   ἀκούσας
                                                        τῶν παρθένων,
ἐξέστην, ἐνθυμήσεις   καὶ λογισμοὺς ἀνακινῶν,
πῶς τὴν τῆς ἀχράντου   παρθενίας ἀρετὴν
αἱ δέκα μὲν ἐκτήσαντο,
ταῖς πέντε δὲ παρθένοις   ἐγένετο   ἄκαρπος ὁ πόνος,
αἱ δὲ ἄλλαι ταῖς λαμπάσιν   ἐξήστραπτον   τῆς
                                                        φιλανθρωπίας.
Διὸ προτρέπεται   αὐτὰς ὁ νυμφίος
καὶ εἰσάγει ἐν χαρᾷ   ἐν τῷ νυμφῶνι,
ὅτε οὐρανοὺς   ἀνοίγει καὶ διανέμει
πᾶσι δικαίοις
τὸν ἄφθαρτον στέφανον.

Prelude 6

to: You who were lifted up on the cross

The time for virtues has come and is here!
The Judge is at the door. Come, without gloom,
as we fast, let us offer
tears, contrition, and alms as we cry,
"Our sins outweigh the sands of the sea,
but, Maker of all, remit them for all,
so that we may obtain
the imperishable wreath!"

I

to: In Galilee of the nations

When I heard the sacred parable about the virgins in the
    gospel,
I was startled, stirred in my mind and my thoughts,
by how the ten had attained the virtue
of spotless virginity,
yet for five of the virgins the toil was fruitless,
while the others dazzled with lamps of benevolence.
The bridegroom therefore urges them on
and leads them into the bridal chamber
with joy, as he opens the heavens, conferring
on all the righteous
the imperishable wreath.

2

Οὐκοῦν ζητήσωμεν ἡμεῖς   τῆς θείας γραφῆς
                    ταύτης   τὴν χάριν καὶ τὸν τρόπον·
ἀφθάρτου γὰρ νυμφῶνος   ὑπάρχει πᾶσιν ὁδηγός,
ὥσπερ οὖν καὶ πᾶσα   ἡ θεόπνευστος γραφὴ
καθέστηκεν ὠφέλιμος.
Χριστῷ οὖν τῷ Σωτῆρι   προσπίπτοντες,   κράξωμεν
                                              προθύμως·
"Βασιλεῦ βασιλευόντων,   φιλάνθρωπε,   δὸς πᾶσι τὴν
                                              γνῶσιν·
ὁδήγησον ἡμᾶς   πρὸς τὰς ἐντολάς σου,
ἵνα γνῶμεν τὴν ὁδὸν   τῆς Βασιλείας·
ταύτην γὰρ ἡμεῖς   ὁδεῦσαι ἐπιποθοῦμεν,
ἵνα καὶ σχῶμεν
τὸν ἄφθαρτον στέφανον."

3

Ὑπὸ τῆς πίστεως αὐτῆς   καὶ τῆς ἐπαγγελίας   οἱ
                              πλεῖστοι τῶν ἀνθρώπων
ποθοῦσιν ἐφικέσθαι   τῆς Βασιλείας τοῦ Θεοῦ·
ὅθεν διὰ τοῦτο   παρθενίας ἀρετὴν
φυλάττειν κατεπείγονται·
ἀσκοῦσι καὶ νηστείας,   κατόρθωμα   μέγιστον ἐν βίῳ,
ταῖς εὐχαῖς προσκαρτεροῦσι,   τὸ δόγμα δὲ   ἄχραντον
                                              τηροῦσιν·
ἐλλείπει δὲ αὐτοῖς   ἡ φιλανθρωπία

2

Let us explore the grace and the style of the godly parable;
it guides us all to a bridal chamber
that does not perish, beneficial as all
divinely inspired scripture.
Let us fall down before Christ the Savior and eagerly cry,
"Grant insight to all, benevolent King of kings!
Lead us toward your own commandments,
showing us thus the path of your Kingdom.
This we fervently yearn to travel,
so we may obtain
the imperishable wreath."

3

Due to faith itself and to its promise, the majority of
    humans
long to reach the Kingdom of God,
and so, for that reason they eagerly guard
the virtue of virginity.
And they practice fasting, the greatest work of perfection,
and persist in prayer and safeguard the undefiled doctrine.
But if they lack benevolence,

καὶ εὑρίσκεται λοιπὸν   μάταια πάντα·
πᾶς γὰρ ἐξ ἡμῶν   μὴ ἔχων τὴν εὐσπλαγχνίαν
οὔτε λαμβάνει
τὸν ἄφθαρτον στέφανον.

4

Τὸν πλοῦν ποιούμενοί τινες   πάντων
                           κατηρτισμένων,   λιπόντες τὴν ὀθόνην
εὐθεῖαν ἐν θαλάσσῃ   πορείαν οὐ κτῶνταί ποτε·
τότε γὰρ τοῦ δρόμου   ἐμποδίζεται ἡ ναῦς
καὶ ἄπρακτος καθίσταται,
οὐ τέχνῃ κυβερνήτου   δουλεύουσα,   οὔτε δὲ οἰάκων.
Τὸν αὐτὸν δὴ τρόπον πάντες   οἱ σπεύδοντες   πρὸς τὴν
                                              Βασιλείαν,
κἂν πάσης ἀρετῆς   σωρεύσουσι φόρτον,
εὐσπλαγχνίας δέ εἰσι   γεγυμνωμένοι,
τοῖς πρὸς οὐρανὸν   λιμέσιν οὐ προσορμῶσιν,
οὐ κομιοῦνται
τὸν ἄφθαρτον στέφανον.

5

Ἀπασῶν μεῖζον ἀρετῶν   τὴν Ἐλεημοσύνην   ὁ πάντων
                                              Κριτὴς κρίνας
παρέδωκεν ἀνθρώποις   διδάξας τὴν παραβολήν·
πέντε μὲν φρονίμους   τὰς τὸ ἔλαιον σαφῶς
βαστασάσας ἐκάλεσε,
μωρὰς δὲ τὰς τὸν δρόμον   τελεσάσας   ἄνευ τοῦ ἐλαίου.

they will find that all is vain.
And each of us too, without compassion,
fails to take
the imperishable wreath.

4

If, when making preparations for a voyage, some leave out
    the sail,
they can never hold a proper course at sea.
The ship is then hindered in its journey
and is left unmanageable.
It obeys neither the skill of the captain nor that of the
    helm.
It's the same for all who rush toward the Kingdom:
if they load up with the cargo of every virtue
and yet are deprived of compassion,
they will not anchor in the heavenly harbor
nor carry off
the imperishable wreath.

5

The Judge of all, having judged Mercy the greatest of
    virtues,
gave her to humans when teaching the parable:
the five who clearly carried the oil
he called wise,
and foolish those who completed their course without oil.

Καὶ τὴν δύναμιν τὴν ταύτης   ἠκούσαμεν   κράζοντος
                                                    Ματθαίου·
ἧς πάλιν ἐπελθεῖν   τὰ ῥήματα πάντα
πρὸς εἰδότας τὰς γραφὰς   ἄτοπον κρίνω·
ὅθεν τὸν σκοπὸν   τὸν ταύτης ἀναζητῶμεν,
ἵνα καὶ σχῶμεν
τὸν ἄφθαρτον στέφανον.

6

Πολλὴ ἡ τῆς παραβολῆς   ἐστι διδασκαλία,   πάσης
                                                    φιλανθρωπίας
καὶ ταπεινοφροσύνης   ὁδὸς καὶ πᾶσιν ὁδηγός·
ἄνακτας ῥυθμίζει,   ἡγουμένους τοῦ λαοῦ
διδάσκει τὴν συμπάθειαν.
Καθάπερ γάρ τις οἶκον   ὑπέρλαμπρον   κτίσας καὶ
                                                    πληρώσας,
εἰ μὴ τοῦτον ὀροφώσῃ,   ἀνόνητος   γίνεται ὁ πόνος,
οὕτως τὰς ἀρετὰς   ὁ οἰκοδομήσας,
καὶ τὸν ὄροφον εἰ μὴ   τῆς συμπαθείας
προσθήσῃ αὐταῖς,   ἀπόλλυσι τοὺς καμάτους,
ὥστε μὴ ἔχειν
τὸν ἄφθαρτον στέφανον.

7

Εἰδεῖν ἰσχύομεν τὸν νοῦν   τῆς θείας γραφῆς
                                        ταύτης,   εἰ τὰ τῆς διανοίας
ὄμματα γρηγοροῦντα   ἐπανατείνωμεν Χριστῷ·

We have heard the story's power, as proclaimed by
    Matthew;
to review again all its words for those
who know the scriptures, I judge unnecessary.
But let us examine the parable's point,
so we may obtain
the imperishable wreath.

6

Great is the parable's lesson—for all a path and a guide
to true benevolence and a humble mind.
It educates rulers; to the leaders of the people
it teaches sympathy.
If when someone has built and furnished a splendid house,
he has not roofed it, then his labor is futile.
Thus one who's built walls with the virtues
ruins his work if he does not add
the roof of sympathy to their structure;
hence he won't obtain
the imperishable wreath.

7

We may glimpse the meaning of the godly parable if we lift
the wakeful eyes of our mind toward Christ.

δόξωμεν οὖν βλέπειν   τῆς ψυχῆς τοῖς ὀφθαλμοῖς
τὴν πάγκοσμον ἀνάστασιν,
Χριστὸν δὲ τὸν Σωτῆρα   δεικνύμενον   πάντων
                                                    Βασιλέα,
ὃς καὶ νῦν γὰρ βασιλεύει   καὶ Κύριός   ἐστι καὶ
                                                    Δεσπότης.
Κἂν στασιάζουσί   τινες ἀγνοοῦντες,
ἀλλ᾽ ἡ φλὸξ ἡ τοῦ πυρὸς   πάντας χωνεύσει·
τότε οὖν οὐδεὶς   δυνήσεται ἀντιστῆναι,
ὅτε παρέξει
τὸν ἄφθαρτον στέφανον.

                        8

Ἴσμεν γὰρ πάντες ὡς φωνῇ   ἡ σάλπιγξ
                        ἐξαπίνης   ἠχοῦσα δι᾽ ἀγγέλου
νεκροὺς τοὺς ἀπ᾽ αἰώνων   ἐγερεῖ μένοντας Χριστὸν
τὸν καλὸν νυμφίον,   υἱὸν τὸν τοῦ Θεοῦ,
τὸν ἄναρχον Θεὸν ἡμῶν·
κραυγῆς τε γινομένης   αἰφνίδιον,   πάντες ἀπαντῶσι,
καὶ ἑτοίμους τὰς λαμπάδας   οἱ ἔχοντες   τὰς
                                                    ἐλαιοθρέπτους
εἰσέρχονται εὐθὺς   μετὰ τοῦ νυμφίου,
Βασιλείαν οὐρανῶν   κληρονομοῦντες·
τότε γὰρ αὐτοῖς   ἡ πίστις μετὰ τῶν ἔργων
δώσει ἀξίως
τὸν ἄφθαρτον στέφανον.

Let's imagine we see, with the gaze of our soul,
the universal resurrection,
and Christ the Savior appearing as King of all,
he who reigns even now and is Master and Lord.
Though some may even ignorantly rebel,
the flaming fire will still melt all,
for nobody will be able to resist
when he awards
the imperishable wreath.

8

The call of the trumpet will sound, as we know, without
    warning from an angel,
and wake the dead who've for ages awaited
the beautiful bridegroom, the son of God,
our sovereign God.
As a sudden cry breaks out, all will present themselves,
and those who have their lamps prepared with oil
will enter at once together with the bridegroom,
thus inheriting the Kingdom of heaven.
Then faith together with works will make them
worthy to receive
the imperishable wreath.

9

Νικᾷ τὰς ἄλλας ἀρετὰς   ἡ Ἐλεημοσύνη   ἡ ὄντως
                                      λαμπροτέρα
πασῶν προκαθημένη   τῶν ἀρετῶν παρὰ Θεῷ·
τέμνει τὸν ἀέρα,   ὑπερβαίνει μετ' αὐτὸν
σελήνην καὶ τὸν ἥλιον,
καὶ φθάνει ἀπροσκόπως   τὴν εἴσοδον   τῶν ἐπουρανίων,
καὶ οὐχ ἵσταται οὐδ' οὕτως,   ἀλλ' ἔρχεται   μέχρι τῶν
                                      ἀγγέλων,
ἐκτρέχει τοὺς χοροὺς   καὶ τῶν ἀρχαγγέλων,
ἐντυγχάνει τῷ Θεῷ   ὑπὲρ ἀνθρώπων,
παρίσταται δὲ   τῷ θρόνῳ τοῦ Βασιλέως,
τοῦτον αἰτοῦσα
τὸν ἄφθαρτον στέφανον.

10

Οὐκοῦν κατίδωμεν ἡμεῖς   τὰς πέντε τὰς πανσόφους   ἐξ
                                      ὕπνου ἀναστάσας
καθάπερ ἐκ παστάδος   καὶ οὐκ ἐκ τάφου τῶν νεκρῶν·
ἔλαιον γὰρ εἶχον,   καὶ εὐθὺς τὰς τῆς ψυχῆς
λαμπάδας κατεκόσμησαν.
Αἱ ἄλλαι δὲ ὁμοίως   ἀνέστησαν   ἀθρόον σὺν ταύταις,
σκυθρωπὰ προσκεκτημέναι   τὰ πρόσωπα   καὶ
                                      συμπεπτωκότα·
ἐσβέσθησαν μὲν γὰρ   αἱ τούτων λαμπάδες,
τὰ ἀγγεῖα δὲ αὐτῶν   κοῦφα ἐδείχθη·

9

Mercy vanquishes the other virtues; being more brilliant,
she presides before God above all the virtues.
She cuts through the air and rises higher
than the moon and the sun,
reaches the entrance of heaven without stumbling,
and does not remain there but continues to the angels;
she exceeds the choirs of archangels too,
intercedes before God on humanity's behalf;
she stands in front of the King's throne,
asking him for
the imperishable wreath.

10

So let us consider the five wisest ones, arisen from sleep,
as from the nuptial bed, not the tomb of the dead.
They had their oil and immediately trimmed
the lamps of their souls.
The others likewise arose with them abruptly,
their faces dazed and gloomy.
And as their lamps had now gone out,
it was obvious that their vessels were empty.

ἔλαιον λαβεῖν   ἐζήτουν ἐκ τῶν φρονίμων
τῶν δρεψαμένων
τὸν ἄφθαρτον στέφανον.

11

Ὑπολαβοῦσαι αἱ σοφαί,   φησὶ ταῖς ἀνοήτοις·   "Μήποτε
οὐκ ἀρκέσῃ
ὃ ἔσχομεν ἐν κόσμῳ   ἡμῖν τε πᾶσι καὶ ὑμῖν;
οὔτε γὰρ θαρροῦμεν   οὔτε ἔχομεν σαφῶς
ἐνέχυρον τὴν ἔκβασιν."
Καὶ γὰρ ὁ τῶν δικαίων   νῦν σύλλογος   ἅπας
ἀμφιβάλλει
καὶ φοβεῖται ἐν τῇ κρίσει   τὸ ἄδηλον   τὸ τοῦ κριτηρίου,
ἕως ἂν πρόδηλος   φανῇται ἡ ψῆφος
καὶ λυτρώσηται αὐτοὺς   πάσης δουλείας·
τὸν ἔλεον οὖν   μερίζει ὁ πάντων Κτίστης,
ὅστις δωρεῖται
τὸν ἄφθαρτον στέφανον.

12

Ῥητῶς αἱ φρόνιμοί φησιν·   "Ἀπέλθατε, ζητεῖτε   ἐκεῖ
πρὸς τοὺς πωλοῦντας
εἰ ἄρα δυνηθῆτε   ἔλαιον πρίασθαι νυνί."
Αὗται δ᾽ ἀπατῶνται   ὡς ἀνόητοι ἀεὶ
καὶ σπεύδουσιν ὠνήσασθαι,
ὅτε τῆς πραγματείας   τοῖς ἄπασι   κέκλεισται ὁ Χρόνος,

They tried to obtain oil from the prudent ones,
who took for themselves
the imperishable wreath.

II

The wise ones replied to the foolish, "Perhaps what we have
    in this world
may not be enough for us all and for you?
We cannot be certain; we do not for sure
have a safe exit."
And now the whole assembly of the righteous are in doubt,
and they fear the uncertain outcome of the tribunal,
until the verdict is openly declared
and sets them free from every bond.
The Creator of all shares the oil of his mercy,
that which confers
the imperishable wreath.

12

The wise ones speak out: "Go that way to the dealers, and
    see
if you might still buy oil at this hour."
As the imprudent tend to, they are deceived
and rush to go shopping,
but Time overtakes them and blocks their futile

παροδεύσας καὶ συγκλείσας   τὸν ἄκαρπον   δρόμον
                                                     τῶν ἀφρόνων·
τὴν τότε ταραχὴν   αὐτῶν ὑπογράφει
καὶ τὸν θόρυβον σαφῶς   τούτων ἐλέγχει·
ἀδύνατον γὰρ   ἐζήτουν ὡς μὴ φρονοῦσαι,
ὅθεν οὐκ ἔσχον
τὸν ἄφθαρτον στέφανον.

13

Ὡς δὲ τοῦ δρόμου τὸ κενὸν   ἐπέγνωσαν εἰς
                                     τέλος,   ὑπέστρεψαν αἱ πέντε
καὶ εὗρον τὸν νυμφῶνα   ἀποκλεισθέντα τοῦ Χριστοῦ·
κράξασαι δὲ πᾶσαι   ἐν φωνῇ ὀδυνηρᾷ
καὶ στεναγμοῖς καὶ δάκρυσι·
"Τῆς σῆς φιλανθρωπίας,   Ἀθάνατε,   ἄνοιξον τὴν θύραν
καὶ ἡμῖν ταῖς δουλευσάσαις   τῷ κράτει σου   ἐν τῇ
                                               παρθενίᾳ,"
τότε ὁ Βασιλεὺς   πρὸς ταύτας κραυγάζει·
"Οὐκ ἀνοίγεται ὑμῖν   ἡ Βασιλεία·
οὐκ οἶδα ὑμᾶς   —ὑπάγετε οὖν ἐκ μέσου·
οὐ γὰρ φορεῖτε
τὸν ἄφθαρτον στέφανον."

14

Μόνον δὲ ἤκουσαν Χριστοῦ   τοῦ πάντων
                                     Βασιλέως   βοῶντος πρὸς τὰς πέντε·
"Τίνες ἐστέ, οὐκ οἶδα,"   πληροῦνται πάσης ταραχῆς·

path and closes down business for everyone.
He underscores their confusion then
and clearly condemns their commotion.
Unwise as they were, they sought the impossible
and did not obtain
the imperishable wreath.

13

When they finally realized they were running in vain, the
      five returned
but found Christ's bridechamber closed.
They all cried out in tormented voices,
with groans and tears,
"Open the door of your benevolence, Immortal one,
to us as well, who with our virginity have served your
      majesty."
The King then exclaimed to them,
"The Kingdom is not open for you.
I do not know you—go away from here,
for you won't wear
the imperishable wreath!"

14

Once they heard Christ, the King of all, exclaim to the five,
"I don't know who you are," they were full of confusion.

κλαύσασαι βοῶσι· "Δικαιότατε Κριτά,
ἁγνείαν ἐτηρήσαμεν·
ἐγκράτειαν δὲ πᾶσαν ἠσκήσαμεν, μετὰ προθυμίας
κατετάκημεν νηστείαις, ἐστέρξαμεν τὴν ἀκτημοσύνην·
τὴν φλόγα τοῦ πυρὸς τῆς ἀκολασίας
ἐνικήσαμεν ἡμεῖς καὶ τὰς ὀρέξεις·
ἄχραντον ἀεὶ μετήλθομεν πολιτείαν,
ἵνα καὶ σχῶμεν
τὸν ἄφθαρτον στέφανον.

15

"Ἀλλὰ μετὰ τὰς ἀρετὰς καὶ χάριν παρθενίας καὶ τὸ
καταπατῆσαι
τὸ πῦρ τὸ τῆς λαγνείας καὶ φλόγα τὴν τῶν ἡδονῶν,
μετὰ πλείστους πόνους, ὅτε τῶν ἐν οὐρανοῖς
τὸν βίον ἐζηλώσαμεν—
καὶ γὰρ τῶν ἀσωμάτων ἐσπεύσαμεν ἔχειν πολιτείαν—
τὰ τοιαῦτα καὶ τοσαῦτα, ὡς ἔοικεν, ἄτιμα εὑρέθη·
πολλῆς γὰρ ἀρετῆς ἐδείξαμεν πόνον,
καὶ ματαία ἡ ἐλπὶς πᾶσα ἐδείχθη.
Τί οὖν προσποιεῖ τὴν ἄγνοιαν, ὁ παρέχων
πᾶσιν οἷς θέλεις
τὸν ἄφθαρτον στέφανον;

Weeping, they exclaimed, "Judge most just,
we've preserved our chastity.
Self-mastery of every kind we have readily practiced;
we are shriveled by fasts, have cherished poverty.
We have conquered the flaming fire
of licentiousness and our desires.
We have always pursued a life undefiled,
that we may obtain
the imperishable wreath!

15

"But after these virtues and the grace of virginity, our
     stamping out
the fire of lust and the flame of pleasures,
all this toiling to emulate the life
of those in the heavens —
for we strove to lead the life of the bodiless ones! —
this all and all such things, it seems, are found to be
     worthless?
We demonstrated the toil of abundant virtue,
but every hope has been shown to be idle.
Why pretend you do not know us,
you who give as you will
the imperishable wreath?

16

"Νεῦσον, Σωτήρ, καὶ ἐφ' ἡμᾶς,   μόνε
                    Δικαιοκρίτα,   ἄνοιξόν σου τὴν θύραν·
δέξαι εἰς τὸν νυμφῶνα   τὰς σὰς παρθένους, Λυτρωτά,
καὶ μὴ ἀποστρέψῃς   τὸ σὸν πρόσωπον, Χριστέ,
τῶν ἐπικαλουμένων σε,
ἵνα μὴ στερηθῶμεν   τῆς χάριτός   σου τῆς ἀθανάτου,
μὴ γενώμεθα αἰσχύνη   καὶ ὄνειδος   ἐπὶ τῶν ἀγγέλων·
μὴ μέχρις οὖν παντὸς   ἡμᾶς παρεάσῃς
τοῦ νυμφῶνός σου, Χριστέ,   ἵστασθαι ἔξω·
πάρεξ γὰρ ἡμῶν   οὐκ ἤσκησαν τὴν ἁγνείαν,
αἷς καὶ παρέσχες
τὸν ἄφθαρτον στέφανον."

17

Οὕτως ἐρούσαις ταῖς μωραῖς   πρὸς τὸν κριτὴν
                    ἁπάντων,   πρὸς ταύτας Χριστὸς ἔφη·
"Πρόκειται νῦν ἡ κρίσις   δικαία καὶ ἀληθινή·
τῆς φιλανθρωπίας   ἀπεκλείσθη ὁ καιρός,
οὐκ ἔστι νῦν συμπάθεια·
οὐκέτι εὐσπλαγχνίας   ἠνέῳκται   θύρα τοῖς ἀνθρώποις,
ἐπειδήπερ μετανοίας   οὐ δέδοται   τόπος τοῖς ἐνταῦθα·
οὐκέτι συμπαθὴς   ὁ πρώην οἰκτίρμων,
ἀλλ' ἀπότομος κριτὴς   ὁ ἐλεήμων·
ἄσπλαγχνοι ὑμεῖς   ἐδείχθητε ἐν τῷ κόσμῳ·
πῶς οὖν ζητεῖτε
τὸν ἄφθαρτον στέφανον;

16

"Beckon us, too! Savior, open your door, our Judge most
    just!
Redeemer, receive your virgins in your chamber!
Christ, do not turn away your face
from those who call upon you,
so we're not deprived of your immortal grace
or appear before the angels in shame and disgrace!
And do not forever neglect us, Christ,
standing outside your bridal chamber!
They practiced chastity no more than us,
these ones who received
the imperishable wreath."

17

To the foolish who questioned the judge of all, Christ
    replied,
"The judgment delivered is right and just.
The season for benevolence has now passed;
there is no more sympathy.
The door of compassion is no longer open for humans;
there's no place of repentance for those who are here.
He who pitied before is no longer sympathetic,
but the merciful one is a severe judge.
In the world, you five proved to be heartless;
how can you seek
the imperishable wreath?

18

"Ὑμῖν οὖν λέγω φανερῶς   ἐπὶ τῶν ἀρχαγγέλων   καὶ
                                         πάντων τῶν ἁγίων
ἃ πέπονθα ἐκ τούτων   τῶν σὺν ἐμοὶ συνελθουσῶν·
εὑρόν με ἐν θλίψει   καὶ πεινάσαντα σφοδρῶς,
ἐσπούδασαν χορτάσαι με·
διψήσαντα δὲ πάλιν   ἐπότισαν   πάσῃ προθυμίᾳ·
ξενιτεύσαντα ἰδοῦσαι   συνήγαγον   ὥσπερ ἐγνωσμένον·
δεσμοῖς κρατούμενον   περιεποιοῦντο·
ἐσκέψαντο δέ με   καὶ ἀσθενοῦντα·
πᾶσαν ἀκριβῶς   ἐφύλαξαν ἐντολήν μου·
ὅθεν καὶ εὗρον
τὸν ἄφθαρτον στέφανον.

19

"Τοιοῦτον οὖν οὐδὲν ὑμεῖς   ἐδράσατε ἐν
                                κόσμῳ,   φυλάξασαι νηστείαν,
ἀσκοῦσαι παρθενίαν   καὶ τὴν ἐν λόγοις ἀρετήν·
ἄνευ τοίνυν ἔργων   εὐσεβῶν καὶ ἐντελῶν
εἰκῇ κεκοπιάκατε·
τοὺς ξένους δεομένους   παρείδετε   καὶ τοὺς
                                         ἀσθενοῦντας,
οὐδεμίαν τοῖς πεινῶσιν   ὠρέξατε   χεῖρα βοηθείας·
ὑπόκρισις ὑμᾶς   ἐξέθρεψε μόνη·
ἐσεμνύνεσθε ἀεὶ   τῇ ἀπηνείᾳ·

18

"I'll tell you openly, before archangels and all the saints,
what I experienced from these who have entered with me:
They found me in affliction; I was truly hungry
and they hastened to feed me.
When I thirsted, then, they eagerly gave me drink;
seeing a stranger, they welcomed me as a friend.
I was held in chains, and they tended to me.
They also cared for me when I was sick.
All my commandments they faithfully observed.
And so they found
the imperishable wreath.

19

"You did no such thing in the world when observing the
    fast;
you practiced virginity and virtue in theory.
Now, without works, pious and perfect,
you have labored in vain.
You failed to notice the strangers begging and the sick;
you never stretched out a helping hand to the hungry.
It's hypocrisy alone that has sustained you.
You always prided yourself on your rigor.

κρούουσι πτωχοῖς   ὅλως οὐκ ἐβοηθεῖτε·
πῶς οὖν ζητεῖτε
τὸν ἄφθαρτον στέφανον;

20

"Ὅλως πρὸς οἶκτον ἑαυτὰς   οὐκ ἠνέσχεσθε
                    δοῦναι,   γυμνοὺς καὶ προσηλύτους
καὶ ξένους ὑπὸ σκέπην   μὴ εἰσαγαγοῦσαί ποτε·
πρὸς τοὺς πικρῶς ὄντας   ἐν δεσμοῖς καὶ φυλακαῖς
τὴν ἀκοὴν ἐφράξατε·
τοὺς μὲν ἐν ἀσθενείᾳ   οὐκ εἴδατε·   τοὺς δὲ ἐν πτωχείᾳ
καὶ ἐνδείᾳ δεομένους   οὐδ' ἱλαρᾷ   ὄψει ἑωρᾶτε,
ἀλλ' εἴχετε ἀεὶ   τὴν ἀπανθρωπίαν
καὶ παρῆν ὑμῖν ὀργὴ   ἀντ' εὐσπλαγχνίας·
πῶς οὖν οἱ ποτὲ   τοιαῦτα ἐν βίῳ δρῶντες
ἄρτι ζητεῖτε
τὸν ἄφθαρτον στέφανον;

21

"Ὑπερηφάνοις ὀφθαλμοῖς   προσείχετε τοὺς
                    πάντας,   πτωχοὺς κατεφρονεῖτε·
γεγόνατε τοῖς πᾶσιν   ἀσυμπαθεῖς, ἀνηλεεῖς·
κατὰ τῶν πταιόντων   ἐκινεῖσθε ἀφειδῶς
αἱ καθ' ἑκάστην πταίουσαι·
κατὰ τῶν ὁμοφύλων   ἀπάνθρωποι   ὡς μὴ
                                πλημμελοῦσαι
ἐφρονεῖτε τὰ μεγάλα,   κομπάζουσαι   τοῖς
                                κατωρθωμένοις·

To the poor who came knocking you offered no help.
How can you seek
the imperishable wreath?

20

"You could never bear to grant your pity; the naked and the
    sojourners—
no stranger was ever received under your roof.
To those who languished in chains or in prisons
you barred your ears.
Those in sickness you did not see, and those who were
    begging
in poverty and need you regarded with a cheerless gaze,
but you always had inhumanity to spare.
Anger took the place of kindheartedness among you.
You behaved like this back then in life,
do you now seek
the imperishable wreath?

21

"You would glare at everyone with arrogant eyes, look down
    on the poor.
Heartless, unmerciful you were to them all.
Though falling daily, you came down unsparingly
on those who fell.
As if you never failed, you viewed your fellows inhumanly
with a swollen head, proudly flaunting your morality.

τοὺς μὴ νηστεύοντας ὡς ἀπερριμμένους,
τοὺς ἐν γάμῳ βδελυκτοὺς εἴχετε πάλιν·
μόνας ἑαυτὰς ἡγεῖσθε ὥσπερ δικαίας,
μήπω λαβοῦσαι
τὸν ἄφθαρτον στέφανον.

22

"Τὴν μὲν νηστείαν εἴχετε μὴ θίγοντες βρωμάτων· τῇ
δὲ πρὸς τοὺς ἀνθρώπους
ἐχρῆσθε λοιδορίᾳ καὶ συκοφαντίαις ἀεί·
ἦν ὑμῖν Ἁγνεία καὶ αὐτὴ οὐ καθαρά·
τῷ ῥύπῳ γὰρ τῶν ῥήσεων
ταύτην καθ᾽ ἡμέραν ἐχραίνετε· τίς οὖν ὠφελία
ἡ Σεμνότης, εἰ μὴ ἔχει τὴν ἔννοιαν πᾶσαν
σεμνοτάτην;
Συμφέρει οὖν τινα ἐσθίειν καὶ πίνειν
καὶ διάγειν συνετῶς ἤπερ νηστεύειν
καὶ μὴ ἐκ πάντων νηστεύειν τῶν βλαπτόντων·
πῶς γὰρ αἰτήσει
τὸν ἄφθαρτον στέφανον;

23

"Οὐκ οἰκοδομεῖταί ποτε Νηστεία, εἰ μὴ ἔχει τὰ πάντα
ἐξελοῦσα
ἐκ λογισμῶν ἀτόπων καὶ πράξεων τῶν χαλεπῶν,
οὐδὲ στερεοῦται ἡ Ἐγκράτεια σαρκὶ
ἐν ἀκρατεῖ διάγουσα.

You considered those not fasting as outcasts
and those who were married as being detestable.
You only believed yourselves to be righteous,
though you had not received
the imperishable wreath.

22

"You kept the fast, touching no food. But you always
    treated
other people to insults and slander.
Chastity was with you, but she was not pure;
you defiled her daily
with the dirt of words. What use is Holiness
if her mind is not also filled with what's holy?
It is better for one to eat and drink
and lead a wise life than to abstain but not abstain
from everything harmful;
how can you request
the imperishable wreath?

23

"Fasting builds nothing unless she keeps discarding
all inappropriate thoughts and harmful deeds,
and neither can Continence be buttressed in flesh
if she lives in incontinence.

Ὑπάρχει γὰρ Νηστείας   θεμέλιος,   καὶ ἐν ἀσφαλείᾳ
δέον ταύτην καταθεῖναι,   ὡς ὅρμον   οἶκον ἀνεγεῖραι·
Ὁ Ἔλεος αὐτὴν   λαμπρύνει μεγάλως
καὶ Εὐσέβεια αὐτὴν   πάλιν πιαίνει·
αὗται οὖν αὐτὴν   ὡς τείχη περιφρουροῦσι
καὶ προξενοῦσι
τὸν ἄφθαρτον στέφανον.

24

"Τί οὖν ὠφέλησεν ὑμᾶς   Νηστεία καὶ Ἁγνεία   μετὰ
                                                    Ἀλαζονείας;
Πραότητα ἠρνεῖσθε,   Θυμὸν ἐστέργετε ἀεί·
πρᾶος δὲ ὑπάρχων,   ἐπεπόθουν τοὺς πραεῖς,
διδοὺς αὐτοῖς τὴν ἄφεσιν·
ἀρνοῦμαι τοὺς νηστείαν   φυλάττοντας   μετὰ
                                                    ἀσπλαγχνίας,
καὶ προσδέχομαι δὲ μᾶλλον   τοὺς ἔσθοντας   μετὰ
                                                    εὐσπλαγχνίας·
παρθένους δὲ μισῶ   ὄντας ἀπανθρώπους,
φιλανθρώπους δὲ τιμῶ   γεγαμηκότας·
τίμιός ἐστιν   ὁ γάμος ἐν σωφροσύνῃ,
ὅθεν καὶ ἔχει
τὸν ἄφθαρτον στέφανον.

25

"Οὐ ξίφος ὤξυνα ἐγὼ   πρὸς τοὺς ἡμαρτηκότας,   ἀλλ'
                                                    ἔσχον ἀεὶ βλέμμα
πρᾶον πρὸς τοὺς ἀνθρώπους   ὁ τῶν ἀνθρώπων ποιητής·

Fasting forms a foundation, but she needs to lay it
on stable ground, to erect her house as a haven.
Pity adorns her with grandeur;
Piety also enriches her.
Like solid walls, the two of them will
secure for her
the imperishable wreath.

24

"What have Fasting and Chastity done for you together
  with Arrogance?
Always fond of Anger, you rejected Mildness.
But I who am mild long for the mild
and grant them forgiveness.
I reject the ones who keep the fast heartlessly,
and welcome instead those who eat kindheartedly.
I hate virgins who are inhumane,
and honor the married who show benevolence.
Marriage is honorable with self-control;
thus it also obtains
the imperishable wreath.

25

"I've never sharpened a sword against sinners, but have
  always regarded
humans with gentleness, I who made them.

κλαύσασαν τὴν πόρνην   ἐδεξάμην εὐμενῶς
καὶ δέδωκα τὴν ἄφεσιν·
στενάξαντα τελώνην   ἠλέησα   καὶ οὐκ ἀπωσάμην,
ὅτι εἶδον τὴν βεβαίαν   μετάνοιαν   τούτῳ ἐνοικοῦσαν·
πρὸς πάντας συμπαθὴς   ἐδείχθην ὁ Κτίστης,
ἀρνησάμενον ἐμὲ   ᾤκτειρα Πέτρον,
δάκρυσιν ἐγὼ   συνέπαθον τοῖς ἐκείνου
ὅτι ἐζήτει
τὸν ἄφθαρτον στέφανον.

26

"Περὶ δὲ τῶν συνελθουσῶν   ἐμοὶ ἐν τῷ νυμφῶνι   εἴπω
                                             ἐπὶ τοῦ πλήθους·
Ἐφύλαξαν σπουδαίως   τὰς ἐντολάς μου ἐπὶ γῆς·
γέγοναν ταῖς χήραις   ἀντιλήπτορες ἀεὶ
καὶ ὀρφανοὺς ἠλέησαν·
τοῖς ἐν στενοχωρίαις   συνέπασχον   καὶ τοῖς
                                             θλιβομένοις,
καὶ οὐδέποτε τὴν θύραν   ἀπέκλεισαν   πένησιν ἢ ξένοις·
ἰάτρευον ἀεὶ   τοὺς ἐν ἀσθενείαις,
οὓς ἡγήσασθε ὑμεῖς   ἀπερριμμένους.
Οὐκ οἶδα ὑμᾶς·   ἀρνοῦμαι τὰς ἀπανθρώπους,
ταύταις δὲ δώσω
τὸν ἄφθαρτον στέφανον.'"

The harlot who wept, I welcomed with favor
and granted forgiveness.
The publican wailed; I had mercy and did not reject him,
for I saw the firm repentance that dwelled inside him.
As Creator I showed sympathy to all.
I took pity on Peter, the one who denied me;
I suffered along with his tears,
for he sought
the imperishable wreath.

26

"Of those who have come to the chamber with me I'd say to
    the multitude,
'They carefully kept my commandments on earth.
They protected widows all the time,
took pity on orphans.
They suffered with those in anguish and those in hardship,
and never closed their door to the poor or the strangers.
They always provided cures for the sick,
the ones that you considered as outcasts.
I do not know you. I deny the inhumane,
but on these I'll bestow
the imperishable wreath.'"

27

Ὁ τῶν ἀγγέλων δὲ χορὸς   θαυμάζει
                    ὑπακούων   Χριστοῦ τοῦ Βασιλέως
ταῖς πέντε μαρτυροῦντος   ταῖς εἰσελθούσαις σὺν αὐτῷ.
Ὦ τῆς παρρησίας   τῶν ἁγίων τοῦ Χριστοῦ
μεγίστου τε καυχήματος·
ἐπὶ τοσούτων δήμων   κομίζονται   ψῆφον ἀφθαρσίας·
ἐπὶ τούτων καὶ αἱ ἄλλαι   ἀπόφασιν   δέχονται ἐσχάτην
καὶ κλαύσωσι πικρῶς   ἀτέλεστον θρῆνον,
ὅτι βλέπουσι χοροὺς   τοὺς τῶν ἁγίων
ἔχοντας ἐκ τοῦ ἐλέου τὴν παρρησίαν,
πάντας φοροῦντας
τὸν ἄφθαρτον στέφανον.

28

Ἰδοὺ οὖν πρόδηλά εἰσι   τὰ εἰς τὴν
                    Βασιλείαν   καλοῦντα τοὺς ἀνθρώπους·
σπεύσωμεν οὖν φυλάξαι   τὰς ἐντολὰς τὰς τοῦ Χριστοῦ·
πρόκειται εἰς πρᾶσιν,   ἂν θελήσωμεν λαβεῖν,
ἐν ἀγοραῖς τὸ ἔλαιον·
εἰσὶ δὲ οἱ πωλοῦντες   οἱ χρῄζοντες   ἐλεημοσύνην·
καθ' ἑκάστην τὴν ἡμέραν   πιπράσκουσι·   τί οὖν
                                        ἀμελοῦμεν;
Καὶ δύο γὰρ λεπτῶν   λαμβάνομεν πάντως
ὅσον λάβῃ τις διδοὺς   χρήματα πλεῖστα·

27

The angels' choir marvels when they hear Christ the King
testify for the five who have entered with him.
Oh, for the confidence of Christ's saints
and their great glory!
In front of so many they gain the verdict of imperishability.
In front of them the others are given a final sentence;
they bitterly wail a futile lament,
for they witness how the choirs of holy ones
possess the confidence that comes from mercy;
all of them wear
the imperishable wreath.

28

Look, they are plain to see, the things that call us to the
     Kingdom:
let us hasten to keep Christ's commandments!
If we wish to obtain it, the oil is available
for sale in the market.
Its vendors are those who ask for charity.
They trade every day; why are we neglectful?
For two small coins we'll receive in full
the same as one who gives large sums.

μέτρα γὰρ ἡμῶν   ἐτάζει ὁ πάντων Κτίστης,
οὕτως παρέχων
τὸν ἄφθαρτον στέφανον.

29

Ἡ ἐντολὴ ἡ τοῦ Θεοῦ   βαρεῖα οὐχ ὑπάρχει· οὐδὲ γὰρ
                                                    παραγγέλλει
δοῦναι ὃ οὐκ ἰσχύεις,   ἀλλὰ προαίρεσιν ζητεῖ·
δύο μόνον ἔχεις   ὀβολοὺς ἐπὶ τῆς γῆς;
Οὐδὲν δὲ ἄλλο κέκτησαι;
Τούτους ὁ πανοικτίρμων   προσδέχεται   πάντως ὡς
                                                    Δεσπότης,
καὶ προτίμησίν σοι δώσει   τοῦ χρήματα   πλεῖστα
                                                    δεδωκότος.
Οὐκ ἔχεις ὀβολὸν   ἵνα προσενέγκῃς;
Δὸς ποτήριον ψυχροῦ   τῷ δεομένῳ·
δέχεται αὐτὸ   Χριστὸς μετ' εὐχαριστίας,
πάντως διδούς σοι
τὸν ἄφθαρτον στέφανον.

30

Μικρὰ λαμβάνων ὁ Σωτὴρ   μεγάλα ἀντιδώσει· ἀντὶ
                                                    γὰρ τῶν προσκαίρων
ἀπόλαυσιν δωρεῖται   τῶν αἰωνίων ἀγαθῶν.
Δὸς βραχύ τι ἄρτου   καὶ λαμβάνεις ἀντ' αὐτοῦ
τὸν τῆς τρυφῆς παράδεισον·
οὐ βλάψει σε ἡ πενία,   οὐκ ἔνδεια,   ἐὰν ὑπομείνῃς,
οὐδὲ γὰρ λογοθεσίῳ   ὑπόκεισαι·   μὴ ζήτει ἐντεῦθεν·

The Creator of all examines our means
and thus offers
the imperishable wreath.

29

The commandment of God is not demanding, and it does
    not require
that you give what you cannot, but it seeks the intention.
Do you only have two obols on this earth?
And you own nothing more?
These the all-merciful Ruler will fully accept
and prefer you to the one who gave larger sums.
Do you not have an obol to offer? Then, give
a cup of cold water to the one in need.
Christ accepts it with his cup of thanksgiving
and certainly gives you
the imperishable wreath.

30

Receiving small gifts, the Savior gives great ones. In return
    for the temporal,
he gives back the enjoyment of eternal treasures.
Give a piece of bread, and receive in return
the paradise of delight.
Neither poverty nor need will harm you if you persist,
nor will you be subject to audit. Do not ask for it!

ὁ γὰρ ἐλάχιστος   συγγνώμην λαμβάνει,
δυνατοὶ δὲ δυνατῶς   λογοθετοῦνται·
εὐγνώμων γενοῦ,   ἵν' εὕρῃς τὴν Βασιλείαν
καὶ ἵνα λάβῃς
τὸν ἄφθαρτον στέφανον.

31

Ἄνες μοι, ἄνες μοι, Σωτήρ,   τῷ κατακεκριμένῳ   παρὰ
πάντας ἀνθρώπους·
οὐ πράττω γὰρ ἃ λέγω   καὶ συμβουλεύω τοῖς λαοῖς,
ὅθεν σοι προσπίπτω·   δὸς κατάνυξιν, Σωτήρ,
κἀμοὶ καὶ τοῖς ἀκούουσιν,
ἵνα τὰς ἐντολάς σου   φυλάξωμεν   πάσας ἐν τῷ βίῳ
καὶ μὴ μείνωμεν θρηνοῦντες   καὶ κράζοντες   ἔξω τοῦ
νυμφῶνος·
ἐλέησον ἡμᾶς   τῇ σῇ εὐσπλαγχνίᾳ,
ὁ βουλόμενος ἀεὶ   πάντας σωθῆναι·
κάλεσον ἡμᾶς,   Σῶτερ, εἰς τὴν Βασιλείαν,
πᾶσιν παρέχων
τὸν ἄφθαρτον στέφανον.

The least one is granted exemption,
while the mighty are held strictly to account.
Be prudent, so you may find the Kingdom
and thus receive
the imperishable wreath.

31

Release me, release me, Savior; condemned as I am by
    everyone.
I don't practice what I preach and advise the people,
so I fall down before you. Savior, grant contrition
to me and my listeners,
so that we may keep all your commandments in life
and not remain outside the bridechamber wailing and
    crying.
Have mercy on us in your compassion,
you who always wish all to be saved!
Call us, Savior, into your Kingdom,
and bestow upon all
the imperishable wreath!

ἦχος πλ. δ΄

Προοίμιον 1

ἰδιόμελον

Ὁ πόρνην καλέσας   "θυγατέραν," Χριστὲ ὁ Θεός,
υἱὸν μετανοίας   κἀμὲ ἀναδείξας,
δέομαι, ῥῦσαί με
τοῦ βορβόρου τῶν ἔργων μου.

Προοίμιον 2

ἰδιόμελον

Κατέχουσα ἐν κατανύξει   ἡ πόρνη τὰ ἴχνη σου
ἐβόα σοι ἐν μετανοίᾳ   τῷ εἰδότι τὰ κρύφια,   Χριστὲ ὁ
Θεός·
"Πῶς σοι ἀτενίσω   τοῖς ὄμμασιν
ἡ πάντας ἀπατῶσα   τοῖς νεύμασιν;
Πῶς σε δυσωπήσω   τὸν εὔσπλαγχνον
ἢ σὲ παροργίσασα   τὸν Κτίστην μου;
Ἀλλὰ δέξαι τοῦτο τὸ μύρον   πρὸς δυσώπησιν, Δέσποτα,
καὶ δώρησαί μοι ἄφεσιν   τῆς αἰσχύνης
τοῦ βορβόρου τῶν ἔργων μου."

218

ON THE HARLOT

in fourth plagal mode

Prelude 1

to its own melody

You called a harlot "daughter," Christ my God,
and identified me as a son of repentance.
Free me, I beg you,
from the filth of my deeds!

Prelude 2

to its own melody

With compunction the harlot followed in your footsteps,
    Christ;
in repentance she cried out to you, who knows all secrets:
"How can I even look you in the eye,
I who beguiled everyone with a wink?
Can I win you over, kindhearted one,
I who have angered you, my Creator?
Yet, Master, accept the appeal of this perfume,
and grant me release from the shame
of the filth of my deeds."

I

ἰδιόμελον

Τὰ ῥήματα τοῦ Χριστοῦ   καθάπερ ἀρώματα
ῥαινόμενα πανταχοῦ,   βλέπων ἡ πόρνη ποτέ,
καὶ τοῖς πιστοῖς πᾶσι   πνοὴν ζωῆς χορηγοῦντα,
τῶν πεπραγμένων αὐτῇ τὸ δυσῶδες ἐμίσησεν,
ἐννοοῦσα τὴν αἰσχύνην   τὴν ἑαυτῆς·
καὶ σκοποῦσα τὴν ὀδύνην   τὴν δι᾽ αὐτῶν ἐγγιγνομένην,
πολλὴ γὰρ θλῖψις γίνεται   τότε τοῖς πόρνοις ἐκεῖ,
ὧν εἷς εἰμι, καὶ ἕτοιμος   πέλω εἰς μάστιγας
ἃς πτοηθεῖσα ἡ πόρνη   οὐκέτι ἔμεινε πόρνη,
ἐγὼ δὲ καὶ πτοούμενος   ἐπιμένω
τῷ βορβόρῳ τῶν ἔργων μου.

2

Οὐδέποτε τῶν κακῶν   ἀποστῆναι βούλομαι·
οὐ μνήσκομαι τῶν δεινῶν   ὧν ἐκεῖ μέλλω ὁρᾶν,
οὔτε λογίζομαι   τὴν τοῦ Χριστοῦ εὐσπλαγχνίαν,
πῶς περιῆλθε ζητῶν με τὸν γνώμῃ πλανώμενον·
δι᾽ ἐμὲ γὰρ πάντα τόπον   ἐξερευνᾷ,
δι᾽ ἐμὲ καὶ Φαρισαίῳ   συναριστᾷ ὁ τρέφων πάντας,
καὶ δείκνυσι τὴν τράπεζαν   θυσιαστήριον·
ἐν ταύτῃ ἀνακείμενος   καὶ χαριζόμενος
τὴν ὀφειλὴν τοῖς χρεώσταις,   ἵνα θαρρῶν πᾶς χρεώστης
προσέλθῃ λέγων· "Κύριε,   λύτρωσαί με
τοῦ βορβόρου τῶν ἔργων μου."

I

to its own melody

When the harlot saw the words of Christ
like fragrance sprinkling everywhere,
providing a breath of life for all the faithful,
she came to detest the stench of her acts;
she considered her shame
and heeded the pain she had wrought by her actions.
In the next world, affliction awaits fornicators.
Being one of them, I should be ready for the scourges,
which the harlot feared. She stopped being a harlot,
while I, although fearful, remain
in the filth of my deeds.

2

I never willingly refrain from evils,
nor remember the horrors I will see in that place.
I do not give thought to the kindhearted Christ,
how he went looking for me when I'd strayed on purpose.
For my sake he searches everywhere;
for my sake the nourisher of all shares a meal with a
     Pharisee
and shows the table to be an altar,
where he is reclining as well as forgiving
what's owed by the debtors, so that all may be bold,
approach him and say, "Release me, Lord,
from the filth of my deeds."

3

Ὑπέκνισεν ἡ ὀσμὴ   τῆς τραπέζης τοῦ Χριστοῦ
τὴν πρώην μὲν ἄσωτον,   νυνὶ δὲ καρτερικήν,
τὴν ἐν ἀρχῇ κύνα   καὶ ἐν τῷ τέλει ἀμνάδα,
τὴν δούλην καὶ θυγατέρα, τὴν πόρνην καὶ σώφρονα,
διὰ τοῦτο λίχνῳ δρόμῳ   φθάνει αὐτήν,
καὶ λιποῦσα τὰ ψιχία   τὰ ὑπ᾽ αὐτήν, τὸν ἄρτον ᾖρε·
τῆς πάλαι Χανανίτιδος   πλέον πεινάσασα,
ψυχὴν κενὴν ἐχόρτασεν,   οὕτω πιστεύσασα·
ἀλλ᾽ οὐ κραυγῇ ἐλυτρώθη,   σιγῇ δὲ μᾶλλον ἐσώθη,
κλαυθμῷ γὰρ εἶπε· "Κύριε,   ἔγειρόν με
τοῦ βορβόρου τῶν ἔργων μου."

4

Τὴν φρένα δὲ τῆς σοφῆς   ἐρευνῆσαι ἤθελον
καὶ γνῶναι, πῶς ἐν αὐτῇ   ἔλαμψεν ὁ Ἰησοῦς,
ὁ ὡραιότατος   καὶ τῶν ὡραίων ὁ ἐργάτης,
οὗ τὴν ἰδέαν πρὶν ἴδῃ ἡ πόρνη ἐπόθησεν.
ὡς ἡ τῶν εὐαγγελίων   βίβλος βοᾷ,
τοῦ Χριστοῦ ἀνακειμένου   ἐν οἰκίᾳ τοῦ Φαρισαίου,
γυνή τις τότε ἤκουσεν,   ἅμα καὶ ἔσπευσεν,
ὠθήσασα τὴν ἔννοιαν   πρὸς τὴν μετάνοιαν·
"Ἄγε, λοιπόν, ὦ ψυχή μου,   ἰδοὺ καιρὸς ὃν ἐζήτεις·
ἐπέστη ὁ καθαίρων σε·   τί προσμένεις
τῷ βορβόρῳ τῶν ἔργων σου;

3

The scent from the table of Christ excited
the straying woman, who was now steadfast:
in the beginning a dog, in the end a lamb,
a slave and a daughter, both harlot and chaste.
So, in greedy pursuit, she arrives at the table,
and forsaking the crumbs underneath, she takes up the
    bread.
Hungrier than the Canaanite woman once was,
she fed her empty soul, and thus she believed.
Not released by a shout, she was saved in silence,
for through tears she said, "Lord, raise me up
from the filth of my deeds."

4

I wanted to examine her wise mind
and understand how, in her, Jesus shone,
the loveliest one and the craftsman of all that is lovely,
whose looks she desired before she saw him.
Just as the book of the gospels proclaims,
when Christ reclined in the house of the Pharisee,
a woman heard and hurried at once,
driving her thoughts directly toward repentance:
"Go, my soul! It's the moment you've sought.
He is here who can cleanse you. Why do you stick
to the filth of your deeds?

5

"Ἀπέρχομαι πρὸς αὐτόν,   δι' ἐμὲ γὰρ ἤλυθεν·
ἀφίημι τούς ποτε,   τὸν γὰρ νῦν πάνυ ποθῶ·
καὶ ὡς φιλοῦντά με   μυρίζω καὶ κολακεύω,
κλαίω, στενάζω καὶ πείθω δικαίως ποθῆσαί με·
ἀλλοιοῦμαι πρὸς τὸν πόθον   τοῦ ποθητοῦ,
καὶ ὡς θέλει φιληθῆναι,   οὕτως φιλῶ τὸν ἐραστήν μου·
πενθῶ καὶ κατακάμπτομαι,   τοῦτο γὰρ βούλεται·
σιγῶ καὶ περιστέλλομαι,   τούτοις γὰρ τέρπεται·
ἀναχωρῶ τῶν ἀρχαίων   ἵνα ἀρέσω τῷ νέῳ·
συντόμως ἀποτάσσομαι   ἐμφυσῶσα
τῷ βορβόρῳ τῶν ἔργων μου.

6

"Προσέλθω οὖν πρὸς αὐτόν·   φωτισθῶ, ὡς γέγραπται·
ἐγγίσω νῦν τῷ Θεῷ,   καὶ οὐ μὴ καταισχυνθῶ·
οὐκ ὀνειδίζει με,   οὐ λέγει μοι· "Ἕως ἄρτι
ἦς ἐν τῷ σκότει, καὶ ἦλθες ἰδεῖν με τὸν ἥλιον.'
Διὰ τοῦτο μύρον αἴρω   καὶ πορευθῶ·
φωτιστήριον ποιήσω   τὴν οἰκίαν τοῦ Φαρισαίου·
ἐκεῖ γὰρ ἀποπλύνομαι   τὰς ἁμαρτίας μου·
ἐκεῖ καὶ καθαρίζομαι   τὰς ἀνομίας μου·
κλαυθμῷ, ἐλαίῳ καὶ μύρῳ   κεράσω μου κολυμβήθραν
καὶ λούομαι καὶ σμήχομαι   καὶ ἐκφεύγω
τοῦ βορβόρου τῶν ἔργων μου.

5

"I am going to him; he has come here for me!
I'm leaving the others; I want him so much.
I'll anoint him and dote on this one who loves me.
I'll weep and I'll sigh and urge him to yearn for me in
     return.
I've turned to the desire of the one I desire,
and as he wants to be kissed, I'll kiss my lover.
I'll lament and bow down, for that is what he wants.
I'll stay silent and covered, for in such he delights;
I'll move on from the old ones to satisfy my new one.
I will readily part from and blow
on the filth of my deeds.

6

"Let me come to him and be enlightened, as is written,
let me draw near to God, not be put to shame.
He neither rebukes me nor tells me, 'Until now
you've been in darkness, but you've come to see me, the
     sun.'
So let me now pick up some perfume and go
and make the Pharisee's house one of enlightenment.
There I am washing my sins away,
There I am cleansed of all my iniquities.
With tears and oil and fragrance I mix my bath,
and I bathe and wipe myself clean, and I flee
from the filth of my deeds.

7

"Ἐδέξατο ἡ Ῥαὰβ   κατασκόπους πρότερον
καὶ τῆς δοχῆς τὸν μισθὸν   ὡς πιστὴ εὗρε ζωήν·
τῆς γὰρ ζωῆς τύπος   ὁ πέμψας τούτους ὑπῆρχε,
τοῦ Ἰησοῦ μου βαστάζων τὸ τίμιον ὄνομα·
Σωφρονοῦντας τότε πόρνη   ξενοδοχεῖ,
νῦν παρθένον ἐκ παρθένου   πόρνη ζητεῖ ἀλεῖψαι μύρῳ·
ἐκείνη μὲν ἀπέλυσεν   οὕσπερ ἀπέκρυψεν,
ἐγὼ δὲ ὃν ἠγάπησα   μένω κατέχουσα,
οὐχ ὡς κατάσκοπον κλήρων,   ἀλλ' ὡς ἐπίσκοπον πάντων
κρατῶ, καὶ ἐξεγείρομαι   ἐκ τῆς ἰλύος
τοῦ βορβόρου τῶν ἔργων μου.

8

"Ἰδοὺ καιρὸς ἔφθασεν   ὃν ἰδεῖν ἐπόθησα·
ἡμέρα μοι ἔλαμψε   καὶ δεκτὸς ἐνιαυτός·
ἐν τοῖς τοῦ Σίμωνος   αὐλίζεται ὁ Θεός μου·
σπεύσω πρὸς τοῦτον καὶ κλαύσω, ὡς Ἄννα, τὴν

στείρωσιν·

κἂν λογίσηταί με Σίμων   ἐν μεθυσμῷ,
ὡς Ἠλὶ τὴν Ἄνναν τότε,   μένω κἀγὼ προσευχομένη,
σιγῇ βοῶσα 'Κύριε,   τέκνον οὐκ ᾔτησα,
ψυχὴν μονογενῆ ζητῶ   ἥνπερ ἀπώλεσα·
ὡς Σαμουὴλ τῆς ἀτέκνου,   Ἐμμανουὴλ τῆς ἀνάνδρου,
τῆς στείρας ᾖρες ὄνειδος·   ῥῦσαι πόρνην
τοῦ βορβόρου τῶν ἔργων μου.'"

7

"Rahab once received spies, and, faithful,
she got life as payment for her entertainment,
for the man who sent them was a figure of life;
he bore the honorable name of my Jesus.
Then a harlot showed hospitality to the upright ones;
Now a harlot seeks the virgin of a virgin to anoint with
        perfume.
The former released the men she'd concealed,
but I will hold on to the one that I love;
the overseer of all, not a spy of the land,
is the one I embrace, and I'm raised from the slime
of the filth of my deeds.

8

"The moment I longed to see has come;
a day has shone forth for me, a favorable year.
My God is staying in the house of Simon.
I shall hurry to him and weep like Anna in her barrenness.
Though Simon may think I am drunk,
as Eli once thought Anna, I too will continue praying
in silence, calling out, 'I have not asked for a child, Lord;
I'm seeking my one and only soul that I've lost!
As the childless woman by Samuel, the unmarried one by
        you, Emmanuel,
was relieved from barrenness; deliver me, a harlot,
from the filth of my deeds.'"

9

Νευροῦται μὲν ἡ πιστὴ   τοῖς τοιούτοις ῥήμασι,
ποιεῖται δὲ τὴν σπουδὴν   πρὸς τὴν τοῦ μύρου ὠνήν,
καὶ παραγίνεται   βοῶσα τῷ μυροπράτῃ·
"Δός μοι, εἰ ἔχεις, ἐπάξιον μύρον τοῦ φίλου μου,
τοῦ δικαίως φιλουμένου   καὶ καθαρῶς,
τοῦ πυρώσαντός μου μέλη   καὶ τοὺς νεφροὺς καὶ τὴν
                                                        καρδίαν·
μηδὲν περὶ τιμήματος   νῦν ἀμφιβάλλεις μοι·
Κἂν δέοι, μέχρι δέρματος   καὶ τῶν ὀστέων μου,
ἑτοίμως ἔχω τοῦ δοῦναι   ἵν' εὕρω τί ἀποδοῦναι
τῷ σπεύσαντι καθᾶραί με   ἐκ τῆς ὕλης
τοῦ βορβόρου τῶν ἔργων μου."

IO

Ὁ δὲ ἰδὼν τῆς σεμνῆς   τὸ θερμὸν καὶ πρόθυμον,
φησὶν αὐτῇ· "Λέξον μοι   τίς ἐστιν ὃν ἀγαπᾷς,
ὅτι τοσοῦτόν σε   ἐπέθελξε πρὸς τὸ φίλτρον;
ἆρα κἂν ἔχει τι ἄξιον τούτου τοῦ μύρου μου;"
Παραυτὰ δὲ ἡ ὁσία   ἦρε φωνὴν
καὶ βοᾷ σὺν παρρησίᾳ   τῷ σκευαστῇ τῶν ἀρωμάτων·
"Ὦ ἄνθρωπε, τί λέγεις μοι;   Ἔχει τι ἄξιον;
Οὐδὲν αὐτοῦ ἀντάξιον   τοῦ ἀξιώματος·
οὐκ οὐρανός, οὔτε γαῖα,   οὐδ' ὅλος τούτῳ ὁ κόσμος
συγκρίνεται τῷ σπεύσαντι   ῥύσασθαί με
τοῦ βορβόρου τῶν ἔργων μου.

9

With such words the faithful woman nerves herself
and hurries to purchase the perfume.
To the perfume seller she comes and cries out,
"Give me, if you can, a scent my beloved deserves,
he who is rightfully and purely kissed,
he who has kindled my limbs, my guts, and my heart.
Now, don't haggle with me over price!
If needed, even my skin and my bones
I would readily pay to find something to repay
the one who has hastened to wipe off the dirt
of the filth of my deeds."

10

Seeing her noble fervor and ardor,
he asked her, "Tell me, who is it you love,
who has cast such a potent love spell on you?
Does he really have something worthy of my perfume?"
The holy one immediately raised her voice,
and called out frankly to the fragrance supplier,
"What are you saying, sir? 'Have something worthy'?
Nothing is worthy of what he is worth;
neither heaven, nor earth, nor the whole universe
compares to the one who is eager to free me
from the filth of my deeds.

11

"Υἱός ἐστι τοῦ Δαυίδ,   δι' αὐτὸ καὶ εὔοπτος·
Υἱὸς Θεοῦ καὶ Θεός,   δι' αὐτὸ σφόδρα τερπνός·
ὃν οὐχ ἑώρακα,   ἀλλ' ἤκουσα, καὶ ἐτρώθην
πρὸς τὴν ἰδέαν τοῦ ἔχοντος φύσιν ἀνείδεον.
Τὸν Δαυὶδ ποτε ἰδοῦσα   στέργει Μελχόλ·
ἐγὼ δὲ μὴ κατιδοῦσα   τὸν ἐκ Δαυὶδ ποθῶ καὶ στέργω·
ἐκείνη τὰ βασίλεια   πάντα παρέδραμε,
καὶ τῷ Δαυὶδ πτωχεύοντί   ποτε προσέδραμεν·
κἀγὼ τὸν ἄδικον πλοῦτον   ὑπερορῶ καὶ ὠνοῦμαι
τὸ μύρον τῷ καθαίροντι   τὴν ψυχήν μου
τοῦ βορβόρου τῶν ἔργων μου."

12

Ῥημάτων δὲ τὸν εἱρμὸν   σιωπῇ διέτεμε
καὶ ἔλαβεν ἡ σεμνὴ   τὸ τερπνὸν μύρον αὐτῆς
καὶ εἰς τὸν θάλαμον   εὑρέθη τοῦ Φαρισαίου
τρέχουσα, ὥσπερ κληθεῖσα, μυρίσαι τὸ ἄριστον.
Ὁ δὲ Σίμων θεωρήσας   τοῦτο αὐτό,
τὸν Δεσπότην καὶ τὴν πόρνην   καὶ ἑαυτὸν ἤρξατο

ψέγειν,

τὸν μὲν ὡς ἀγνοήσαντα   τὴν προσεγγίσασαν,
τὴν δὲ ἀναισχυντήσασαν   καὶ προσκυνήσασαν,
καὶ ἑαυτὸν ὡς ἀσκέπτως   δεξάμενον τοὺς τοιούτους,
καὶ μάλιστα τὴν κράζουσαν·   "Ἐξελοῦ με
τοῦ βορβόρου τῶν ἔργων μου."

11

"He is the son of David and therefore good-looking,
Son of God, and God, and thus extremely handsome.
I haven't laid my eyes on him, but I've heard and been struck
by the appearance of one who is really invisible.
Michal loved David after she had seen him;
I haven't looked at him, but I love and desire David's
        progeny.
That woman fled all the trappings of royalty
in order to flee to David's poverty.
I too disdain unrighteous wealth
and buy perfume for the one who cleanses my soul
from the filth of my deeds."

12

But she cut off the flow of words with silence.
The noble woman grabbed her delightful perfume
and found her way to the Pharisee's chamber,
hurrying to anoint at the meal as if she'd been asked to.
When Simon saw this, he started to blame
the Master, and the harlot, and even himself;
the first for ignorance regarding her advance,
and her for impudence and the kissing of feet,
and himself for unadvisedly welcoming both,
but especially her, who was crying, "Rescue me
from the filth of my deeds!"

13

Ὦ ἄγνοια. Τί φησιν;   "Τοῦτο μὲν ἐτέλεσα·
ἐκάλεσα Ἰησοῦν   ὥς τινα τῶν προφητῶν,
καὶ οὐκ ἐνόησεν·   ἣν ἕκαστος ἡμῶν οἶδεν,
οὗτος καὶ οὐκ ἔγνω· εἰ ἦν γὰρ προφήτης, ἐγίνωσκεν."
Ὁ ἐτάζων δὲ καρδίας   καὶ τοὺς νεφρούς,
θεωρῶν τοῦ Φαρισαίου   τοὺς λογισμοὺς σαλευομένους,
εὐθέως τούτῳ γίνεται   ῥάβδος εὐθύτητος,
"Ὦ Σίμων," λέγων, "ἄκουσον   τὸ τῆς χρηστότητος
τῆς ἐπὶ σὲ γενομένης   καὶ ἐπὶ ταύτην, ἣν βλέπεις
κλαυθμῷ βοῶσαν· Κύριε,   ἔγειρόν με
τοῦ βορβόρου τῶν ἔργων μου.'

14

"Μεμπτέος σοι ἔδοξα   ἐπειδὴ οὐκ ἤλεγξα
τὴν σπεύδουσαν ἐκφυγεῖν   τῶν αὐτῆς ἀνομιῶν·
ἀλλ' οὐ καλῶς, Σίμων,   οὐκ εὔλογος ἡ μομφή σου·
σύγκρινον τοῦτο ὃ θέλω εἰπεῖν σοι, καὶ δίκασον·
Ὀφειλέται δύο ἦσαν   τῷ δανειστῇ,
ὁ μὲν εἷς πεντακοσίων,   ἕτερος δὲ πενῆντα μόνον,
καὶ τούτοις ἀπορήσασι   πρὸς τὴν ἀπόδοσιν
ὁ χρήσας ἐχαρίσατο   ὅ τι ἐχρήσατο·
Τίς οὖν αὐτὸν ἐκ τῶν δύο   ποθήσει πλέον; εἰπέ μοι·
Τίς ὤφειλε βοᾶν αὐτῷ·   Ἔσωσάς με
τοῦ βορβόρου τῶν ἔργων μου';"

13

Oh, what ignorance! What is he saying?
"I accomplished this: I invited Jesus as one of the prophets,
and he doesn't understand! All of us know her,
but he hasn't figured her out; if he were a prophet, he would
    surely have known."
The one who examines hearts and minds,
observing the Pharisee's wavering thoughts,
becomes now a scepter of righteousness for him.
"Simon," says Jesus, "listen to the goodness
that has come to you and the woman you see
crying and weeping, 'Raise me, Lord,
from the filth of my deeds.'

14

"I've seemed blameworthy to you, since I did not condemn
the woman hastening to escape her offenses,
but it isn't right, Simon; your complaint is not fair.
Consider now what I will say to you and judge:
A certain creditor had two debtors;
one owed five hundred, the other only fifty.
Since they were both unable to repay him,
the lender canceled the debtors' debts.
Tell me, which of the two would love him more?
Which would owe him the cry, 'You have released me
from the filth of my deeds'?"

15

Ἀκούσας δὲ ὁ σοφὸς   Φαρισαῖος ἔφησε·
"Διδάσκαλε, ἀληθῶς   φανερὸν πᾶσίν ἐστιν
ὅτι πλειότερον   ὀφείλει τοῦτον ποθῆσαι,
ᾧ περισσότερον χρέος ὁ χρήσας κεχάρισται."
Ὁ δὲ Κύριος πρὸς ταῦτα   εἶπεν αὐτῷ·
"Ὀρθῶς ἀπεκρίθης, Σίμων·   οὕτως ἐστὶ καθάπερ λέγεις·
ὃν σὺ γὰρ οὐκ ἐπήλειψας,   αὕτη ἐμύρισεν·
ὃν ὕδασιν οὐκ ἔνιψας,   αὕτη τοῖς δάκρυσιν·
ὃν οὐκ ἠσπάσω φιλήσας,   καταφιλοῦσά με κράζει·
''Εκράτησα τοὺς πόδας σου,   μὴ ἐμπέσω
τῷ βορβόρῳ τῶν ἔργων μου.'

16

"Νῦν ὅτι σοι ἔδειξα   τὴν ποθοῦσάν με στοργῇ,
διδάξω σε, βέλτιστε,   τίς ἐστιν ὁ δανειστής,
καὶ ὑποδείξω σοι   τοὺς τούτου χρεωφειλέτας,
ὧν εἷς ὑπάρχεις, καὶ αὕτη ἣν βλέπεις δακρύουσαν·
δανειστὴς δὲ ἀμφοτέρων   πέλω ἐγώ,
καὶ οὐ μόνον ἀμφοτέρων,   ἀλλὰ καὶ τῶν ἀνθρώπων
                                                                πάντων
ἐγὼ γὰρ πᾶσιν ἔχρησα   ταῦτα ἃ ἔχουσιν,
πνοήν, ψυχὴν καὶ αἴσθησιν,   σῶμα καὶ κίνησιν·
τὸν δανειστὴν οὖν τοῦ κόσμου,   ἐν ὅσῳ ἔχεις, ὦ Σίμων,
ἱκέτευσον καὶ βόησον·   Λύτρωσαί με
τοῦ βορβόρου τῶν ἔργων μου.'

15

The wise Pharisee listened and said,
"Teacher, it is truly obvious to all:
the one for whom a larger debt was canceled
owes his lender greater love."
The Lord then said regarding these things,
"You answered correctly; it is as you say, Simon.
The man you did not anoint, she has rubbed with perfume.
The man you did not wash with water, she has with tears.
The man you did not greet with a kiss, she kisses tenderly,
        crying,
'I have grasped your feet, let me not fall
into the filth of my deeds.'

16

"Now that I've shown you who loves me with longing,
I'll prove, my good man, who the creditor is,
and point out to you who his debtors are:
You are one, as is she, whom you see weeping.
I am the creditor for both of you,
and not just for you both, but for every human,
for I have lent to all whatever they have,
breath, soul, and senses, body and movement.
With all you have, Simon, beseech and cry out
to the creditor of the world, 'Deliver me
from the filth of my deeds.'

17

"Οὐ δύνασαι δοῦναί μοι   ἅπερ ἐποφείλεις μοι·
κἂν σίγησον, ἵνα σοι   χαρισθῇ ἡ ὀφειλή·
μὴ καταδίκαζε   τὴν καταδεδικασμένην,
μὴ εὐτελίσῃς τὴν εὐτελισμένην—ἡσύχασον·
οὐ τῶν σῶν, οὐδὲ τῶν ταύτης   βούλομαί τι·
χρεωλύτης γὰρ τῶν δύο ἐγώ εἰμι—μᾶλλον δὲ πάντων·
νομίμως, Σίμων, ἔζησας,   ἀλλ᾽ ἐχρεώστησας·
ἐλθὲ οὖν πρὸς τὴν χάριν μου   ἵν᾽ ἀποδώσῃς μοι·
ἴδε τὴν πόρνην ἣν βλέπεις   καθάπερ τὴν Ἐκκλησίαν
βοῶσαν· Ἀποτάσσομαι,   ἐμφυσῶσα
τῷ βορβόρῳ τῶν ἔργων μου.᾽

18

"Ὑπάγετε· τὸ λοιπὸν   τῶν χρεῶν ἐλύθητε·
πορεύθητε· ἐνοχῆς   παρεκτὸς πάσης ἐστέ·
ἠλευθερώθητε·   μὴ πάλιν ὑποταγῆτε·
τοῦ χειρογράφου σχισθέντος, μὴ ἄλλο ποιήσητε."
Τὸ αὐτὸ οὖν, Ἰησοῦ μου,   λέξον κἀμοί,
ἐπειδή σοι ἀποδοῦναι   ἃ χρεωστῶ οὐκ ἐξισχύω·
σὺν τόκῳ γὰρ ἀνήλωσα   καὶ τὸ κεφάλαιον·
διὸ μὴ ἀπαιτήσῃς με   ὅσον παρέσχες μοι,
τοῦ τῆς ψυχῆς κεφαλαίου   καὶ τῆς σαρκός μου τοῦ

                                        τόκου·
κουφίσας με ὡς εὔσπλαγχνος,   ἄνες, ἄφες
τοῦ βορβόρου τῶν ἔργων μου.

17

"You are not able to give what you owe me,
but at least keep silent, so the debt may be canceled!
Do not condemn the one who's condemned herself.
Do not disparage the one who's disparaged herself—hold
    your peace!
I do not want anything from you or from her.
I am the forgiver of debts for you both—or rather for all.
You've lived lawfully, Simon, but not without debt,
so come to my grace to pay it back to me.
See, the harlot you're looking at is crying out,
just like the Church, 'I reject and blow
on the filth of my deeds.'

18

"Depart, you have now been freed from debts!
Go, you're exempt from every obligation!
You have been liberated. Never again let yourself be
    subjugated!
The promissory note has been torn up, do not sign
    another!"
My Jesus, say this also to me now,
for I don't have the strength to repay what I owe you.
I have spent the capital as well as the interest.
So do not demand from me as much as you gave to me,
the capital of my soul, the interest of my flesh.
Relieve me, kindhearted one, wipe away and blot out
all the filth of my deeds.

Προοίμιον 1

ἰδιόμελον

Εἰ καὶ ἐν τάφῳ   κατῆλθες, ἀθάνατε,
ἀλλὰ τοῦ Ἅιδου   καθεῖλες τὴν δύναμιν
καὶ ἀνέστης   ὡς νικητής,   Χριστὲ ὁ Θεός,
γυναιξὶ μυροφόροις   τὸ "Χαῖρε" φθεγξάμενος
καὶ τοῖς σοῖς ἀποστόλοις   εἰρήνην δωρούμενος,
ὁ τοῖς πεσοῦσι   παρέχων ἀνάστασιν.

Προοίμιον 2

ἰδιόμελον

Καταλαβοῦσαι   γυναῖκες τὸ μνῆμά σου
καὶ μὴ εὑροῦσαι   τὸ ἄχραντον σῶμά σου
ἐλεεινὰ   δακρύουσαι ἔλεγον·
"Ἆρα ἐκλάπη   ὁ συληθεὶς
ἐκ τῆς αἱμόρρου   τὴν ἴασιν;
Ἆρα ἠγέρθη   ὁ προειπὼν
καὶ πρὸ τοῦ πάθους   τὴν ἔγερσιν;
Ἀληθῶς ἀνέστη Χριστὸς
ὁ τοῖς πεσοῦσι   παρέχων ἀνάστασιν."

ON THE WOMEN AT THE TOMB

in fourth plagal mode

Prelude 1

to its own melody

You descended into the grave, immortal one,
and rescinded the power of Hades.
As victor you arose, Christ, our God.
To the women with perfumes you said "Rejoice!"
and to your own apostles you granted peace,
you who let those who have fallen arise.

Prelude 2

to its own melody

When the women arrived at your tomb
unable to find your undefiled body,
they wept wretchedly and said,
"Could he be stolen, he whom the bleeding
and faithful woman robbed of a cure?
Could he be risen, he who once even
before his passion spoke of arising?
Indeed, Christ has risen,
the one who lets those who have fallen arise."

I

ἰδιόμελον

Τὸν πρὸ ἡλίου ἥλιον   δύναντά ποτε ἐν τάφῳ
προέφθασαν πρὸς ὄρθρον   ἐκζητοῦσαι ὡς ἡμέραν,
μυροφόροι κόραι   καὶ πρὸς ἀλλήλας ἐβόων·
"Ὦ φίλαι, δεῦτε,   τοῖς ἀρώμασιν ὑπαλείψωμεν
σῶμα ζωηφόρον   καὶ τεθαμμένον,
σάρκα ἀνιστῶσαν   τὸν παραπεσόντα Ἀδὰμ
κειμένην ἐν τῷ μνήματι.
Ἄγωμεν,   σπεύσωμεν   ὥσπερ οἱ Μάγοι,
καὶ προσκυνήσωμεν   καὶ προσκομίσωμεν
τὰ μύρα ὡς δῶρα   τῷ μὴ ἐν σπαργάνοις,
ἀλλ᾽ ἐν σινδόνι   ἐνειλημένῳ·
καὶ κλαύσωμεν καὶ κράξωμεν·
'Ὦ Δέσποτα,   ἐξεγέρθητι,
ὁ τοῖς πεσοῦσι   παρέχων ἀνάστασιν.'"

2

Ὅτε δὲ ταῦτα ἑαυταῖς   ἔφησαν αἱ θεοφόροι,
ἐσκόπησαν καὶ ἄλλο   ὅ ἐστι σοφίας πλήρης
καί φησιν ἀλλήλαις·   "Γυναῖκες, τί ἀπατᾶσθε;
Πάντως γάρ, ὅτι   ἐν τῷ τάφῳ πέλει ὁ Κύριος.
Ἄρα ἕως ἄρτι   εἶχε κρατεῖσθαι
ὁ ἡνιοχεύων   τὴν τῶν κινουμένων πνοήν;
Ἀκμὴν νεκρὸς κατάκειται;
Ἄπιστον,   ἄστατον   τοῦτο τὸ ῥῆμα·

I

to its own melody

The maidens with perfume hastened toward dawn,
seeking the day of the sun that had risen
before the sun, once set in the grave; they called to each
    other,
"Come, let us anoint with spices, friends,
a body bearing life although buried,
a flesh raising Adam, the fallen,
yet lying in the tomb!
Let us go, let us hurry, just like the Magi!
Let us bow and bring perfumes
as presents for the one
not swaddled but wrapped in a shroud!
Let us weep and cry out:
'Awaken, Master,
you who let those who have fallen arise!'"

2

Speaking among themselves, these God-bearing women
considered something else, filled with wisdom,
and said to each other, "Ladies, what have we missed?
Something, surely, for the Lord is in the grave!
Could the one that directs the breath
of all moving beings be confined until now?
Is he still lying dead?
An incredible thing, insane to say!

διὸ συνήσωμεν   καὶ οὕτω πράξωμεν·
ἀπέλθῃ Μαρία   καὶ ἴδῃ τὸν τάφον
καὶ οἷς ἂν εἴπῃ   ἀκολουθῶμεν·
πολλάκις γάρ, ὡς προεῖπεν,
ἐγήγερται   ὁ ἀθάνατος,
ὁ τοῖς πεσοῦσι   παρέχων ἀνάστασιν."

3

Ὑπὸ δὲ τούτου τοῦ σκοποῦ   αἱ συνεταὶ ῥυθμηθεῖσαι
προέπεμψαν, ὡς οἶμαι,   τὴν Μαγδαληνὴν Μαρίαν
ἐπὶ τὸ μνημεῖον,   ὡς λέγει ὁ Θεολόγος.
Ἦν δὲ σκοτία,   ἀλλ᾽ ἐκείνην πόθος κατέλαμπεν·
ὅθεν καὶ κατεῖδε   τὸν μέγαν λίθον
ἐκκεκυλισμένον   ἀπὸ τῆς θύρας τῆς ταφῆς
καὶ εἶπεν ὑποστρέψασα·
"Μαθηταί,   μάθετε   τοῦτο ὃ εἶδον
καὶ μή με κρύψητε,   ἐὰν νοήσητε·
ὁ λίθος οὐκέτι   καλύπτει τὸν τάφον·
μὴ ἄρα ἦραν   τὸν Κύριόν μου;
Οἱ φρουροὶ γὰρ οὐ φαίνονται,
ἀλλ᾽ ἔφυγον·   μὴ ἐγήγερται
ὁ τοῖς πεσοῦσι   παρέχων ἀνάστασιν;"

4

Τούτων ὡς ἤκουσε Κηφᾶς   καὶ ὁ υἱὸς Ζεβεδαίου,
ἐξέδραμον εὐθέως   ὡς ἐρίζοντες ἀλλήλοις,
καὶ τοῦ Πέτρου πρῶτος   εὑρέθη ὁ Ἰωάννης·

So, let us rejoice and proceed in this way:
Let Mary go ahead and see the grave,
and let us follow whatever she says.
As he promised so often,
the immortal one has risen,
the one who lets those who have fallen arise."

3

The sensible women agreed on this plan
and sent forth, I imagine, Mary Magdalene
to the tomb, as also the Theologian says.
It was dark, but longing illumined her,
and so she detected the great stone
rolled away from the grave's opening.
Returning, she said,
"Disciples, hear what I saw,
and don't hide from me whatever you may think.
The stone no longer covers the grave.
Surely they haven't taken my Lord away?
The guards can't be spotted; no, they have fled.
Could he have risen,
the one who lets those who have fallen arise?"

4

As Kephas heard this and Zebedee's son,
they ran on at once, as vying with each other,
and John arrived ahead of Peter.

ὅμως καὶ φθάσας   οὐκ εἰσῆλθεν ἔνδον τοῦ μνήματος,
ἀλλὰ ἀναμένει   τὸν κορυφαῖον,
ἵνα ὡς ποιμένι   ἀκολουθήσῃ ὁ ἀμνός·
καὶ ὄντως οὕτως ἔπρεπε.
Πέτρῳ γὰρ   εἴρηται·   "Πέτρε, φιλεῖς με;"
καί· "Τὰ ἀρνία μου   ὡς θέλεις ποίμαινε"·
τῷ Πέτρῳ ἐρρέθη·   "Μακάριε Σίμων,
τὰς κλεῖς σοι δώσω   τῆς Βασιλείας."
Τῷ Πέτρῳ πρὶν ὑπέταξε
τὰ κύματα   ἃ ἐπέζευσεν
ὁ τοῖς πεσοῦσι   παρέχων ἀνάστασιν.

5

Ἀλλ' ὡς προεῖπον πρὸ μικροῦ,   Πέτρος τε καὶ Ἰωάννης
κατέλαβον τὸ μνῆμα   δι' ὃ εἶπεν ἡ Μαρία,
καὶ εἰσῆλθον ἔνδον·   τὸν Κύριον δὲ οὐχ εὗρον.
Ὅθεν πρὸς ταῦτα   πτοηθέντες εἶπον οἱ ἅγιοι·
"Ἆρα τίνος χάριν   ἡμῖν οὐκ ὤφθη;
Μὴ τὴν παρρησίαν   ἡμῶν ἡγήσατο πολλήν;
Πολὺ γὰρ ἐτολμήσαμεν·
ἔδει γὰρ   ἔξωθεν   ἡμᾶς σταθῆναι
καὶ περιβλέψασθαι   τὰ ἐν τῷ μνήματι·
ὁ τάφος γὰρ οὗτος   οὐκέτι ὡς τάφος,
ἀλλ' ὄντως οἶκος   Θεοῦ ὑπάρχει·
ἐν τούτῳ γὰρ ἐγένετο
καὶ ᾤκησεν   ὡς εὐδόκησεν
ὁ τοῖς πεσοῦσι   παρέχων ἀνάστασιν.

Having outrun him, though, he did not enter
the tomb, but awaited the leader,
so the lamb would follow the shepherd,
as was indeed appropriate.
For Peter was asked, "Peter, do you love me?
Then, as you wish, tend my lambs."
And Peter was told, "Blessed are you, Simon,
I will give you the keys of the Kingdom."
For Peter, Christ once subdued the waves
on which he had walked,
the one who lets those who have fallen arise.

5

But as I said a moment ago, Peter and John
reached the tomb because of Mary's words.
They went inside but did not find the Lord.
Then, terrified, the holy men said:
"Why can we not see the Lord?
Did he consider our boldness too great?
We have been truly daring;
we ought to have stayed outside
and merely gazed at the tomb's secrets,
for the grave is no longer like a grave
but has truly become a house of God.
He came into it
and dwelt as he pleased,
the one who lets those who have fallen arise.

6

"Περιετράπη οὖν ἡμῖν   ἡ παρρησία εἰς τόλμαν
καὶ μᾶλλον ἐλογίσθη   καταφρόνησις τὸ θάρσος;
διὰ τοῦτο τάχα   οὐκ ὤφθη ὡς ἀναξίοις;"
Ταῦτα λαλούντων   τῶν γνησίων φίλων τοῦ Πλάσαντος,
εἶπεν ἡ Μαρία   ἀκολουθοῦσα·
"Μύσται τοῦ Κυρίου   καὶ ὄντως θερμοὶ ἐρασταί,
μὴ ὡς ὑπολαμβάνητε,
ἀλλ' ὑπομείνατε,   μὴ ἀθυμεῖτε·
τὸ γὰρ γενόμενον   οἰκονομία ἦν
ἵνα αἱ γυναῖκες   ὡς πρῶται πεσοῦσαι
ἴδωσι πρῶται   τὸν ἀναστάντα·
ἡμῖν θέλει χαρίσασθαι
τὸ 'Χαίρετε'   ταῖς πενθήσασιν
ὁ τοῖς πεσοῦσι   παρέχων ἀνάστασιν."

7

Ἐπειδὴ οὕτως ἑαυτὴν   ἐπληροφόρει Μαρία,
παρέμεινε τῷ τάφῳ   ἀπελθόντων τῶν ἁγίων·
ἀκμὴν γὰρ ἐδόκει   ὅτι ἐπήρθη τὸ σῶμα·
ὅθεν ἐβόα   οὐχὶ ῥήμασιν, ἀλλὰ δάκρυσιν·
"Οἴμοι, Ἰησοῦ μου,   ποῦ σε μετῆραν;
Πῶς δὲ κατεδέξω   κεκηλιδωμέναις χερσὶν
βαστάζεσθαι, ἀμώμητε;
'Ἅγιος,   ἅγιος,   ἅγιος' κράζει
τὰ ἑξαπτέρυγα   καὶ πολυόμματα·

6

"Has our boldness been turned into audacity,
and our courage regarded rather as contempt?
Perhaps, then, we are unworthy of seeing him?"
When the true friends of the Maker had spoken,
Mary, who was following, said,
"Initiates of the Lord, his truly ardent lovers,
do not take it this way,
but rather take courage, don't despair.
What has happened was part of the plan,
so that women, the first to fall,
might be first to see the risen one.
He wishes to grant us mourners
the grace of his own 'Rejoice!'
the one who lets those who have fallen arise."

7

When Mary had thus made known her insights,
she remained at the grave, though the saints had departed.
It still seemed that the body had been taken,
and so she cried out, not with words but with tears:
"Alas my Jesus, where have they put you?
How could you accept being carried away
by sullied hands, my unblemished one?
'Holy, holy, holy!' they cry,
the six winged and many eyed,

καὶ τούτων οἱ ὦμοι   μόλις φέρουσί σε,
καὶ πλάνων χεῖρες   ἐβάστασάν σε;
ὁ Πρόδρομος βαπτίζων σε
ἐκραύγαζε· 'Σύ με βάπτισον,
ὁ τοῖς πεσοῦσι   παρέχων ἀνάστασιν.'

8

"'Ἰδοὺ τριήμερος νεκρὸς   πέλεις, ὁ πάντα καινίζων·
ὁ Λάζαρον ἐγείρας   μετὰ τέσσαρας ἡμέρας
καὶ δρομαῖον δείξας   τὸν κηριαῖς δεδεμένον,
κεῖσαι ἐν τάφῳ,   καὶ ὡς εἴθε ᾔδειν ποῦ τέθαψαι,
ἵνα ὡς ἡ πόρνη   δάκρυσι βρέξω
μὴ μόνον τοὺς πόδας,   ἀλλὰ καὶ ὅλον ἀληθῶς
τὸ σῶμα καὶ τὸ μνῆμά σου,
λέγουσα· Δέσποτα,   ὡς τὸν τῆς χήρας
υἱὸν ἀνέστησας,   σαυτὸν ἀνάστησον·
ὁ τὴν Ἰαείρου   παιδίσκην ζωώσας,
τί ἔτι μένεις   ἐν τῷ μνημείῳ;
Ἀνάστηθι, ἐπίστηθι,
ἐμφάνηθι   τοῖς ζητοῦσί σε,
ὁ τοῖς πεσοῦσι   παρέχων ἀνάστασιν.'"

9

Νενικημένην τῷ κλαυθμῷ   καὶ ἡττημένην τῷ πόθῳ
ἰδὼν ὁ πάντα βλέπων   τὴν Μαγδαληνὴν Μαρίαν,
ἐσπλαγχνίσθη τότε   καὶ ὤφθη λέγων τῇ κόρῃ·
"Γύναι, τί κλαίεις;   Τίνα θέλεις ἔνδον τοῦ μνήματος;"

and their shoulders can hardly bear you,
yet deceitful hands could carry you off?
As the Forerunner was baptizing you,
he exclaimed, 'You should baptize me,
you who let those who have fallen arise!'

8

"You, who should renew it all, are a corpse on the third day.
You raised Lazarus after four days
and presented him running, bound with graveclothes.
You're laid in a grave. If I only knew where,
so that I, like the harlot, might drench with tears
not only your feet, but really your whole
body and tomb!
'Master,' I'd say, 'as you resurrected
the widow's son, resurrect yourself!
You brought Jairus's girl to life;
why do you still remain in the tomb?
Arise and be near,
and to seekers appear,
you who let those who have fallen arise!'"

9

Overcome with tears and overwhelmed by longing
was Mary Magdalene when the All-Seer saw her;
with loving-kindness he appeared, addressing the maiden:
"Woman, why are you weeping? Whom do you want inside
    the tomb?"

Εἶτα ἡ Μαρία   στραφεῖσα εἶπε·
"Κλαίω ὅτι ἦραν   τὸν Κύριόν μου τῆς ταφῆς   καὶ οὐκ
οἶδα ποῦ κατάκειται.
Πάντως δὲ   σόν ἐστι   τοῦτο τὸ ἔργον;
εἰ μὴ πλανῶμαι γάρ,   ὁ κηπουρὸς εἶ σύ·
λοιπὸν εἰ ἐπῆρες   τὸ σῶμα, εἰπέ μοι,
κἀγὼ λαμβάνω   τὸν λυτρωτήν μου·
ἐμὸς πέλει διδάσκαλος
καὶ Κύριος   ὁ ἐμός ἐστιν
ὁ τοῖς πεσοῦσι   παρέχων ἀνάστασιν."

10

Ὁ τὰς καρδίας ἐρευνῶν   καὶ τοὺς νεφροὺς ἐμβατεύων,
εἰδὼς ὅτι γνωρίζει   τὴν φωνὴν αὐτοῦ Μαρία,
ὡς ποιμὴν ἐφώνει   τὴν μηκωμένην ἀμνάδα
λέγων· "Μαρία."   Ἡ δ' εὐθέως εἶπε γνωρίσασα·
"Ὄντως ὁ καλός μου   ποιμὴν φωνεῖ με
ἵνα τοῖς ἐννέα   καὶ ἐνενήκοντα ἀμνοῖς
λοιπὸν συναριθμήσῃ με·
βλέπω γὰρ   ὄπισθεν   τοῦ με καλοῦντος
ἁγίων σώματα,   ἀγγέλων τάγματα·
διὸ οὔτε λέγω   'Τίς εἶ ὁ καλῶν με;'·
σαφῶς γὰρ ἔγνων   τίς ὁ καλῶν με·
αὐτός ἐστιν, ὡς προεῖπον,
ὁ Κύριος   ὁ ἐμός ἐστιν,
ὁ τοῖς πεσοῦσι   παρέχων ἀνάστασιν."

Then Mary turned around and said,
"I weep, for they've taken my Lord from the grave,
and I do not know where he lies.
Undoubtedly this must be your doing,
for, unless I'm mistaken, you are the gardener?
So if you've removed the body, tell me,
and I will take my redeemer back.
He is my teacher
and my Lord is he,
the one who lets those who have fallen arise."

10

He searches hearts and penetrates minds,
and knowing that Mary knew his voice,
he called as a shepherd to the bleating lamb.
"Mary!" he said. And she knew him at once
and exclaimed, "Truly my good shepherd
is calling to me, so he may number me
with the other ninety-nine lambs.
Behind the one who calls me, I see
bodies of saints, ranks of angels;
thus I do not ask, 'Who is calling me?'
for I know precisely who is calling.
It is he, as I said,
my Lord, he who is
the one who lets those who have fallen arise."

11

Ὑπὸ δὲ πόθου τοῦ θερμοῦ   καὶ τῆς ἐμπύρου ἀγάπης
ἡ κόρη κατεπείχθη   καὶ κρατῆσαι ἠβουλήθη
τὸν ἀπεριγράπτως   τὴν κτίσιν πᾶσαν πληροῦντα·
ὅμως ὁ Πλάστης   τὴν σπουδὴν αὐτῆς οὐκ ἐμέμψατο,
ἀλλ᾽ ἐπὶ τὰ θεῖα   αὐτὴν ἀνάγει
λέγων· "Μή μου ἅπτου· ἢ μόνον βροτόν με νοεῖς;
Θεός εἰμι, μὴ ἅπτου μου.
Ὦ σεμνή,   πέτασον   ἄνω τὸ ὄμμα
καὶ κατανόησον   τὰ ἐπουράνια·
ἐκεῖ ζήτησόν με·   καὶ γὰρ ἀναβαίνω
πρὸς τὸν Πατέρα   ὃν οὐκ ἀφῆκα·
αὐτοῦ πέλω ὁμόθρονος
ὡς σύγχρονος   καὶ συνάναρχος,
ὁ τοῖς πεσοῦσι   παρέχων ἀνάστασιν.

12

"Ῥητορευέτω δὲ λοιπὸν   ταῦτα ἡ γλῶσσά σου, γύναι,
καὶ διερμηνευέτω   τοῖς υἱοῖς τῆς Βασιλείας
τοῖς καραδοκοῦσι   τὴν ἔγερσίν μου τοῦ ζῶντος.
Σπεῦσον, Μαρία,   καὶ τοὺς μαθητάς μου συνάθροισον·
σάλπιγγί σοι χρῶμαι   μεγαλοφώνῳ·
ἤχησον εἰρήνην   εἰς τὰς ἐμφόβους ἀκοὰς
τῶν κεκρυμμένων φίλων μου,
ἔγειρον   ἅπαντας   ὥσπερ ἐξ ὕπνου,
ἵν᾽ ὑπαντήσωσι   καὶ δᾷδας ἅψωσιν·

11

Ardent longing and burning love
had seized the maiden, who wished to lay hold
of the one who, ungraspably, fills all creation.
Now, the Maker did not fault her zeal,
but lifted her up to divine things:
"Do not touch me—or do you think I am only mortal?
I am God. Do not touch me!
Noble woman, let your eye fly
upward to contemplate heavenly matters!
Seek me there, for I am ascending
toward my Father, whom I have not left.
With him am I enthroned,
as coeval and co-unoriginate,
the one who lets those who have fallen arise.

12

"So, let your tongue, woman, preach these things
to the sons of the Kingdom and interpret them
for those who expect me, the living, to rise.
Hurry, Mary, assemble my disciples!
I'm engaging you as a loud-voiced trumpet.
Make peace resound in the terrified ears
of my friends in hiding!
Arouse them all as if from slumber,
that they may gather and light their torches.

εἰπέ· Ὁ νυμφίος   ἠγέρθη τοῦ τάφου
καὶ οὐδὲν ἀφῆκεν   ἐντὸς τοῦ τάφου·
ἀπώσασθε, ἀπόστολοι,
τὴν νέκρωσιν,   ὅτι ἐγήγερται
ὁ τοῖς πεσοῦσι   παρέχων ἀνάστασιν.'"

<h2 style="text-align:center">13</h2>

Ὡς οὖν ἀκήκοε σαφῶς   ὅλων τῶν λόγων τοῦ Λόγου,
ὑπέστρεψεν ἡ κόρη   καί φησι ταῖς ὁμοτρόποις·
"Θαυμαστά, γυναῖκες,   ἃ εἶδον καὶ διηγοῦμαι·
μή τις οὖν δόξῃ   ὡς ληρήματά μου τὰ ῥήματα·
οὐ γὰρ ἐφαντάσθην,   ἀλλ' ἐνεπνεύσθην·
πέπλησμαι τῆς θέας   καὶ τῆς ὁμιλίας Χριστοῦ,
καὶ πῶς καὶ πότε μάθετε.
Ὅτε με   ἔλιπον   οἱ περὶ Πέτρον,
ἱστάμην κλαίουσα   ἐγγὺς τοῦ μνήματος·
ἐδόκουν γὰρ ὅτι   ἐπήρθη τοῦ τάφου
τὸ θεῖον σῶμα   τοῦ ἀθανάτου·
ἀλλ' εὐθέως οἰκτείρας μου
τὰ δάκρυα,   ἐπεφάνη μοι
ὁ τοῖς πεσοῦσι   παρέχων ἀνάστασιν.

<h2 style="text-align:center">14</h2>

"Μετεποιήθη ἀθρόον   εἰς εὐφροσύνην ἡ λύπη
καὶ γέγονέ μοι πάντα   ἱλαρὰ καὶ γεγηθότα·
οὐκ ὀκνῶ δὲ λέγειν·   Ὥσπερ Μωσῆς ἐδοξάσθην·
εἶδον γάρ, εἶδον,   —οὐκ ἐν ὄρει, ἀλλ' ἐν τῷ μνήματι,

Say, 'The groom was raised from the grave,
and nothing was left inside the grave.
Apostles, dispel
death, for he has risen,
the one who lets those who have fallen arise.'"

13

When she heard clearly all the words of the Word,
the maiden returned to her like-minded friends:
"Ladies, I'm telling you the wonders I've seen;
let no one regard them as idle tales!
Not fantasizing, but rather inspired,
I was filled with the sight of Christ and his speech.
Let me tell you how and when!
When those around Peter left me, I stayed,
weeping, close to the tomb,
for I thought the immortal one's divine body
had been stolen from the grave,
but taking pity on my tears,
he immediately appeared,
the one who lets those who have fallen arise.

14

"Suddenly grief was transformed to joy,
and all for me became cheer and rejoicing.
I'm not afraid to say I'm shining like Moses.
I saw, yes, I saw—not on a mount, but inside the tomb,

οὐχ ὑπὸ νεφέλην,   ἀλλ᾽ ὑπὸ σῶμα—
τὸν τῶν ἀσωμάτων   Δεσπότην καὶ τῶν νεφελῶν
τὸν πρὶν καὶ νῦν καὶ πάντοτε
λέγοντα· 'Μαριάμ,   σπεῦσον καὶ φράσον
τοῖς ἀγαπῶσί με   ὅτι ἐγήγερμαι·
ὡς κάρφος ἐλαίας   λαβοῦσά με γλώσσῃ,
τοῖς ἐκ τοῦ Νῶε   εὐαγγελίζου
σημαίνουσα ὡς πέπαυται
ὁ θάνατος   καὶ ἐγήγερται
ὁ τοῖς πεσοῦσι   παρέχων ἀνάστασιν.'"

15

Ἀκούσας τούτων ὁ χορὸς   τῶν εὐσεβῶν νεανίδων
συμφώνως ἀπεκρίθη   τῇ Μαγδαληνῇ Μαρίᾳ·
"Ἀληθὲς ὃ εἶπας;   καὶ συναινοῦμέν σοι πᾶσαι
οὐκ ἀπιστοῦμεν,   ἀλλὰ τοῦτο μᾶλλον θαυμάζομεν
ὅτι ἕως ἄρτι   ἦν ἐν τῷ τάφῳ
καὶ συναριθμεῖσθαι   τοῖς τεθνεῶσιν ἡ Ζωὴ
ἠνείχετο τριήμερον·
ὅτι γὰρ   ἤμελλεν   ἐκ τῶν χθονίων
ἐλθεῖν ἠλπίζομεν·   διὸ ἐλέγομεν·
'Τοῦ κήτους οἰκέτην   ἐξήγαγε τότε,
καὶ πῶς κρατεῖται   ὑπὸ Θανάτου;'
Εἰ τοῦ θηρὸς ἀνήρπασεν,
ἀνίσταται   καὶ ἐκ μνήματος
ὁ τοῖς πεσοῦσι   παρέχων ἀνάστασιν.

not in a cloud but instead in a body—
the Master of the bodiless ones and the clouds,
who was before, is now, and always,
saying, 'Mary, hurry and tell
those who love me that I have risen!
Take me, like an olive twig, on your tongue,
bringing good news to Noah's descendants,
and signal that death has been put to rest
while another has risen,
the one who lets those who have fallen arise.'"

15

When the choir of devout and youthful women
heard Mary Magdalene, they replied in unison:
"Is it true what you said? We agree with it all
and don't disbelieve, but we marvel at this,
that up till now, Life was entombed
and for three days endured
being counted among the dead.
We hoped to see this life force come
out from the underworld; thus we were asking,
'How could the one who once freed his servant
from the sea monster be captured by Death?'
If he could snatch from the beast,
he can rise from the tomb,
the one who lets those who have fallen arise.

16

"Νῦν οὖν μὴ νόμιζε, σεμνή,   ὅτι χωλεύει ἃ λέγεις·
ὀρθῶς ἡμῖν ἐφθέγξω   καὶ οὐδὲν ἐν τούτοις σκάζον·
ἀληθὴς ὁ λόγος   καὶ προσηνής σου ὁ τρόπος·
ὅμως, Μαρία,   κοινωνῆσαί σοι βουλευόμεθα
ἵνα μὴ ἓν μέλος   ἡμῶν τρυφήσῃ,
μείνῃ δὲ τὰ ἄλλα   νεκρὰ καὶ ἄγευστα ζωῆς
ἐκείνης ἧς ἀπήλαυσας·
γένωνται   ἅμα σοι   στόματα πλεῖστα
ἐπισφραγίζοντα   τὴν μαρτυρίαν σου·
ἀπέλθωμεν πᾶσαι   ἐπὶ τὸ μνημεῖον
καὶ βεβαιοῦμεν   τὴν ὀπτασίαν·
κοινὸν ἔστω, συνόμιλε,
τὸ καύχημα   ὃ παρέσχε σοι
ὁ τοῖς πεσοῦσι   παρέχων ἀνάστασιν."

17

Οὕτω λαλῶν ὁ σύλλογος   τῶν θεοφόρων θηλείων
ἐξήρχετο τὴν πόλιν   μετὰ τῆς διηγουμένης
καὶ ἰδὼν τὸν τάφον   ἀπὸ μακρόθεν ἐβόα·
"Ἴδε ὁ τόπος—μᾶλλον δὲ ὁ κόλπος ὁ ἄφθαρτος·
ἴδε ὁ βαστάσας   τὸν Βασιλέα,
ἴδε ὁ χωρήσας   ὃν οὐ χωροῦσιν οὐρανοί,
χωροῦσι δὲ οἱ ἅγιοι.
Αἶνός σοι,   ὕμνος σοι,   ἅγιε τάφε,
μικρὲ καὶ μέγιστε,   πτωχὲ καὶ πλούσιε,

16

"Do not think, noble one, what you say is a problem;
you have told us correctly, and no one's upset by it.
Your speech is truthful and your behavior gentle;
it is just that we'd like to take part in this with you,
so one of our limbs isn't nourished, Mary,
while the rest remain dead, with no taste of the life
you have come to enjoy.
Let many mouths be with you,
to set a seal on your testimony.
Let us all go off to the tomb
and confirm the vision!
Let us share, companion,
the boast he granted you,
the one who lets those who have fallen arise."

17

Thus spoke the gathering of God-bearing women
as they went out of the city, with the one who had told
        them,
and seeing the grave from afar, they exclaimed,
"See, the tomb—or rather the womb, uncorrupted!
See, it bore the King!
See, it contained the one whom the heavens
cannot contain, while the saints do!
Praise be to you, a hymn to you, holy tomb,
small yet great, poor yet rich,

ζωῆς ταμιεῖον, εἰρήνης δοχεῖον,
χαρᾶς σημεῖον, Χριστοῦ μνημεῖον·
ἑνὸς μνῆμα, τοῦ κόσμου δὲ
τὸ καύχημα, ὡς ηὐδόκησεν
ὁ τοῖς πεσοῦσι παρέχων ἀνάστασιν."

18

Ὑμνολογήσασαι λοιπὸν τοῦ Ζωοδότου τὸν τάφον,
ἐστράφησαν καὶ εἶδον τὸν καθήμενον τῷ λίθῳ
καὶ ἀπὸ τοῦ φόβου εἰς τὰ ὀπίσω ἀπῆλθον,
εὐλαβηθεῖσαι, κάτω κλίνασαι καὶ τὰ πρόσωπα
καὶ μετὰ δειλίας λαλοῦσαι ταῦτα·
"Τί τοῦτο τὸ εἶδός ἐστιν, ἢ τίνος ἡ μορφή;
Τίς πέφυκεν ὃν βλέπομεν;
ἄγγελος; ἄνθρωπος; ἄνωθεν ἦλθεν
ἢ τάχα κάτωθεν ἡμῖν ἀνέτειλεν;
Πῦρ πέλει, φῶς πέμπει, ἀστράπτει, αὐγάζει·
φύγωμεν, κόραι, μὴ φλογισθῶμεν·
ὄμβρε θεῖε, οὐράνιε,
ἐπίσταξον ταῖς διψῶσί σε,
ὁ τοῖς πεσοῦσι παρέχων ἀνάστασιν.

19

"Ψυχαγωγήσουσιν ἡμᾶς νῦν ὡς σταγόνες οἱ λόγοι
τοῦ στόματός σου, Λόγε, ἡ χαρὰ τῶν θλιβομένων,
ἡ ζωὴ τῶν πάντων, μὴ νεκρωθῶμεν τῷ φόβῳ."

chamber of life, cistern of peace,
symbol of joy, grave of Christ!
A tomb to one, a boast to the world,
as in it delighted
the one who lets those who have fallen arise."

18

Having sung their praises to the Life-Giver's grave,
they turned and saw someone sitting on the stone,
and fearful, then, they stepped back in awe,
bowing down their faces,
and with fear they said,
"What is this figure; whose is this shape?
Who may the one we see be?
An angel? A human? Has it come from above
or perhaps from below it has risen for us?
Fire has flared; light glares, dazzles, and blazes.
Let us flee, maidens, or we'll be aflame!
Rain, you divine and heavenly storm,
on those thirsting for you,
the one who lets those who have fallen arise!

19

"The words from your mouth, like drops of rain,
will refresh us, Word, joy of the troubled,
life of the world, so we don't die of fear."

Ταῦτα, ὡς οἶμαι,   ἐλιτάνευον αἱ θεόπνευστοι·
ὅθεν ἐμειλίχθη   ὁ ἐν τῷ λίθῳ
καὶ πρὸς τὰς ὁσίας   φησί· "Μὴ φοβεῖσθε ὑμεῖς,
ἀλλ' οὗτοι οἱ φυλάσσοντες
φρίξουσι,   πτήξουσι   καὶ νεκρωθῶσιν
ἀπὸ τοῦ φόβου μου,   ἵνα καὶ μάθωσιν
ὅτι τῶν ἀγγέλων   Δεσπότης ὑπάρχει
ὃν νῦν φρουροῦσιν,   ἀλλ' οὐ κρατοῦσιν·
ἀνέστη γὰρ ὁ Κύριος
καὶ οὐκ ἔγνωσαν   πῶς ἐγήγερται
ὁ τοῖς πεσοῦσι   παρέχων ἀνάστασιν.

20

"Ἀθανατίσθητε λοιπόν,   θήλειαι, μὴ νεκρωθῆτε·
τὸν κτίστην τῶν ἀγγέλων   ἐζητεῖτε θεωρῆσαι,
καὶ ἑνὸς ἀγγέλου   τὴν ὄψιν τί δειλιᾶτε;
Δοῦλος ὑπάρχω   τοῦ τὸν τάφον τοῦτον οἰκήσαντος,
τάξιν ὑπηρέτου   καὶ φύσιν ἔχω·
ἅπερ προσετάχθην   ἐπέστην κηρῦξαι ὑμῖν·
Ἐγήγερται ὁ Κύριος,
ἔτριψε   τὰς χαλκᾶς   πύλας τοῦ Ἅιδου
καὶ σιδηροῦς μοχλοὺς   αὐτοῦ συνέθλασε,
καὶ τῇ προφητείᾳ   ἐπέθηκε πέρας,
καὶ τῶν ἁγίων   ὕψωσε κέρας.
Δεῦτε, κόραι, καὶ ἴδετε
ποῦ ἔκειτο   ὁ ἀθάνατος,
ὁ τοῖς πεσοῦσι   παρέχων ἀνάστασιν."

Thus, I imagine, were the God-inspired praying,
and so the one on the stone was appeased.
To the holy women he said, "You need not fear,
but these guards here
will shudder, shrink, and be as dead
from fear of me, in order for them
to learn that it is the angels' Master
whom they try to keep, but do not hold.
The Lord is risen,
yet they don't know how he rose,
the one who lets those who have fallen arise.

20

"Be immortal, women, not mortified.
You sought to behold the creator of angels,
and the sight of a single angel scares you?
I serve the one who dwelt in this grave;
I have a servant's rank and nature.
As I was assigned, I am here to proclaim to you:
The Lord has arisen.
He has shattered Hades's gates of bronze
and crushed its iron bars.
He's set an end to prophesying
and raised the horn of the holy ones.
Come, maidens, see where
the immortal one lay,
the one who lets those who have fallen arise!"

21

Λαβοῦσαι θάρσος ἄμεμπτον   ἐκ τῆς φωνῆς τοῦ ἀγγέλου,
φρονίμως αἱ γυναῖκες   ἀπεκρίθησαν πρὸς τοῦτον·
"Ἀληθῶς ἀνέστη   ὁ Κύριος, καθὼς ἔφης·
ἔδειξας ἡμῖν   καὶ τῷ ῥήματι καὶ τῷ σχήματι
ὅτιπερ ἀνέστη   ὁ ἐλεήμων·
εἰ μὴ γὰρ   ἠγέρθη καὶ ἐπορεύθη τῆς ταφῆς,
οὐκ ἂν αὐτὸς ἐκάθισας·
πότε γὰρ   στρατηγός,   τοῦ βασιλέως
παρόντος, κάθηται   ἢ διαλέγεται;
Εἰ δὲ καὶ τελεῖται   ἐν γῇ τὰ τοιαῦτα,
ἀλλ' ἐν ὑψίστοις   οὐκ ἔστι ταῦτα,
ὅπου θρόνος ἀθέατος
καὶ ἄφραστος   ὁ καθήμενος,
ὁ τοῖς πεσοῦσι   παρέχων ἀνάστασιν."

22

Μίξασαι φόβῳ τὴν χαρὰν   καὶ εὐφροσύνην τῇ λύπῃ
ὑπέστρεψαν τοῦ τάφου,   ὡς διδάσκει τὸ Βιβλίον,
πρὸς τοὺς ἀποστόλους   καὶ ἔλεγον αἱ γυναῖκες·
"Τί ἀθυμεῖτε;   Τί τὰ πρόσωπα συγκαλύπτετε;
Ἄνω τὰς καρδίας·   Χριστὸς ἀνέστη.
Στήσατε χορείας   καὶ εἴπατε ἅμα ἡμῖν·
'Ἐγήγερται ὁ Κύριος'·
ἔλαμψεν   ὁ τεχθεὶς   πρὸ Ἑωσφόρου·

21

Taking irreproachable courage from his voice,
the women wisely answered the angel,
"Truly, as you said, the Lord has risen!
By your speech and your conduct you've shown us
that the merciful one has risen.
Had he not stood up and departed the tomb,
you yourself would not be sitting down,
for does a general, when the king is present,
remain seated, engaged in conversation?
And though such things might occur on earth,
they do not, surely, up on high,
where the throne is invisible
and the ineffable one is seated,
the one who lets those who have fallen arise."

22

Mixing joy with fear and gladness with grief,
they returned from the grave, as the Bible teaches,
and to the apostles the women said,
"Why are you downcast? Why hide your faces?
Lift up your hearts! Christ has risen!
Stand in choirs and exclaim with us,
'The Lord has arisen!'
He shines who was born before the Morning Star,

μὴ οὖν στυγνάσητε,   ἀλλ' ἀναθάλλετε·
τὸ ἔαρ ἐφάνη·   ἀνθήσατε, κλῶνες,
καρποφορίαν,   μὴ δυσφορίαν·
πάντες χεῖρας κροτήσωμεν
καὶ εἴπωμεν·   Ἐξεγήγερται
ὁ τοῖς πεσοῦσι   παρέχων ἀνάστασιν.'"

23

Οἱ δὲ ἀκούσαντες σαφῶς   καὶ εὐφρανθέντες τῷ λόγῳ
ἐξέστησαν εὐθέως   καί φησι πρὸς τὰς γυναῖκας·
"Πόθεν τοῦτο, κόραι,   ἐμάθετε ὃ λαλεῖτε;
Ἄγγελος εἶπεν;"   "Ναί," φησίν, "καὶ εἶπε καὶ ἔδειξε,
καὶ ὁ τῶν ἀγγέλων   Θεὸς καὶ Πλάστης
ὤφθη τῇ Μαρίᾳ   καὶ ἔφη· Λέξον τοῖς ἐμοῖς·
"ἐγήγερται ὁ Κύριος."'"
Δεῦτε οὖν,   ὡς κριοὶ   καὶ ὡς ἀρνία
προβάτων ἅπαντες   σκιρτῶντες εἴπωμεν·
"Ποιμὴν ἡμῶν, δεῦρο,   συνάγαγε ἡμᾶς
τοὺς σκορπισθέντας   ὑπὸ δειλίας·
ἐπάτησας τὸν Θάνατον,
ἐπίστηθι   τοῖς ποθοῦσί σε,
ὁ τοῖς πεσοῦσι   παρέχων ἀνάστασιν.'"

24

Συναναστήτω σοι, Σωτήρ,   ἡ νεκρωθεῖσα ψυχή μου,
μὴ φθείρῃ ταύτην λύπη   καὶ λοιπὸν εἰς λήθην ἔλθῃ
τῶν ᾀσμάτων τούτων   τῶν ταύτην ἁγιαζόντων·

so don't hang your heads, but bloom anew!
Spring has come! Blossom, twigs,
bear fruit, not gloom!
Let's all clap hands and say,
'He's awoken again,
the one who lets those who have fallen arise!'"

23

Those who listened and heard and rejoiced at the words
immediately turned and said to the women,
"Maidens, where did you learn what you're telling us?
Did an angel say it?" "Yes," they replied, "both said it and
     showed it.
And the angels' God and Maker was seen
by Mary and said, 'Tell my people:
"The Lord has arisen!"'
Come, then, like rams, like lambs of the sheep,
let us all thus say as we leap,
'Come, our shepherd, gather us in,
we who were scattered abroad by fright!
You trampled Death;
be present to those who long for you,
you who let those who have fallen arise.'"

24

Let my mortified soul arise with you, Savior.
May grief not defile it so it ends up forgetful
of these songs that sanctify it. Merciful one,

ναί, ἐλεῆμον,   ἱκετεύω σε μὴ παρίδῃς με
τὸν ταῖς πλημμελείαις   κατεστιγμένον·
ἐν γὰρ ἀνομίαις   καὶ ἐν ἁμαρτίαις ἐμὲ
ἐκίσσησεν ἡ μήτηρ μου,
Πάτερ μου   ἅγιε   καὶ φιλοικτίρμον,
ἁγιασθήτω σου   ἀεὶ τὸ ὄνομα
ἐν τῷ στόματί μου   καὶ τοῖς χείλεσί μου,
ἐν τῇ φωνῇ μου   καὶ τῇ ᾠδῇ μου·
δός μοι χάριν κηρύττοντι
τοὺς ὕμνους σου,   ὅτι δύνασαι,
ὁ τοῖς πεσοῦσι   παρέχων ἀνάστασιν.

I beg you, do not neglect me,
although I am stained by transgressions.
In iniquities and in sins
my mother conceived me.
Our Father, holy and compassionate,
hallowed always be your name
in my mouth and on my lips,
in my voice and by my song!
Give me grace proclaiming your hymns,
for yours is the power,
you who let those who have fallen arise.

Προοίμιον

ἰδιόμελον

Ἐπὶ τὸ φρέαρ   ὡς ἦλθεν ὁ Κύριος,
ἡ Σαμαρεῖτις   ἠρώτα τὸν εὔσπλαγχνον·
"Παράσχου μοι   τὸ ὕδωρ τῆς πίστεως,
καὶ λήψομαι   τῆς κολυμβήθρας τὰ νάματα,
ἀγαλλίασιν καὶ ἀπολύτρωσιν."

I

ἰδιόμελον

Τὸ τάλαντον τὸ δοθέν σοι,   ψυχή μου, μὴ ἀποκρύψῃς,
ἵνα μὴ τῆς ῥαθυμίας   ὑπενέγκῃς τὴν αἰσχύνην,
ἐν ἡμέρᾳ   ἐν ᾗ κρίνει ὁ Θεὸς   τὴν οἰκουμένην.
Ἐρχόμενος γὰρ τότε,   τὸ χρῆμα παραχρῆμα   ἀπαιτήσει
                                                                                    σε·
οὐχ ὅσον ἐκομίσω,   ἀλλ' ὅσον ἐπορίσω
ψηφίσας μεθοδεύσει σε·
σὺν τόκῳ γὰρ τὸ δάνειον   παρ' ἑκάστου λαμβάνει·
ψυχή μου, μὴ ἀμέλει,   ψυχή μου, ἐμπορεύου,   ψυχή
                                                        μου, δὸς καὶ λάβε,

270

ON THE SAMARITAN WOMAN

in second mode

Prelude

to its own melody

When the compassionate Lord came to the well,
the woman of Samaria asked him herself,
"Give me, please, the water of faith,
and I shall receive the streams of the font,
jubilance and deliverance!"

I

to its own melody

My soul, do not hide the talent you were granted
and be weighed down with indolent shame
on the day God judges the world!
When he comes, he will demand his money back.
Not only what you got, but also what you gained,
he will calculate and exact your debt;
he collects his loan from each with interest.
My soul, don't be careless; my soul, do business; my soul,
    give and take,

ἵν' ὅταν ἔλθῃ   ὁ Βασιλεύς σου,
ἀντὶ τῆς πραγματείας   σοι παράσχῃ
ἀγαλλίασιν καὶ ἀπολύτρωσιν.

2

Οὐκ ἧς ἀξία τοῦ ἔχειν,   καὶ ἔχεις ἅπερ κατέχεις
σὺ τὴν χάριν του δόντος·   μὴ οὖν ὄκνει τοῖς αἰτοῦσιν
μεταδοῦναι,   ὡς μετέδωκέ ποτε   ἡ Σαμαρεῖτις.
Ἀντλήσασα γὰρ μόνη   παρέσχε καὶ ἑτέροις   οὕπερ
ἔλαβεν·
οὐδεὶς αὐτὴν ᾐτεῖτο,   καὶ πᾶσιν ἐδωρεῖτο
ἀφθόνως τοῦ χαρίσματος·
διψᾷ καὶ δαψιλεύεται,   μὴ πιοῦσα ποτίζει·
ἀγμὴν μὴ γευσαμένη,   ἀλλ' ὡς μεμεθυσμένη   τοῖς
ὁμοφύλοις κράζει·
"Δεῦτε, ὁρᾶτε   νᾶμα ὃ εὗρον·
μὴ οὗτος ἄρα πέλει   ὁ παρέχων
ἀγαλλίασιν καὶ ἀπολύτρωσιν;"

3

Ὑδάτων οὖν ἀθανάτων,   ὧν ἡ πιστὴ Σαμαρεῖτις
γέγονε μὲν ὡς εὑροῦσα,   ἡμεῖς ἄρτι [. . .]
πιόντες ἐρευνήσωμεν καλῶς   ὅλας τὰς φλέβας·
μικρὸν δὲ καὶ τὰς λέξεις   τὰς τοῦ
εὐαγγελίου   ἀναλάβωμεν,
Χριστὸν τὸ φῶς ὁρῶντες,   τὸ ὕδωρ ὅπερ πάλαι

so when your King comes, he may grant you,
in return for your commerce,
jubilance and deliverance!

2

You're not entitled to having, and what you have you have
as a favor from the giver, so don't be slow to share it
with those who ask you, as the woman of Samaria once was
     sharing.
She drew the water alone, but offered to others what she
     had taken;
though no one requested, she freely gave
her gift to all.
She thirsts, yet pours till it spills, hasn't drunk, but offers a
     drink,
has not tasted, but shouts like a drunk to all her
     compatriots,
"Come, see the stream which I have discovered!
Is this not the one that is offering
jubilance and deliverance?"

3

Since we just drank from the waters of immortality
that the faithful Samaritan woman discovered,
let's examine all the sources with care
and recall for a moment the passage from the gospel,
and in Christ, the light, we'll perceive the water

ἡ Σαμαρεῖτις ἔπιεν,
καὶ πῶς αὕτη ἐξ ὕδατος   ὕδωρ ἄλλο παρέσχε,
καὶ τίνος χάριν τότε   διψῶντα οὐ ποτίζει,   καὶ τί ἦν τὸ
κωλῦον.

Πάντα γὰρ ταῦτα   τὸ μεγαλεῖον,
ἡ Βίβλος, περιέχει   καὶ παρέχει
ἀγαλλίασιν καὶ ἀπολύτρωσιν.

4

Τί οὖν διδάσκει ἡ Βίβλος;   Χριστός, φησίν, ὁ πηγάζων
πηγὴν ζωῆς τοῖς ἀνθρώποις,   ἀπὸ τῆς ὁδοιπορίας
κοπιάσας   ἐπεκάθητο πηγῇ   τῆς Σαμαρείας,
καὶ καύσωνος ἦν ὥρα·   ὡς ἕκτη γὰρ ὑπῆρχε,   καθὼς
γέγραπται,
μεσούσης τῆς ἡμέρας,   Μεσσίας ὅτε ἦλθε
τοὺς ἐν νυκτὶ καταυγάσαι·
Πηγὴ πηγὴν κατέλαβεν,   ἀποπλύνων, οὐ πίνων·
κρουνὸς ἀθανασίας   τῷ ῥείθρῳ τῆς ἀθλίας   ὡς ἐνδεὴς
ἐπέστη·
κάμνει βαδίζων   ὁ ἐν θαλάσσῃ
πεζεύσας ἀκαμάτως,   ὁ παρέχων
ἀγαλλίασιν καὶ ἀπολύτρωσιν.

5

Ἀλλ' ὅτε ἦν ὁ οἰκτίρμων   ἐπὶ τὸ φρέαρ, ὡς εἶπον,
τότε γύνη Σαμαρεῖτις   ἐπὶ ὤμων τὴν ὑδρίαν
ἦρε καὶ ἦλθεν   ἐξελθοῦσα τὴν Συχάρ,   πόλιν ἰδίαν.

the woman was drinking,
how she from water gave a different water,
why she did not give drink when he was thirsting, and what
  held her back.
All this the magnificent book, the Bible,
contains; it offers
jubilance and deliverance.

4

So what does the Bible teach? It says that Christ, gushing
  forth
a spring of life for humans, grew weary from his journey
and sat down at the spring of Samaria.
This was the hot hour, around noon, as it's written,
in the middle of the day, when the Messiah came
to shine on those in the night.
The Spring came to the spring, to cleanse and not to drink.
The fount of immortality halted in need by the needy one's
  stream;
he was tired from walking, the one who had tirelessly
traversed the sea, the one who is offering
jubilance and deliverance.

5

When the merciful one was at the well, as I said,
a Samaritan woman, gone out from her city of Sychar,
came carrying a pot on her shoulders.

Καὶ τίς οὐ μακαρίζει   τὴν ἔξοδον ἐκείνης   καὶ τὴν
                                       εἴσοδον;
Ἐξῆλθε γὰρ ἐν ῥύπῳ,   εἰσῆλθε δὲ ἐν τύπῳ
τῆς Ἐκκλησίας ἄμωμος·
ἐξῆλθε καὶ ἐξήντλησε   τὴν ζωὴν ὥσπερ σπόγγος·
ἐξῆλθεν ὑδροφόρος,   εἰσῆλθε θεοφόρος·   καὶ τίς οὐ
                                       μακαρίζει
τοῦτο τὸ θῆλυ,   μᾶλλον δὲ σέβει
τὴν ἐξ ἐθνῶν, τὸν τύπον,   τὴν λαβοῦσαν
ἀγαλλίασιν καὶ ἀπολύτρωσιν;

6

Προσῆλθεν οὖν ἡ ὁσία   καὶ ἤντλησεν ἐν σοφίᾳ·
τὸν γὰρ Δεσπότην ἰδοῦσα   κεκμηκότα καὶ διψῶντα
καὶ βοῶντα· "Γύναι, δός μοι πιεῖν,"   οὐκ ἐτραχύνθη,
ἀλλ᾽ εἶπεν εἰλημμένως· "Καὶ πῶς σύ, Ἰουδαῖος   ὤν,
                                     ᾐτήσω με;"
Ὑπέμνησε τὸ δόγμα,   μετέπειτα τὸ πόμα
φρονίμως ἐπηγγείλατο.
Οὐκ εἶπε γάρ· "Οὐ δίδωμι   ἀλλοφύλῳ σοι πίνειν,"
ἀλλ᾽ εἶπεν· "Πῶς ᾐτήσω;"   ὥς ποτε τῷ ἀγγέλῳ   ἡ
                                     Θεοτόκος ἔφη·
"Πῶς ἔσται τοῦτο;   Πῶς ὁ ἀμήτωρ
μητέρα με λαμβάνει   ὁ παρέχων
ἀγαλλίασιν καὶ ἀπολύτρωσιν;"

Who would not call blessed her going and coming?
She went out in filth, but came back in the figure
of the Church, unblemished;
she went out and sucked up life like a sponge;
she went to bear water and came back bearing God. Who
     does not bless
this woman and even revere the one from the nations,
a figure, the one who receives
jubilance and deliverance?

6

So the holy one came forward and wisely drew water,
for she saw the Master, tired and thirsty,
calling, "Woman, give me a drink!" She was not annoyed,
yet said in surprise, "But how can you, a Jew, ask me?"
She recalled the precept and then, with prudence,
promised the drink.
She did not say, "I won't give you, a foreigner, a drink,"
but, "How can you ask?" Just as the God-Bearer said to the
     angel,
"How can this be? How can the motherless
take me as mother, he who will offer
jubilance and deliverance?"

7

Ἰδού μοι δύο εἰκόνων   ζωγράφος ἡ Σαμαρεῖτις
ἐκ τῆς Συχὰρ ἀνεφάνη·   Ἐκκλησίας καὶ Μαρίας.
Διὰ τοῦτο   μὴ παρέλθωμεν αὐτήν·   ἔχει γὰρ τέρψιν.
Λεγέτω οὖν τὸ θῆλυ   καὶ πάλιν πρὸς τὸν
                             Πλάστην·   "Πῶς ἠτήσω με;
Ἐάν σοι δώσω πίνης,   πιὼν δὲ μεταβαίνης
τὸν Ἰουδαϊκὸν θεσμόν,
καὶ λήψομαι ἐξ ὕδατος   σὲ ὁμόφρονα ἄνδρα."
Ὅτι καλοί οἱ λόγοι   τῆς
                    Σαμαρείτιδος·   ὑποσκιογραφοῦσιν
ἐπὶ τὸ φρέαρ   τὴν κολυμβήθραν
ἐξ ἧς λαμβάνει δούλην   ὁ παρέχων
ἀγαλλίασιν καὶ ἀπολύτρωσιν.

8

"Νῦν ἄκουσόν μου, ὦ γύναι,"   ὁ Ἰησοῦς ἀνεβόα·
"εἰ ἤδεις τὴν δωρεάν μου   καὶ τίς ἐστιν ὁ εἰπών σοι·
'Ὕδωρ δός μοι,'   σὺ ἂν ᾔτησας αὐτὸν   νάματα ζῶντα·
ὕδωρ γὰρ ζῶν παρέχει."   Πρὸς ταῦτα
                             ἀπεκρίθη   ἀμφιβάλλουσα·
"Οὐκ ἄντλημα βαστάζεις,   βαθὺ δὲ καὶ τὸ φρέαρ,
καὶ πόθεν σοι τὰ ὕδατα;
Μὴ μείζων εἶ σὺ ἢ καλλίων   Ἰακὼβ τοῦ γενέτου;
Αὐτὸς γὰρ ἡμῖν ταύτην   τὴν πηγὴν πρὶν παρέσχε·   καὶ
                             πῶς σὺ λέγεις ἄρτι·

7

As I see it, the Samaritan woman from Sychar
is painting two pictures: of the Church and of Mary.
So let's not pass her by, for she offers delight.
Let her say to her Maker again, "How can you ask me?
If I give you a drink, you will alter the law
of the Jews when you are drinking,
and from water I'll receive you as a like-minded man."
What lovely words! On the well they sketch
the font from which he receives her as servant,
he who is offering
jubilance and deliverance.

8

"Listen, woman," Jesus exclaimed,
"If you knew my gift, and who is saying to you,
'Give me water,' you would have asked him for living
      streams,
for he offers living water." To this she retorted with doubt,
"You carry no bucket, and the well is deep;
where do you get water from?
Are you greater or better than our ancestor Jacob?
It was he who gave us this spring long ago; and you're saying
      now,

"Ἔχω σοι δοῦναι   νάματα ζῶντα
οὐ λήγοντα διδοῦντα   τῷ αἰτοῦντι
ἀγαλλίασιν καὶ ἀπολύτρωσιν';"

9

"Οὐκ οἶδας, γύναι, ὃ λέγω,   οὐκ ἔφθασας ὅπου θέλω·
διὸ τὰ ὦτά σου κλῖνον   καὶ τὰς φρένας ἄνοιξόν μοι,
ἵν' εἰσέλθω   καὶ οἰκήσω ἐν αὐταῖς·   οὕτω γὰρ θέλω·
τοῦ ὕδατος γὰρ τούτου   ὁ πίνων καθ' ἑκάστην   πάλιν
                                                  διψήσεται·
τὸ ὕδωρ δέ, ὃ δώσω   τοῖς πίστει φλεγομένοις
ἐκ δίψης μὲν ἀνάψυξις·
γενήσεται γὰρ ἔνδοθεν   τοῖς πιοῦσι τὸ ῥεῖθρον
κρουνὸς ἀθανασίας   ἁλλόμενος καὶ βρύων   ζωὴν τὴν
                                                  αἰωνίαν·
τοῦτο γὰρ πρώην   ἐν τῇ ἐρήμῳ
οἱ ἐξ Ἑβραίων ἦραν,   ἀλλ' οὐχ εὗρον
ἀγαλλίασιν καὶ ἀπολύτρωσιν."

10

Ὑφήφθη τούτοις τοῖς λόγοις   ἡ Σαμαρεῖτις πρὸς δίψαν,
καὶ μετηλλάγη ἡ τάξις·   ἡ ποτίζουσα γὰρ πρώην
νῦν ἐδίψα,   καὶ ὁ διψήσας ἐξ ἀρχῆς   ἄρτι ποτίζει·
προσπίπτει οὖν τὸ θῆλυ·   "Τὸ ὕδωρ τοῦτο," φησί,   "δός
                                                  μοι, Κύριε,
ἵνα μηκέτι τούτῳ   τῷ φρέατι προστρέχω,
ὃ Ἰακὼβ παρέσχε μοι.

'I can give you streams that are living,
which do not cease giving to anyone seeking
jubilance and deliverance'?"

9

"You're not understanding what I'm saying, woman, not
    getting to where I want.
Incline your ears, now, and open your mind to me,
so that I may enter and dwell inside it. That's what I want.
Someone who drinks this water daily will again be thirsty,
but the water I'll give is relief from thirst
for those burning with faith.
When they drink from the stream, a spring of immortality
will be bubbling up, gushing forth eternal life.
This the Hebrews in the desert once
obtained, but they did not attain
jubilance and deliverance."

10

By these words the Samaritan was inflamed with thirst,
and the order was reversed: she who offered water first
was thirsting now, and he who thirsted from the start,
    suddenly offers it.
She falls down before him: "Give me this water, sir,
so I need no longer run to this well
that Jacob has granted me!

Ἀργείτω τὰ γηράσαντα   καὶ ἀνθείτω τὰ νέα·
παρέλθῃ τὰ πρὸς ὥραν·   καὶ γὰρ ἦλθεν ἡ ὥρα   τοῦ
         ὕδατος οὗ ἔχεις·
τοῦτο βρυέτω   καὶ ἀρδευέτω
ἐμοὶ καὶ τοῖς ἐν πίστει   ἐκζητοῦσιν
ἀγαλλίασιν καὶ ἀπολύτρωσιν."

II

"Ῥοὰς ἀχράντων ὑδάτων   εἰ θέλεις ἵνα σοι δώσω,
πορεύου, φώνει τὸν ἄνδρα.   Οὐ μιμοῦμαί σου τὴν
         γνώμην,
οὐκ ἐρῶ σοι·   'Σαμαρεῖτις εἶ, καὶ πῶς   ᾔτησας ὕδωρ;'
Οὐ θλίβω σου τὴν δίψαν·   ἐγὼ γάρ σε πρὸς
        δίψαν   δίψῃ εἵλκυσα·
διψῶντα ὑπεκρίθην   καὶ ὡς διψῶν ἐτρώθην,
ἵνα διψῶσαν δείξω σε.
Πορεύθητι οὖν, φώνησον   τὸν σὸν ἄνδρα καὶ ἐλθέ."
Τὸ γύναιον δὲ ἔφη·   "Οὐκ ἔχω ἄνδρα, οἴμοι."   Καὶ
       πρὸς αὐτὴν ὁ Πλάστης·
"Ὄντως οὐκ ἔχεις·   πέντε γὰρ ἔσχες,
τὸν ἕκτον δὲ οὐκ ἔχεις   ἵνα λάβῃς
ἀγαλλίασιν καὶ ἀπολύτρωσιν."

12

Ὦ τῶν σοφῶν αἰνιγμάτων,   ὦ τῶν σοφῶν χαρακτήρων·
δι' ὧν τὰ τῆς Ἐκκλησίας   ἐν τῇ πίστει τῆς ὁσίας
ζωγραφεῖται   ἐκ χρωμάτων ἀληθῶν,   ἀπαλαιώτων·

Let the old things go fallow and the new things flower!
Let the momentary pass; the moment has come for the
     water you have.
Let it gush forth and water me,
along with all who seek out in faith
jubilance and deliverance."

11

"If you want me to give you unpolluted streams,
go, call your husband! I won't mimic your attitude;
I will not say to you: 'How can you, Samaritan, ask me for
     water?'
I won't censure your thirst, I who with thirst drew you to
     thirsting.
I acted out thirst, and I did feel thirsty,
to show you your thirsting.
So, go, call your husband and come back here!"
The woman said, "Alas, I have no husband." Then the
     Maker replied,
"Truly you don't; you've had five,
but a sixth you won't have when you accept
jubilance and deliverance."

12

What clever conundrums! What clever features,
through which those of the Church are depicted
with true, unfading colors in the holy woman's faith.

283

ὃν τρόπον γὰρ τὸ θῆλυ   ἠρνήσατο τὸν ἄνδρα   ἡ
                                            πολύανδρος,
οὕτως ἡ Ἐκκλησία   πολλοὺς θεοὺς ὡς ἄνδρας
ἠρνήσατο καὶ ἔλιπεν,
καὶ ἕνα ἐμνηστεύσατο   ἐξ ὑδάτων Δεσπότην·
ἐκείνη ἄνδρας πέντε   καὶ τὸν ἕκτον οὐκ ἔσχε·   καὶ
                                            αὕτη δὲ τοὺς πέντε
τῆς ἀσεβείας   ἄρτι λιποῦσα
τὸν ἕκτον ἐξ ὑδάτων   σὲ λαμβάνει,
ἀγαλλίασιν καὶ ἀπολύτρωσιν.

13

Μισήσωμεν τὰ εἴδη   τῆς εἰδωλολατρίας·
ἡ ἐξ ἐθνῶν νυμφευθεῖσα   ὡς πικρὰν ἀποστρέφεται
καὶ ἀρνεῖται   τὴν ἀμείνην, ὅ ἐστι   ῥίζα γλυκεῖα.
Ἀλλ᾽ ἴσως ἐρωτᾷ τις·   "Τὰ πέντε εἴδη ταῦτα   τί
                                            ὑπάρχουσιν;"
Ἡ τῶν εἰδώλων πλάνη   πολυειδὴς μέν ἐστιν,
ἔχει δὲ πέντε κεραίας·
ἀσέβειαν, ἀσέλγειαν   καὶ τὴν ἐπιμιξίαν,
πρὸς τούτοις ἀσπλαγχνίαν   καὶ τὴν τεκνοφονίαν,   ὡς
                                            καὶ Δαυὶδ διδάσκει·
"Ἔθυσαν," λέγων,   "τοῖς δαιμονίοις
υἱοὺς καὶ θυγατέρας," καὶ οὐχ εὗρον
ἀγαλλίασιν καὶ ἀπολύτρωσιν.

As she with many husbands disowned her husband,
so the Church disowned and abandoned many
gods like husbands
and, from the water, espoused herself to one Master.
That one had five, but not a sixth;
this one abandoned fivefold impiety,
and is taking you, the sixth, from the water,
jubilance and deliverance.

13

Let us all abhor idolatry's forms!
The bride from the nations renounces its lavishness,
and the sweet root she rejects as bitter.
But someone may ask: "What are these five forms?"
The error of idols is certainly multiform,
yet it has five horns:
impiety, impudence, and intercourse too;
heartlessness, also, and murder of children, as David
        teaches:
"They sacrificed," he says, "their sons and their daughters
to the demons," and didn't find
jubilance and deliverance.

14

Ἀφῆκεν οὖν τὰ τοσαῦτα   ἡ ἐξ ἐθνῶν μνηστευθεῖσα,
καὶ πρὸς τὸ τῆς κολυμβήθρας   φρέαρ τρέχει ἐκεῖσε
καὶ ἀρνεῖται   τὰ ποτέ, ὥσπερ ποτὲ   ἡ Σαμαρεῖτις·
οὐκ ἔκρυψε γὰρ αὕτη   τὸν πάντα πρὶν
                        γενέσθαι   ἐπιστάμενον,
ἀλλ' ἔφησεν· "Οὐκ ἔχω"· οὐκ εἶπε γάρ· "Οὐκ ἔσχον,"
νομίζω, τοῦτο λέγουσα·
"Κἂν ἔσχον ἄνδρας πρότερον,   ἀλλ' οὐ θέλω νῦν ἔχειν
ἐκείνους οὕσπερ εἶχον·   σὲ γὰρ ἄρτι κατέχω   τὸν
                        σαγηνεύσαντά με
ἐκ τοῦ βορβόρου   τῶν πονηρῶν μου
πιστῶς ἀντλησαμένη,   ἵνα λάβω
ἀγαλλίασιν καὶ ἀπολύτρωσιν."

15

Νοήσασα ἡ ὁσία   τὴν τοῦ Σωτῆρος ἀξίαν
ἐκ τῶν ἀποκαλυφθέντων,   ἐπὶ πλεῖον ἐπεπόθει
ἐπιγνῶναι   τί ἐστι καὶ τίς ἐστιν ὁ πρὸς τὸ φρέαρ·
καὶ τάχα τοῖς τοιούτοις   συνείχετο
                        εἰκότως   ἐνθυμήμασιν·
"Θεὸς ὑπάρχει ἄρα   ἢ ἄνθρωπος ὃν βλέπω;
Οὐράνιος ἢ γήϊνος;
Ἰδοὺ γὰρ τὰ ἀμφότερα   ἐν ἑνί μοι γνωρίζει,
διψῶν τε καὶ ποτίζων,   μανθάνων καὶ προλέγων,   καὶ
                        πάλιν προσκαλῶν με

14

The betrothed from the nations abandoned all these,
and there to the well of the font she runs;
she disowns past liaisons, like the woman of Samaria.
The latter was not trying to hide anything from the
     foreknowing one,
but said, "I do not have," not, "I have not had."
I think that she meant,
"I've had husbands before, but will no longer have
the ones that I had. Now I've seized you, who caught me in
     your net;
I've been drawn from the filth of my wicked deeds
by faith, so I'll embrace
jubilance and deliverance."

15

When the holy one recognized the dignity of the Savior
from what had been disclosed, she yearned even more
to grasp what he was and who was there at the well.
And perhaps she was occupied with thoughts such as these:
"Is he whom I see a god or a human?
From heaven or from earth?
See how he shows me the two at once:
he both thirsts and gives drink, listens and foretells, and he
     even invites me,

τὴν παρὰ νόμον   καὶ προσδεικνύς μοι
τὰ σφάλματά μου πάντα,   ἵνα λάβω
ἀγαλλίασιν καὶ ἀπολύτρωσιν.

16

"Οὐκοῦν οὐράνιος πέλει   καὶ τὸ ἐπίγειον φέρει;
εἰ οὖν Θεὸς καὶ βροτὸς ὤν,   ὡς ἄνθρωπός μοι ἐδείχθη,
καὶ διψήσας   με ποτίζει ὡς θεὸς   καὶ προφητεύει.
Οὐκ ἦν γὰρ ἐν ἀνθρώπῳ   τὸ γνῶναί μου τὸν βίον   καὶ
                                      ἐνθυμήσασθαι,
ἀλλὰ τοῦ ἀοράτου   καὶ νῦν θεωρουμένου
ἐνδεῖξαι καὶ ἐλέγξαι με·
αὐτοῦ ἦν καὶ εἰδέναι με   καὶ κηρῦξαι ὃ πέλω·
αὐτοῦ τὸν νοῦν ἀντλήσω,   αὐτοῦ τὴν γνῶσιν
                              πίω,   αὐτοῦ τοῖς λόγοις πλύνω
πάντα τὸν ῥύπον   τῶν ἁμαρτιῶν μου,
ἵν' ἀμωμήτῳ γνώμῃ   ἀπολάβω
ἀγαλλίασιν καὶ ἀπολύτρωσιν.

17

"Υἱὲ βροτοῦ ὡς ὁρῶ σε,   υἱὲ Θεοῦ ὡς νοῶ σε,
σὺ φώτισόν μου τὰς φρένας,   Κύριε, δίδαξόν με
τίς ὑπάρχεις,"   χρηστῶς παρεκάλει Χριστὸν   ἡ
                                      Σαμαρεῖτις.
"Ἰδοὺ σαφῶς σε βλέπω   πιστῶς κατανοοῦσα   καὶ μὴ
                                      κρύψῃς μοι·
μὴ ἄρα σὺ ὑπάρχεις   Χριστὸς ὃν οἱ προφῆται
προεῖπον ὅτι ἔρχεται;

who am outside the law, and lays out for me also
all of my faults, so I may receive
jubilance and deliverance.

16

"Surely someone from heaven does not bear an earthly
    form?
If he's God, he's also mortal, for he looks human to me;
though he's thirsty, he offers me drink as a god, and
    prophesizes.
A human would not be able to know my life and ponder it,
but if the invisible one is now being seen,
he could reveal
and expose me, he'd know and proclaim what I am.
I will draw from his mind, drink of his knowledge, wash
    with his words
all the dirt of my sins, so I may obtain,
with unblemished intent,
jubilance and deliverance.

17

"Son of mortals, as I see you, son of God, as I understand
    you,
enlighten my thoughts, sir; teach me who you are!"
the woman of Samaria politely asked him.
"I see you clearly when observing with faith—do not hide
    from me!
Are you not the Christ whom the prophets foretold
was going to come?

Ἐὰν σὺ εἶ, ὡς ἔφησαν,   παρρησίᾳ εἰπέ μοι·
ὁρῶ γὰρ ὅτι ὄντως   ἃ ἔπραξα γνωρίζεις   καὶ τὰ τῆς
καρδίας μου
κρύφια πάντα·   καὶ διὰ τοῦτο
καθικετεύω γνώμῃ,   ἵνα λάβω
ἀγαλλίασιν καὶ ἀπολύτρωσιν."

18

Ἀλλ' ὅτε εἶδεν ὁ βλέπων   τὰς τῆς σοφῆς διαλέξεις
καὶ τὸ πιστὸν τῆς καρδίας,   παρευθὺς ἀπεκρίθη
πρὸς τὸ θῆλυ·   "Ὃν μὲν λέγεις Μεσσίαν,   ὃν οἱ
προφῆται
νῦν ἔρχεσθαι προεῖπον,   ὁρᾷς μὲν καὶ ἀκούεις   τῆς
φωνῆς αὐτοῦ.
Ἐγώ εἰμι ὃν βλέπεις,   ἐγώ εἰμι ὃν ἔχεις
ἐν μέσῳ τῆς καρδίας σου·
ἐγὼ ποθῶν σε ἤλυθα   σὲ ἑλκύσαι καὶ σῶσαι·
νῦν κήρυξον τοῖς πᾶσι   τοῖς θέλουσι σωθῆναι   ἐν τῇ
Συχὰρ τῇ πόλει,
τοῖς συγγενέσι   καὶ συμπολίταις
καὶ δεῦτε πάντες ἅμα   οἱ διψῶντες
ἀγαλλίασιν καὶ ἀπολύτρωσιν.

19

"Ἰδοὺ ἤντλησαι, γύναι,   ἐκ λάκκου ταλαιπωρίας·
ὁ μηδὲ ἄντλημα ἔχων   τὴν καρδίαν σου καθῆρα
ἄνευ ῥείθρου   καὶ ἀπέπλυνα τὸν νοῦν   ἄνευ ναμάτων·

If you are, as they said, speak freely to me,
for I see that in truth you know all I've done
and the secrets of my heart. So I beg you resolutely
that I may receive
jubilance and deliverance."

18

Now when the seer considered the wise one's speech
and the faithfulness of her heart, he replied directly
and said to the woman, "The one you call Messiah, whom
 the prophets foretold
would be coming, you are beholding; you're hearing his
 voice.
I am he, the one you see; it is I whom you hold
in the depth of your heart.
Since I longed for you I came to attract and to save you.
Proclaim this to all who wish to be saved in the city of
 Sychar,
to kinsfolk and townsfolk,
and come, all who thirst for
jubilance and deliverance!

19

"Look, woman, you've been drawn from a desolate pit.
Not even carrying a bucket, I have cleansed your heart,
without running water; I have washed your mind without
 any streams.

καὶ ᾤκισά σε θέλων,   καὶ ἔδειξα ὃ πέλω   καὶ οὐκ
                                                          ἔπιον."
Καὶ τούτων λεγομένων   ὁμοῦ καὶ τελουμένων,
οἱ μαθηταὶ ἐλήλυθαν·
οὐκ ἦσαν γάρ, ὡς γέγραπται,   πρὸς τὸ φρέαρ ἐν
                                                          τούτοις,
ἀλλ᾽ ἦλθον μετὰ ταῦτα   καὶ γνόντες ταῦτα πάντα
                                              ἐθαύμασαν βοῶντες·
"Ὦ τῆς ἀφάτου   φιλανθρωπίας·
γυναίῳ συγκατέβη   ὁ παρέχων
ἀγαλλίασιν καὶ ἀπολύτρωσιν."

20

Νευροῦται ἡ Σαμαρεῖτις   καὶ τρέχει πρὸς Σαμαρείτας,
καταλιποῦσα τὴν κάλπιν   καὶ λαβοῦσα ἐπὶ ὤμων
τῆς καρδίας   τὸν ἐτάζοντα νεφροὺς   καὶ τὰς καρδίας·
καὶ φθάσασα τὴν πόλιν,   ἐσάλπισε τοῖς πᾶσιν   οὕτως
                                                          κράζουσα·
"Πρεσβῦται μετὰ παίδων,   νεανίσκοι καὶ παρθένοι,
ἐπὶ τὸ φρέαρ δράμετε·
τὸ ὕδωρ ἐπεπόλευσε   καὶ προχεῖται τοῖς πᾶσιν·
ἐκεῖ κατεῖδον ἄνδρα,   ὃν οὐ χρὴ λέγειν 'ἄνδρα'·   Θεοῦ
                                              γὰρ ἔχει ἔργα
πάντα μοι λέγων   καὶ προφητεύων,
ὁ πάντας σῶσαι θέλων   καὶ παρέχων
ἀγαλλίασιν καὶ ἀπολύτρωσιν."

I've willingly come and dwelt in you, and shown who I am,
    yet I have not drunk."
And when these things were said and done,
the disciples came,
for, as is written, they were not near the well when this
    happened,
but arrived after. When they learned of it all, they marveled
    and cried,
"What ineffable loving-kindness! He abased himself
to a woman; he is offering
jubilance and deliverance."

20

Encouraged, the Samaritan woman runs to the Samaritans.
She leaves the pitcher, but on her heart's shoulders
she takes the one who examines human minds and hearts.
When she reaches the city, she trumpets loudly, calling to
    all,
"Elders and children, young men and maidens,
hurry to the well!
The water's flowed over and pours forth for all.
I saw a man there, or I shouldn't say 'man,' for his deeds are
    God's;
he spoke in prophesies and told me everything
and offered, as he wished to save everyone,
jubilance and deliverance."

21

Οὐδὲν ὅλως οὐκ εἶπον   οἱ κήρυκες τοῦ Σωτῆρος,
ὅτι συνόμιλον εὗρον   τῷ γυναίῳ τὸν ἐλθόντα
καὶ τεχθέντα   ἐκ παρθένου ἐπὶ γῆς   οἰκονομίᾳ·
τροφὰς γὰρ ἀπελθόντες   κομίσαι, εὗρον
                                    βρῶσιν   ἀγεώργητον,
διδοῦντα τοῖς αἰτοῦσι   τροφὴν ἀθανασίας·
πρὸς οὓς καὶ ἀπεκρίνατο·
"Ἐμὸν βρῶμα τὸ θέλημα   τοῦ Πατρός μου ὑπάρχει·
διὸ ἣν ἀγνοεῖτε   τροφὴν ἐγὼ ἐσθίω,   ἥπερ ἐσθιομένη
πᾶσι πηγάζει   πνοὴν τελείαν
καὶ πίστιν ἀναφαίρετον, διδοῦντα
ἀγαλλίασιν καὶ ἀπολύτρωσιν."

22

Συνῆλθε τῆς Σαμαρείας   τὸ πλῆθος ἐπὶ τὸν Πλάστην,
καταλιπόντα τοὺς οἴκους,   καὶ ἐδείχθησαν τῇ πίστει
ὥσπερ οἶκοι   τοῦ εἰπόντος ἐν γραφαῖς   ταῖς
                                    θεοπνεύστοις
ὡς λέγει· "Ἐνοικήσω   καὶ ἐμπεριπατήσω,"   καθὼς
                                    γέγραπται,
"ἐν οἴκοις τοιούτοις   καταλιποῦσι πάντα,
ἀγρούς, γονεῖς καὶ φίλτατα,
καὶ ἔσομαι αὐτῶν Θεὸς   καὶ σωτὴρ ἐκ παγίδων·

21

The heralds of the Savior did not say anything at all
when they found him consorting with the woman, he
who was born of a virgin in the earthly household.
Having gone to get something to eat, they found food no
     farmer produced,
feeding the needy with edible immortality.
And to them he said,
"My own food is the will of my Father;
so you do not know that which I eat. When it is eaten,
it gushes a perfect spirit for all
and indissoluble faith, which gives
jubilance and deliverance."

22

The crowd from Samaria gathered around the Maker.
They had left their houses, and appeared, in their faith,
as houses for the one who had spoken in divinely inspired
     scriptures,
when he said, "I will dwell and walk," as it is written,
"in those houses that have left all behind,
fields, parents, and loved ones.
I shall be their God and save them from snares;

αὐτοὶ δὲ ἔσονταί μοι   λαὸς ἡγιασμένος,   κατοίκησιν
                                                ποιοῦντες
τῇ ἀϊδίᾳ   καὶ ἀχωρίστῳ
Τριάδι τῇ ἀφθόνως   πηγαζούσῃ
ἀγαλλίασιν καὶ ἀπολύτρωσιν."

they will be to me a hallowed people, who make their
    dwelling
in the eternal, inseparable Trinity
that gushes abundant
jubilance and deliverance."

Προοίμιον

Ὡς ἡ αἱμόρρους   προσπίπτω σοι, Κύριε,
ὅπως τοῦ ἄλγους   με ῥύσῃ, φιλάνθρωπε,
καὶ πταισμάτων μοι   παράσχῃς συγχώρησιν,
ἵνα ἐν κατανύξει   καρδίας κραυγάζω σοι·
"Σῶτερ σῶσόν με."

I

πρός· Οἱ ἐν πάσῃ τῇ γῇ μαρτυρήσαντες

Ψάλλω σοι ἐν ᾠδαῖς, Ἄναξ ὕψιστε,   ὅτιπερ οὐ στερεῖς
με τῆς δόξης σου·
παρορᾷς μου γὰρ τὰ ἁμαρτήματα,   θέλων μετανοοῦντα
εὑρεῖν με,
ὑπάρχων φύσει ἀναμάρτητος·   ὅθεν λίττομαί σου ἐμοὶ
γενέσθαι
τὴν σὴν μακροθυμίαν εἰς ἐπιστροφὴν
καὶ μὴ εἰς καταφρόνησιν, ὅτι βοῶ·
"Σῶτερ σῶσόν με."

298

ON THE BLEEDING WOMAN

in fourth plagal mode

Prelude

to its own melody

As the bleeding woman, I fall down before you:
free me from suffering, compassionate Lord,
and grant me forgiveness for my mistakes,
so I may cry to you with a contrite heart,
"Healer, heal me!"

I

to: Those who testify in the whole world

I praise you in song, exalted King, for you do not deprive
    me of your glory.
You overlook my sins and want to see me repent,
as you are sinless by nature. I pray that your patience
may bring me to correction and not to contempt,
since I call out to you,
"Healer, heal me!"

2

Ἀφθαρσίας ποσὶν γῆς ἐπέβης νῦν   πᾶσι καταμερίζων
                                              ἰάματα·
πηροῖς γὰρ ἐδωρήσω ἀνάβλεψιν,   παρειμένοις δὲ
                                              ἔδωκας σύσφιγξιν
χειρὶ καὶ λόγῳ καὶ θελήματι·   οὕτως οὖν ἐπακούσασα ἡ
                                              αἱμόρρους
σοὶ προσῆλθε σωθῆναι, σιγῶσα φωνῇ,
τῇ παλάμῃ δὲ κράζουσά σοι ἐκτενῶς·
"Σῶτερ σῶσόν με."

3

Λανθανόντως, Σωτήρ, σοὶ προσήρχετο,   καὶ γὰρ
                                              ἄνθρωπον μόνον ἐνόμιζεν·
ἰωμένη δὲ ἐξεπαιδεύετο   ὅτι σὺ Θεὸς ἅμα καὶ ἄνθρωπος.
Λαθραίως ψαύει τοῦ κρασπέδου σου—τῇ παλάμῃ
                                              κρατοῦσα, ψυχῇ δειλιῶσα·
σὲ ἐνόμιζεν ἀποσυλᾶν τῇ χειρί,
ὑπὸ σοῦ ἐσυλήθη δὲ κράζουσά σοι·
"Σῶτερ σῶσόν με."

4

Μαθεῖν θέλεις σαφῶς πῶς σεσύληται   ὁ Σωτὴρ καὶ
                                              ἐσύλησεν, ἀκροατά;
Ὅπερ εἶχε ποιῆσαι ἠπίστατο   ἡ γυνή, καὶ σιγᾷ κλοπῆς
                                              ἕνεκα·

2

You set your incorruptible feet on the earth and distributed
    remedies to all.
The blind received sight, the paralyzed strength
at your hand, your word, your will alone. Thus the bleeding
    one heard
and came for your healing; her voice was silent,
yet she cried out with fervor, with the palm of her hand,
"*Healer, heal me!*"

3

She approached you furtively, Healer, and thought you were
    only a human,
but, cured, she learned and inferred that you are both God
    and human.
Secretly she touches your hem—her palm seizing, her soul
    trembling.
While she thought her hand was robbing you,
you robbed her, who was crying to you,
"*Healer, heal me!*"

4

Do you want to know, listener, just how the Healer robbed
    and was robbed?
The woman knew what she had to do and kept silent
    regarding the theft.

εἰ γὰρ ἐγνώρισεν, ἐμάνθανεν   ὁ ἐχθρὸς τὴν τῆς κόρης
σωτηρίαν
καὶ εἰς ἀπόγνωσιν ταύτην ἐνέβαλλε·
διὰ τοῦτο σιγῇ ὑπακούει αὐτῆς
"Σῶτερ σῶσόν με."

5

Οὐ γὰρ μόνον εἰκὸς ἐλογίζετο   ἡ αἱμόρρους καὶ ἔλεγε
καθ' ἑαυτήν·
"Πῶς ὀφθήσομαι τῷ παντεπόπτῃ μου   φέρουσα τὴν
αἰσχύνην πταισμάτων ἐμῶν;
Αἱμάτων ῥύσιν ὁ ἀμώμητος   ἐὰν ἴδῃ, χωρεῖ μου ὡς
ἀκαθάρτου,
καὶ δεινότερον ἔσται μοι τοῦτο πληγῆς,
ἐὰν ἀποστραφῇ με βοῶσαν αὐτῷ·
'Σῶτερ σῶσόν με.'

6

"Συνωθοῦσί με πάντες ὁρῶντές με,   'Ποῦ νυνὶ σὺ
προσέρχει;' βοῶντές μοι.
'Κατανόησον, γύναι, τὸ αἶσχός σου,   γνῶθι τίς τίνι
θέλεις ἐγγίσαι νυνί;
τῷ ἀμωμήτῳ ἡ ἀκάθαρτος;   Ἄπιθι καὶ καθάρθητι ἀπὸ
ῥύπου,
καὶ τὸν σπίλον τὸν σὸν ἀποσμήξασα,
τότε τούτῳ προσέρχει βοῶσα φωνῇ·
"Σῶτερ σῶσόν με."'

If she had told, the enemy would have learned of her
     healing
and driven her into despair.
Thus, in silence he grants her request,
"*Healer, heal me!*"

5

The bleeding woman not only wondered, but probably also
     said to herself,
"How will I be perceived by my all-seeing one, when I bear
     the shame of my faults?
If the unblemished one sees the flow of blood, he will avoid
     me as being unclean.
It will terrify me more than a blow
if he turns away when I cry to him,
'*Healer, heal me!*'

6

"When they see me, everyone crowds around me. 'Where
     are you going now?'
they're yelling. 'Consider your shame, woman! Don't you
     realize whom you want to approach?
The unclean to the unblemished? Go and purify yourself
     from filth,
and when you have wiped away your stain,
then go closer and call out with your voice,
"*Healer, heal me!*"'"

7

"Τοῦ ἐμοῦ πάθους τάχα βουλεύεσθε   χαλεπώτεροι,
                                   ἄνδρες, γενέσθαι μοι;
Μὴ γὰρ νῦν τῇ ἀγνοίᾳ κεκράτημαι;   Οἶδα ὅτι αὐτὸς
                                   καθαρός ἐστιν—
ὅθεν αὐτῷ καὶ προσελεύσομαι   τῶν ὀνειδισμῶν
                                   ῥυσθῆναι καὶ τῶν κηλίδων·
μὴ κωλύσητε οὖν ῥῶσιν δρέψασθαί με·
διό λίττομαι ἄφετε κράξαι ἐμέ·
'Σῶτερ σῶσόν με.'

8

"'Οὐ νοεῖς τί αἰτεῖς, γύναι· ἄπιθι,   μὴ ἡμεῖς ὑπὸ μέμψιν
                                   γενώμεθα.
Ἄν ἐάσωμέν σε, πάντες αἴτιοι   τῆς αὐτοῦ ἀτιμίας
                                   δεικνύμεθα·
ἐὰν δὲ πάλιν σε θεάσωνται   οἱ φοιτῶντες αὐτῷ νῦν
                                   προσιοῦσαν,
ὥσπερ καταφρονοῦντας μέμψονται ἡμᾶς
καὶ ὡς ἄφρονας κρινοῦσιν, ὅτι βοᾷς·
"Σῶτερ σῶσόν με."'

9

"'Ὑμεῖς, δύσμοροι, φθόνῳ κεκράτησθε,   ὅθεν ἐμὲ
                                   σωθῆναι οὐ βούλεσθε·
ἡ πηγὴ πᾶσι βλύζει τὰ νάματα·   χάριν τίνος αὐτὴν
                                   ἀποφράττετε;

7

"Perhaps you men want to be harsher on me than my
    suffering is?
I am not seized with ignorance, am I? I know he is pure—
that is why I'll approach him, to be delivered from insults
    and stains.
So do not hinder me from gathering my strength,
but, please, let me cry out,
'Healer, heal me!'

8

"'You do not know what you're asking, woman. Go away or
    we will be blamed.
If we were to let you, we'd all be found guilty of dishonoring
    him.
And if those who gather around him see that you are
    approaching,
they will condemn us as being contemptuous
and judge us idiots when you call out,
"Healer, heal me!"'

9

"You wretches are in the grip of envy and do not want me to
    be healed.
The streams gush from the spring for all. Why do you block
    it?

Ἰδοὺ προσέρχομαι τῷ Πλάστῃ μου,   καὶ ἐὰν θυμωθῇ
                                         οὔκ ἐστιν ὑπὸ μέμψιν·
ἐὰν δὲ σώσῃ με τῆς πληγῆς τῆς ἐμῆς,
τὴν αἰσχύνην κομίσησθε, ὅτι βοῶ·
'Σῶτερ σῶσόν με.'

10

"Καθορᾶτε αὐτοῦ τὰ ἰάματα,   καὶ τί τοὺς προσιόντας
                                         κωλύετε;
Καθ' ἑκάστην βοᾷ καὶ προτρέπεται·   Δεῦτε πρός με
                                 νῦν, οἱ κοπιῶντες κακοῖς·
ἐγὼ γὰρ ὑμᾶς ἀναπαύσοιμι.'   Χαίρει δῶρον διδοὺς πᾶσι
                                         τὴν ὑγείαν,
καὶ ὑμεῖς τί κεντᾶσθε κωλύοντές με,
ὡς προφάσει τιμῆς, μὴ βοῆσαι αὐτῷ·
'Σῶτερ σῶσόν με';

11

"'Υμῶν ὄμμασι τί ἐνεφάνησα;   Ῥῶσιν γὰρ ὡς οὐκ
                                         οἴδατε λήψομαι·
μὴ γὰρ μύσται ὑπάρχετε τοῦ Χριστοῦ;   Τί δὲ
                                 ἀκολουθεῖτε στυγοῦντες αὐτῷ;
Ὑμεῖς πτερνίζετε τὸν ἄχραντον·   ὅθεν ἀπόστητε, καὶ
                                         μόνος οὐκ ἔνι·
φθόνου, φόνου δυσοσμίαν πνέετε·
διὰ τοῦτο κωλύετέ με τοῦ βοᾶν·
'Σῶτερ σῶσόν με.'"

Look, I'm going to my Maker, and if he is angry, he is not to
    blame,
but if he heals the wound that I have,
you'll be left with the shame, for I am calling out,
'Healer, heal me.'

10

"You observe his remedies, so why hinder those who
    approach him?
Daily he calls and exhorts, 'Come to me, you who are weary
    from ills,
for I'll give you rest.' He enjoys bestowing the gift of health
on all, so why do you, as for the sake of honor,
bully and hinder me from calling to him,
'Healer, heal me'?

11

"Why have I let your eyes see? I will gain a strength you
    have never known.
Are you not the initiates of Christ? Then why follow him so
    grudgingly?
You are tripping up the undefiled one. But step aside. He is
    not alone!
Your breath reeks of envy, of murder;
that is why you prevent me from exclaiming,
'Healer, heal me!'"

12

Ῥήσεις ταύτας αἱμόρρους ἐλάλησε   τάχα πρὸς τοὺς
                                            σοβεῖν αὐτὴν θέλοντας,
καὶ λαθραίως κρασπέδου προσήψατο·   ὥσπερ ἄνθρωπον
                                            γὰρ ἐπειρᾶτο συλᾶν
τὸν τῇ θεότητι ἀκοίμητον·   ὅμως Χριστὸς ἠνέσχετο τοῦ
                                            κλαπῆναι
πρὶν ὁ κλέψας πλευρὰν ἐν Ἐδὲμ τοῦ Ἀδὰμ
καὶ μορφώσας τὴν κράξασαν νῦν ἐν κλοπῇ·
"Σῶτερ σῶσόν με."

13

Ὁ τὰ πάντα εἰδὼς πρὶν γενέσεως,   ὅστις πρὶν οὐκ
                                            ἠγνόει τί πέπονθε,
στραφεὶς εἶπε πρὸς τοὺς μαθητὰς αὐτοῦ·   "Τίς ἥψατο
                                            νῦν τοῦ κρασπέδου μου
καὶ ἔλαβεν ὅπερ ἠθέλησε;   Πῶς φυλάττετε οὖν τὸν
                                            θησαυρόν μου;
Γρηγορούντων ὑμῶν τῶν ἐμῶν μαθητῶν
μὴ κλαπεὶς ἐσυλήθην βοώσῃ χειρί·
'Σῶτερ σῶσόν με.'

14

"'Ὑπὸ τίνος αὐτὸ τοῦτο γέγονεν;   Ὑμεῖς γνῶναι
                                            ὀφείλετε, φίλοι μου·
νῦν ἐγνώρισα τὸ δραματούργημα,   νῦν ὑμῖν ἐκκαλύπτω
                                            τὸν κλέψαντα

12

Perhaps the bleeding woman spoke such words to those
    who wished to drive her away,
yet she secretly grasped his hem. She tried to rob him as a
    human
who in divinity is always wakeful. Still Christ accepted the
    theft,
he who stole once the rib of Adam in Eden
and shaped the woman who now stealthily cries,
"Healer, heal me!"

13

He who knows all before its beginning was not unaware of
    what had happened.
He turned to his disciples and said, "Who touched my hem
    just now
and took what they wanted? Is this how you guard my
    treasure?
While you kept watch to protect me from theft,
I was robbed, my disciples, by a hand calling out,
'Healer, heal me!'

14

"By whom was this done? You, my friends, should know.
I just disclosed the plot, and now I reveal to you who stole

δυνάμεις τρόπῳ πῶς ἐχρήσατο·   ἀφωνίᾳ προσῆλθεν ἐμοὶ
                                                                        βοῶσα
καὶ κρατοῦσα στολὴν ὥσπερ ἐπιστολήν,
θεραπείαν ἐδρέψατο κράζουσά μοι·
Ἀωτερ σῶσόν με.ʼ

15

"Ῥῶσιν ἔλαβεν ἡ προσελθοῦσά μοι,   δύναμιν ἐξ ἐμοῦ
                                                                        γὰρ ἐλήστευσεν·
τί μοι φθέγγει, ὦ Σίμων Βαριωνᾶ,   ὅτι ὄχλοι πολλοί με
                                                                        συνέχουσιν;
Οὐ ψαύουσί μου τῆς θεότητος·   αὕτη, ψαύσασα δὲ
                                                                        στολῆς ὁρωμένης,
θείας φύσεως σαφῶς ἐδράξατο
καὶ ὑγείαν ἐκτήσατο κράξασά μοι·
Ἀωτερ σῶσόν με.ʼ"

16

Ὡς κατεῖδεν δὲ ὅτι οὐκ ἔλαθεν,   ἡ γυνὴ ταῦτα
                                                                        συνελογίζετο,
φησὶν ὅτι "Ὀφθῶ τῷ Σωτῆρί μου   Ἰησοῦ, καθαρθεῖσα
                                                                        τοὺς σπίλους μου·
οὐκέτι φόβος γὰρ οὐκ ἔστι μοι·   τῇ βουλῇ γὰρ αὐτοῦ
                                                                        ἐξετέλεσα τοῦτο·
ὃ ἠθέλησε, τοῦτο καὶ ἔδρασα·
ἐν γὰρ πίστει προσῆλθον βοῶσα αὐτῷ·
Ἀωτερ σῶσόν με.ʼ

my powers, how she did it. She came to me, crying
     speechlessly,
and grabbed my robe like a request.
She snatched treatment by calling to me,
'Healer, heal me!'

15

"The woman who came to me gathered strength, stole
     power from me.
Why do you tell me, Simon son of Jonah, that great crowds
     surround me?
They don't touch my divinity, but she, who touched a visible
     robe,
clearly grasped my divine nature
and acquired health as she cried out to me,
'Healer, heal me!'"

16

Seeing she could not escape notice, the woman reasoned
     and said:
"I was seen by my Healer, Jesus; I was cleansed of my stains.
I am no longer afraid; by his will I carried this out.
What he intended, I accomplished;
in faith I approached him and cried,
'Healer, heal me!'

17

"Μὴ οὐκ ᾔδει ὁ Πλάστης ὃ ἔπραττον,   ἀλλ' ἠνέσχετό
                                   μου ὡς καὶ εὔσπλαγχνος·
μόνον ψαύσασα ῥῶσιν ἐτρύγησα,   ἐπειδήπερ ἡδέως
                                                        σεσύλητο.
Διὸ οὐ δέδοικα ὀφθῆναι νῦν   τῷ Θεῷ μου κηρύττουσα
                                                  ὅτι ἔστιν
ἰατρὸς ἀσθενῶν καὶ σωτὴρ τῶν ψυχῶν
καὶ δεσπότης τῆς φύσεως, ᾧπερ βοῶ·
'Σῶτερ σῶσόν με.'

18

"Ἀγαθῷ Ἰατρῷ σοι προσέφυγον   ἀπορρίψασά μου νῦν
                                              τὸ ὄνειδος.
Κατ' ἐμοῦ τὸν θυμὸν μὴ ἐγείρῃς σου,   μηδὲ τῇ
                                θεραπαίνῃ τῇ σῇ ὀργισθῇς·
ὃ γὰρ ἠθέλησας ἐτέλεσα·   πρὶν λογίσωμαι γὰρ ποιῆσαι
                                              τὸ δρᾶμα,
σὺ ὑπῆρχες συμβιβάζων με πρὸς αὐτό·
τὴν καρδίαν μου ᾔδεις κραυγάζουσάν σοι·
'Σῶτερ σῶσόν με.'"

19

"Νῦν νευρώθητι, γύναι, τῇ πίστει σου   θέλοντά με
                                συλήσασα· θάρσει λοιπόν·
οὐ γὰρ ἕνεκεν τοῦ ἐλεγχθῆναί σε   τούτων πάντων εἰς
                                        μέσον παρήγαγόν σε,

312

17

"As Maker, he knew what I had done, but, being merciful,
    he accepted me;
by touch alone, I gathered strength, while he was gladly
    robbed.
So I no longer fear to be seen by my God;
I proclaim him doctor of sufferers, healer of souls,
and master of nature, to whom I call out,
'*Healer, heal me!*'

18

"I fled to you, good Doctor, having thrown the reproach
    aside.
Don't rouse your fury against me, nor be angered by your
    servant.
I have done what you wanted. Before I considered
doing the deed, you arranged for me to do it.
You knew that my heart was crying to you,
'*Healer, heal me!*'"

19

"Be strong, woman! With your faith you robbed me, and I
    was willing. Take heart!
It was not to accuse you that I brought you into the midst
    of the crowd,

ἀλλ' ἵνα τούτους νῦν πιστώσωμαι   ὅτι συλούμενος
                                    χαίρω—οὐκ ἀπελέγχω·
ὅθεν ἔσο λοιπὸν ὑγιαίνουσα,
μέχρι τέλους τῆς νόσου σου κράζουσά μοι·
'Σῶτερ σῶσόν με.'

20

"Οὐ χειρὸς τῆς ἐμῆς τοῦτο ἔργον νῦν,   ἀλλὰ πίστεως
                                    τῆς σῆς τὸ κάτεργον·
πολλοὶ ἥψαντο γὰρ τοῦ κρασπέδου μου,   τῆς δυνάμεως
                                    δὲ οὐκ ἐπέτυχον,
ἐπειδὴ πίστιν οὐ προσήγαγον·   σὺ δὲ πίστει πολλῇ ἐμοῦ
                                    ἁψαμένη
τὴν ὑγείαν ἐδρέψω, ὅθεν σε νῦν
ἐπὶ πάντων προήγαγον, ἵνα βοᾷς·
'Σῶτερ σῶσόν με.'"

21

Υἱὲ τοῦ Θεοῦ ἀκατάληπτε,   δι' ἡμᾶς σαρκωθεὶς ὡς
                                    φιλάνθρωπος,
ὡς ἐκείνην αἱμάτων τὸ πρότερον,   οὕτως ἁμαρτημάτων
                                    με λύτρωσαι,
ὑπάρχων μόνος ἀναμάρτητος·   ταῖς εὐχαῖς καὶ
                                    πρεσβείαις τῶν ἁγίων
κλῖνόν μου τὴν καρδίαν, μόνε δυνατέ,
ἐπὶ τὸ μελετᾶν σου τοὺς λόγους ἀεί,
ἵνα σώσῃς με.

but to prove to them that I am glad to be robbed—
I do not refute it. So recover your health,
crying to me till your illness ends,
'Healer, heal me!'

20

"Now, this was not the act of my hand, but the work of your
　　　faith.
Many have touched my hem but not obtained power,
since they offered no faith; while you, who touched me with
　　　much,
snatched health. And thus I have brought you
before everybody, so you may call out
'Healer, heal me!'"

21

Ungraspable Son of God, who became flesh in compassion
　　　for us,
as you once saved the woman from bleeding, save me now
　　　from my sins,
you who alone are free from sin. By saintly prayers and
　　　intercessions,
you who alone are powerful, incline
my heart to meditate always on your words,
so you may heal me.

Προοίμιον

Ἰωακεὶμ καὶ Ἄννα   ὀνειδισμοῦ ἀτεκνίας,
καὶ Ἀδὰμ καὶ Εὖα   ἐκ τῆς φθορᾶς τοῦ θανάτου
ἠλευθερώθησαν, ἄχραντε,   ἐν τῇ ἁγίᾳ γεννήσει σου·
αὐτὴν ἑορτάζει   καὶ ὁ λαός σου,
ἐνοχῆς τῶν πταισμάτων   λυτρωθῆναι τῷ κράζειν σοι·
"Ἡ στεῖρα τίκτει   τὴν Θεοτόκον   καὶ τροφὸν τῆς ζωῆς
ἡμῶν."

I

Ἡ προσευχὴ   ὁμοῦ καὶ στεναγμὸς   τῆς στειρώσεως
καὶ ἀτεκνώσεως
Ἰωακείμ τε καὶ Ἄννης εὐπρόσδεκτος
καὶ εἰς ὦτα Κυρίου ἐλήλυθεν   καὶ ἐβλάστησε
καρπὸν   ζωηφόρον τῷ κόσμῳ·
ὁ μὲν γὰρ προσευχὴν   ἐν τῷ ὄρει ἐτέλει,
ἡ δὲ ἐν τῷ παραδείσῳ   ὄνειδος φέρει·
ἀλλὰ μετὰ χαρᾶς
ἡ στεῖρα τίκτει   τὴν Θεοτόκον   καὶ τροφὸν τῆς ζωῆς
ἡμῶν.

ON THE NATIVITY OF THE THEOTOKOS

Prelude

Joachim and Anna from childless disgrace,
Eve along with Adam from deadly decay,
all were delivered by your holy birth,
and your people, undefiled one, are celebrating too;
released from the debt of their wrongs they cry to you,
"The barren one bears the Mother of God and nurse of our life!"

1

Joachim and Anna's prayer with their groaning for their
    barren and childless state
was acceptable, and so it entered
the ears of the Lord and yielded the fruit of life to the
    world.
The husband performs his prayer on the mountain,
while she is carrying her disgrace in the garden,
but then with joy
the barren one bears the Mother of God and nurse of our life.

317

2

Ὦ τοκετὲ   τῆς Ἄννης ἀγαθέ,   πῶς ὑμνήσω σε ἢ πῶς
δοξάσω σε,
ὅτι ὑπάρχεις τεχθεὶς ναὸς ἅγιος;
Ἰωακεὶμ ἐν τῷ ὄρει ἱκέτευε   τὸν καρπὸν ἀπολαβεῖν   ἐκ
κοιλίας τῆς Ἄννης·
καὶ γίνεται δεκτὴ   ἡ εὐχὴ τοῦ ὁσίου,
καὶ μετὰ κυοφορίαν   ἡ μακαρία
ἐν τῷ κόσμῳ χαρά·
ἡ στεῖρα τίκτει   τὴν Θεοτόκον   καὶ τροφὸν τῆς ζωῆς
ἡμῶν.

3

Δῶρά ποτε   προσῆγεν ἐν ναῷ   καὶ ἀπρόσδεκτα ταῦτα
γεγόνασι,
τῶν ἱερέων μὴ θελόντων προσδέξασθαι
ὡς ἀτέκνου καὶ σπέρμα μὴ ἔχοντος·   καὶ ἐν τοῖς υἱοῖς
Ἰσραὴλ   Ἰωακεὶμ ἐβδελύχθη·
ἀλλ' ἦλθεν ἐν καιρῷ   καὶ προσάγει τὴν Παρθένον
σὺν δώροις εὐχαριστίας   ἅμα τῇ Ἄννῃ,
ὅτι χαίρουσα νῦν
ἡ στεῖρα τίκτει   τὴν Θεοτόκον   καὶ τροφὸν τῆς ζωῆς
ἡμῶν.

2

How can I praise you, how can I extol you, Anna's noble
    offspring,
for you are born a holy temple?
On the mountain Joachim begged for fruit from Anna's
    womb,
and the prayer of the holy man is pleasing,
and after the pregnancy, the blessed joy
appears in the world:
the barren one bears the Mother of God and nurse of our life.

3

Joachim once offered gifts in the temple, yet they were not
    acceptable.
The priests were unwilling to receive them from a childless
man without seed, and he was despised among the sons of
    Israel.
But when the right time comes, he offers the Virgin
with gifts of thanksgiving, and Anna is with him,
for now she rejoices,
the barren one bears the Mother of God and nurse of our life.

4

Ἤκουσαν οὖν   φυλαὶ τοῦ Ἰσραὴλ   ὅτι ἔτεκεν Ἄννα τὴν
ἄχραντον,
καὶ εὐφροσύνῃ αἱ πᾶσαι συνέχαιρον·
πότον Ἰωακεὶμ ἐποίησε   καὶ ηὐφραίνετο λαμπρῶς   ἐπὶ
τῷ παραδόξῳ·
καλέσας εἰς εὐχὴν   ἱερεῖς καὶ Λευίτας
καὶ τὴν Μαρίαν μέσον   ἤγαγε πάντων
ὅπως μεγαλυνθῇ·
ἡ στεῖρα τίκτει   τὴν Θεοτόκον   καὶ τροφὸν τῆς ζωῆς
ἡμῶν.

5

Ῥεῖθρον ζωῆς   ἐξέβλυσας ἡμῖν   ἡ τραφῆναι δοθεῖσα εἰς
ἅγια
καὶ τὴν ἀγγέλου τροφὴν ἀπολαύσασα,
ἐν ἁγίοις ἁγία ὑπάρχουσα,   ὡς ὡρίσθη, καὶ ναὸς   καὶ
δοχεῖον Κυρίου.
Αἱ παρθένοι τὴν Παρθένον   προσῆγον μετὰ λαμπάδων
τὸν Ἥλιον τυποῦσαι,   ὅνπερ προσφέρειν
ἤμελλε τοῖς πιστοῖς·
ἡ στεῖρα τίκτει   τὴν Θεοτόκον   καὶ τροφὸν τῆς ζωῆς
ἡμῶν.

4

Israel's tribes heard that Anna had borne the undefiled one,
and all were congratulating her with joy.
Joachim hosted a party and celebrated the wonder with
    splendor.
He called priests and Levites to prayer
and led Mary into their midst
to be magnified thus:
The barren one bears the Mother of God and nurse of our life.

5

You released a stream of life for us, you who were nurtured
    in holy places
and there enjoyed an angel's nourishment.
You are holy among the holy, as ordained, and a temple and
    a vessel of the Lord.
Virgins led the Virgin with lamps
prefiguring the Sun, the one she was going
to offer the faithful.
The barren one bears the Mother of God and nurse of our life.

6

"Ὦ μυστικὸν   τελούμενον ἐν γῇ".   μετὰ τόκον ἡ Ἄννα
                                                    ἐβόησε
πρὸς τὸν προγνώστην Ποιητὴν καὶ Θεὸν ἡμῶν·
"Εἰσήκουσάς μου, Δέσποτα,   ὥσπερ τῆς Ἄννης τοῦ
                                        Ἠλὶ   μεμφομένου ἐν μέθῃ·
αὕτη τὸν Σαμουὴλ   ὑπέσχετο τεχθέντα
Κυρίῳ ἱερατεύειν·   σὺ οὖν ὡς πρώην
ἐδωρήσω κἀμοί·
ἡ στεῖρα τίκτει   τὴν Θεοτόκον   καὶ τροφὸν τῆς ζωῆς
                                                    ἡμῶν.

7

"Μέγα μοι νῦν   ὑπάρχει, ἀγαθέ,   ὅτι τέτοκα παῖδα τὴν
                                                    τίκτουσαν
τὸν πρὸ αἰώνων Δεσπότην καὶ Κύριον,
τὸν μετὰ τόκον φυλάττοντα   τὴν μητέρα
                                        ἑαυτοῦ   ὥσπερ ἔστι παρθένον·
αὐτὴν ἐν τῷ ναῷ   προσφέρω σοι, οἰκτίρμων·
αὐτὴ καὶ πύλη σὴ ἔσται   τοῦ ἐξ ὑψίστων,
ἥνπερ μετὰ χαρᾶς
ἡ στεῖρα τίκτει,   τὴν Θεοτόκον   καὶ τροφὸν τῆς ζωῆς
                                                    ἡμῶν.

6

"Oh, mystical accomplishment on earth!" Anna exclaimed,
    after the birth,
to our foreknowing Maker and God:
"You have heard me, Master, like the Anna whom Eli
    accused of drunkenness.
She promised Samuel to the Lord as a priest
when he was born. Like her, I have now
received your gift:
The barren one bears the Mother of God and nurse of our life.

7

"It is great for me, that I've given birth to the child who
    gives birth, noble one,
to the Lord and Master before the ages,
who protects his mother in his own childbirth so that she is
    a virgin.
Her I offer to you in the temple, compassionate one,
and she'll be your gate when you come from on high,
she whom in joy
the barren one bears, the Mother of God and nurse of our life.

8

"Ἀρά ποτε   καὶ Σάρρα ἡ πιστὴ   ἐπεθύμει γεννῆσαι
                                            στειρεύουσα
πρὶν ἢ τεχθῆναι Ἰσαὰκ τὸν υἱὸν αὐτῆς;
Αὕτη μὲν θεὸν ὑπεδέξατο   ἐν ἀνθρωπίνη μορφῇ   σὺν
                                            δυσὶν ἀρχαγγέλοις,
καὶ λόγος πρὸς αὐτὴν   Εἰς τὸν καιρὸν τοῦτον
τῇ Σάρρᾳ ἔσται τέκνον.'   Νῦν δὲ τῷ κόσμῳ
χαίρουσα ἐκβοᾷ·
'Ἡ στεῖρα τίκτει   τὴν θεοτόκον   καὶ τροφὸν τῆς ζωῆς
                                            ἡμῶν.'"

9

Νῦν Μαριὰμ   ἐκλάμπει τοῖς καιροῖς   καὶ ναὸν τῶν
                                            ἁγίων οὐκ ἔλιπεν·
ἣν Ζαχαρίας θεωρῶν ὑπερακμάζουσαν
μνηστῆρα λαχμῷ καθυπέβαλεν   Ἰωσὴφ τὸν ἐκ
                                            Θεοῦ   μνηστευσάμενον ταύτην·
ἐδόθη γὰρ αὐτῷ   ἐν ῥάβδῳ δηλωθεῖσα
ἐκ Πνεύματος Ἁγίου,   δι' ἣν καὶ Ἄννα
χαίρουσα ἐκβοᾷ·
"Ἡ στεῖρα τίκτει   τὴν θεοτόκον   καὶ τροφὸν τῆς ζωῆς
                                            ἡμῶν."

8

"Did not the faithful yet barren Sarah also once long to have
    children,
before her son Isaac was born?
And she received God, in human form, with two
    archangels,
and a word in reply: 'At this time Sarah
shall have a child.' Now, to the world
she rejoices and cries,
'*The barren one bears the Mother of God and nurse of our life!*'"

9

Mary shone with time and never left the temple of the holy
    ones.
When Zechariah saw her in full bloom,
he assigned her Joseph by lot as betrothed, the one
    entrusted with her by God.
She was given to him, revealed in a rod
by the Holy Spirit. For her also Anna
rejoices and cries,
"*The barren one bears the Mother of God and nurse of our life!*"

10

Ὅλος σεπτὸς   ὁ τόκος σου, σεμνή·   τοῦ γὰρ κόσμου τὸ
                                              καύχημα ἔτεκες
καὶ τῶν ἀνθρώπων πρεσβείαν εὐπρόσδεκτον·
αὐτὴ γὰρ τεῖχος καὶ στήριγμα   καὶ λιμὴν τῶν ἐπ’
                                  αὐτῇ   πεποιθότων ὑπάρχει,
ἣν πᾶς Χριστιανὸς   ἔχει προστασίαν
καὶ σκέπην σωτηρίας   καὶ ἐλπίδα,
ἥνπερ ἐκ τῆς γαστρὸς
ἡ στεῖρα τίκτει,   τὴν Θεοτόκον   καὶ τροφὸν τῆς ζωῆς
                                              ἡμῶν.

11

Ὕψιστε Θεέ,   ὁ πάντων Πλαστουργός,   ὁ τῷ Λόγῳ
                                              ποιήσας τὰ σύμπαντα
καὶ σῇ Σοφίᾳ σκευάσας τὸν ἄνθρωπον,
αὐτὸς ὡς μόνος φιλάνθρωπος   τὴν σὴν εἰρήνην σῷ
                                  λαῷ   ὡς οἰκτίρμων παράσχου,
φυλάττων βασιλεῖς   πιστούς, σὺν τῷ ποιμένι
ἀτάραχον τὴν ποίμνην   φρουρῶν καὶ σκέπων,
ἵνα πᾶς τις βοᾷ·
"Ἡ στεῖρα τίκτει   τὴν Θεοτόκον   καὶ τροφὸν τῆς ζωῆς
                                              ἡμῶν."

10

Your offspring is wholly sacred, noble one; you bore the
    boast of the world
and a welcome advocate on behalf of humans.
She is a wall and support and a harbor for those who trust in
    her,
she whom each Christian has as protection,
both a shelter of salvation and a hope
whom, from the womb,
the barren one bears, the Mother of God and nurse of our life.

11

God most high, the Fashioner of all, who composed the
    whole world by the Word,
who with your Wisdom enrobed humanity,
as the only benevolent one, grant your peace to your
    people, for you are compassionate,
guard the faithful rulers, with the shepherd
watch and protect the flock undisturbed,
so everyone may cry,
"The barren one bears the Mother of God and nurse of our life!"

Προοίμιον

ἰδιόμελον

Ὅτι οὐκ ἔστιν ὡς σὺ ἐλεήμων
ἔγνωμεν, Κύριε, ἀφ' οὗ ἐτέχθης
καὶ υἱὸς ὠνομάσθης   γυναικὸς ἣν ἐποίησας,
ἣν μακαρίζοντες   καθ' ἑκάστην βοῶμεν·
"Χαῖρε, νύμφη ἀνύμφευτε."

I

ἰδιόμελον

Τῷ ἀρχαγγέλῳ Γαβριὴλ   δεῦτε καὶ
        συμπορευθῶμεν   πρὸς τὴν Παρθένον Μαρίαν
καὶ ταύτην ἀσπασώμεθα   ὡς μητέρα   καὶ τροφὸν τῆς
                                                    ζωῆς ἡμῶν·
οὔτε γὰρ μόνῳ πρέπον   τῷ στρατηγῷ   τὴν βασιλίδα
                                                    ἀσπάσασθαι,
ἀλλὰ καὶ τοῖς ταπεινοῖς   ἔξεστι ταύτην ἰδεῖν καὶ
                                                    προφθέγξασθαι,
ἣν ὡς Μητέρα Θεοῦ   αἱ γενεαὶ πᾶσαι   μακαρίζουσαι
                                                    βοῶσι·

ON THE ANNUNCIATION

in first mode

Prelude

to its own melody

That no one is merciful like you, Lord,
we learned when you were born
and were called the son of a woman you created,
the one we call blessed, as daily we cry,
"*Hail, unwedded bride!*"

I

to its own melody

Come, let us follow the archangel Gabriel to Mary the
    Virgin
and greet her as the mother and nurse of our life!
It is right not only for the general to greet the empress,
but even the humble are able to see and salute her,
she whom all peoples call blessed as Mother of God, and
    cry,

"Χαῖρε, ἀκήρατε,   χαῖρε, κόρη θεόκλητε,
χαῖρε, σεμνή,   χαῖρε, τερπνὴ καὶ καλή,
χαῖρε, εὔειδε,   χαῖρε, ἄσπορε,   χαῖρε ἄφθορε,
χαῖρε, μῆτερ ἄνανδρε,
χαῖρε, νύμφη ἀνύμφευτε."

2

Ὁ ἀρχιστράτηγός ποτε   τῶν οὐρανίων
                    ταγμάτων   σύνθημα φιλανθρωπίας
δεξάμενος, ἐπείγετο   ἐμφανίσαι   τῇ Παρθένῳ, ὡς
                                        γέγραπται·
καὶ ἐλθὼν εἰς Ναζαρὲτ   πρὸς τὴν σκηνὴν   τοῦ Ἰωσὴφ
                                        ἐξεπλήττετο,
ὅτι πῶς ὁ ὑψηλὸς   τοῖς ταπεινοῖς ἀγαπᾷ συνεπάγεσθαι·
"Ὅλος," φησίν, "ὁ οὐρανὸς   καὶ ὁ πύρινος θρόνος   οὐ
                              χωρεῖ μου τὸν Δεσπότην·
καὶ ἡ εὐτελὴς   αὕτη πῶς ὑποδέχεται;
ἄνω φρικτὸς   καὶ κάτω πῶς ὁρατός;
πάντως ὡς βούλεται·   τί οὖν ἵσταμαι   καὶ οὐχ ἵπταμαι
καὶ τῇ κόρῃ φθέγγομαι·
'Χαῖρε, νύμφη ἀνύμφευτε';"

3

Ὑπὸ τὴν σκέπην τῆς σεμνῆς   ταῦτα λαλήσας,
                    εἰσῆλθε   τῶν οὐρανῶν ὁ οἰκήτωρ
καὶ πρόσειπε τὴν ἄγαμον   λέγων· "Χαῖρε·   μετὰ σοῦ ὁ
                                        Κύριος."

"Hail, untouched one, hail, divinely summoned maiden,
hail, noble one, hail, delightful and fair,
hail, beautiful one, hail, unseeded one, hail, you without
    corruption,
hail, mother without man,
hail, unwedded bride!"

2

The commander in chief of the heavenly ranks received a
    benevolence signal
and hurried, as is written, to appear before the Virgin,
but when he arrived in Nazareth, at Joseph's hovel, he was
    stunned
that the exalted one could enjoy consorting with the
    humble.
"The whole heaven," he says, "and the fiery throne cannot
    contain my Master,
so how may this simple girl conceive him?
How can he be frightful on high, yet visible below?
But in any event—as he wishes! So why do I stay and not fly,
and proclaim to the maiden,
'*Hail, unwedded bride*'?"

3

Having said this, the one who lives in heaven entered her
    house
and addressed the holy unmarried one: "Hail, the Lord is
    with you!"

331

ἡ δὲ παῖς πρὸς τὴν μορφὴν   τοῦ φαεινοῦ   οὐδὲ ὅλως
                                                    ἐθάρρησεν,
ἀλλ' εὐθὺς ἐπὶ τὴν γῆν   ἔκλινε τὴν κεφαλὴν καὶ
                                                    ἡσύχασε·
νοῦν δὲ συνῆψεν εἰς νοῦν   καὶ φρένα εἰς
                            φρένα   συμβιβάζει ἐκβοῶσα·
"Τί ἐστι τοῦτο   ὅπερ βλέπω; τί σκέψομαι;
εἶδος πυρός,   φωνὴν δὲ ἔχει ἀνδρὸς
ὁ παριστάμενος,   καὶ ταράττει με   καὶ θαρρύνει με
ὅτι τοῦτο λέγει μοι·
'Χαῖρε, νύμφη ἀνύμφευτε.'"

4

Τοιαύτην ὕλην λογισμῶν   τῆς Μαρίας
                        στοιβαζούσης   ἐν τῇ ἰδίᾳ καρδίᾳ,
ἐνέπνευσεν ὁ πύρινος   καὶ ὡς χαίτην   τὴν δειλίαν
                                                    κατέκαυσε
καί φησι· "Ὦ φαεινή,   μὴ πτοηθῇς·   εὗρες γὰρ χάριν
                                        πρὸς Κύριον·
μὴ πτοοῦ τὸν λειτουργόν·   τὸν Πλαστουργὸν γὰρ ἥκω
                                        φέρων σοι·
μέλλεις γεννᾶν υἱόν,   καὶ τί σε ταράττει   ἡ πυρίνη ἰδέα
                                                    μου;
τίκτεις τὸν Κύριον,   τί πτοεῖσαι τὸν σύνδουλον;
τί δειλιᾷς   ἐμὲ τὸν τρέμοντά σε
διὰ τὰ μέλλοντα   ἃ πεπίστευμαι καὶ τεθάρρημαι;
ταῦτα ἦλθον λέγων σοι·
'Χαῖρε, νύμφη ἀνύμφευτε.'"

Facing his radiant figure, the girl was not bold;
she immediately bowed her head to the ground and kept
    quiet.
Meaning she tied to meaning, thought she joined to
    thought and exclaimed,
"What am I seeing? What shall I think?
The one before me has the appearance of fire,
yet the voice of a man; he both stirs me and spurs me
when he says this to me:
'*Hail, unwedded bride!*'"

4

These were the matters piling up in Mary's heart
when the fiery one breathed, burning her worries like
    leaves.
He said, "Do not be alarmed, radiant one; you've found
    favor with the Lord.
Don't let his servant alarm you; I have brought you the
    Maker;
you are about to bear a son, so why does my fiery
    appearance agitate you?
You are giving birth to the Lord; why be alarmed by your
    fellow servant?
Why do you fear me, who trembles before you,
on account of the things to come, entrusted and confided
    to me,
for which I have come to say to you,
'*Hail, unwedded bride*'?"

5

Ἀλλ' ὅτε τούτων τῶν λόγων ἤκουσεν ἡ
                     παναγία, εἶπεν ἐν τῇ διανοίᾳ·
"Τὰ πρότερα ἤκουσα καὶ οὐ συνῆκα· καὶ πῶς μάθω
                     τὰ ὕστερα;
ἀσπασμὸν εἶπεν ἐμοὶ ὁ παρεστώς, καὶ οὐ νοῶ τὸ
                     τελούμενον·
καὶ ἰδού, ἄλλο φρικτὸν ἐν τοῖς ὠσί μου ἐπέθηκεν·
εἶπε γὰρ ὅτι· 'Υἱὸν βαστάζεις καὶ τίκτεις'· καίτοι
                     ἄνδρα οὐ γινώσκω.
τάχα οὐκ ἔμαθεν οὗτος ὅτι ἐσφράγισμαι;
ἆρα ἀγνοεῖ ὅτι παρθένος εἰμί;
ὄντως οὐ πείθομαι· εἰ μὴ ἔμαθε καὶ κατέμαθεν,
οὐκ ἂν ἦλθε λέγων μοι·
'Χαῖρε, νύμφη ἀνύμφευτε.'

6

"Πῶς ἔσται τοῦτο ὃ λαλεῖς; φράσον μοι νῦν ὃ
                     ὑπάρχεις· ἄγγελον ἢ ἄνθρωπον εἴπω;
οὐράνιον ἢ γήϊνον; δίδαξόν με, καὶ ὃ εἶ καὶ ὃ εἴρηκας·
ἐὰν γὰρ φθάσω μαθεῖν τίς ὁ λαλῶν, πάντως νοῶ τὸ
                     λαλούμενον·
καὶ διὰ τοῦτο φράσον μοί· πόθεν εἶ; ἄνωθεν ἦλθες ἢ
                     κάτωθεν;
ἔλαβον θάρσος λοιπόν· πολλὴν παρρησίαν κεκτημένη
                     συζητῶ σοι·

5

But when she heard this, the all-holy maiden said to herself,
"I've heard what he said but don't understand it; so what of
his next words?
He stood there and gave me his greeting, but I am not sure
what it leads to.
And look, he's given my ears another shock,
for he said, 'You'll carry and bear a son'; yet I know no man.
Has he maybe not heard that I am sealed?
Is he unaware that I am a virgin?
I can hardly believe that; had he not known and grasped it,
he would not have come and addressed me,
'*Hail, unwedded bride!*'

6

"How can this be? Tell me what you are. Angel or human?
From heaven or earth? And explain who you are and what
you have said!
If I learn first who's speaking, then I shall certainly grasp
what you say.
So tell me where you are from, above or below?
I've grown bolder, with freedom to speak; let me speak with
you now:

τοῦτο ὃ εἴρηκας   ποῦ ἐρρέθη μὴ κρύψῃς μοι·
ἐν οὐρανῷ   ἐρρέθη τὸ κατ' ἐμέ;
τί οὖν οὐ λέγεις μοι   ὅτι ἄγγελος   καὶ οὐκ ἄνθρωπος
πέλεις σὺ ὁ λέγων μοι·
'Χαῖρε, νύμφη ἀνύμφευτε';"

7

Εὐθὺς ἀκούσας Γαβριὴλ   τῶν τῆς παρθένου
                    ῥημάτων   πρὸς ἑαυτὸν ἐταράχθη·
οὐ μέντοι γε ἐλάλησε   σκληρὸν ῥῆμα   τῇ τικτούσῃ τὸν
                                      Κύριον·
ἀλλ' αὐτὸς καθ' ἑαυτὸν   οὕτω φησίν·   "Οὐδὲ ὧδε
                                      πιστεύομαι,
ἀλλ' ὡς πρὶν ἐν τῷ ναῷ   νῦν ἐν τῷ οἴκῳ τῆς κόρης
                                      ἠπίστημαι·
ἴσως ἐδίστασεν ἐκεῖ ὁ Ζαχαρίας,   καὶ ἐνταῦθα ἡ Μαρία·
ὅμως οὐ δύναμαι,   οὐ τολμῶ ἀποφήνασθαι,
οὐχ ἱκανῶ   ταύτης δεσμεῦσαι φωνὴν
ὡς τὴν τοῦ γέροντος·   τότε ἴσχυσα   καὶ ἐφίμωσα,
νῦν δὲ τρέμων φθέγγομαι·
'Χαῖρε, νύμφη ἀνύμφευτε.'

8

"'Ιδοὺ κωφὸς ὁ ἱερεύς,   καὶ κυοφόρος ἡ στεῖρα,   καὶ
                                      Μαρία ἀπιστεῖ μοι·
καὶ τίς εἰμι καὶ τί λαλῶ   ἀπαιτεῖ με,   καὶ μὴ θέλων
                                      ἀνέχομαι,

336

What you have told me, do not conceal where it was
    decreed.
Was that decreed about me in heaven?
Why don't you tell me that you are an angel,
not a human, who says to me,
'*Hail, unwedded bride*'?"

7

When Gabriel heard the words of the Virgin he was
    instantly unsettled;
he had certainly not said anything harsh to her who would
    birth the Lord.
But he said to himself, "I am not believed here either.
No, I am distrusted; as before in the temple, so now in this
    maiden's house.
Zechariah was hesitant there, and likewise Mary in this
    place;
still I cannot, I dare not tell her off,
I am not able to fetter her voice,
as I did with the old man; then I was strong and muzzled
    him,
now I am trembling as I say,
'*Hail, unwedded bride!*'

8

"Look, the priest is mute, the barren woman pregnant, but
    Mary doesn't believe me!
And she's asking who I am and what I'm saying! Against my
    will I endure this,

337

ἵνα μὴ ὁ ἐν αὐτῇ   ἐπιδημῶν   ἀγανακτῶν ἀπολέσῃ με,
ὥς ποτε ἀπ᾽ οὐρανῶν   πταίσαντας ἀγγέλους εἰς Ἅιδην
                                  ἔρριψεν·
στέργω οὖν ἐγκαρτερῶν   καὶ τῇ συζητούσῃ   τὴν
                                ἀπόκρισιν δίδωμι"·
"Πῶς ἔσται τοῦτο,   ὅπερ λέγω, ἀμώμητε;
πῶς τῷ λαῷ   θάλασσα ὤφθη ξηρὰ
πάλιν δὲ θάλασσα;   οὕτως γίνεται   καὶ ἡ μήτρα σου,
ἵνα πᾶς τις λέξῃ σοι·
ʽΧαῖρε, νύμφη ἀνύμφευτε.᾽"

9

Νοῆσαι θέλουσα σαφῶς   τὸ λαληθὲν ἡ ἁγία   πάλιν
                                βοᾷ τῷ ἀγγέλῳ·
"Τὴν θάλασσαν ἣν ἔφης μοι,   ὁ προφήτης   ἐν τῇ
                                ῥάβδῳ διέρρηξεν·
οὐδὲ γὰρ δίχα τινὸς   τοῦ μεταξὺ   τοῦτο τὸ θαῦμα
                                ἐγένετο·
ἀλλὰ ἦν πρῶτος Μωσῆς,   ἔπειτα εὐχαὶ καὶ ῥάβδος
                                μεσάζουσα.
νῦν εἰς μέσον οὐδέν·   καὶ πῶς ἔσται   ἐπεὶ ἄνδρα οὐ
                                γινώσκω;
Ἡ ἀναρότρευτος   ἄρουρα ἀγεώργητος,
δώσω καρπὸν   μὴ δεξαμένη σπορὰν
μηδὲ τὸν σπείραντα;   τοῦτο λέξον μοι,   τοῦτο φράσον
                                μοι,
ὁ ἑστὼς καὶ λέγων μοι·
ʽΧαῖρε, νύμφη ἀνύμφευτε.᾽"

so that he who resides in her does not destroy me in anger,
as he once threw the fallen angels from the heavens down
    to Hades.
I am happy to persevere, then, and give my questioner her
    answer":
"How can this be, all I have said, unblemished one?
How did the sea appear dry to the people,
and then again sea? Thus it will be with your womb as well,
so that everyone may say to you,
'*Hail, unwedded bride!*'"

9

Wanting to get a clearer sense of what he meant, the Virgin
    replies:
"The sea that you mentioned the prophet split apart with
    his rod.
This wonder did not happen without some intermediary
    tool.
First there was Moses, and then there were prayers and a
    rod was inserted.
Now there is nothing going in, and how can there be when I
    do not know man?
How will I, the unplowed and untilled field,
give fruit when I have not received seed,
and not even its sower? Tell me this, explain it to me,
you who stand and say to me,
'*Hail, unwedded bride!*'"

10

Ὁ ἐν ὑψίστοις θαρρηθεὶς   τὸν ἀσπασμόν, οὐ τὸν
                                  τόκον   τῆς παναγίας Μαρίας,
ὡς ἤκουσεν ὃ ἔφησεν   ἡ Παρθένος,   πρὸς αὐτὴν
                                       ἀπεκρίνατο·
"Ἐπειδὴ ἔφης, σεμνή,   μέσον τινὰ   ἔχειν τὰ πάλαι
                                       γενόμενα,
τὸ παρὸν μεῖζόν ἐστιν·   ὅθεν οὐκ ἔστι χρεία
                                       μεσιτεύοντος·
ἄγγελος πέλω ἐγὼ   καὶ οὐκ ἐθαρρήθην   μεσιτεῦσαι τὸ
                                       τοιοῦτον·
πῶς οὖν ταλαίπωρος   ἄνθρωπος μεσιτεύσει σοι;
ῥάβδος ποτὲ   καὶ ὁ προφήτης Μωσῆς
τύποι τούτων ἐγένοντο·   νῦν ἀλήθεια   ἐπιλάμψει σοι·
ὅθεν ἦλθον λέγων σοι·
Χαῖρε, νύμφη ἀνύμφευτε.'"

11

"Ὑψόθεν ἦλθες ἀληθῶς   —σύγγνωθι, νῦν σε
                          ἐπέγνων·   φόβῳ γὰρ νῦν συνεσχέθην
τοῦ κάλλους σου, τῆς θέας σου,   τῆς φωνῆς
                          σου   διαφόρως θροούντων με·
εἰ μὴ γὰρ ἄνωθεν ἦς,   τὰ τῆς γραφῆς   ῥήματα οὐ
                                       διερμήνευες,
ἀλλ' ὡς ὢν ἐκ τοῦ φωτὸς   πάντα τὰ σκολιὰ ἐξωμάλισας·
γένοιτο οὖν τοῦτό μοι   ὅπερ εἶπας ἄρτι·   τὴν γὰρ
                                       ἀλήθειαν ἔχεις·

10

He who was entrusted in the highest with the embrace but
    not with her offspring,
heard what the all-holy Mary was saying and answered,
"You said, noble Virgin, that the events of the past needed a
    tool,
yet the present is greater, for it needs no intermediary.
I am an angel, and have not been entrusted to act as
    intermediary.
So how could a miserable human intermediate?
The rod back then and the prophet Moses
were prefiguring all this. Now truth is making you shine.
It's for this I came and said to you,
'*Hail, unwedded bride!*'"

11

"You really have come from on high—forgive me; I see now!
    I was seized by fear
of your beauty, your looks, your voice; they completely
    terrified me.
Were you not from above, you would not have interpreted
    words of scripture,
but being from light you straightened out all that was
    tangled.
Let it be for me, then, as you've just said, for you hold the
    truth!

γένοιτό μοι, ἄγγελε, γένοιτό μοι τὸ ῥῆμα σου·
δούλη εἰμὶ τοῦ ἀποστείλαντός σε·
φράσον ἃ βούλεται, καὶ οἰκήσει μοι καὶ τηρήσει με,
ἵνα πᾶς τις λέξῃ μοι·
'Χαῖρε, νύμφη ἀνύμφευτε.'"

12

Ῥυθμῷ λαλήσας Γαβριὴλ καὶ ἀντακούσας εὐθέως τῶν
                                                    τῆς παρθένου ῥημάτων,
ἀνίπταται καὶ ἔφθασε τὸ πύρινον καὶ φαιδρὸν
                                                              ἐνδιαίτημα·
ἡ δὲ παῖς τότε ἴσως πρὸς ἑαυτὴν τὸν Ἰωσὴφ
                                                        μετεπέμψατο
καί φησι· "Ποῦ ἦς, σοφέ; πῶς οὐκ ἐφύλαξας τὴν
                                                      παρθενίαν μου;
ἦλθεν γάρ τις πτερωτὸς καὶ ἔδωκε μοι
                                  μνῆστρα, μαργαρίτας τοῖς ὠσί μου·
οὗτος ἐνεῖρέ μοι λόγους ὥσπερ ἐνώτια·
βλέπε, ἰδὲ πῶς ἐκαλλώπισέ με
τούτῳ ὡραΐσας με, ὅτι ἔφη μοι ὅτι λέξεις μοι
μετ' ὀλίγον, ὅσιε·
'Χαῖρε, νύμφη ἀνύμφευτε.'"

Let it be for me, angel, according to your word!
I am the servant of the one who has sent you;
explain what he wishes, and how he'll dwell in and safeguard
    me,
so everyone will say to me,
'*Hail, unwedded bride!*'"

12

When he had spoken in due measure and immediately
    heard the Virgin's replies,
Gabriel flew off and reached his fiery and shining abode.
And then, perhaps, the girl summoned Joseph and said,
"Where were you, wise man? How did you not guard my
    virginity?
Someone with wings came with pearls for my ears as a gift
    of betrothal;
he hung his words on me like earrings.
Look, see how beautiful he has made me,
how he's adorned me like this! He said that you'd say to me
in a short while, holy one,
'*Hail, unwedded bride!*'"

13

Ὡς δὲ κατεῖδεν Ἰωσὴφ   τὴν θεοκόσμητον κόρην   μάλα
κεχαριτωμένην,
ἐτρόμασεν, ἐθαύμασεν,   ἐθαμβήθη   καὶ εἰς νοῦν
ἐλογίσατο·
"Ποταπὴ εἶ αὕτη;" φησίν·   "σήμερον γὰρ   ὥσπερ χθὲς
οὐχ ὁρᾶταί μοι·
φοβερὰ καὶ γλυκηρὰ   φαίνεται ἡ σὺν ἐμοὶ καὶ συνέχει
με·
καύσωνι καὶ νιφετῷ   ἐγὼ ἐνατενίζω,   παραδείσῳ καὶ
καμίνῳ·
ὄρει καπνίζοντι,   θείῳ ἄνθει χλοάζοντι,
θρόνῳ φρικτῷ,   ὑποποδίῳ οἰκτρῷ
τοῦ πανοικτίρμονος·   ἥνπερ ἔλαβον,   οὐ κατέλαβον·
πῶς οὖν ταύτῃ φθέγξομαι·
'Χαῖρε, νύμφη ἀνύμφευτε';

14

"Μεγάλη οὖν καὶ ταπεινή,   δέσποινα ἅμα καὶ
δούλη,   φράσον μοι νῦν ὃ ὑπάρχεις·
τί εἴπω σε; τί λέξω σοι;   πῶς ὑμνήσω,   πῶς αἰνέσω τὸ
κάλλος σου;"
Ἀληθῶς τοῦτό ἐστιν,   ὅπερ ἡμῖν   ἔφησε τὸ εὐαγγέλιον·
ὁ Ἰωσὴφ ἕως καιροῦ   τὴν σὺν αὐτῷ Μαρίαν οὐκ
ἐγίνωσκεν,

13

As Joseph gazed at the divinely adorned and richly favored
    maiden,
he trembled, marveled, and, astonished, thought to himself,
"What being is she? Today she looks nothing like yesterday.
She is with me but enthralling me, she seems frightening
    and sweet to me.
I am staring into burning heat and a snowstorm, a garden
    and a furnace,
a smoking mountain, a divine flower in bloom,
an awesome throne, a pitiful footstool
for the one who pities all. She whom I took, I did not grasp;
so how can I say to her,
'*Hail, unwedded bride!*'?

14

"Both great and humble, at once mistress and servant,
    explain what you are now!
What shall I say to you? What shall I call you? How can I
    laud and praise your beauty?"
This truly is what the gospel has told us:
Until it was time, Joseph did not know Mary who was with
    him,

ἕως οὗ ἔτεκε σαφῶς   τὸν τοῦ Θεοῦ Λόγον,   ὅπερ ἦν
                                      καὶ ἐδηλώθη,
ἕως οὗ ἔτεκεν,   ἀλλὰ οὐδὲ μετέπειτα·
ἔμεινε γὰρ   κεκαλυμμένη αὐτή,
καὶ ὃν ἔτεκεν   καὶ οὔτε ἔγνωσται   οὔτε γνωσθήσεται,
ἢ δικαίως λέξομεν·
"Χαῖρε, νύμφη ἀνύμφευτε."

15

Αὐτὸς οὖν οὗτος ὁ Ἰωσὴφ   ποτὲ μὴ γνοὺς τὴν
                            Παρθένον   πρὸς τὴν αὐτῆς εὐδοξίαν
ἱστάμενος ἐξίστατο   καὶ ἀτενίζων   τῷ φωτὶ τῆς μορφῆς
                                    αὐτῆς
ἔφησεν· "Ὦ φαεινή,   φλόγα ὁρῶ   καὶ ἀνθρακιὰν
                                κυκλοῦσάν σε·
διὰ τοῦτο, Μαριάμ,   ἐκπλήττομαι· φύλαξόν με καὶ μὴ
                                φλέξῃς με·
κλίβανος πλήρης πυρὸς   ἐγένετο ἄφνω   ἡ ἄμεμπτος
                                γαστήρ σου·
μὴ οὖν χωνεύσῃ με   δέομαι, ἀλλὰ φεῖσαί μου·
θέλεις κἀγὼ   λύσω, ὡς πάλαι Μωσῆς,
τὰ ὑποδήματα   καὶ ἐγγίσω σοι   καὶ ἀκούσω σου
καὶ μαθὼν λέξω σοι·
'Χαῖρε, νύμφη ἀνύμφευτε';"

until she gave birth to the Word of God, with which it was
      clear;
until she gave birth—but not thereafter,
she remained concealed,
as the one she bore, neither known nor to be known,
she who's rightly addressed,
"*Hail, unwedded bride!*"

15

This Joseph, who had not known the Virgin, stood there
      startled,
facing her splendor and staring into the light of her form.
He said, "I see a flame, radiant one, a fiery glow around you;
so, Mary, I'm bewildered. Protect me, do not set me on fire!
Your faultless womb has become all of a sudden a furnace
      full of fire.
Do not melt me, I beg you, but spare me!
Do you want me too, like Moses of old,
to undo my sandals and come near to you and hear
and learn from you and say to you,
'*Hail, unwedded bride*'?"

16

"Νῦν προσεγγίσαι μοι ζητεῖς   καὶ διδαχθῆναι ὃ
                    πέλω,"   τῷ Ἰωσὴφ ἡ Μαρία·
"προσέγγισον καὶ ἄκουσον   ὃ ὑπάρχω   καί εἰμι ὅπερ
                          βλέπεις με,
πτερωτὸς ὤφθη μοί τις,   οὗ ἡ μορφὴ   ὅλον τὸν
                       θάλαμον ἔπλησε
καὶ ἐμὲ ἅμα αὐτῷ·   τῶν γὰρ θυρῶν κεκλεισμένων
                        ἐπέστη μοι·
ἔλεξε δ᾽ οὕτως ἐμοί·   Κεχαριτωμένη,   μετὰ σοῦ ὁ
                          Κύριος.᾽
ὅτε δὲ ἤκουσα   τοῦ Κυρίου τὸ ὄνομα,
τότε μικρὸν   λαβοῦσα παραψυχὴν
εἶδον ᾧ ἔβλεπον   φαεινόμορφον,   φλόγινον ὅλον,
δροσινὰ λαλοῦντά μοι·
Χαῖρε, νύμφη ἀνύμφευτε.᾽

17

"Ὁ οὖν τοιοῦτος ἀσπασμὸς   ἐνηχηθεὶς τοῖς ὠσί
                    μου   πλήρης, φαεινὴν ἀπαρτίσας
ἐγκύμονα ἀπέδειξεν·   τοῦ ἐμβρύου   οὖν οὐκ οἶδα τὴν
                          σύλληψιν,
καὶ ἰδοὺ κυοφορῶ   καὶ ὡς ὁρᾷς   ἄθικτος ἡ παρθενία
                          μου·
οὔτε γὰρ ἔγνωσμαι·   τίς τούτων μάρτυς ἢ σὺ ὁ
                        φυλάττων με;

16

"So, you seek to come near me and be taught who I am,"
    said Mary to Joseph.
"Come near and hear what I am: I am what you see.
Someone with wings appeared before me; his form filled
    the whole room
and me as well. Although the doors were closed, he came to
    me.
He spoke to me like this: 'Favored one, the Lord is with
    you.'
When I heard the name of the Lord,
I was slightly relieved
and I saw whom I saw, a shining form all on fire,
saying to me tenderly,
Hail, unwedded bride!'

17

"That greeting, resounding in my ears, completely filled me
    with radiance
and rendered me pregnant. How the baby was conceived I
    do not know,
but look, I am with child, and you see, my virginity is
    unviolated.
I have not been known. Who could testify to this except
    you, my protector?

δὸς οὖν ὑπὲρ ἐμοῦ   τὴν ἀπολογίαν,   ἵνα εὕρῃς
                                                ἀνάπαυσιν."
τοῦτο ὡς ἤκουσεν   Ἰωσήφ, ἀνεκραύγασε·
"Τοῦτο ἐγὼ   μαρτυρῶ ὄντως σαφῶς·
ὅμως δὲ ἄκουσον·   τίς πιστεύσει μοι,   ὅτι ἄνωθεν
ἦλθεν ὁ βοήσας σοι·
'Χαῖρε, νύμφη ἀνύμφευτε';

18

"Υἱοὶ λοιμοὶ καὶ πονηροὶ   οἱ ἱερεῖς τοῦ λαοῦ
                      σου·   τοῦτο δὲ οἶδας πρὶν εἴπω,
καὶ ἐμοὶ ἀπιστήσουσιν   ὅτι δίχα   συναφείας συνέλαβες·
παρ' ἐμοὶ δῆλόν ἐστιν   ὅτι τὸ φῶς   λάμπει τὸ τῆς
                                                παρθενίας σου·
παρὰ δὲ τοῖς σκοτεινοῖς   ἔσβεσται ὡς ἀναξίοις τοῦ
                                                γνῶναί σε·
τοῦτο οὖν ἔσται καλόν,   νομίζω, Παρθένε,   ἀπολῦσαί
                                                σε λαθραίως·
θέλω δικαίως   μὴ παραδειγματίσαι σε·
στέργω γὰρ σὲ   καὶ τὸν λαὸν δειλιῶ·
ὅθεν οὐ ἐκπέμπω σε   δυνατός ἐστιν   ἀθῳῶσαί σε·
θέλων καὶ λαλήσω σοι·
'Χαῖρε, νύμφη ἀνύμφευτε.'"

So make apologies for me, and you'll find peace."
When he heard this, Joseph cried out,
"I shall attest this, clearly and truthfully,
but listen, who will believe that he came from above,
the one who called out to you,
'*Hail, unwedded bride*'?

18

"Your people's priests are sick and wicked sons—you know
    that already.
They will not believe me if I say you conceived without
    union.
To me it is clear that the light of your virginity shines,
yet to those in the dark, it is quenched; they're unworthy of
    knowing you.
The best thing, I think, is to part from you quietly.
I want to be just and avoid exposing you;
I am fond of you, Virgin, but I fear the people.
The one for whom I'm sending you away has the power to
    exonerate you;
that's my wish when I say to you,
'*Hail, unwedded bride!*'"

Προοίμιον

Κατεπλάγη Ἰωσὴφ   τὸ ὑπὲρ φύσιν θεωρῶν,
καὶ ἐλάμβανεν εἰς νοῦν   τὸν ἐπὶ πόκον ὑετὸν
ἐν τῇ ἀσπόρῳ κυήσει σου,   Θεοτόκε,
βάτον ἐν πυρὶ   ἀκατάφλεκτον,
ῥάβδον Ἀαρὼν   τὴν βλαστήσασαν·
καὶ μαρτυρῶν ὁ μνήστωρ σου   καὶ φύλαξ τοῖς ἱερεῦσιν
ἐκραύγαζεν·
"Παρθένος τίκτει   καὶ μετὰ τόκον   πάλιν μένει παρθένος."

I

πρός· Ἡ προσευχὴ ὁμοῦ καὶ στεναγμός

Ὅπερ ὁρῶ   νοῆσαι οὐ χωρῶ·   ὑπὲρ νοῦν γὰρ ὑπάρχει
ἀνθρώπινον
πῶς πῦρ φέρων ὁ χόρτος οὐ φλέγεται,
ἀμνὰς βαστάζει λέοντα,   ἀετὸν δὲ χελιδών,   καὶ
δεσπότην ἡ δούλη·
γαστρὶ θνητῇ Θεὸν   ἀπεριγράπτως

ON THE VIRGIN

in fourth mode

Prelude

to its own melody

Joseph was astounded by the vision beyond nature
but called to mind the rain upon the fleece
in your conceiving without seed, Theotokos,
a bush unburned in flames,
the budding rod of Aaron;
as your witness, your betrothed and guardian exclaimed to
    the priests,
"A virgin gives birth and remains afterward a virgin still!"

I

to: Joachim and Anna's prayer with their groaning

What I observe, I cannot comprehend; it surpasses the
    human mind,
how the grass filled with flames is not burned,
a lamb carries a lion, the swallow an eagle, and the servant
    her master.
Mary carries my willing Savior,

Μαρία ἐμὸν Σωτῆρα ἑκόντα φέρει,
ὅθεν χαίρων βοῶ·
"Παρθένος τίκτει   καὶ μετὰ τόκον   πάλιν μένει παρθένος."

2

Ὕβριν οὐδεὶς   ἡγεῖται βασιλεύς,   ὅταν τὸν ἐχθρὸν
θέλῃ χειρώσασθαι,
κἂν σχῆμα στρατιώτου ἐνδύσηται·
διὸ Θεὸς τὸν τρώσαντα   τὸν Ἀδὰμ τρῶσαι ζητῶν   ἐκ
παρθένου σαρκοῦται,
καὶ γίνεται παγὶς   τῷ παμπανούργῳ
μορφὴν ἡμετέραν λαβὼν ὁ πρὸ αἰώνων,
ὅνπερ δίχα σπορᾶς
παρθένος τίκτει   καὶ μετὰ τόκον   πάλιν μένει παρθένος.

3

Μάννα ποτὲ   καὶ στάμνον τὴν χρυσῆν   κιβωτὸν
Μωσῆς γράφει βαστάζουσαν·
τί βούλεται δὲ ταῦτα ζητήσωμεν·
οὐδὲν γὰρ ἀργὸν ἔγκειται   τῇ γραφῇ οὐδ᾽
ἀσαφές,   ἀλλὰ πάντα εὐθέα.
Ἡ στάμνος ἡ χρυσῆ   Χριστοῦ τὸ σῶμα,
τὸ μάννα θεῖος Λόγος ᾧπερ ἡνώθη·
τίς δὲ ἡ κιβωτός;
Παρθένος τίκτει   καὶ μετὰ τόκον   πάλιν μένει παρθένος.

God unbounded, in a mortal womb
and with joy I cry,
"*A virgin gives birth and remains afterward a virgin still!*"

2

No king ever considers it an outrage to put on a soldier's
     garb
at a time when he wishes to conquer his enemy.
So to wound the one who wounded Adam, God takes flesh
     from a virgin
and becomes a trap for the cunning deceiver.
The one before the ages is taking our form;
to him, without seed,
a virgin gives birth and remains afterward a virgin still.

3

An ark once carried manna and even a golden jar, writes
     Moses;
let us explore what these things mean,
for nothing lies fallow in scripture, nor is obscure, but all
     has a point.
The golden jar is the body of Christ,
the manna, the Word divine, that united with it.
But who is the ark?
A virgin gives birth and remains afterward a virgin still.

4

Νῦν θεωρῶ   τὴν ῥάβδον Ἀαρὼν   τὴν ἀνθήσασαν δίχα
                                                    ἀρδεύοντος,
ἣν Ἀμὼς Ἡσαΐας μοι ἔγραψεν.
"Ἰδού," φησιν, "ἐλεύσεται   ῥάβδος ἐκ τοῦ Ἰεσσαὶ   καὶ
                                                    ἐκ ῥίζης τὸ ἄνθος."
Ἡ ῥάβδος Ἀαρὼν   καὶ Ἰεσσαὶ τίς;
Μαρία ἡ ἀνθοῦσα ἀγεωργήτως
τὸν καρπὸν ὃν ἐμοὶ
παρθένος τίκτει,   καὶ μετὰ τόκον   πάλιν μένει παρθένος.

5

Οὕτω ποτὲ   καὶ πῦρ ἐν βάτῳ ἦν   φωταυγοῦν καὶ μὴ
                                                    καῖον τὴν ἄκανθα,
ὡς νῦν ἐν τῇ Παρθένῳ ὁ Κύριος·
οὐ γὰρ φαντάσαι ἤθελε   τὸν Μωσέα ὁ Θεὸς   οὐδὲ
                                                    καταπτοῆσαι·
γνωρίζων δὲ αὐτῷ   τὰ μετὰ ταῦτα,
ἐδείκνυε πυρφόρον τὴν βάτον, ὅπως
μάθῃ ὅτι Χριστὸν
παρθένος τίκτει   καὶ μετὰ τόκον   πάλιν μένει παρθένος.

6

Σέ, Ἰησοῦ,   δηλοῦσιν αἱ γραφαί,   ἡ μὲν μάννα καὶ
                                                    στάμνον σημαίνουσα,
ἡ δὲ ἐκ ῥίζης ἄνθος γνωρίζουσα·

4

I'm seeing now Aaron's rod, which blossoms without being
    watered,
as Amoz's son Isaiah wrote for me:
"Behold, a rod shall come from Jesse, and from his root a
    flower."
Who is the rod of Aaron and Jesse?
Mary, who produces for me without husbandry
the fruit, for to it
a virgin gives birth and remains afterward a virgin still.

5

As fire once shone in a bush, without consuming its thorns,
so the Lord is now in the Virgin.
God did not wish to deceive Moses, nor to frighten him,
but revealing to him what was to come,
he showed him the bush bearing fire
to teach that, to Christ,
a virgin gives birth and remains afterward a virgin still.

6

You, Jesus, the scriptures elucidate; one gives manna and a
    jar;
another makes known a flower from a root.

καὶ σὴν μητέρα λέγουσιν   ἄνθος, ῥάβδον,
                  κιβωτόν,   τὴν σὲ φέρουσαν κόλποις,
τὴν διὰ Πνεύματος   ἀνεωχθεῖσαν
καὶ μετὰ τοῦτο μείνασαν κεκλεισμένην,
ἵνα πᾶς τις ἐρεῖ·
"Παρθένος τίκτει   καὶ μετὰ τόκον   πάλιν μένει παρθένος."

7

Ῥῆμα χαρᾶς   εἰπὼν ὁ Γαβριὴλ   τῇ Παρθένῳ τὸν
                              Λόγον ἐνέσπειρε,
τὴν ἄγαμον λοχὸν δείξας Πνεύματι·
"Ἰδοὺ μετὰ σοῦ Κύριος,   καὶ ἐκ σοῦ ὁ καὶ πρὸ σοῦ,   ὁ
                              πατήρ σου υἱός σου,
ὁ πέμψας με πρὸς σὲ   καὶ προλαβών με,
ὁ καὶ μετὰ τὸν τόκον ἁγνὴν τηρῶν σε,
ἵνα πᾶς τις ἐρεῖ·
'Παρθένος τίκτει   καὶ μετὰ τόκον   πάλιν μένει παρθένος.'

8

"Ὤσθη Ἀδάμ,   διὸ Θεὸς Ἀδὰμ   τῷ Ἀδὰμ μηχανώμενος
                              ἔγερσιν
τῆς σῆς κοιλίας τοῦτον ἀνέλαβε."
Γυνὴ τὸ πρὶν κατέβαλε   καὶ γυνὴ νῦν ἀνιστᾷ,   ἐκ
                              παρθένου παρθένος·
τὴν Εὔαν ὁ Ἀδὰμ   οὐκ ἔγνω τότε,
οὐδὲ τὴν Θεοτόκον ὁ Ἰωσὴφ νῦν,
ἀλλὰ δίχα σπορᾶς
παρθένος τίκτει   καὶ μετὰ τόκον   πάλιν μένει παρθένος.

358

And your mother, they say, is a flower, a rod, an ark with you
     in her womb,
who was opened up by the Spirit
and after that remained closed,
so all may say,
"A virgin gives birth and remains afterward a virgin still."

7

As Gabriel uttered a greeting of joy, he sowed the Word in
     the Virgin,
and gestured with the Spirit toward the unwed mother:
"Behold, the Lord is with you, and from you and before you;
     your father is your son,
the one who sent me, and also preceded me,
the one who keeps you pure after childbirth,
so all may say,
'A virgin gives birth and remains afterward a virgin still.'

8

"Adam was banished, so Adam's God, contriving Adam's
     revival,
recovered him from your womb."
A woman once subdued him; now a woman will raise him, a
     virgin from a virgin;
Adam had not then known Eve,
nor Joseph now the Theotokos,
but without seed
a virgin gives birth and remains afterward a virgin still.

9

Μόνον δὲ τῶν   ῥημάτων ἤκουσε   τοῦ ἀγγέλου, ἡ κόρη
ἐβόησε·
"Πῶς ἔσται, ὅτι πέλω ἀπείρανδρος;
ὁ νῦν θαλάμοις ἔχων με   —ὡς μνηστήρ, οὐκ ὡς
ἀνήρ—   ἑαυτῷ με φυλάττει·
εἰ δὲ γενήσεται   ὅπερ σὺ λέγεις,
σωματικοῦ μοι γάμου τὸ πρᾶγμα κρεῖττον,
ὅπως πᾶς τις ἐρεῖ·
'Παρθένος τίκτει   καὶ μετὰ τόκον   πάλιν μένει παρθένος.'"

10

"Ἄκουσόν μου,"   φησίν, "ὦ Μαριάμ·   πρὸς γὰρ σὲ
ἀπεστάλην ὁ ἄσαρκος
ὡς ἄλλον πόλον μέλλουσαν γίνεσθαι.
Μὴ θῇς ἐν τῇ καρδίᾳ σου   ὅτι μέλλει Ἰωσὴφ   σὲ
γυναῖκα λαμβάνειν·
προώρισέ σε γὰρ   ὁ πλαστουργός σου
βαστᾶσαι τοῦτον ὥσπερ ὁ θρόνος ἄνω,
ἵνα πᾶς τις ἐρεῖ·
'Παρθένος τίκτει   καὶ μετὰ τόκον   πάλιν μένει παρθένος.'"

9

As soon as she heard the words of the angel, the maiden
    herself exclaimed:
"How can this be when I've had no man?
He who keeps me here—my betrothed, not husband—
    protects me as his own.
If it will happen, as you are saying,
it will be greater for me than a bodily marriage,
so that all may say,
'A *virgin gives birth and remains afterward a virgin still*.'"

10

"Listen, to me, Mary," he says, "I, who am fleshless, was sent
    to you,
as you're going to become another heaven.
Do not expect in your heart that Joseph will take you as his
    wife.
For he who formed you has preordained you
to carry him like the throne on high,
so all may say,
'*A virgin gives birth and remains afterward a virgin still*.'"

11

"Νὺξ ἀμειδὴς   ἡ φύσις ἡ ἐμή—   καὶ πῶς ἐξ αὐτῆς
                                           λάμψει ὁ ἥλιος;
Ὡς ἄπιστον ὃ λέγεις μοι, ἄνθρωπε·
γυνὴ ἡ πρὶν τὸν θάνατον   προξενήσασα βροτοῖς,   πῶς
                                           ζωὴν νῦν βλαστήσει;
Πηλὸν ὁ πλαστουργὸς   πῶς μοι οἰκήσει;
Τὴν ἀκανθώδη φύσιν τὸ πῦρ οὐ φλέγει;
Ὄντως πᾶς τις ἐρεῖ·
'Παρθένος τίκτει   καὶ μετὰ τόκον   πάλιν μένει παρθένος';"

12

"'Ὅλον Θεὸς   βεβούλευται ἐκ σοῦ   καινουργῆσαι
                                           φθαρέντα τὸν ἄνθρωπον.
Μὴ λέγε· 'Πῶς οἰκεῖ καὶ οὐ φλέγει με;'
Τὸ πῦρ ὅπερ σὺ δέδοικας   ἔσται ὄμβρος ἐπὶ σέ,   ὡς
                                           Δαυὶδ προανεφώνει·
ὡς ὑετός,' φησίν,   'ὁ ἐπὶ τὸν πόκον'·
οὕτως οἰκεῖ τὴν κόρην Θεὸς ἡσύχως,
ἵνα πᾶς τις ἐρεῖ·
'Παρθένος τίκτει   καὶ μετὰ τόκον   πάλιν μένει παρθένος.'

11

"A gloomy night is my nature—how can the sun shine forth
     from that?
What you are saying to me, sir, is incredible.
How will woman, who once procured death for mortals,
     now produce life?
How will the craftsman inhabit the clay?
Will the fire not burn my thorny nature?
Will all really say,
'*A virgin gives birth and remains afterward a virgin still*'?"

12

"God has resolved to renew corrupted humanity wholly
     through you.
Don't ask, 'How can he inhabit and not burn me?'
The fire you fear will be a shower upon you, as David
     foretold,
'as rain,' he says, 'upon the fleece.'
Thus quietly God dwells in the maiden
so all will say,
'*A virgin gives birth and remains afterward a virgin still.*'

13

"Ὕμνησον οὖν   Χριστόν, ὦ Μαριάμ,   τὸν καὶ κάτω σοι
                                          κόλποις φερόμενον
καὶ ἄνω τῷ Πατρὶ συγκαθήμενον,
μαστὸν τὸν σὸν μὲν ἕλκοντα,   χορηγοῦντα δὲ
                          θνητοῖς   βρῶσιν θείαν ὑψόθεν·
τὸν ἄνω, ὡς σκηνήν,   οἰκοῦντα πόλον,
καὶ κάτω ἐν σπηλαίῳ ἀνακλιθέντα
διὰ πόθον βροτῶν
παρθένος τίκτει   καὶ μετὰ τόκον   πάλιν μένει παρθένος."

13

"So, Mary, praise the Christ who is carried below by you in a
    womb
and seated above with the Father.
He sucks at your breast, while providing divine food from
    on high for mortals.
To the one who dwells in the heavenly vault
and is laid down below here in a cave
through desire for mortals,
a virgin gives birth and remains afterward a virgin still."

Προοίμιον

ἰδιόμελον

Ἡ Παρθένος σήμερον   τὸν ὑπερούσιον τίκτει,
καὶ ἡ Γῆ τὸ σπήλαιον   τῷ ἀπροσίτῳ προσάγει·
ἄγγελοι μετὰ ποιμένων   δοξολογοῦσι,
Μάγοι δὲ μετὰ ἀστέρος   ὁδοιποροῦσι·
δι’ ἡμᾶς γὰρ   ἐγεννήθη
παιδίον νέον,   ὁ πρὸ αἰώνων Θεός.

I

ἰδιόμελον

Τὴν Ἐδὲμ Βηθλεὲμ   ἤνοιξε, δεῦτε ἴδωμεν·
τὴν τρυφὴν ἐν κρυφῇ   ηὕραμεν, δεῦτε λάβωμεν
τὰ τοῦ παραδείσου   ἐντὸς τοῦ σπηλαίου·
ἐκεῖ ἐφάνη   ῥίζα ἀπότιστος   βλαστάνουσα ἄφεσιν,
ἐκεῖ ηὑρέθη   φρέαρ ἀνόρυκτον,
οὗ πιεῖν Δαυὶδ   πρὶν ἐπεθύμησεν·
ἐκεῖ παρθένος   τεκοῦσα βρέφος
τὴν δίψαν ἔπαυσεν εὐθὺς   τὴν τοῦ Ἀδὰμ καὶ τοῦ Δαυίδ·
διὰ τοῦτο πρὸς τοῦτο   ἐπειχθῶμεν ποῦ ἐτέχθη
παιδίον νέον,   ὁ πρὸ αἰώνων Θεός.

366

ON THE NATIVITY
(MARY AND THE MAGI)

in third mode

Prelude

to its own melody

The Virgin today gives birth to the unworldly one,
and Earth offers the cave to the unapproachable one.
Angels give glory with shepherds;
Magi journey with a star.
To us has been born
a little child, God before the ages.

I

to its own melody

Bethlehem opened Eden—come, let us see!
We've found hidden delight—come, let us seize
the pleasure of paradise inside the cave!
There an unwatered root buds with deliverance;
there an undug well was discovered,
from which David yearned to drink;
there a virgin who gave birth to a baby
quenched both Adam's and David's thirst.
Let us, then, hurry to where there was born
a little child, God before the ages.

2

Ὁ πατὴρ τῆς μητρὸς   γνώμῃ υἱὸς ἐγένετο,
ὁ σωτὴρ τῶν βρεφῶν   βρέφος ἐν φάτνῃ ἔκειτο·
ὃν κατανοοῦσά   φησιν ἡ τεκοῦσα·
"Εἰπέ μοι, τέκνον,   πῶς ἐνεσπάρης μοι   ἢ πῶς ἐνεφύης
                                                        μοι;
ὁρῶ σε, σπλάγχνον,   καὶ καταπλήττομαι,
ὅτι γαλουχῶ   καὶ οὐ νενύμφευμαι·
καὶ σὲ μὲν βλέπω   μετὰ σπαργάνων,
τὴν παρθενίαν δὲ ἀκμὴν   ἐσφραγισμένην θεωρῶ·
σὺ γὰρ ταύτην φυλάξας   ἐγεννήθης εὐδοκήσας
παιδίον νέον,   ὁ πρὸ αἰώνων Θεός.

3

"Ὑψηλὲ Βασιλεῦ,   τί σοι καὶ τοῖς πτωχεύσασι;
Ποιητὰ οὐρανοῦ,   τί πρὸς γηΐνους ἤλυθας;
Σπηλαίου ἠράσθης   ἢ φάτνῃ ἐτέρφθης;
Ἰδοὺ οὐκ ἔστι   τόπος τῇ δούλῃ σου   ἐν τῷ καταλύματι·
οὐ λέγω τόπον,   ἀλλ᾽ οὐδὲ σπήλαιον,
ὅτι καὶ αὐτὸ   τοῦτο ἀλλότριον·
καὶ τῇ μὲν Σάρρᾳ   τεκούσῃ βρέφος
ἐδόθη κλῆρος γῆς πολλῆς,   ἐμοὶ δὲ οὔτε φωλεός·
ἐχρησάμην τὸ ἄντρον   ὃ κατῴκησας βουλήσει,
παιδίον νέον,   ὁ πρὸ αἰώνων Θεός."

2

The mother's father chose to become her son;
the savior of infants lay as an infant in a manger.
Gazing at him the mother exclaims,
"Tell me, my child, how were you sown or planted in me?
Astounded, I look at you, my flesh and blood—
I nurse yet I am not married;
although I see you in swaddling clothes,
I find my virginity still sealed;
you guarded it when you deigned to be born,
my little child, God before the ages.

3

"What are the poor to you, exalted King?
Why have you come to mortals, heavenly Maker?
Were you enticed by a cave, or attracted by a manger?
Look! There's no room for your servant at the inn—
no room, for sure, no, not even a cave,
for that belongs to another as well.
A great land was once allotted to Sarah
when she had a baby—to me not even a fox hole.
I borrowed the den you have settled in willingly,
my little child, God before the ages."

4

Τὰ τοιαῦτα ῥητὰ   ἐν ἀπορρήτῳ λέγουσα
καὶ τὸν τῶν ἀφανῶν   γνώστην καθικετεύουσα
ἀκούει τῶν Μάγων   τὸ βρέφος ζητούντων·
εὐθὺς δὲ τούτοις·   "Τίνες ὑπάρχετε;"   ἡ κόρη ἐβόησεν·
οἱ δὲ πρὸς ταύτην·   "Σὺ γὰρ τίς πέφυκας,
ὅτι τὸν τοιοῦτον ἀπεκύησας;
Τίς ὁ πατήρ σου,   τίς ἡ τεκοῦσα,
ὅτι ἀπάτορος υἱοῦ   ἐγένου μήτηρ καὶ τροφός;
Οὗ τὸ ἄστρον ἰδόντες   συνήκαμεν ὅτι ὤφθη
παιδίον νέον,   ὁ πρὸ αἰώνων Θεός.

5

"Ἀκριβῶς γὰρ ἡμῖν   ὁ Βαλαὰμ παρέθετο
τῶν ῥημάτων τὸν νοῦν   ὧνπερ προεμαντεύσατο,
εἰπὼν ὅτι μέλλει   ἀστὴρ ἀνατέλλειν,
ἀστὴρ σβεννύων   πάντα μαντεύματα   καὶ τὰ
                                                    οἰωνίσματα·
ἀστὴρ ἐκλύων   παραβολὰς σοφῶν,
ῥήσεις τε αὐτῶν   καὶ τὰ αἰνίγματα·
ἀστὴρ ἀστέρος   τοῦ φαινομένου
ὑπερφαιδρότερος πολύ,   ὡς πάντων ἄστρων ποιητής,
περὶ οὗ προεγράφη·   'Ἐκ τοῦ Ἰακὼβ ἀνατέλλει
παιδίον νέον,   ὁ πρὸ αἰώνων Θεός.'"

4

As she is speaking such words in silence,
beseeching the one who knows every secret,
she hears the Magi searching for the infant.
"Who are you?" she called out at once,
and they called back, "And who might you be,
that you've given birth to such a child?
Who is your father, and who is your mother,
that you've become mother and nurse of a fatherless son?
We saw his star, and we knew he'd appeared,
a little child, God before the ages.

5

"Balaam explained for us precisely
the meaning of the words he spoke in divination.
He said that a star was going to rise,
a star to extinguish all the oracles and all the auguries,
a star to dissolve the wise ones' parables,
their sayings, and even their riddles;
a star far outshining the star that appeared,
as he's the maker of all the stars,
about whom was proclaimed, 'From Jacob shall rise
a little child, God before the ages.'"

6

Παραδόξων ῥητῶν   ἡ Μαριὰμ ὡς ἤκουσε,
τῷ ἐκ σπλάγχνων αὐτῆς   κύψασα προσεκύνησε
καὶ κλαίουσα εἶπε·   "Μεγάλα μοι, τέκνον,
μεγάλα πάντα   ὅσα ἐποίησας   μετὰ τῆς πτωχείας μου·
ἰδοὺ γὰρ Μάγοι   ἔξω ζητοῦσί σε·
τῶν ἀνατολῶν   οἱ βασιλεύοντες
τὸ πρόσωπόν σου   ἐπιζητοῦσι,
καὶ λιτανεύουσιν ἰδεῖν   οἱ πλούσιοι τοῦ σοῦ λαοῦ·
ὁ λαός σου γὰρ ὄντως   εἰσὶν οὗτοι οἷς ἐγνώσθης,
παιδίον νέον,   ὁ πρὸ αἰώνων Θεός.

7

"Ἐπειδὴ οὖν λαὸς   σός ἐστι, τέκνον, κέλευσον
ὑπὸ σκέπην τὴν σὴν   γένωνται, ἵνα ἴδωσι
πενίαν πλουσίαν,   πτωχείαν τιμίαν·
αὐτόν σε δόξαν   ἔχω καὶ καύχημα·   διὸ οὐκ αἰσχύνομαι·
αὐτὸς εἶ χάρις   καὶ ἡ εὐπρέπεια
τῆς σκηνῆς κἀμοῦ·   νεῦσον εἰσέλθωσιν·
οὐδέν μοι μέλει   τῆς εὐτελείας·
ὡς θησαυρὸν γὰρ σὲ κρατῶ,   ὃν βασιλεῖς ἦλθον ἰδεῖν,
βασιλέων καὶ Μάγων   ἐγνωκότων ὅτι ὤφθης
παιδίον νέον,   ὁ πρὸ αἰώνων Θεός."

6

When Mary heard these astonishing words,
she bowed and adored the one she had borne
and, weeping, she said, "You've done great things for me,
great things in the midst of my poverty, child.
Look, Magi are outside searching for you;
the kings of the east
are seeking your face,
the rich among your people are begging to see you.
These are truly your people who have recognized you,
my little child, God before the ages.

7

"Since they are your people, ask them, my child,
to come under your roof, so they may perceive
a wealthy neediness, a precious poverty!
I have you for glory and pride; so I'm not ashamed.
You are yourself the grace and the beauty
of me and my dwelling place; beckon them
to come in! I do not mind the shabbiness,
for I have you as my treasure that kings came to see,
kings and Magi who learned you'd appeared,
a little child, God before the ages."

8

Ἰησοῦς ὁ Χριστὸς   ὄντως καὶ ὁ Θεὸς ἡμῶν
τῶν φρενῶν ἀφανῶς   ἥψατο τῆς μητρὸς αὐτοῦ,
"Εἰσάγαγε," λέγων,   "οὓς ἤγαγον λόγῳ·
ἐμὸς γὰρ λόγος   τούτοις ἐπέλαμψε   τοῖς ἐπιζητοῦσί με·
ἀστὴρ μέν ἐστιν   πρὸς τὸ φαινόμενον,
δύναμις δέ τις   πρὸς τὸ νοούμενον·
συνῆλθε Μάγοις   ὡς λειτουργῶν μοι,
καὶ ἔτι ἵσταται πληρῶν   τὴν διακονίαν αὐτοῦ
καὶ ἀκτῖσι δεικνύων   τὸν τόπον ὅπου ἐτέχθη
παιδίον νέον,   ὁ πρὸ αἰώνων Θεός.

9

"Νῦν οὖν δέξαι, σεμνή,   δέξαι τοὺς δεξαμένους με·
ἐν αὐτοῖς γάρ εἰμι   ὥσπερ ἐν ταῖς ἀγκάλαις σου·
καὶ σοῦ οὐκ ἀπέστην   κἀκείνοις συνῆλθον."
Ἡ δὲ ἀνοίγει   θύραν καὶ δέχεται   τῶν Μάγων τὸ
                                                    σύστημα·
ἀνοίγει θύραν   ἡ ἀπαράνοικτος
πύλη, ἣν Χριστὸς   μόνος διώδευσεν·
ἀνοίγει θύραν   ἡ ἀνοιχθεῖσα
καὶ μὴ κλαπεῖσα μηδαμῶς   τὸν τῆς ἁγνείας θησαυρόν·
αὐτὴ ἤνοιξε θύραν,   ἀφ' ἧς ἐγεννήθη θύρα,
παιδίον νέον,   ὁ πρὸ αἰώνων Θεός.

8

Jesus the Christ, who is truly our God,
invisibly grasped his mother's thoughts:
"Lead them in," were his words, "whom I led with a word!
It was my word that shone when they sought me;
to the eyes it is indeed a star,
but to the mind it is a power.
Ministering to me, it traveled with the Magi
and it still remains, fulfilling its service,
and it points with its rays to the place where there was born
a little child, God before the ages.

9

"Receive, then, noble one, those who received me!
I am within them, as I am in your arms,
and I never left you, though I came here with them."
So she opens the door and receives the group of Magi;
she opens the door, she, the unopened
gate through which Christ alone passed;
she opens the door, she who was opened
yet by no means robbed of her purity's treasure;
she opened a door, giving birth to a door,
a little child, God before the ages.

10

Οἱ δὲ Μάγοι εὐθὺς   ὥρμησαν εἰς τὸν θάλαμον,
καὶ ἰδόντες Χριστὸν   ἔφριξαν, ὅτι εἴδοσαν
τὴν τούτου μητέρα,   τὸν ταύτης μνηστῆρα,
καὶ φόβῳ εἶπον·   "Οὗτος υἱός ἐστιν   ἀγενεαλόγητος·
καὶ πῶς, Παρθένε,   τὸν μνηστευσάμενον
βλέπομεν ἀκμὴν   ἔνδον τοῦ οἴκου σου;
Οὐκ ἔσχε μῶμον   ἡ κύησίς σου·
μὴ ἡ κατοίκησις ψεχθῇ   συνόντος σοι τοῦ Ἰωσήφ·
πλῆθος ἔχεις φθονούντων   ἐρευνώντων ποῦ ἐτέχθη
παιδίον νέον,   ὁ πρὸ αἰώνων Θεός.

11

"Ὑπομνήσω ὑμᾶς,"   Μάγοις Μαρία ἔφησε,
"τίνος χάριν κρατῶ   τὸν Ἰωσὴφ ἐν οἴκῳ μου·
εἰς ἔλεγχον πάντων   τῶν καταλαλούντων·
αὐτὸς γὰρ λέξει   ἅπερ ἀκήκοε   περὶ τοῦ παιδίου μου·
ὑπνῶν γὰρ εἶδεν   ἄγγελον ἅγιον
λέγοντα αὐτῷ   πόθεν συνέλαβον·
πυρίνη θέα   τὸν ἀκανθώδη
ἐπληροφόρησε νυκτὸς   περὶ τῶν λυπούντων αὐτόν·
δι' αὐτὸ σύνεστί μοι   Ἰωσὴφ δηλῶν ὡς ἔστι
παιδίον νέον   ὁ πρὸ αἰώνων Θεός.

10

The Magi immediately rushed into the room.
Seeing Christ, they trembled, for they also glimpsed
both his mother and her betrothed,
and fearfully they said, "This is the son without genealogy.
Then, how is it, Virgin, that we still see
a husband-to-be within your house?
Your conception had no blemish; nor should your abode
be flawed by the presence of Joseph!
Many search with envy for the place where there was born
a little child, God before the ages.

11

"I'll let you know," said Mary to the Magi.
"The reason I keep Joseph in my house
is to censure all those slandering me.
He can relate what he has heard concerning my child.
In his sleep he saw a holy angel
who recounted to him how I had conceived.
A fiery vision gave reassurance in the night
to the anxious man regarding what troubled him.
Joseph is with me to show that this is
a little child, God before the ages.

12

"Ῥητορεύει σαφῶς   ἄπαντα ἄπερ ἤκουσεν·
ἀπαγγέλλει τρανῶς   ὅσα αὐτὸς ἑώρακεν
ἐν τοῖς οὐρανίοις   καὶ τοῖς ἐπιγείοις·
τὰ τῶν ποιμένων,   πῶς συνανύμνησαν   πηλίνοις οἱ
                                          πύρινοι·
ὑμῶν τῶν Μάγων,   ὅτι προέδραμεν
ἄστρον φωταυγοῦν   καὶ ὁδηγοῦν ὑμᾶς·
διὸ ἀφέντες   τὰ προρρηθέντα,
ἐκδιηγήσασθε ἡμῖν   τὰ νῦν γενόμενα ὑμῖν,
πόθεν ἤκατε, πῶς δὲ   συνήκατε ὅτι ὤφθη
παιδίον νέον,   ὁ πρὸ αἰώνων Θεός."

13

Ὡς δὲ ταῦτα αὐτοῖς   ἡ φαεινὴ ἐλάλησεν,
οἱ τῆς ἀνατολῆς   λύχνοι πρὸς ταύτην ἔφησαν·
"Μαθεῖν θέλεις πόθεν   ἠλύθαμεν ὧδε;
Ἐκ γῆς Χαλδαίων,   ὅθεν οὐ λέγουσι·   'Θεὸς θεῶν
                                          Κύριος,'
ἐκ Βαβυλῶνος,   ὅπου οὐκ οἴδασιν
τίς ὁ Ποιητὴς   τούτων ὧν σέβουσιν·
ἐκεῖθεν ἦλθε   καὶ ἦρεν ἡμᾶς
ὁ τοῦ παιδίου σου σπινθὴρ   ἐκ τοῦ πυρὸς τοῦ Περσικοῦ·
πῦρ παμφάγον λιπόντες,   πῦρ δροσίζον θεωροῦμεν,
παιδίον νέον,   τὸν πρὸ αἰώνων Θεόν.

12

"He recounts precisely all that he heard
and reports clearly what he himself saw
of both heavenly and earthly things:
how those of fire sang hymns with those of clay, the
    shepherds,
and of you, Magi, that a star went before you,
lighting and guiding your way.
So leaving aside all that's been said,
tell us in detail what happened to you,
where you're from, and how you knew that here could be
    seen
a little child, God before the ages."

13

As the radiant one said this to them,
those lamps from the east replied to her,
"You want to learn where we started our journey?
From the land of Chaldeans, where they do not say, 'The
    God of gods is Lord';
from Babylon, where they do not know
who has made the ones they worship.
And there came your child's spark,
which took us out of the Persian fire;
leaving behind a voracious fire, we see a refreshing one,
a little child, God before the ages.

14

"Ματαιότης ἐστὶ   ματαιοτήτων ἅπαντα,
ἀλλ' οὐδεὶς ἐν ἡμῖν   ταῦτα φρονῶν εὑρίσκεται·
οἱ μὲν γὰρ πλανῶσιν,   οἱ δὲ καὶ πλανῶνται·
διό, Παρθένε,   χάρις τῷ τόκῳ σου,   δι' οὗ ἐλυτρώθημεν
οὐ μόνον πλάνης,   ἀλλὰ καὶ θλίψεως
τῶν χωρῶν πασῶν   ὧνπερ διήλθομεν,
ἐθνῶν ἀσήμων,   γλωσσῶν ἀγνώστων,
περιερχόμενοι τὴν γῆν   καὶ ἐξερευνῶντες αὐτὴν
μετὰ λύχνου τοῦ ἄστρου,   ἐκζητοῦντες ποῦ ἐτέχθη
παιδίον νέον,   ὁ πρὸ αἰώνων Θεός.

15

"Ἀλλ' ὡς ἔτι αὐτὸν   τοῦτον τὸν λύχνον εἴχομεν,
τὴν Ἰερουσαλὴμ   πᾶσαν περιωδεύσαμεν,
πληροῦντες εἰκότως   τὰ τῆς προφητείας·
ἠκούσαμεν γὰρ   ὅτι ἠπείλησε   Θεὸς ἐρευνᾶν αὐτήν·
καὶ μετὰ λύχνου   περιηρχόμεθα,
θέλοντες εὑρεῖν   μέγα δικαίωμα·
ἀλλ' οὐχ εὑρέθη,   ὅτι ἐπήρθη
ἡ κιβωτὸς αὐτῆς μεθ' ὧν   συνεῖχε πρότερον καλῶν·
τὰ ἀρχαῖα παρῆλθεν,   ἀνεκαίνισε γὰρ πάντα
παιδίον νέον,   ὁ πρὸ αἰώνων Θεός."

14

"Vanity of vanities, all is vanity,
but no one there thinks like that.
Some mislead, while others are misled.
So, thanks be to your birth-giving, which has freed us,
    Virgin,
not only from being misled, but also from misfortune
in all the regions which we traversed
among undiscovered peoples with unintelligible tongues,
while we traveled the earth and thoroughly searched it
with the lamp of the star, while we were seeking to find
a little child, God before the ages.

15

"But while we still possessed this lamp,
we visited the whole of Jerusalem
and so fulfilled the words of the prophecy,
for we have heard that God threatened to search the city.
So we were roaming about with the lamp,
wishing to find outstanding righteousness,
but it couldn't be found, for its ark had been removed,
together with the wonders it used to hold.
The old things have passed; he renewed all things,
a little child, God before the ages."

16

"Ναί," φησί, τοῖς πιστοῖς   Μάγοις Μαρία ἔφησε,
"τὴν Ἰερουσαλὴμ   πᾶσαν περιωδεύσατε,
τὴν πόλιν ἐκείνην   τὴν προφητοκτόνον;
Καὶ πῶς ἀλύπως   ταύτην διήλθατε   τὴν πᾶσι
                                                    βασκαίνουσαν;
Ἡρώδην πάλιν   πῶς διελάθετε
τὸν ἀντὶ θεσμῶν   φόνων ἐμπνέοντα;"
Οἱ δὲ πρὸς ταύτην   φησί· "Παρθένε,
οὐ διελάθομεν αὐτόν,   ἀλλ᾿ ἐνεπαίξαμεν αὐτῷ·
συνετύχομεν πᾶσιν   ἐρωτῶντες ποῦ ἐτέχθη
παιδίον νέον,   ὁ πρὸ αἰώνων Θεός."

17

Ὅτε ταῦτα αὐτῶν   ἡ Θεοτόκος ἤκουσεν,
τότε εἶπεν αὐτοῖς·   "Τί ὑμᾶς ἐπηρώτησεν
Ἡρώδης ὁ ἄναξ   καὶ οἱ Φαρισαῖοι;"
"Ἡρώδης πρῶτον,   εἶτα, ὡς ἔφησας,   οἱ πρῶτοι τοῦ
                                                    ἔθνους σου
τὸν χρόνον τούτου   τοῦ φαινομένου νῦν
ἄστρου παρ᾿ ἡμῶν   ἐξηκριβώσαντο·
καὶ ἐπιγνόντες   ὡς μὴ μαθόντες
οὐκ ἐπεθύμησαν ἰδεῖν   ὃν ἐξηρεύνησαν μαθεῖν,
ὅτι τοῖς ἐρευνῶσιν   ὀφείλει θεωρηθῆναι
παιδίον νέον,   ὁ πρὸ αἰώνων Θεός.

16

"Is it true," says Mary to the faithful Magi,
"that you visited the whole of Jerusalem,
that prophet-killing city? How did you pass
unharmed through that place which casts its evil eye on all?
And how, again, did you avoid Herod,
who breathes murder instead of order?"
And they say to her, "Virgin,
we did not avoid him; rather we tricked him.
We went around and asked where there was born
a little child, God before the ages."

17

When the God-Bearer heard their words
she said to them, "What questions did they pose,
Herod the king and then the Pharisees?"
"Herod first, and then, as you said, the first among your
     people,
diligently inquired of us
at what exact time the star had appeared.
And they heard, but as if without listening;
they did not wish to see the one they had sought to know,
because those who seek are going to behold
a little child, God before the ages.

18

"Ὑπενόουν ἡμᾶς   ἄφρονας οἱ ἀνόητοι
καὶ ἠρώτων, φησί·   'Πόθεν καὶ πότε ἥκατε;
πῶς μὴ φαινομένας   ὡδεύσατε τρίβους;'
Ἡμεῖς δὲ τούτοις   ὅπερ ἠπίσταντο   ἀντεπηρωτήσαμεν·
"Ὑμεῖς τὸ πάρος   πῶς διωδεύσατε
ἔρημον πολλὴν   ἥνπερ διήλθετε;'
Ὁ ὁδηγήσας   τοὺς ἀπ' Αἰγύπτου
αὐτὸς ὡδήγησε καὶ νῦν   τοὺς ἐκ Χαλδαίων πρὸς αὐτόν,
τότε στύλῳ πυρίνῳ,   νῦν δὲ ἀστέρι δηλοῦντι
παιδίον νέον,   τὸν πρὸ αἰώνων Θεόν.

19

"Ὁ ἀστὴρ πανταχοῦ   ἦν ἡμῶν προηγούμενος
ὡς ὑμῖν ὁ Μωσῆς   ῥάβδον ἐπιφερόμενος,
τὸ φῶς περιλάμπων   τῆς θεογνωσίας·
ὑμᾶς τὸ μάννα   πάλαι διέθρεψε   καὶ πέτρα ἐπότισεν·
ἡμᾶς ἐλπὶς ἡ   τούτου ἐνέπλησε·
τῇ τούτου χαρᾷ   διατρεφόμενοι,
οὐκ ἐν Περσίδι   ἀναποδίσαι
διὰ τὸ ἄβατον ὁδὸν   ὁδεύειν ἔσχομεν ἐν νῷ,
θεωρῆσαι ποθοῦντες,   προσκυνῆσαι καὶ δοξάσαι
παιδίον νέον,   τὸν πρὸ αἰώνων Θεόν."

18

"The idiots there assumed we were fools
and asked us, 'Where did you come from and when?
How did you travel unknown paths?'
Then we asked them about things they knew:
'How did you make your way through
the great desert that you once crossed?'
The one who once led them from Egypt
has now led others from Chaldea to himself,
then with a fiery pillar, now with a star to reveal
a little child, God before the ages.

19

"All the way the star was leading us,
like Moses carrying a rod for you,
spreading the light of divine knowledge.
Whereas long ago the rock gave you drink and the manna
        nourishment,
we were filled with his hope.
Fed with his joy,
we did not think of returning to Persia,
facing the inaccessible roads we had to travel,
for we yearned to see, adore, and glorify
a little child, God before the ages."

20

Ὑπὸ τῶν ἀπλανῶν   Μάγων ταῦτα ἐλέγετο·
ὑπὸ δὲ τῆς σεμνῆς   πάντα ἐπεσφραγίζετο,
κυροῦντος τοῦ βρέφους   τὰ τῶν ἀμφοτέρων,
τῆς μὲν ποιοῦντος   μετὰ τὴν κύησιν   τὴν μήτραν
                                                    ἀμίαντον,

τῶν δὲ δεικνύντος   μετὰ τὴν ἔλευσιν
ἄμοχθον τὸν νοῦν   ὥσπερ τὰ βήματα·
οὐδεὶς γὰρ τούτων   ὑπέστη κόπον,
ὡς οὐκ ἐμόχθησεν ἐλθὼν   ὁ Ἀμβακοὺμ πρὸς Δανιήλ·
ὁ φανεὶς γὰρ προφήταις   ὁ αὐτὸς ἐφάνη Μάγοις,
παιδίον νέον,   ὁ πρὸ αἰώνων Θεός.

21

Μετὰ ταῦτα αὐτῶν   πάντα τὰ διηγήματα,
δῶρα ἦραν χερσὶν   Μάγοι καὶ προσεκύνησαν
τῷ δώρῳ τῶν δώρων,   τῷ μύρῳ τῶν μύρων·
χρυσὸν καὶ σμύρναν   εἶτα καὶ λίβανον   Χριστῷ
                                                    προσεκόμισαν
βοῶντες· "Δέξαι   δώρημα τρίϋλον,
ὡς τῶν σεραφὶμ   ὕμνον τρισάγιον·
μὴ ἀποστρέψῃς   ὡς τὰ τοῦ Κάϊν,
ἀλλ᾽ ἐναγκάλισαι αὐτὰ   ὡς τὴν τοῦ Ἄβελ προσφοράν,
διὰ τῆς σε τεκούσης,   ἐξ ἧς ἡμῖν ἐγεννήθης
παιδίον νέον,   ὁ πρὸ αἰώνων Θεός."

20

Thus spoke the Magi, who had never strayed;
the noble Mary approved it with her seal,
and the infant himself ratified both:
He left her a spotless womb after her pregnancy,
and he showed them to have tireless minds,
just like their feet upon arrival.
None of them endured hardship,
just as Habakkuk came to Daniel without being tired.
For the one who appeared to prophets has now appeared to
      Magi,
a little child, God before the ages.

21

When they had related all their stories, the Magi
lifted up gifts in their hands, adoring
the gift of gifts, the balm of balms.
Gold and myrrh, then also frankincense they offered to
      Christ,
exclaiming, "Receive a threefold present,
like the thrice-holy hymn you receive from seraphim!
Do not reject it like those of Cain,
but embrace it instead like Abel's offering,
through her who gave birth and bore you for us,
a little child, God before the ages."

22

Νέα νῦν καὶ φαιδρὰ   βλέπουσα ἡ ἀμώμητος
Μάγους δῶρα χερσὶ   φέροντας καὶ προσπίπτοντας,
ἀστέρα δηλοῦντα,   ἀγγέλους ὑμνοῦντας,
τὸν πάντων τούτων   Κτίστην καὶ Κύριον   ἱκέτευε
                                         λέγουσα·
"Τριάδα δώρων,   τέκνον, δεξάμενος,
τρεῖς αἰτήσεις δὸς   τῇ γεννησάσῃ σε·
ὑπὲρ ἀέρων   παρακαλῶ σε
καὶ ὑπὲρ τῶν καρπῶν τῆς γῆς   καὶ τῶν οἰκούντων ἐν
                                         αὐτῇ·
διαλλάγηθι πᾶσι   δι' ἐμοῦ, ὅτι ἐτέχθης
παιδίον νέον,   ὁ πρὸ αἰώνων Θεός.

23

"Οὐχ ἁπλῶς γάρ εἰμι   μήτηρ σου, Σῶτερ εὔσπλαγχνε·
οὐκ εἰκῇ γαλουχῶ   τὸν χορηγὸν τοῦ γάλακτος,
ἀλλὰ ὑπὲρ πάντων   ἐγὼ δυσωπῶ σε·
ἐποίησάς με   ὅλου τοῦ γένους μου   καὶ στόμα καὶ
                                         καύχημα·
ἐμὲ γὰρ ἔχει   ἡ οἰκουμένη σου
σκέπην κραταιάν,   τεῖχος καὶ στήριγμα·
ἐμὲ ὁρῶσιν   οἱ ἐκβληθέντες
τοῦ παραδείσου τῆς τρυφῆς,   ὅτι ἐπιστρέφω αὐτοὺς
λαβεῖν αἴσθησιν πάντων   δι' ἐμοῦ τῆς σε τεκούσης
παιδίον νέον,   ὁ πρὸ αἰώνων Θεός.

22

When the immaculate one saw the Magi
bearing new and shining gifts in their hands
and bowing before the Creator and Lord of all things,
and a star revealing and angels praising him, she begged,
"Child, as you are receiving a trinity of gifts,
grant three requests to the one who bore you:
for the air, I implore you,
for the fruits of the earth, and for those who inhabit it:
bring all into harmony through me, for I bore
a little child, God before the ages.

23

"I am not only your mother, compassionate Savior;
I do not nurse the provider of milk without reason,
but I'm winning you over on behalf of everyone.
You have made me the mouthpiece and the pride of my
      whole race,
and your world has me
as a strong roof, a wall and foundation.
Those driven out from the garden of delight
look to me, because I lead them all back
to receive a taste through me who bore you,
a little child, God before the ages.

24

"Σῶσον κόσμον, Σωτήρ· τούτου γὰρ χάριν ἤλυθας·
στῆσον πάντα τὰ σά· τούτου γὰρ χάριν ἔλαμψας
ἐμοὶ καὶ τοῖς Μάγοις καὶ πάσῃ τῇ κτίσει·
ἰδοὺ γὰρ Μάγοι, οἷς ἐνεφάνισας τὸ φῶς τοῦ
προσώπου σου,
προσπίπτοντές σοι δῶρα προσφέρουσι
χρήσιμα, καλά, λίαν ζητούμενα·
αὐτῶν γὰρ χρήζω, ἐπειδὴ μέλλω
ἐπὶ τὴν Αἴγυπτον μολεῖν καὶ φεύγειν σὺν σοὶ διὰ σέ,
ὁδηγέ μου, υἱέ μου, ποιητά μου, πλουτιστά μου,
παιδίον νέον, ὁ πρὸ αἰώνων Θεός."

24

"Savior, save the world! That is why you have come.
Raise up all that is yours! That is why you have shone
for me and the Magi and the whole creation.
See, the Magi, to whom you have shown the light of your
        face,
bow down before you and offer gifts—
useful, beautiful, and highly desirable.
I will need them now; I must go down to Egypt,
in order to flee—with you and for you,
my leader, my son, my maker, my treasure,
my little child, God before the ages."

Προοίμιον

ἰδιόμελον

Ὁ πρὸ Ἑωσφόρου   ἐκ Πατρὸς ἀμήτωρ γεννηθεὶς
ἐπὶ γῆς ἀπάτωρ   ἐσαρκώθη σήμερον ἐκ σοῦ·
ὅθεν ἀστὴρ   εὐαγγελίζεται Μάγοις,
ἄγγελοι δὲ   μετὰ ποιμένων ὑμνοῦσι
τὸν ἄφραστον τόκον σου,
ἡ κεχαριτωμένη.

I

ἰδιόμελον

Τὸν ἀγεώργητον βότρυν   βλαστήσασα ἡ Ἄμπελος
ὡς ἐπὶ κλάδων ἀγκάλαις   ἐβάσταζε καὶ ἔλεγεν·
"Σὺ καρπός μου,   σὺ ζωή μου,
ἀφ' οὗ ἔγνων   ὅτι καὶ ὃ ἤμην εἰμί·   σύ μου Θεός·
τὴν σφραγῖδα τῆς παρθενίας μου   ὁρῶσα ἀκατάλυτον,
κηρύττω σε ἄτρεπτον   Λόγον σάρκα γενόμενον.
Οὐκ οἶδα σποράν,   οἶδά σε λύτην τῆς φθορᾶς·
ἁγνὴ γάρ εἰμι,   σοῦ προελθόντος ἐξ ἐμοῦ·

ON THE NATIVITY
(MARY WITH ADAM AND EVE)

in second plagal mode

Prelude

to its own melody

Born before the Morning Star, with no mother, from the
    Father,
he became flesh on earth today, from you without a father.
A star brings glad tidings to Magi,
and angels with shepherds are praising
your ineffable childbirth,
most favored one.

I

to its own melody

The Vine held in her arms, as in branches,
the cluster of grapes she grew without cultivation
and said, "You are my fruit, you are my life,
from whom I know I still am what I was; you are my God!
As I see the seal of my virginity inviolable,
I proclaim you unchangeable, Word made flesh.
I know no sowing; I know you, who deliver from
    corruption;
for I am pure though you came forth from me.

ὡς γὰρ εὗρες ἔλιπες   μήτραν ἐμὴν   φυλάξας σώαν
                                                        αὐτήν·
διὰ τοῦτο συγχορεύει   πᾶσα κτίσις βοῶσά μοι·
'Η κεχαριτωμένη.'

2

"Οὐκ ἀθετῶ σου τὴν χάριν   ἧς ἔσχον πεῖραν, Δέσποτα·
οὐκ ἀμαυρῶ τὴν ἀξίαν   ἧς ἔτυχον τεκοῦσά σε·
τοῦ γὰρ κόσμου   βασιλεύω·
ἐπειδὴ κράτος   τὸ σὸν ἐβάστασα γαστρί,   πάντων
                                                        κρατῶ·
μετεποίησας τὴν πτωχείαν μου   τῇ συγκαταβάσει σου·
σαυτὸν ἐταπείνωσας   καὶ τὸ γένος μου ὕψωσας.
Εὐφράνθητέ μοι   νῦν ἅμα, Γῆ καὶ Οὐρανός·
τὸν γὰρ Ποιητὴν   ὑμῶν βαστάζω ἐν χερσί·
γηγενεῖς, ἀπόθεσθε   τὰ λυπηρὰ   θεώμενοι τὴν χαράν,
ἣν ἐβλάστησα ἐκ κόλπων   ἀμιάντων καὶ ἤκουσα·
'ἡ κεχαριτωμένη.'"

3

Ὑμνολογούσης δὲ τότε   Μαρίας ὃν ἐγέννησεν,
κολακευούσης δὲ βρέφος   ὃ μόνη ἀπεκύησεν,
ἤκουσεν ἡ   ἐν ὀδύναις
τεκοῦσα τέκνα,   καὶ γηθομένη τῷ Ἀδὰμ   Εὔα βοᾷ·
"Τίς ἐν τοῖς ὠσί μου νῦν ἤχησεν   ἐκεῖνο ὃ ἤλπιζον,
παρθένον τὴν τίκτουσαν   τῆς κατάρας τὴν λύτρωσιν;
ἧς μόνη φωνὴ   ἔλυσέ μου τῶν δυσχερῶν

You left my womb as you found it and kept it safe,
so the whole of creation joins the choir and cries to me,
'*The favored one!*'

2

"I shall not reject the favor you have granted to me, Master;
I shall not conceal the dignity I received giving birth to you,
for I rule the world.
Since I bore your power in my womb, I have power over all.
By your descent you transformed my poverty;
humbling yourself, you exalted my race.
Celebrate with me now, Earth and Heaven,
for I carry your Maker in my arms!
Lay aside your sadness, people of earth, and see the joy
sprung from my undefiled womb; I was called
'*the favored one.*'"

3

As Mary sang praises to the one she had borne,
pampering the baby she had birthed on her own,
Eve, who, in pain, gave birth to children,
heard her and rejoiced, exclaiming to Adam,
"Who has now made hope resound in my ears—
a virgin giving birth to deliverance from the curse?
Her voice alone has freed me from my troubles;

καὶ ταύτης γονὴ   ἔδησε τὸν τρώσαντά με·
ταύτην ἣν προέγραψεν   υἱὸς Ἀμώς,   ἡ ῥάβδος τοῦ
                                                                    Ἰεσσαί,
ἡ βλαστήσασά μοι κλάδον   οὗ φαγοῦσα οὐ θνήξομαι,
ἡ κεχαριτωμένη.

4

"Τῆς χελιδόνος ἀκούσας   κατ' ὄρθρον κελαδούσης μοι,
τὸν ἰσοθάνατον ὕπνον,   Ἀδάμ, ἀφεὶς ἀνάστηθι·
ἄκουσόν μου   τῆς συζύγου·
ἐγὼ ἡ πάλαι   πτῶμα προξενήσασα βροτοῖς   νῦν ἀνιστῶ.
Κατανόησον τὰ θαυμάσια,   ἰδὲ τὴν ἀπείρανδρον
διὰ τοῦ γεννήματος   ἰωμένην τοῦ τραύματος·
ἐμὲ γάρ ποτε   εἷλεν ὁ ὄφις καὶ σκιρτᾷ,
ἀλλ' ἄρτι ὁρῶν   τοὺς ἐξ ἡμῶν φεύγει συρτῶς·
κατ' ἐμοῦ μὲν ὕψωσε   τὴν κεφαλήν,   νυνὶ δὲ
                                                                    ταπεινωθεὶς
κολακεύει, οὐ χλευάζει,   δειλιῶν ὃν ἐγέννησεν
ἡ κεχαριτωμένη."

5

Ἀδὰμ ἀκούσας τοὺς λόγους   οὓς ὕφανεν ἡ σύζυγος,
ἐκ τῶν βλεφάρων τὸ βάρος   εὐθέως ἀποθέμενος
ἀνανεύει   ὡς ἐξ ὕπνου
καὶ οὓς ἀνοίξας   ὃ ἔφραξε παρακοὴ   οὕτως βοᾷ·
"Λιγυροῦ ἀκούω κελαδήματος,   τερπνοῦ μινυρίσματος,

her child has bound the one who wounded me.
It was her that the son of Amoz foretold, the rod of Jesse;
I shall not die if I eat of the branch she has produced for
    me,
the favored one.

4

"You heard the swallow, it sang for me at dawn,
so shed your deathlike sleep, Adam, and get up!
Listen to me, your spouse!
I, who long ago caused mortals to fall, am now arising.
Consider the wonders! See the woman without man
healing the wound with the offspring she's produced!
I was once conquered by the serpent that quivered with joy,
but seeing our descendants, it now flees, slithering away.
It reared its head against me; but now it's been brought low,
groveling, not sneering, fearing the child of
the favored one."

5

When Adam heard the words his spouse had woven,
he wiped the drowsy weight from his eyelids at once
and looked up as if from sleep;
unstopping the ear that disobedience had clogged, he cried
    out,
"I hear a clear song, a delightful warbling,

ἀλλὰ τοῦ μελίζοντος   νῦν ὁ φθόγγος οὐ τέρπει με·
γυνὴ γάρ ἐστιν,   ἧς καὶ φοβοῦμαι τὴν φωνήν·
ἐν πείρᾳ εἰμί,   ὅθεν τὸ θῆλυ δειλιῶ·
ὁ μὲν ἦχος θέλγει με   ὡς λιγυρός,   τὸ ὄργανον δὲ
                                                 δονεῖ,
μὴ ὡς πάλαι με πλανήσῃ   ἐπιφέρουσα ὄνειδος
ἡ κεχαριτωμένη."

6

"Πληροφορήθητι, ἄνερ,   τοῖς λόγοις τῆς συζύγου σου·
οὐ γὰρ εὑρήσεις με πάλιν   πικρά σοι συμβουλεύουσαν·
τὰ ἀρχαῖα   γὰρ παρῆλθε
καὶ νέα πάντα   δείκνυσιν ὁ τῆς Μαριὰμ   γόνος
                                                 Χριστός.
Τούτου τῆς νοτίδος ὀσφράνθητι   καὶ εὐθέως ἐξάνθησον,
ὡς στάχυς ὀρθώθητι·   τὸ γὰρ ἔαρ σε ἔφθασεν,
Ἰησοῦς Χριστὸς   πνέει ὡς αὔρα γλυκερά·
τὸν καύσωνα ᾧ ἧς   ἀποφυγὼν τὸν αὐστηρόν,
δεῦρο ἀκολούθει μοι   πρὸς Μαριάμ,   καὶ τῶν
                                                 ἀχράντων αὐτῆς
ποδῶν ἅψαι σὺν ἐμοὶ νῦν,   καὶ εὐθέως
                                                 σπλαγχνισθήσεται
ἡ κεχαριτωμένη."

7

"Ἔγνων, ὦ γύναι, τὸ ἔαρ   καὶ τῆς τρυφῆς αἰσθάνομαι
ἧς ἐξεπέσαμεν πάλαι·   καὶ γὰρ ὁρῶ παράδεισον
νέον, ἄλλον,   τὴν παρθένον

yet the sound of the singer does not delight me;
for it's a woman, and her voice makes me scared.
I've encountered it before, so I fear all women.
The clear tone enchants me, but the instrument upsets me.
May she not, as of old, lead me astray, inflicting disgrace,
the favored one."

6

"Trust the words of your spouse, husband;
you will not find me giving bitter advice again!
The old has passed away,
and Christ, the child of Mary, reveals everything as new.
Inhale his moist breath and burst into flower,
stand up straight like grain—spring has arrived!
Jesus Christ exhales a sweet breeze.
Free from the burning fever you had,
come, follow me to Mary and touch with me
her immaculate feet; at once she'll take pity,
the favored one."

7

"I feel the spring, wife, and I sense the delight
we fell from in the past; for I am seeing paradise—
a new one, another, a virgin

φέρουσαν κόλποις   αὐτὸ τὸ Ξύλον τῆς Ζωῆς   ὅπερ
                                                        ποτὲ
χερουβὶμ ἐτήρει τὸ ἅγιον   πρὸς τὸ μὴ ψαῦσαι ἐμέ·
τοῦτο τοίνυν ἄψαυστον   ἐγὼ βλέπων φυόμενον,
ᾐσθόμην πνοῆς,   σύζυγε, τῆς ζωοποιοῦ
τῆς κόνιν ἐμὲ   ὄντα καὶ ἄψυχον πηλὸν
ποιησάσης ἔμψυχον·   ταύτης νυνὶ   τῇ εὐοσμίᾳ ῥωσθείς,
πορευθῶ πρὸς τὴν ἀνθοῦσαν   τὸν καρπὸν τῆς ζωῆς
                                                        ἡμῶν,
τὴν κεχαριτωμένην.

8

"Ἰδού εἰμι πρὸ ποδῶν σου,   Παρθένε, μῆτερ ἄμωμε,
καὶ δι' ἐμοῦ πᾶν τὸ γένος   τοῖς ἴχνεσί σου πρόσκειται.
Μὴ παρίδῃς   τοὺς τεκόντας,
ἐπειδὴ τόκος   ὁ σὸς ἀνεγέννησε νῦν   τοὺς ἐν φθορᾷ·
τὸν ἐν Ἅιδῃ παλαιωθέντα με,   Ἀδὰμ τὸν πρωτόπλαστον
οἰκτείρησον, θύγατερ,   τὸν πατέρα σου στένοντα·
τὰ δάκρυά μου   βλέπουσα, σπλαγχνίσθητί μοι
καὶ τοῖς ὀδυρμοῖς   κλῖνον τὸ οὖς σου εὐμενῶς·
τὰ δὲ ῥάκη βλέπεις μου   ἅπερ φορῶ,   ἃ ὄφις ὕφανέ μοι·
ἄμειψόν μου τὴν πενίαν   ἐνώπιον οὗ ἔτεκες,
ἡ κεχαριτωμένη."

9

"Ναί, ἡ ἐλπὶς τῆς ψυχῆς μου,   κἀμοῦ τῆς Εὔας ἄκουσον
καὶ τῆς ἐν λύπαις τεκούσης   τὸ αἶσχος ἀποσόβησον,

carrying in her bosom the Tree of Life, which cherubim
  once
guarded as sacred and stopped me from touching,
this untouchable plant I now see growing.
I've sensed, my spouse, the life-giving breath
that turned me, dust and lifeless clay, into a living being.
Quickened by the fragrance, I'm drawn to her
who yields the fruit of our life,
the favored one.

8

"See, here I am at your feet, unblemished Virgin mother,
and, through me, the whole race clings to you.
Do not overlook your parents,
now that your childbirth has given rebirth to those in
  decline.
Take pity, daughter, on me your groaning father,
the first-formed Adam, grown old in Hades!
Have sympathy for me as you witness my tears
and turn a kind ear toward my weeping!
See, the rags I wear, the serpent wove for me.
In the presence of your child, transform my poverty,
most favored one."

9

"Yes, hear me, Eve, as well, hope of my soul,
and chase away the shame from me who gave birth in
  suffering!

ὡς ἰδοῦσα   ὅτι πλέον
ἐγὼ ἡ τλήμων   τοῖς ὀδυρμοῖς τοῦ Ἀδὰμ   τήκω τὴν
ψυχήν·
τῆς τρυφῆς γὰρ οὗτος μνησκόμενος   ἐμοὶ ἐπανίσταται
κραυγάζων ὡς· Εἴθε μὴ   τῆς πλευρᾶς μου ἐβλάστησας·
καλὸν ἦν μή σε   λαβεῖν εἰς βοήθειάν μου·
οὐκ ἔπιπτον γὰρ   νυνὶ εἰς τοῦτον τὸν βυθόν.'
Καὶ λοιπὸν μὴ φέρουσα   τοὺς ἐλεγμοὺς   μηδὲ τὸν
ὀνειδισμόν,
κατακάμπτω τὸν αὐχένα   ἕως οὗ ἀνορθώσῃς με,
ἡ κεχαριτωμένη."

10

Οἱ ὀφθαλμοὶ δὲ Μαρίας   τὴν Εὔαν θεωρήσαντες
καὶ τὸν Ἀδὰμ κατιδόντες   δακρύειν κατηπείγοντο·
ὅμως στέγει   καὶ σπουδάζει
νικᾶν τὴν φύσιν   ἡ παρὰ φύσιν τὸν Χριστὸν   σχοῦσα
υἱόν·
ἀλλὰ τὰ σπλάγχνα ἐταράττετο   γονεῦσι συμπάσχουσα·
τῷ γὰρ ἐλεήμονι   μήτηρ ἔπρεπεν εὔσπλαγχνος.
Διὸ πρὸς αὐτούς·   "Παύσασθε τῶν θρήνων ὑμῶν,
καὶ πρέσβις ὑμῖν   γίνομαι πρὸς τὸν ἐξ ἐμοῦ·
ὑμεῖς δὲ ἀπώσασθε   τὴν συμφοράν,   τεκούσης μου τὴν
χαράν·
ὡς γὰρ πάντα τὰ τῆς λύπης   ἐκπορθήσουσα ἥκω νῦν
ἡ κεχαριτωμένη.

As you have seen, wretch that I am,
my heart is melting even more with Adam's weeping.
When he recalls the delight, he attacks me, shouting,
'I wish you had never sprung from my rib!
It would have been better if I hadn't received you as my
    helper;
for I would not now have fallen into these depths.'
Unable to bear his reproaches and humiliation,
I bow my head—till you raise me up,
most favored one."

10

Seeing Eve and gazing on Adam,
Mary's eyes were driven to tears,
though she held them in check, for she was eager
to conquer nature, she who bore her son against nature.
But compassion for her parents unsettled her heart,
for a kindhearted mother befits the child of loving-
    kindness,
so she said to them, "Cease your laments,
and I'll be an ambassador for you to him who comes from
    me!
Shake off your misfortune—I've given birth to joy!
For to plunder the realm of grief I've come,
the favored one.

11

"Υἱὸν οἰκτίρμονα ἔχω   καὶ λίαν ἐλεήμονα,
ἐξ ὧν τῇ πείρᾳ ἐπέγνων·   προσέχω ὅπως φείδεται·
πῦρ ὑπάρχων,   ᾤκησέ με
τὴν ἀκανθώδη   καὶ οὐ κατέφλεξεν ἐμὲ   τὴν ταπεινήν·
ὡς πατὴρ οἰκτείρει υἱοὺς αὐτοῦ,   οἰκτείρει ὁ γόνος μου
τοὺς φοβουμένους αὐτόν,   ὡς Δαυὶδ προεφήτευσε.
Τὰ δάκρυα οὖν   στείλαντες, ἐκδέξασθέ με
μεσῖτιν ὑμῶν   γενέσθαι πρὸς τὸν ἐξ ἐμοῦ·
χαρᾶς γὰρ παραίτιος   ὁ γεννηθεὶς   ὁ πρὸ αἰώνων Θεός·
ἡσυχάσατε ἀλύπως,   πρὸς αὐτὸν γὰρ εἰσέρχομαι
ἡ κεχαριτωμένη."

12

Ῥήμασι τούτοις Μαρία   καὶ ἄλλοις δὲ τοῖς πλείοσι
παρακαλέσασα Εὕαν   καὶ ταύτης τὸν ὁμόζυγα,
εἰσελθοῦσα   πρὸς τὴν φάτνην,
αὐχένα κάμπτει   καὶ δυσωποῦσα τὸν υἱὸν   οὕτω φησί·
"Ἐπειδή με, ὦ τέκνον, ὕψωσας   τῇ συγκαταβάσει σου,
τὸ πενιχρὸν γένος μου   δι' ἐμοῦ νῦν σοῦ δέεται.
Ἀδὰμ γὰρ πρός με   ἤλυθε στενάζων πικρῶς·
Εὕα δὲ αὐτῷ   ὀδυνωμένη συνθρηνεῖ·
ὁ δὲ τούτων αἴτιος   ὄφις ἐστὶν   τιμῆς γυμνώσας αὐτούς·
διὰ τοῦτο σκεπασθῆναι   ἐξαιτοῦσι βοῶντές μοι·
Ἡ κεχαριτωμένη.'"

11

"The son I have is compassionate and truly gracious;
I know from experience; I've observed his gentleness:
Although he is fire, he dwelt within
my thorny flesh, but did not consume my humble self.
As a father has compassion for his sons, so my child
has compassion for those who fear him, as David
        prophesied.
Hold back your tears, then, and wait for me
to be your intercessor with the one who comes from me!
The infant is a source of joy, God before the ages.
Be still, don't be sad, for I'm turning to him as
the favored one."

12

Mary, with these and many more words,
comforted Eve as well as her spouse,
before she then went to the manger.
She bows her head and entreats her son, saying this:
"Since you, my child, have exalted me by your descent,
my needy race now implores you through me.
Adam has come to me groaning bitterly,
and Eve weeps too, in pain with him.
The cause of it all is the serpent, who stripped them of
        honor,
so they're begging to be covered when they cry out to me,
'*The favored one!*'"

13

Ὡς δὲ τοιαύτας δεήσεις   προσήγαγεν ἡ ἄμωμος
Θεῷ κειμένῳ ἐν φάτνῃ,   λαβὼν εὐθὺς ὑπέγραφεν·
ἑρμηνεύων   τὰ ἐσχάτως,
φησίν· "Ὦ μῆτερ,   καὶ διὰ σὲ καὶ διὰ σοῦ   σῴζω αὐτούς.
Εἰ μὴ σῶσαι τούτους ἠθέλησα,   οὐκ ἂν ἐν σοὶ ᾤκησα,
οὐκ ἂν ἐκ σοῦ ἔλαμψα,   οὐκ ἂν μήτηρ μου ἤκουσας·
τὴν φάτνην ἐγὼ   διὰ τὸ γένος σου οἰκῶ,
μαζῶν δὲ τῶν σῶν   βουλόμενος νῦν γαλουχῶ,
ἐν ἀγκάλαις φέρεις με   χάριν αὐτῶν·   ὃν οὐχ ὁρᾷ
                                                    χερουβὶμ
ἰδοὺ βλέπεις καὶ βαστάζεις   καὶ ὡς υἱὸν κολακεύεις με,
ἡ κεχαριτωμένη.

14

"Μητέρα σε ἐκτησάμην   ὁ Πλαστουργὸς τῆς κτίσεως
καὶ ὥσπερ βρέφος αὐξάνω   ὁ ἐκ τελείου τέλειος·
τοῖς σπαργάνοις   ἐνειλοῦμαι
διὰ τοὺς πάλαι   χιτῶνας δερματίνους   φορέσαντας,
καὶ τὸ σπήλαιόν μοι ἐράσμιον   διὰ τοὺς μισήσαντας
τρυφὴν καὶ παράδεισον   καὶ φθορὰν ἀγαπήσαντας·
παρέβησάν μου   τὴν ζωηφόρον ἐντολήν·
κατέβην εἰς γῆν   ἵνα ἔχουσι τὴν ζωήν.
Ἂν δὲ καὶ τὸ ἕτερον   μάθῃς, σεμνή,   ὃ μέλλω δρᾶν δι᾽
                                                    αὐτούς,
μετὰ πάντων τῶν στοιχείων   σὲ δονεῖ τὸ γενόμενον,
ἡ κεχαριτωμένη."

13

When the immaculate woman presented these pleas to the
     God
whom she'd laid in a manger, he accepted directly and
     agreed.
Explaining what had just happened, he said,
"Mother, both for you and through you I save them;
were that not my wish, I wouldn't have dwelt in you,
wouldn't have shone from you, nor had you as my mother.
It is for your race that I dwell in the manger,
and at your breasts I now suckle for them voluntarily.
You carry me in your arms, who's unseen by cherubim;
you hold and behold me, soothe me as your son,
most favored one.

14

"I, the Shaper of creation, have taken you as mother;
I'm perfect and hail from perfection, but develop like a
     baby.
I have wrapped myself in swaddling clothes
for those who long ago wore coats of skin;
I was drawn to the cave for those who hated
delight and paradise and loved corruption.
They disobeyed my life-giving commandment,
but I have come to earth so that they may live.
If you learned, noble mother, what else I shall do for them,
it would shake you, together with all the elements,
most favored one!"

15

Ἀλλὰ τοιαῦτα εἰπόντος   τοῦ πᾶσαν γλῶσσαν πλάσαντος
καὶ τῆς μητρὸς τῇ δεήσει   ταχέως ὑπογράψαντος,
ἔτι εἶπεν   ἡ Μαρία·
"Ἐὰν λαλήσω,   μὴ ὀργισθῇς μοι τῇ πηλῷ,   ὦ
                                        Πλαστουργέ·
ὡς πρὸς τέκνον παρρησιάσομαι·   θαρρῶ ὡς σὲ
                                        γεννήσασα·
σύ μοι γὰρ τῷ τόκῳ σου   πᾶσαν καύχησιν δέδωκας.
Ὃ μέλλεις τελεῖν   τί ἐστι θέλω νῦν μαθεῖν·
μὴ κρύψῃς ἐμοὶ   τὴν ἀπ᾽ αἰῶνός σου βουλήν·
ὅλον σε ἐγέννησα·   φράσον τὸν νοῦν   ὃν ἔχεις περὶ
                                        ἡμᾶς,
ἵνα μάθω καὶ ἐκ τούτου   ὅσης ἔτυχον χάριτος
ἡ κεχαριτωμένη."

16

"Νικῶμαι διὰ τὸν πόθον   ὃν ἔχω πρὸς τὸν ἄνθρωπον,"
ὁ Ποιητὴς ἀπεκρίθη.   "Ἐγώ, δούλη καὶ μῆτέρ μου,
οὐ λυπῶ σε·   γνωριῶ σοι
ἃ θέλω πράττειν   καὶ θεραπεύσω σου ψυχήν,   ὦ
                                        Μαριάμ.
Τὸν ἐν ταῖς χερσί σου φερόμενον   τὰς χεῖρας ἡλούμενον
μετὰ μικρὸν ὄψει με,   ὅτι στέργω τὸ γένος σου·
ὃν σὺ γαλουχεῖς   ἄλλοι ποτίσουσι χολήν·

15

When he who shaped every tongue had spoken
and immediately approved his mother's plea,
Mary spoke to him again:
"If I speak, don't be angry, Shaper, with me, the clay!
I'll speak freely, as to a child; I'm emboldened as your
     mother,
for you gave me, by your birth, every reason to boast.
I would like to learn now what you're going to accomplish.
Don't hide from me your ancient plan—
I gave birth to all of you! Reveal to me, then, your intention
     for us,
that I may again learn what favor I enjoy,
the favored one!"

16

"I am overcome by my longing for humanity,"
the Maker replied, "and, servant and mother,
I shall not upset you. I will let you know
what I want to achieve, dear Mary, and I shall tend your
     soul.
The one you hold in your hands, you will see in a little while
with his hands nailed, since I love your race.
The one you give milk to, others will serve gall;

ὃν καταφιλεῖς   μέλλει πληροῦσθαι ἐμπτυσμῶν·
ὃν ζωὴν ἐκάλεσας,   ἔχεις ἰδεῖν   κρεμάμενον ἐν σταυρῷ
καὶ δακρύσεις ὡς θανόντα,   ἀλλ᾽ ἀσπάσει με ἀναστάντα,
ἡ κεχαριτωμένη.

17

"Ὅλων δὲ τούτων ἐν πείρᾳ   βουλήσει μου γενήσομαι,
καὶ πάντων τούτων αἰτία   διάθεσις γενήσεται
ἣν ἐκ πάλαι   ἕως ἄρτι
πρὸς τοὺς ἀνθρώπους   ἐπεδειξάμην ὡς Θεός,   σῶσαι
                                                  ζητῶν."
Μαριὰμ δὲ τούτων ὡς ἤκουσεν   ἐκ βάθους ἐστέναξε
βοῶσα· "Ὦ βότρυς μου,   μὴ ἐκθλίψωσί σε ἄνομοι·
βλαστήσαντός σου   μὴ ὄψωμαι τέκνου σφαγήν."
Ὁ δὲ πρὸς αὐτὴν   ἔφησεν οὕτως εἰπών·
"Παῦσαι, μῆτερ, κλαίουσα   ὃ ἀγνοεῖς·   ἐὰν γὰρ μὴ
                                                  τελεσθῇ,
ἀπολοῦνται οὗτοι πάντες   ὑπὲρ ὧν ἱκετεύεις με,
ἡ κεχαριτωμένη.

18

"Ὕπνον δὲ νόμισον εἶναι   τὸν θάνατόν μου, μῆτέρ μου·
τρεῖς γὰρ ἡμέρας τελέσας   ἐν μνήματι θελήματι,
μετὰ ταῦτα   σοὶ ὁρῶμαι
ἀναβιώσας   καὶ ἀνακαινίσας τὴν γῆν   καὶ τοὺς ἐκ γῆς.

the one you kiss will be covered in spit;
the one you called life, you must see on a cross
and weep for as dead. But you'll greet me when I've risen,
most favored one!

17

"All these things I shall willingly undergo,
and they will happen due to the disposition
that from olden days until the present
I, as God, have shown toward humans, seeking to save
    them."
When Mary heard this, she groaned deeply
and cried, "My sweet bunch of grapes, don't let the lawless
    crush you!
Don't let me see the slaughter of the child that grew from
    me!'"
But he spoke to her and said this:
"Stop weeping over what you don't understand, mother! If
    it is not finished,
all those for whom you implore me will perish,
most favored one!

18

"Think of my death, dear mother, as sleep.
When I've willingly completed three days in a tomb,
I will show myself to you
returned to life and having renewed the earth and its
    offspring.

Ταῦτα, μῆτερ, πᾶσιν ἀνάγγειλον,   ἐν τούτοις
                                              πλουτίσθητι,
ἐκ τούτων βασίλευσον,   διὰ τούτων εὐφράνθητι."
Ἐξῆλθεν εὐθὺς   ἡ Μαριὰμ πρὸς τὸν Ἀδάμ,
εὐαγγελισμὸν   φέρουσα τῇ Εὔᾳ φησί·
"Τέως ἡσυχάσατε   ὅσον μικρόν·   ἠκούσατε γὰρ αὐτοῦ
ἅπερ εἶπεν ὑπομεῖναι   δι' ὑμᾶς τοὺς βοῶντάς μοι·
Ἡ κεχαριτωμένη.'"

Announce these things, mother! Be rich in them,
rule by them, rejoice through them!"
Mary went off to Adam straight away
and brought glad tidings, saying to Eve,
"Be still a little while longer! For you heard from him what
      he said
awaits, through you, those who cry to me,
'*The favored one!*'"

Προοίμιον

ἰδιόμελον

Ὁ τὸ ὕδωρ εἰς οἶνον ὡς δυνατὸς μεταποιήσας,
τὴν ἐξ ἁμαρτημάτων συνέχουσάν με θλῖψιν
εἰς χαρὰν μεταποίησον διὰ τῆς Θεοτόκου,
Χριστὲ ὁ Θεός,
ὁ τὰ πάντα ἐν σοφίᾳ ποιήσας.

I

πρός· Τῷ τυφλωθέντι Ἀδάμ

Τὴν παρθενίαν τιμήσας Θεὸς γαστέραν ᾤκησε
παρθενικήν·
τεχθεὶς δὲ ἐξ αὐτῆς ἀσπόρως, τῆς ἁγνείας αὐτῆς τὰς
σφραγῖδας οὐκ ἔλυσεν·
οὗτος τὴν Ἐκκλησίαν ἄμωμον καὶ παρθένον
ἑαυτῷ ἐμνηστεύσατο.
Ἡ μήτηρ οὖν Χριστοῦ καὶ παρθένος καὶ νύμφη,
παρθένος καὶ αὐτός· ἡ παστὰς δὲ ἁγία,
οὐρανὸν γὰρ νυμφῶνα εἰργάσατο.
Κἂν οὖν ἐτέχθη ἐκ παρθενικῆς καὶ παναγίας γαστρός,

ON THE WEDDING AT CANA

in second plagal mode

Prelude

to its own melody

As you with power turned water into wine,
turn the sinful misery that clutches me
into joy through your own God-bearing mother,
Christ our God,
the one who has made all in wisdom.

I

to: On the blinded Adam

God, who honored virginity, came to dwell in a virginal
    womb.
Born from it without seed, he did not break the seals of its
    purity.
He took the Church, an unblemished virgin,
and betrothed it to himself.
The mother of Christ is both virgin and bride,
as he is a virgin. Yet the marriage bed is holy,
for he made heaven into a bridal chamber.
Though born of a virginal, all-holy womb,

οὐ βδελύττεται ὅμως   τὰς τῶν γάμων συζυγίας
ὁ τὰ πάντα   ἐν σοφίᾳ ποιήσας.

2

Ὅθεν ὁ ἄμοιρος γάμου θνητοῦ,   ὁ μόνος ἅγιος καὶ
                                                φοβερὸς
θαλάμῳ γαμικῷ ἐπέστη,   ὡς ὁ θεῖος ἡμᾶς   Ἰωάννης
                                                ἐδίδαξεν
ὅτι ὁ ἀνυμφεύτους   διαδραμὼν ὠδῖνας
ἐν τοῖς γάμοις ἐλήλυθεν,
ὁ ἐπὶ χερουβὶμ   ἐποχούμενος ὤμοις,
ἐν κόλποις τοῦ Πατρὸς   ἀχωρίστως ὑπάρχων,
ἐν στιβάδι   φθαρτῇ ἀνεκλίνετο·
συνεστιάθη τοῖς ἁμαρτωλοῖς   ὁ ἁμαρτίαν μὴ γνούς,
ἵνα δείξῃ τὸν γάμον   τίμιον τῇ παρουσίᾳ
ὁ τὰ πάντα   ἐν σοφίᾳ ποιήσας.

3

Ἔνθεν εἰκότως λαβὼν ἀφορμὰς   ὁ μέγας ἔγραψε
                                                Παῦλος βοῶν
ὡς τίμιός ἐστιν ὁ γάμος   καὶ τοῦ γάμου ἡ
                                                κοίτη   ὑπάρχει ἀμίαντος·
καὶ γὰρ διὰ τοῦ γάμου   λάμπουσιν αἱ παρθένοι·
διὰ γάμου γὰρ τίκτονται.
Ἡ Θεοτόκος γὰρ   καὶ ἁγία παρθένος
καὶ ἔμεινεν ἁγνὴ   μετὰ τόκον παρθένος,
ἀλλὰ γάμος   αὐτὴν ἀπεκύησεν,

he does not abhor nuptial unions,
the one who has made all in wisdom.

2

So he who alone is holy and awesome, who had no share in
    mortal marriage,
came to the place of the wedding, as the godly John has
    taught us,
he who passed through an unmarried labor,
arrived at the wedding;
he who is borne on the shoulders of cherubim,
being unseparated from the bosom of the Father,
reclined to dine on a perishable couch.
He who knew no sin feasted with sinners
in order to honor marriage with his presence,
the one who has made all in wisdom.

3

Likewise, drawing on this occasion, the great Paul wrote
and proclaimed that marriage is honorable, and the
    marriage bed is undefiled.
And it is from a marriage that virgins can shine,
for through marriage they are born.
The God-Bearer was a holy virgin
and remained a pure virgin after childbirth,
but a marriage gave birth to her;

ὡς καὶ τὸ πλῆθος τῶν διὰ Χριστὸν   παρθενευσάντων ἀεὶ
διὰ γάμου ἐτέχθη,   ὃν ἡγίασεν ἐκ μήτρας
ὁ τὰ πάντα   ἐν σοφίᾳ ποιήσας.

4

Πρόκειται νῦν καὶ τὸ θαῦμα εἰπεῖν   ὃ πρῶτον ἔπραξεν
                                    ἐν τῇ Κανᾷ
ὁ πρώην Αἰγυπτίοις δείξας   καὶ Ἑβραίοις αὐτοῖς   τῶν
                                    θαυμάτων τὴν δύναμιν.
Τότε μὲν γὰρ εἰς αἷμα   ἡ τῶν ὑδάτων φύσις
θαυμαστῶς μετεβάλλετο·
δεκάπληγον ὀργὴν   Αἰγυπτίοις ἐπῆξε,
τὴν θάλασσαν βατὴν   τοῖς Ἑβραίοις παρέσχεν,
ἣν ὡς χέρσον   σπουδαίως διώδευσαν·
ἐν τῇ ἀνύδρῳ ὕδωρ χορηγεῖ   ἀπὸ τῆς πέτρας αὐτοῖς·
ἐν τοῖς γάμοις δὲ ἄρτι   φύσιν πάλιν μεταβάλλει
ὁ τὰ πάντα   ἐν σοφίᾳ ποιήσας.

5

Ὅτε τοῖς γάμοις παρῆν ὁ Χριστὸς   καὶ εὐωχεῖτο
                                    ἀνθρώπων πληθύς,
ἐπέλειψεν αὐτοῖς ὁ οἶνος,   καὶ εἰς λύπην αὐτοῖς   ἡ
                                    χαρὰ μετεβάλετο·
ἤχθετο ὁ νυμφίος,   καὶ οἱ οἰνοχοοῦντες
ἐψιθύριζον ἄπαυστα,
καὶ μία ἦν αὐτοῖς   τραγῳδία πενίας,

indeed, all who, for Christ, remain in perpetual virginity
were born through marriage, which he hallowed from the
 womb,
the one who has made all in wisdom.

4

It is time now to speak of the wonder he first performed in
 Cana,
he who formerly showed Egyptians and the Hebrews
 themselves the power of his wonders.
For at that time the nature of water was wondrously
transformed into blood;
he brought upon the Egyptians a ten-plague wrath;
he offered the Hebrews the sea to walk through,
and they hastily crossed it like dry land.
In the waterless place he provides water from the rock;
at the wedding he again transforms nature,
the one who has made all in wisdom.

5

When Christ was present at the wedding and the crowd of
 people were feasting,
they ran out of wine, and so their joy was transformed to
 grief.
The groom was troubled, and those who served
were whispering incessantly.
To them it was one more tragedy of poverty;

καὶ θόρυβος παρῆν   οὐ μικρὸς τῷ θαλάμῳ·
ὃν καὶ γνοῦσα   Μαρία ἡ πάναγνος
ἦλθεν εὐθὺς καὶ λέγει τῷ υἱῷ·   "Οἶνον οὐκ ἔχουσιν·
ἀλλὰ δέομαι, τέκνον,   δεῖξον ὅτι πάντα δύνῃ,
ὁ τὰ πάντα   ἐν σοφίᾳ ποιήσας."

6

Σὲ δυσωποῦμεν, Παρθένε σεμνή,   ἐκ ποίων ἔγνως
                                        θαυμάτων αὐτοῦ
ὡς δύναται ὁ υἱός σου   σταφυλὴν μὴ τρυγήσας   τὸν
                                        οἶνον χαρίζεσθαι,
οὔπω θαυματουργήσας   πρώην, ὡς Ἰωάννης
ὁ Θεσπέσιος ἔγραψεν;
Ἐκδίδαξον ἡμᾶς   πῶς μὴ θεασαμένη,
πῶς θαύματος αὐτοῦ   μὴ λαβοῦσα τὴν πεῖραν,
προσκαλεῖσαι   αὐτὸν πρὸς τὰ θαύματα·
οὐ γὰρ ἁπλῆ ἡ αἴτησις νυνί   ἐστιν ἐν τούτῳ ἡμῖν,
ὅτι πῶς τῷ υἱῷ σου·   "Δὸς αὐτοῖς," ἐβόας, "οἶνον,
ὁ τὰ πάντα   ἐν σοφίᾳ ποιήσας."

7

Ῥήματα μάθωμεν ἃ πρὸς ἡμᾶς   ἡ Μήτηρ λέγει τοῦ
                                        πάντων Θεοῦ·
"Ἀκούσατε," φησίν, "ὦ φίλοι,   συνετίσθητε,
                                        πάντες,   καὶ γνῶτε μυστήρια.
Εἶδον τὸν υἱόν μου   ἤδη θαυματουργοῦντα
καὶ πρὸ τούτου τοῦ θαύματος·

in the room arose a major commotion.
When the all-pure Mary noticed it,
she went at once and said to her son, "They have no wine!
But show them your powers, I beg you, my child,
the one who has made all in wisdom!"

6

Please, let us know, noble Virgin, from what wonders of his
    did you grasp
that your son was able to offer wine without harvesting
    grapes,
since he hadn't worked wonders before, as John
the Divine wrote?
Teach us how, with no glimpse of his wonders
and without experience, you can summon him
to perform such miracles.
For us it is no simple question how you
can exclaim to your son, "Give them wine, you who are
the one who has made all in wisdom!"

7

Let us learn from the words she speaks to us, the Mother of
    the God of all!
"Listen, my friends," she says, "open your minds and fathom
    the mysteries!
I have seen my son working wonders already,
before this wonder.

οὐδέπω ἦν αὐτοῦ   μαθητὴς Ἰωάννης·
οὐδέπω γὰρ οὐκ ἦν   τῷ Χριστῷ μαθητεύσας,
ὅτε ταῦτα   ἐποίει τὰ θαύματα·
πρώτην αὐτοῦ θαυμάτων ἀπαρχὴν   ταύτην τεθέαται
ἐν Κανᾷ γεναμένην,   ὥσπερ οἶδεν ὁ υἱός μου,
ὁ τὰ πάντα   ἐν σοφίᾳ ποιήσας.

8

"Ὥστε ἐπείπερ ἐκεῖνα οὐδεὶς   ἀνθρώπων ἔχει εἰς πίστιν
                                                σαφῶς
ταῖς βίβλοις μὴ ἐγγεγραμμένα   αἷς αὐτοῦ οἱ
                        αὐτόπται   τῆς χάριτος ἔγραψαν,
ταῦτα μὲν παραλείψω·   ἅψομαι δὲ μειζόνων
ὧνπερ ἔχω τὴν εἴδησιν.
Ἐπίσταμαι ἐγὼ   ὅτι ἄνδρα οὐκ ἔγνων,
καὶ ἔτεκον υἱὸν   ὑπὲρ φύσιν καὶ λόγον,
καὶ ὡς ἤμην   παρθένος μεμένηκα·
τούτου τοῦ τόκου μεῖζον οὖν ζητεῖς   θαῦμα, ὦ ἄνθρωπε;
Γαβριήλ μοι ἐπέστη   λέγων πῶς γεννᾶται οὗτος
ὁ τὰ πάντα   ἐν σοφίᾳ ποιήσας.

9

"Μετὰ τὴν σύλληψιν εἶδον ἐγὼ   τὴν Ἐλισάβετ
                                                καλοῦσαν ἐμὲ
'Μητέρα τοῦ Θεοῦ' πρὸ τόκου·   Συμεὼν δὲ ἐμὲ   μετὰ
                                                τόκον ἀνύμνησεν,
Ἄννα με ἀνευφήμει·   Μάγοι δὲ ἐκ Περσίδος

John was not his disciple yet;
he had not yet come to learn from him
when Christ performed these wonders.
This first one that he witnessed, the first fruit of his
    wonders,
occurred in Cana, as my son well knows,
the one who has made all in wisdom.

8

"Since no one, apparently, has faith in things that are not
    recorded
in the books written by those who witnessed his grace
    directly,
I'll leave those out and turn to something greater
of which I have knowledge.
I know for a fact that I knew no man,
but bore a son, beyond nature and reason,
and, as I was, I have remained a virgin.
Can anyone ask for a wonder greater than this birth?
Gabriel appeared and told me how this child might be born,
the one who has made all in wisdom.

9

"After I'd conceived, I saw Elizabeth, who called me
    'Mother of God'
before I gave birth and, after that, Symeon sang my praises;
Anna lauded me. Magi from Persia

πρὸς τὴν φάτνην ἐξέδραμον,
οὐράνιος ἀστὴρ   προμηνύων τὸν τόκον·
ἐκήρυττον χαρὰν   μετ᾽ ἀγγέλων ποιμένες,
καὶ ἡ κτίσις   σὺν τούτοις ἠγάλλετο·
τί τῶν θαυμάτων τούτων ἐκζητεῖν   μεῖζον δυνήσομαι;
Καὶ ἐντεῦθεν πιστεύω   ὅτι ἐστὶν ὁ υἱός μου
ὁ τὰ πάντα   ἐν σοφίᾳ ποιήσας."

10

Ἀλλ᾽ ὁ Χριστὸς τὴν μητέρα ἰδὼν   "Παράσχου,"
                                    λέγουσαν, "χάριν ἐμοί,"
καὶ εἶπεν πρὸς αὐτὴν εὐθέως·   "Τί ἐμοὶ καὶ σοί,
                                    γύναι;   Οὐχ ἥκει ἡ ὥρα μου."
Τοῦτον τινὲς τὸν λόγον   πρόφασιν ἀσεβείας
ἑαυτοῖς κατεσκεύασαν,
οἱ λέγοντες Χριστὸν   ὑποκεῖσθαι ἀνάγκαις,
οἱ φάσκοντες αὐτὸν   καὶ ταῖς ὥραις δουλεύειν,
οὐ νοοῦντες   τοῦ λόγου τὴν ἔννοιαν·
ἀλλ᾽ ἐνεφράγη στόμα ἀσεβῶν   τῶν μελετώντων κακά,
ἐπειδὴ παραχρῆμα   καὶ τὸ θαῦμα διεξῆλθεν
ὁ τὰ πάντα   ἐν σοφίᾳ ποιήσας.

11

"Νῦν ἀποκρίθητι, τέκνον," φησὶν   ἡ πάναγνος μήτηρ
                                    τοῦ Ἰησοῦ,
"ὁ μέτροις χαλινῶν τὰς ὥρας,   πῶς τὰς ὥρας
                                    ἐκδέχει,   υἱέ μου καὶ Κύριε;

rushed to the manger;
a heavenly star foretold the birth.
With angels, shepherds proclaimed joy,
and creation itself joined in their rejoicing.
What wonders greater than these can I ask for?
And so I believe that my son is that one,
the one who has made all in wisdom."

10

When Christ noticed his mother saying, "Grant me your
    favor!" he replied at once,
"What concern is that to me and you, woman? My hour
    hasn't come."
Some have constructed for themselves a pretext
for impiety with this saying,
for they say that Christ is subject to necessity,
and they claim he is also a slave to time,
as they don't understand the meaning of the saying.
But the mouth of the impious, who contemplate evil, was
    stopped,
for the wonder was accomplished by him straight away,
the one who has made all in wisdom.

11

"Answer me this, child," says Jesus's all-pure mother, "you
    who hold
the hours in check with measures, why wait for the hours,
    my son and my Lord?

Πῶς δὲ καιρὸν προσμένεις,   σὺ ὁ νομοθετήσας
τοῖς καιροῖς διαστήματα;
Ὁ Κτίστης ὁρατῶν   ὁμοῦ καὶ ἀοράτων,
ἡμέρᾳ καὶ νυκτὶ   ὁ ἀλύτους βραβεύσας
ὡς δυνάστης   τροπάς, ὡς ἠθέλησας,
κύκλοις εὐτάκτοις τοὺς ἐνιαυτοὺς   σὺ περιέγραψας·
πῶς καιρὸν ἀναμένεις   πρὸς τὸ θαῦμα ὃ αἰτῶ σε,
ὁ τὰ πάντα   ἐν σοφίᾳ ποιήσας;"

12

"Οἶδα πρὶν μάθῃς, Παρθένε σεμνή,   ὡς οἶνος ἔλειψε
                                        τούτοις νυνί,"
ὁ ἄφραστος καὶ ἐλεήμων   τῇ πανσέμνῳ
                              μητρὶ   παρευθὺς ἀπεκρίνατο.
"Οἶδά σου τῆς καρδίας   πάσας τὰς ἐνθυμήσεις
ἃς ἐν τούτῳ ἐκίνησας·
καὶ γὰρ ἐν ἑαυτῇ   ἐλογίσω τοιαῦτα·
'Ἡ χρεία νῦν καλεῖ   τὸν υἱόν μου πρὸς θαῦμα,
καὶ προφάσει   ὡρῶν ἀναβάλλεται.'
Μήτηρ ἁγνή, τὸν τῆς ἀναβολῆς   νῦν ἐκδιδάχθητι νοῦν·
ὅταν τοῦτον γὰρ μάθῃς,   δώσω σοι τὴν χάριν πάντως,
ὁ τὰ πάντα   ἐν σοφίᾳ ποιήσας.

13

""Ὕψωσόν σου πρὸς τοὺς λόγους τὸν νοῦν   καὶ γνῶθι,
                                        ἄφθορε, ἅπερ ἐρῶ·
ἡνίκα γὰρ ἐκ τῶν μὴ ὄντων   οὐρανόν τε καὶ γῆν   καὶ
                                        τὰ πάντα παρήγαγον,

Why await your time, you who've established
the ages of time with their intervals?
Creator of what is both visible and invisible,
who by day and night directs what's unchangeable
at your own will, as ruler of the seasons,
and has circumscribed the years with orderly cycles,
how can you wait for the hour of your wonder,
the one who has made all in wisdom?"

12

"Noble Virgin, I knew before you that their wine would run
    out now,"
her ineffable and compassionate son replied at once to his
    most noble mother.
"I know all the worries that you have stirred up
in your heart over this;
I believe you were thinking something like this:
'Need calls my son to perform a wonder,
but he puts it off with the pretext of hours!'
Let me explain, pure mother, the point of the delay;
when you've learned it, you'll be granted this favor from me,
the one who has made all in wisdom.

13

"Uplift your mind to my words, uncorrupted one, and hear
    what I'll say:
when I brought heaven and earth and all things out of
    nonexistence,

ὅλα τὰ παραχθέντα   τότε διακοσμῆσαι
παραχρῆμα ἐξίσχυον·
ἀλλ' εὔτακτόν τινα   συνεισήγαγον τάξιν·
συνέστη γὰρ ἐν ἓξ   τὰ κτισθέντα ἡμέραις,
οὐκ ἐπείπερ   οὐ δυνατὸς πέφυκα,
ἀλλ' ἵν' ἀγγέλων βλέπων ὁ χορὸς   ἃ κατὰ μέρος ποιῶ
ἐκθειάζεται ᾄδων,   ὑμνῶν· Δόξα σοι, δυνάστα,
ὁ τὰ πάντα   ἐν σοφίᾳ ποιήσας.'

14

"Ταῦτα σαφῶς ἐνωτίζου, σεμνή,   ὡς ἡδυνάμην ἑτέρᾳ
ὁδῷ
λυτρώσασθαι τοὺς πεπτωκότας   καὶ μὴ δούλου,
πτωχοῦ   τὴν μορφὴν καταδέξασθαι·
ὅμως δὲ ἠνεσχόμην   πρῶτον μὲν συλληφθῆναι
καὶ τεχθῆναι ὡς ἄνθρωπος
καὶ γάλακτος λαβεῖν   ἐκ μαζῶν σου, Παρθένε,
καὶ πάντα δ' ἐν ἐμοὶ   κατὰ τάξιν προέβη·
παρ' ἐμοὶ γὰρ   οὐδέν ἐστιν ἄτακτον.
Οὕτως καὶ νῦν τὸ θαῦμα βούλομαι   τάξει εὐτάκτῳ
ποιεῖν,
ὃ εὐδόκησα πράττειν   πρὸς ἀνθρώπων σωτηρίαν,
ὁ τὰ πάντα   ἐν σοφίᾳ ποιήσας.

I was able to set all of these elements
in place at that very moment,
but I also introduced a regulated order.
Creation came together in six days—
not because I lacked any power,
but so the chorus of angels, seeing what I did piece by
      piece,
might worship with song and praise: 'Glory to you, ruler,
the one who has made all in wisdom!'

14

"Listen carefully, noble one. Although I could have chosen a
      different way
to redeem the fallen, and not embraced the form of a poor
      slave,
I undertook it—first to be conceived
and then to be born as a human being,
and to suck the milk from your breasts, Virgin.
Everything about me developed in order,
for nothing with me is random.
So I want also now to perform this wonder in a regulated
      order,
I who, gladly for human salvation, am doing this,
the one who has made all in wisdom.

15

"Ἄπαντα σύνες ἃ λέγω, σεμνή·   νυνὶ γὰρ ἤθελον
                                    πρῶτον ἐγὼ
κηρῦξαι τοῖς Ἰσραηλίταις   καὶ διδάξαι αὐτοὺς   τὴν
                                    ἐλπίδα τῆς πίστεως,
ἵνα πρὸ τῶν θαυμάτων   οὗτοι ἐκδιδαχθῶσιν
ὅτι τίς με ἀπέστειλε,
καὶ γνῶσιν ἀσφαλῶς   τοῦ Πατρός μου τὴν δόξαν
καὶ τούτου τὴν βουλήν,   ὅτι βούλεται πάντως
σὺν αὐτῷ με   ἐκ πάντων δοξάζεσθαι·
ἃ ὁ γεννήσας γὰρ ἐμὲ ποιεῖ,   ταῦτα ποιῶ καὶ ἐγώ,
ὁμοούσιος τούτου   καὶ τοῦ Πνεύματος ὑπάρχων,
ὁ τὰ πάντα   ἐν σοφίᾳ ποιήσας.

16

"Πάντα γὰρ ταῦτα εἰ ἔγνωσαν αὐτοὶ   ἡνίκα θαύματα
                                    εἶδον φρικτά,
ἐγίνωσκον ὅτι ὑπάρχω   πρὸ αἰώνων Θεός,   κἂν
                                    γεγένημαι ἄνθρωπος·
νῦν δὲ παρὰ τὴν τάξιν,   πρὸ τῆς διδασκαλίας,
ἐπεζήτησας θαύματα,
καὶ διὰ τοῦτό σοι   μικρὸν ἀνεβαλλόμην,
καὶ τοῦ θαυματουργεῖν   ἐπεζήτουν τὴν ὥραν
διὰ ταύτην   καὶ μόνην τὴν πρόφασιν·
ἀλλ' ὅτι χρὴ τιμᾶσθαι τοὺς γονεῖς   παρὰ τῶν τέκνων
                                    αὐτῶν,

15

"Understand all that I say, noble one. For at this point I
        wanted first
to proclaim to the Israelites and teach them the hope of
        faith,
so they might learn, before the wonders,
who it is who has sent me,
and might surely know the glory of my Father
as well as his will, that he certainly wants me
to be glorified by all along with him.
What he who begot me does, this I also do;
consubstantial with him and the Spirit, I am
the one who has made all in wisdom.

16

"If those people had known all this when they saw the
        awesome wonders,
they would have grasped that although I'm human, I am
        God before the ages.
Now, however, contrary to my ordering, before my
        instruction,
you wished for wonders.
That's why I delayed it a moment for you,
and I sought the right time to work the wonder
for this reason and this alone.
But since parents ought to be honored by their children,

θεραπεύσω σε, μῆτερ·   δύναμαι γὰρ πάντα πράττειν,
ὁ τὰ πάντα   ἐν σοφίᾳ ποιήσας.

17

"Εἰπὲ οὖν τάχος τοῖς ἐν τῇ οἰκίᾳ   ἵν' ὑπουργήσωσι τοῖς
                                                      παρ' ἐμοῦ,
καὶ ἔσονται μετὰ ταῦτα   ἑαυτοῖς καὶ τοῖς ἄλλοις   τοῦ
                                                      θαύματος μάρτυρες·
Πέτρον γὰρ ὑπουργῆσαι,   ἀλλ' οὐδὲ Ἰωάννην,
οὐκ Ἀνδρέαν νῦν βούλομαι,
οὐκ ἄλλον οὐδένα   τῶν ἐμῶν ἀποστόλων,
ἵνα μὴ γεννηθῇ   δι' αὐτῶν τοῖς ἀνθρώποις
ὑποψία   ἐντεῦθεν φαυλότητος,
ἀλλὰ αὐτοὺς νῦν θέλω ὑπουργεῖν   τοὺς ὑπηρέτας ἐμοί,
ἵν' αὐτοὶ μαρτυροῦσιν   ὅτι πάντα ἐξισχύω,
ὁ τὰ πάντα   ἐν σοφίᾳ ποιήσας."

18

Εἴξασα τούτοις ἡ μήτηρ Χριστοῦ   τοῖς ὑπηρέταις τοῦ
                                                      γάμου εὐθὺς
ἐφθέγξατο σὺν προθυμίᾳ·   "Ἅπερ λέγει ὑμῖν   ὁ υἱός
                                                      μου ποιήσατε."
Τότε δὲ ἓξ ὑδρίαι,   ὡς ἡ γραφὴ διδάσκει,
ἐν τῷ οἴκῳ ἀπέκειντο·
τοῖς ὑπηρέταις οὖν   ὁ Χριστὸς ἐπιτάττει,
"Γεμίσατε," λέγων,   "τὰς ὑδρίας ὕδατος."
Καὶ εὐθέως   τὸ ἔργον ἐγένετο·

I'll serve you, mother, for I can do anything,
the one who has made all in wisdom.

17

"So quickly tell those in the household to serve as I request,
and after this, they'll be witnesses of the wonder, to
    themselves and to others.
I want neither Peter nor John to serve—
nor Andrew today,
nor anyone else among my apostles,
so that people don't suspect them
of foul play;
but I want those serving me now to serve, so they'll witness
that I have the power to do anything,
the one who has made all in wisdom."

18

Yielding to these words, the mother of Christ willingly said
at once to the servants at the wedding, "Do whatever my
    son tells you."
As scripture teaches, there were six water jars
stored in the house.
Christ then instructed the servants:
"Fill the jars with water!" he said.
And straightaway this was done;

τὰς γὰρ ὑδρίας ὕδατος ψυχροῦ   πάσας ἐπλήρωσαν,
καὶ εἰστήκεσαν γνῶναι   τί βουλεύεται πρὸς τοῦτο
ὁ τὰ πάντα   ἐν σοφίᾳ ποιήσας.

19

Νῦν ὑδρίας ἐπαινέσω ἐγὼ   πῶς ἀπεδείχθησαν οἴνου
                                                    μεσταί,
πῶς ἀθρόον ἡ τῶν ὑδάτων   μεταχώνευσις
                                          οὕτως   αἰφνίδιον γέγονε.
Τότε γὰρ ὁ Δεσπότης   εἶπεν τοῖς ὑπηρέταις
φανερῶς, καθὼς γέγραπται·
"Ἀντλήσατε ὑμεῖς   μὴ τρυγήσαντες οἶνον·
ποτίσατε λοιπὸν   τοὺς ἀνακεκλιμένους,
τὰς ἀβρόχους   φιάλας ἀρδεύσατε·
ἀπολαυέτω πᾶσα ἡ πληθὺς   καὶ ὁ νυμφίος αὐτός·
παραδόξως γὰρ πᾶσιν   ἔδωκα τὴν εὐφροσύνην,
ὁ τὰ πάντα   ἐν σοφίᾳ ποιήσας."

20

Ὅτε τὸ ὕδωρ εἰς οἶνον Χριστὸς   σαφῶς μετέβαλεν ὡς
                                                        δυνατός,
κατευφράνθη ἅπαν τὸ πλῆθος,   θαυμασίαν τὴν
                                          γεῦσιν   αὐτοῦ ἡγησάμενοι·
ἄρτι δὲ ἐν τῷ δείπνῳ   τῷ ἐν τῇ ἐκκλησίᾳ
ἀπολαύομεν ἅπαντες·
εἰς αἷμα γὰρ Χριστοῦ   μεταβάλλεται οἶνος,
καὶ πίνομεν αὐτὸν   εὐφροσύνῃ ἁγίᾳ

434

they filled all the jars with cold water,
and stood there to hear what plans he had,
the one who has made all in wisdom.

19

Let me, now, praise those jars: Oh, how they were shown to
     be full of wine!
How, all at once, the transformation of water suddenly
     happened!
For then the master said to the servants
plainly, as is written:
"Draw out wine, which you have not harvested,
and offer it to the reclining guests—
wet their dry cups!
Let the whole party enjoy it—even the groom himself!
For everyone has miraculously received joy from me,
the one who has made all in wisdom."

20

When Christ transformed water to wine, as he was clearly
     able to,
everybody was delighted, loving its wonderful taste.
And now we are all enjoying the supper,
the one in church.
Wine is transformed into the blood of Christ,
and we drink this with holy joy,

τὸν Νυμφίον   τὸν μέγαν δοξάζοντες·
ὁ γὰρ Νυμφίος ὁ ἀληθινὸς   ὁ ἐκ Μαρίας ἐστίν,
ὁ προάναρχος Λόγος   ὁ λαβὼν μορφὴν τοῦ δούλου,
ὁ τὰ πάντα   ἐν σοφίᾳ ποιήσας.

21

Ὕψιστε ἅγιε, πάντων Σωτήρ,   τὸν οἶνον φύλαξον τὸν
                                    ἐν ἡμῖν
ἀνόθευτον, ὡς παντεπόπτης·   κακοδόξους δὲ
                        πάντας   ἐντεῦθεν ἀπέλασον,
οἵτινες ὡς πανοῦργοι   μίσγουσί σου τὸν οἶνον
τὸν πανάγιον ὕδατι·
τὸ δόγμα γὰρ τὸ σὸν   ἀεὶ ἐξυδαροῦντες,
κατάκριτοί εἰσι   τῷ πυρὶ τῆς Γεέννης·
ἀλλὰ ῥῦσαι   ἡμᾶς, ἀναμάρτητε,
τοῦ ὀδυρμοῦ τῆς κρίσεως τῆς σῆς,   ὡς ἐλεήμων Θεός,
ταῖς εὐχαῖς τῆς ἁγίας   Θεοτόκου καὶ Παρθένου,
ὁ τὰ πάντα   ἐν σοφίᾳ ποιήσας.

glorifying the great Bridegroom.
For the true Bridegroom is the child of Mary,
the beginningless Word who took the form of a slave,
the one who has made all in wisdom.

21

Most high and holy, Savior of all, as you see everything,
preserve the wine undiluted within us, and chase all
     misbelievers away,
those who are cunning and mix your most holy
wine with water.
As they are always watering down your doctrine,
they are condemned to the fire of Gehenna.
But by the holy and God-bearing Virgin's
prayers, sinless one, deliver us from grief
at the hour of your judgment, our merciful God,
the one who has made all in wisdom.

Προοίμιον

ἰδιόμελον

Τὸν δι' ἡμᾶς σταυρωθέντα   δεῦτε πάντες ὑμνήσωμεν·
αὐτὸν γὰρ κατεῖδε Μαρία   ἐπὶ ξύλου καὶ ἔλεγεν·
"Εἰ καὶ σταυρὸν ὑπομένεις,   σὺ ὑπάρχεις
ὁ υἱὸς καὶ Θεός μου."

I

ἰδιόμελον

Τὸν ἴδιον ἄρνα   ἡ ἀμνὰς θεωροῦσα
πρὸς σφαγὴν ἑλκόμενον   ἠκολούθει ἡ
                        Μαρία   τρυχομένη
μεθ' ἑτέρων γυναικῶν,   ταῦτα βοῶσα·
"Ποῦ πορεύῃ, τέκνον;   Τίνος χάριν τὸν ταχὺν   δρόμον
                                        τελέεις;
Μὴ ἕτερος γάμος   πάλιν ἔστιν ἐν Κανᾶ
κἀκεῖ νυνὶ σπεύδεις   ἵν' ἐξ ὕδατος αὐτοῖς οἶνον ποιήσῃς;
Συνέλθω σοι, τέκνον,   ἢ μείνω σε μᾶλλον;
Δός μοι λόγον, Λόγε·   μὴ σιγῶν παρέλθῃς με,
ὁ ἁγνὴν τηρήσας με,
ὁ υἱὸς καὶ Θεός μου.

438

ON THE WAY TO GOLGOTHA

in fourth plagal mode

Prelude

to its own melody

Let us all praise the one who is crucified for us;
Mary saw him on the tree and she said,
"Although you endure the cross, you remain
my son and my God."

I

to its own melody

The young ewe, Mary, saw her own lamb
being dragged to the slaughter; wearily she followed
the other women and cried out these words:
"Where are you going, my child? Why complete your
    course so fast?
Surely there isn't another wedding in Cana
where you are rushing to turn their water into wine?
Should I come with you, child, or wait instead?
Give me a word, Word; don't pass me by in silence;
you who guarded my purity,
my son and my God!

2

"Οὐκ ἤλπιζον, τέκνον,   ἐν τούτοις ἰδεῖν σε,
οὐδ' ἐπίστευόν ποτε   ἕως τούτου τοὺς
                                        ἀνόμους   ἐκμανῆναι
καὶ ἐκτεῖναι ἐπὶ σὲ   χεῖρας ἀδίκως·
ἔτι γὰρ τὰ βρέφη   τούτων κράζουσί σοι
                                        τὸ   Εὐλογημένος·
ἀκμὴν δὲ βαΐων   πεπλησμένη ἡ ὁδὸς
μηνύει τοῖς πᾶσι   τῶν ἀθέσμων τὰς πρὸς σὲ
                                        πανευφημίας.
Καὶ νῦν τίνος χάριν   ἐπράχθη τὸ χεῖρον;
Γνῶναι θέλω, οἴμοι,   πῶς τὸ φῶς μου σβέννυται,
πῶς σταυρῷ προσπήγνυται
ὁ υἱὸς καὶ Θεός μου.

3

"Ὑπάγεις, ὦ τέκνον,   πρὸς ἄδικον φόνον,
καὶ οὐδείς σοι συναλγεῖ·   οὐ συνέρχεταί σοι Πέτρος   ὁ
                                        εἰπών σοι·
'Οὐκ ἀρνοῦμαί σέ ποτε,   κἂν ἀποθνήσκω'·
ἔλιπέ σε Θωμᾶς   ὁ βοήσας· 'Μετ' αὐτοῦ   θάνωμεν
                                        πάντες'·
οἱ ἄλλοι δὲ πάλιν,   οἱ οἰκεῖοι καὶ γνωστοὶ
καὶ μέλλοντες κρίνειν   τὰς δώδεκα φυλάς, ποῦ εἰσιν
                                        ἄρτι;
Οὐδεὶς ἐκ τῶν πάντων,   ἀλλ' εἷς ὑπὲρ πάντων

2

"I did not expect to see you like this, child,
nor did I imagine that those lawless men could ever be
        driven
so mad as to lay their hands on you unjustly.
For their babies still shout to you, 'Blessed is he!'
Filled with palms, the road even now
reveals to all the impious people's rich praises to you.
But now, why is something so much worse going on?
I want to know, alas, how my light is put out,
how he's fastened to a cross,
my son and my God.

3

"You are heading, my child, for an unjust killing,
and no one suffers with you; Peter doesn't follow you, the
        one who said to you,
'I will never deny you, even if I must die.'
Thomas has left you, the one who cried, 'Let us all die with
        him!'
The others, too, your kinsmen and friends,
and those who will judge the twelve tribes, where are they
        now?
Not one of all of them, but one for all of them

θνήσκεις, τέκνον, μόνος,   ἀνθ' ὧν πάντας ἔσωσας,
ἀνθ' ὧν πᾶσιν ἤρεσας,
ὁ υἱὸς καὶ Θεός μου."

4

Τοιαῦτα Μαρίας   ἐκ λύπης βαρείας
καὶ ἐκ θλίψεως πολλῆς   κραυγαζούσης καὶ
                              κλαιούσης,   ἐπεστράφη
πρὸς αὐτὴν ὁ ἐξ αὐτῆς   οὕτω βοήσας·
"Τί δακρύεις, μῆτηρ;   Τί ταῖς ἄλλαις
                              γυναιξὶ   συναποφέρῃ;
Μὴ πάθω; μὴ θάνω;   Πῶς οὖν σώσω τὸν Ἀδάμ;
Μὴ τάφον οἰκήσω;   Πῶς ἑλκύσω πρὸς ζωὴν τοὺς ἐν τῷ
                              Ἅιδη;
Καὶ μήν, καθὼς οἶδας,   ἀδίκως σταυροῦμαι·
τί οὖν κλαίεις, μῆτηρ;   Μᾶλλον οὕτω κραύγασον
ὅτι 'Θέλων ἔπαθεν
ὁ υἱὸς καὶ Θεός μου.'

5

"Ἀπόθου οὖν, μῆτερ,   ἀπόθου τὴν λύπην·
οὐ γὰρ πρέπει σοι θρηνεῖν,   ὅτι
                              'Κεχαριτωμένη'   ὠνομάσθης·
τὴν οὖν κλῆσιν τῷ κλαυθμῷ   μὴ συγκαλύψῃς·
μὴ ταῖς ἀσυνέτοις   ὁμοιώσῃς ἑαυτήν,   πάνσοφε κόρη·
ἐν μέσῳ ὑπάρχεις   τοῦ νυμφῶνος τοῦ ἐμοῦ·

you die, my child, alone. Unlike them, you've saved them
    all;
unlike them, you've pleased them all,
my son and my God."

4

When, in unbearable grief and great affliction,
Mary cried such words and wept, he who came from her
turned to her: "Mother,
why are you weeping? Why are you carried away with the
    other women?
Should I not suffer? Not die? How would I then save Adam?
Should I not dwell in a grave? How would I draw those in
    Hades to life?
And yes, as you know, I am crucified unjustly,
but, mother, why weep? You should rather cry out
that 'He willingly suffered,
my son and my God!'

5

"So cast off your grief, mother, cast it off!
You shouldn't lament, for you were named 'the Favored
    One.'
You should not obscure your title by wailing.
Don't be like the foolish ones, most wise maiden.
You are in the middle of my bridal chamber,

μὴ οὖν ὥσπερ ἔξω   ἰσταμένη τὴν ψυχὴν καταμαράνῃς·
τοὺς ἐν τῷ νυμφῶνι   ὡς δούλους σου φώνει—
πᾶς γὰρ τρέχων τρόμῳ   ὑπακούσει σου, σεμνή,
ὅταν εἴπῃς· 'Ποῦ ἐστιν
ὁ υἱὸς καὶ Θεός μου;'

6

"Πικρὰν τὴν ἡμέραν   τοῦ πάθους μὴ δείξῃς·
δι' αὐτὴν γὰρ ὁ γλυκὺς   οὐρανόθεν νῦν κατῆλθον,   ὡς
τὸ μάννα,
οὐκ ἐν ὄρει τῷ Σινᾷ,   ἀλλ' ἐν γαστρί σου:
ἔνδοθεν γὰρ ταύτης   ἐτυρώθην, ὡς
Δαυὶδ   προανεφώνει·
τὸ τετυρωμένον   ὄρος νόησον, σεμνή·
ἐγὼ γὰρ ὑπάρχω,   ὅτι Λόγος ὢν ἐν σοὶ σὰρξ ἐγενόμην·
ἐν ταύτῃ οὖν πάσχω,   ἐν ταύτῃ καὶ σῴζω·
μὴ οὖν κλαύσῃς, μῆτερ,   μᾶλλον κρᾶξον ἐν χαρᾷ·
'Θέλων πάθος δέχεται
ὁ υἱὸς καὶ Θεός μου.'"

6*

Ἐν τούτοις τοῖς λόγοις   ἡ πάναγνος μήτηρ
τῷ ἀφράστως ἐξ αὐτῆς   σαρκωθέντι καὶ τεχθέντι,   ἐπὶ
πλεῖον
τρυχωθεῖσα τὴν ψυχήν,   οὕτως ἐβόα·
"Τί μοι λέγεις, τέκνον·   Μὴ ταῖς ἄλλαις
γυναιξὶ   συναποφέρῃ;

so don't let your spirits wither as though you were standing
    outside it.
Summon those in the chamber as your servants —
for all will tremble, noble one, and run to obey you
when you say, 'Where is he,
my son and my God?'

6

"Don't let the day of my passion seem bitter;
for this I came down from heaven — sweet, like manna,
not on Mount Sinai, but in your belly.
Within it I was curdled, as David foretold. Think, noble
    one,
of the curdled mountain. I am here,
for as Word I became flesh in you.
In that, I suffer, and in that, I save.
So, mother, don't weep, but cry with joy,
'He willingly embraces the passion,
my son and my God!'"

6*

With the following words the purest mother,
even lower in spirits, cried out to him
who ineffably received flesh and was born of her:
"Why do you say, child, 'Don't be carried away like the
    other women?'

Καὶ γὰρ ὥσπερ αὗται   ἐν κοιλίᾳ υἱὸν
σὲ ἔσχον ἐν μήτρᾳ   καὶ μαστοῖς σοι τοῖς ἐμοῖς γάλα
                                                    παρέσχον.
Πῶς οὖν θέλεις ἄρτι   μὴ κλαύσω σε, τέκνον,
θάνατον ἀδίκως   ὑποστῆναι σπεύδοντα,
τὸν νεκροὺς ἐγείροντα,
ὁ υἱὸς καὶ Θεός μου;

7

"Ἰδού," φησί, "τέκνον,   ἐκ τῶν ὀφθαλμῶν μου
τὸν κλαυθμὸν ἀποσοβῶ,   τὴν καρδίαν μου
                                        συντρίβω   ἐπὶ πλεῖον,
ἀλλ' οὐ δύναται σιγᾶν   ὁ λογισμός μου.
Τί μοι λέγεις, σπλάγχνον·   Εἰ μὴ πάθω, ὁ Ἀδὰμ   οὐχ
                                                    ὑγιαίνει';
Καὶ μὴν ἄνευ πάθους   ἐθεράπευσας πολλούς·
λεπρὸν γὰρ καθῆρας   καὶ οὐκ ἤλγησας οὐδέν, ἀλλ'
                                                    ἠβουλήθης·
παράλυτον σφίγξας   οὐ κατεπονήθης·
πῆρον πάλιν λόγῳ   ὀμματώσας, ἀγαθέ,
ἀπαθὴς μεμένηκας,
ὁ υἱὸς καὶ Θεός μου.

8

"Νεκροὺς ἀναστήσας   νεκρὸς οὐκ ἐγένου
οὐδ' ἐτέθης ἐν ταφῇ,   υἱέ μου καὶ ζωή μου·   πῶς οὖν
                                                    λέγεις·

446

For, just as they had a son in their womb,
so I had you in mine and fed you milk from my own breasts.
How can you not want me to weep for you, child,
as you rush to submit unjustly to a death
that awakens the dead,
my son and my God?

7

"Look, child," she says, "I'll chase the weeping
from my eyes; I'll crush my heart even more,
and yet my thoughts cannot be silent.
Why do you tell me, my love, 'If I don't suffer, Adam won't
       recover'?
Indeed, without suffering, you've healed many:
You cleansed a leper and felt no pain, but only a wish;
you gave strength to a paralytic but weren't tormented;
with only a word you gave sight to the blind man,
while you were unharmed,
my son and my God!

8

"When you raised the dead, you didn't die,
nor lay in a tomb, my son and my life, so how can you say,

Εἰ μὴ πάθω, ὁ Ἀδὰμ   οὐχ ὑγιαίνει';
Κέλευσον, Σωτήρ μου,   καὶ ἐγείρεται εὐθὺς   κλίνην
βαστάζων·
εἰ δὲ καὶ ἐν τάφῳ   κατεχώσθη ὁ Ἀδάμ,
ὡς Λάζαρον τάφου   ἐξανέστησας φωνῇ, οὕτως καὶ
τοῦτον·
δουλεύει σοι πάντα   ὡς Πλάστῃ τῶν πάντων.
Τί οὖν τρέχεις, τέκνον;   Μὴ ἐπείγου πρὸς σφαγήν,
μὴ φιλήσῃς θάνατον,
ὁ υἱὸς καὶ Θεός μου."

9

"Οὐκ οἶδας, ὦ μῆτερ,   οὐκ οἶδας ὃ λέγω·
διὸ ἄνοιξον τὸν νοῦν   καὶ εἰσοίκισον τὸ ῥῆμα   ὃ
ἀκούεις
καὶ αὐτὴ καθ' ἑαυτὴν   νόει ἃ λέγω.
Οὗτος ὃν προεῖπον   ὁ ταλαίπωρος Ἀδάμ,   ὁ
ἀρρωστήσας
οὐ μόνον τὸ σῶμα,   ἀλλὰ γὰρ καὶ τὴν ψυχὴν
ἐνόσησε θέλων·   οὐ γὰρ ἤκουσεν ἐμοῦ καὶ κινδυνεύει·
γνωρίζεις ὃ λέγω·   μὴ κλαύσῃς οὖν, μῆτερ,
μᾶλλον τοῦτο κρᾶξον·   Τὸν Ἀδὰμ ἐλέησον
καὶ τὴν Εὔαν οἴκτειρον,
ὁ υἱὸς καὶ Θεός μου.'

'If I don't suffer, Adam won't recover'?
Command him, my Savior; he'll stand up at once and carry
    his bed.
Even if Adam is buried in a tomb,
rouse him now from the grave with your voice, as you did
    Lazarus!
All things serve you, the Shaper of all.
So why do you rush, child? Don't hurry to slaughter,
don't make friends with death,
my son and my God!"

9

"Mother, you don't get it, don't get what I'm saying.
Open your mind, and let in the word that you hear,
and take what I'm saying to heart:
The one I spoke of before, the miserable Adam, who is sick,
not only in body, but also in soul,
became ill through desire; he's in danger since he didn't
    listen to me.
You hear what I'm saying. So, mother, don't weep!
But cry out instead, 'Have mercy on Adam
and compassion on Eve,
my son and my God!'

10

"Ὑπὸ ἀσωτίας   καὶ ἀδηφαγίας
ἀρρωστήσας ὁ Ἀδὰμ   κατηνέχθη ἕως
                                    Ἅιδου   κατωτάτου,
καὶ ἐκεῖ τὸν τῆς ψυχῆς   πόνον δακρύει·
Εὕα δὲ ἡ τοῦτον   ἐκδιδάξασά ποτε   τὴν ἀταξίαν
σὺν τούτῳ στενάζει,   σὺν αὐτῷ γὰρ ἀρρωστεῖ,
ἵνα μάθωσιν ἅμα   τοῦ φυλάττειν ἰατροῦ παραγγελίαν.
Συνῆκας κἂν ἄρτι;   Ἐπέγνως ἃ εἶπον;
Πάλιν, μήτηρ, κράξον·   Τῷ Ἀδὰμ εἰ συγχωρεῖς,
καὶ τῇ Εὕᾳ σύγγνωθι,
ὁ υἱὸς καὶ Θεός μου.'"

11

Ῥημάτων δὲ τούτων   ὡς ἤκουσε τότε
ἡ ἀμώμητος ἀμνάς,   ἀπεκρίθη πρὸς τὸν ἄρνα·   "Κύριέ
                                                        μου,
ἔτι ἅπαξ ἂν εἴπω,   μὴ ὀργισθῇς μοι·
λέξω σοι ὃ ἔχω,   ἵνα μάθω παρὰ σοῦ   πάντως ὃ θέλω.
Ἂν πάθῃς, ἂν θάνῃς,   ἀναλύσεις πρὸς ἐμέ;
Ἂν περιοδεύσῃς   σὺν τῇ Εὕᾳ τὸν Ἀδάμ, βλέψω σε πάλιν;
Αὐτὸ γὰρ φοβοῦμαι,   μήπως ἐκ τοῦ τάφου
ἄνω δράμῃς, τέκνον,   καὶ ζητοῦσά σε ἰδεῖν
κλαύσω, κράξω· Ποῦ ἐστιν
ὁ υἱὸς καὶ Θεός μου;'"

10

"Extravagance and gluttony made Adam sick
and brought him down all the way to the depths of Hades,
where he weeps for his soul's affliction.
Eve, who once taught him to be disobedient,
groans with him, for she's sick with him,
so that, together, they may learn to heed the doctor's order.
Have you got it now? Have you grasped what I've said?
Again, mother, cry to me, 'If Adam is forgiven,
excuse also Eve,
my son and my God!'"

11

When the unblemished ewe heard
these words, she replied to her lamb: "My Lord,
don't be angry with me if I speak once more.
I'll ask you about what I have on my mind, so I may learn
    from you all I want.
If you suffer and die, will you come back to me?
If you go to treat Adam, and Eve as well, will I see you
    again?
This is my fear, that perhaps from the grave
you will rush on high, my child, and then when I try to see
    you,
I'll weep and cry 'Where's
my son and my God?'"

12

Ὡς ἤκουσε ταῦτα   ὁ πάντα γινώσκων
πρὶν γενέσεως αὐτῶν,   ἀπεκρίθη πρὸς
                    Μαρίαν·   "Θάρσει, μῆτερ,
ὅτι πρώτη με ὁρᾷς   ἀπὸ τοῦ τάφου·
ἔρχομαί σοι δεῖξαι   πόσοις πόνοις τὸν
                            Ἀδὰμ   ἐλυτρωσάμην
καὶ πόσους ἱδρῶτας   ἔσχον ἕνεκεν αὐτοῦ·
δηλώσω τοῖς φίλοις   τὰ τεκμήρια δεικνὺς ἐν ταῖς χερσί
                                        μου·
καὶ τότε θεάσῃ   τὴν Εὔαν, ὦ μῆτερ,
ζῶσαν ὥσπερ πρώην,   καὶ βοήσεις ἐν χαρᾷ·
'Τοὺς γονεῖς μου ἔσωσεν
ὁ υἱὸς καὶ Θεός μου.'

13

"Μικρὸν οὖν, ὦ μῆτερ,   ἀνάσχου, καὶ βλέπεις
πῶς καθάπερ ἰατρὸς   ἀποδύομαι καὶ φθάνω   ὅπου
                                    κεῖνται
καὶ ἐκείνων τὰς πληγὰς   περιοδεύω,
τέμνων ἐν τῇ λόγχῃ   τὰ πωρώματα αὐτῶν   καὶ τὴν
                                        σκληρίαν·
λαμβάνω καὶ ὄξος,   καταστύφω τὴν πληγήν,
τῇ μήλῃ τῶν ἥλων   ἐρευνήσας τὴν τομὴν χλαίνη
                                        μοτώσω·
καὶ δὴ τὸν σταυρόν μου   ὡς νάρθηκα ἔχων,

12

He who knows all before it begins
heard these words and replied to Mary, "Take heart, mother,
for you'll be the first to see me after the tomb.
I will come to show you with how much toil I rescued Adam
and how much I sweated on his account.
I'll reveal it to my friends, displaying the proof in my hands.
And, mother, then you'll see Eve as well,
alive, as before, and you'll cry with joy,
'He saved my forebears,
my son and my God.'

13

"Be patient a little longer, mother, and see
how I, like a doctor, undress and arrive at the place
where they lie, and how I treat their wounds,
excising their calluses and scars with the lance;
how I take vinegar and use it as an astringent for the
        wound, and how,
after examining the incision with the probe of the nails, I'll
        bandage it with the robe;
indeed, I have my cross as a medicine chest,

τούτῳ χρῶμαι, μῆτερ,   ἵνα ψάλλῃς συνετῶς·
Ἱ Πάσχων πάθος ἔλυσεν
ὁ υἱὸς καὶ Θεός μου.'

14

"Ἀπόθου οὖν, μῆτερ,   τὴν λύπην ἀπόθου,
καὶ πορεύου ἐν χαρᾷ·   ἐγὼ γάρ, δι' ὃ κατῆλθον,   ἤδη
                                                                        σπεύδω
ἐκτελέσαι τὴν βουλὴν   τοῦ πέμψαντός με·
τοῦτο γὰρ ἐκ πρώτης   δεδογμένον ἦν ἐμοὶ   καὶ τῷ
                                                                        Πατρί μου,
καὶ τῷ Πνεύματί μου   οὐκ ἀπήρεσέ ποτε
τὸ ἐνανθρωπῆσαι   καὶ παθεῖν με διὰ τὸν παραπεσόντα.
Δραμοῦσα, ὦ μῆτερ,   ἀνάγγειλον πᾶσιν
ὅτι· Πάσχων πλήττει   τὸν μισοῦντα τὸν Ἀδὰμ
καὶ νικήσας ἔρχεται
ὁ υἱὸς καὶ Θεός μου.'"

15

"Νικῶμαι, ὦ τέκνον,   νικῶμαι τῷ πόθῳ,
καὶ οὐ στέγω ἀληθῶς   ἵν' ἐγὼ μὲν ἐν θαλάμῳ,   σὺ δ' ἐν
                                                                        ξύλῳ,
ἵν' ἐγὼ ἐν οἰκίᾳ,   σὺ δ' ἐν μνημείῳ.
Ἄφες οὖν συνέλθω·   θεραπεύει γὰρ ἐμὲ   τὸ θεωρεῖν σε·
κατίδω τὴν τόλμαν   τῶν τιμώντων τὸν Μωσῆν·
αὐτὸν γὰρ ὡς δῆθεν   ἐκδικοῦντες οἱ τυφλοὶ κτεῖναί σε
                                                                        ἦλθον·

I make use of it, mother, so you can sing with insight,
'By suffering he undid suffering,
my son and my God.'

14

"So cast off your grief, mother, cast it off,
and go forth with joy! I'm hurrying to do what I came down
    for,
to complete the plan of the one who sent me.
For this was resolved from the outset, and it was
agreed on by me and my Father and my Spirit
that I'd take the form of a human and suffer for the sake of
    the fallen.
So run, mother, and proclaim to all
that 'By suffering he strikes the one who hates Adam
and, having conquered, he comes,
my son and my God!'"

15

"I'm overcome, my child, overcome by longing.
I could not bear to be in my room with you on the tree,
so that I would be at home but you in the tomb.
So let me come with you, for seeing you comforts me!
Let me observe the audacity of those who revere Moses;
for I suppose that those blind men have come to kill you in
    defense of him.

Μωϋσῆς δὲ τοῦτο τῷ Ἰσραὴλ εἶπεν
ὅτι ʽΜέλλεις βλέπειν ἐπὶ ξύλου τὴν ζωήν.ʼ
Ἡ ζωὴ δὲ τίς ἐστιν;
Ὁ υἱὸς καὶ Θεός μου.ʺ

16

ʺΟὐκοῦν εἰ συνέρχῃ, μὴ κλαύσῃς, ὦ μῆτερ,
μηδὲ πάλιν πτοηθῇς, ἐὰν ἴδῃς σαλευθέντα τὰ στοιχεῖα·
τὸ γὰρ τόλμημα δονεῖ πᾶσαν τὴν κτίσιν.
Πόλος ἐκτυφλοῦται καὶ οὐκ ἀνοίγει ὀφθαλμὸν ἕως
ἂν εἴπω·
ἡ γῆ σὺν θαλάσσῃ τότε σπεύσωσι φυγεῖν·
ναὸς τὸν χιτῶνα ῥήξει τότε κατὰ τῶν τοῦτο τολμώντων·
τὰ ὄρη δονοῦνται, οἱ τάφοι κενοῦνται·
ὅταν ἴδῃς ταῦτα, ἐὰν πτήξῃς ὡς γυνή,
κράξον πρὸς μέ· ʽΦεῖσαί μου,
ὁ υἱὸς καὶ Θεός μου.ʼʺ

17

Υἱὲ τῆς Παρθένου, Θεὲ τῆς Παρθένου,
καὶ τοῦ κόσμου Ποιητά, σὸν τὸ πάθος, σὸν τὸ
βάθος τῆς σοφίας·
σὺ ἐπίστασαι ὃ ἦς καὶ ὃ ἐγένου·
σὺ παθεῖν θελήσας κατηξίωσας ἐλθεῖν ἀνθρώπους
σῶσαι·
σὺ τὰς ἁμαρτίας ἡμῶν ἦρας ὡς ἀμνός,

But this is what Moses said to Israel:
'You are going to see life on a tree.'
Life—who is that?
My son and my God!"

16

"If you come with me, then, don't weep, mother;
no, do not tremble, even if you feel the elements shake.
This audacity agitates all creation.
Heaven is blinded and does not open its eye until I say so.
Then the earth and the sea will hasten to flee.
Then the temple will rend its garment in response to those
    who dare to do this.
The mountains are trembling, the graves emptying.
If, being a woman, you're afraid when you see this,
cry out to me, 'Spare me,
my son and my God!'"

17

Son of the Virgin, God of the Virgin,
and Creator of the world, yours is the passion and the depth
    of all wisdom.
You know what you were and what you became.
You were willing to suffer and deigned to come to save
    humanity.
You took our sins away like a lamb,

σὺ ταύτας νεκρώσας   τῇ σφαγῇ σου, ὁ Σωτήρ, ἔσωσας
                                        πάντας·

σὺ εἶ ἐν τῷ πάσχειν   καὶ ἐν τῷ μὴ πάσχειν,
σὺ εἶ θνήσκων, σῴζων,   σὺ παρέσχες τῇ σεμνῇ
παρρησίαν κράζειν σοι·
"Ὁ υἱὸς καὶ Θεός μου."

you put them to death by your slaughter, Savior, and all
    were saved.
You are there where there's suffering and where there is
    not.
You are saving by dying. You gave the noble one
boldness to cry,
"*My son and my God!*"

Abbreviations

GdM = José Grosdidier de Matons, ed., *Hymnes,* 5 vols., Sources Chrétiennes 99, 110, 114, 128, 283 (Paris, 1964–1981)

MaTr = Paul Maas and Constantine A. Trypanis, eds., *Sancti Romani Melodi cantica,* vol. 1, *Cantica genuina* (Oxford, 1963)

PG = J. P. Migne, *Patrologia Graeca,* 161 vols. (Paris, 1857–1866)

Note on the Texts

SIGLA

P. Vindob. G 29430 = Papyrus Vindobonensis Graecus 29430 [6th–7th c.]

A = Athous Vatopedinus 1041 [10th–11th c.]

B = Athous Laurae Γ 27 [10th–11th c.]

C = Corsinianus 366 [10th–11th c.]

D = Athous Laurae Γ 28 [11th c.]

Δ = The "western" kontakarion manuscripts, copied in Grottaferrata (includes C and V)

G = Sinaiticus 925 [10th c.]

J = Sinaiticus 927 [13th c.]

M = Mosquensis Synod. 437 [12th c., from Vatopedi]

P = Patmiacus 212–13 [late 10th c.; GdM labels the second volume (213) "Q"]

T = Taurinensis 189, previously B VI 34 [11th c.]

V = Vindobonensis, suppl. gr. 96 [12th c.]

b = Cryptensis Δ a I [11th–12th c.]

p = Vaticanus gr. 1829 [11th c.]

w = Marcianus 1264 [16th c.]

GdM = José Grosdidier de Matons, ed., *Hymnes,* 5 vols., Sources Chrétiennes 99, 110, 114, 128, 283 (Paris, 1964–1981)

MaTr = Paul Maas and Constantine A. Trypanis, eds., *Sancti Romani Melodi cantica,* vol. 1, *Cantica genuina* (Oxford, 1963)

Much philological work has gone into establishing editions of Romanos during the past centuries, and there is no need for more. The Greek text printed in the present volume is adapted from the Oxford edition by Paul Maas and Constantine A. Trypanis (1963) and José Grosdidier de Matons's edition in the Sources Chrétiennes series (1964–1981). These two critical editions resemble each other to a large degree and follow the same basic principles of establishing the text.

For centuries, the kontakia constituted a living genre performed orally, and there is no reason to imagine or hope that we have the text exactly as Romanos wrote it, nor can we know how he laid out his songs on the page. That said, he probably did not have the luxury, as modern poetry publications like this one, to play with open space. The earliest witnesses we have are late sixth- or early seventh-century papyrus fragments. The text for *On the Three Children in the Furnace* (MaTr, no. 46; GdM, no. 8, stanza 6) looks like this (in P. Vindob. G 29430):

ΘΕΟΥΣΓΑΡΟΥΣΣΕΒΕΙ·ΕΚΕΙΝΟΙΔΙΑΠΤ
ΥΟΥΣΙ·ΚΑΙΕΙΚΟΝΑ·ΗΝΕΣΤΗΣΑΣΧΡ
ΥΣΗΝ·ΤΗΣΔΕΔΕΞΙΑΣΣΟΥ·ΤΟΚΥΡΟΣΕΥΤ
ΕΛΙΖΟΥΣΙΝ·ΚΑΙΤΗΝΤΑΥΤΗΣ·ΠΡΟΣΔΟΚ
ΩΣΙΚΑΤΑΛΥΣΙΝ·ΚΑΘΕΚΑΣΤΗΝΕΥΧΟΜΕ
ΝΟΙ , ΤΑΧΥΝΟ ΝΟΟΙΚΤΙΡΜΩΝ [. . .]

This illustration, which is not a precise transcription, is based on Günther Zuntz, "The Romanos Papyrus," *Journal of Theological Studies* 16, no. 2 (1965): 463–68. It shows how kontakia were written only decades after Romanos's own lifetime. There are no accents nor spaces between words. According to Zuntz, who studied the papyrus, distinctions between kola are probably marked by a small dot. A clear punctuation mark, which looks like a comma, introduces the refrain. Stanzas seem to have been separated by a small space or a line.

The Middle Byzantine kontakaria render the text in minuscule, as seen in this illustration based on C and P:

θεοὺς γὰρ οὓς σέβει·ἐκεῖνοι διαπτύουσι·καὶ
εἰκόνα·ἣν ἔστησας χρυσῆν·τῆς δὲ δεξιᾶς σου·τὸ
κῦρος εὐτελίζουσιν·καὶ τὴν ταύτης·προσδοκῶσι
κατάλυσιν·καθ' ἑκάστην εὐχόμενοι:—τ ά χ υ ν ο ν
ὁ ο ἰ κ τ ί ρ μ ω ν [. . .]

It is in this later form that the kontakia have been transmitted to us. Accentuation has been introduced, and a slight space between words. Dots still mark the distinction between kola, and the refrain stands out (as does the prelude). Each stanza is also clearly distinguished by a large initial and sometimes a stanza number.

The recent critical editions make further distinctions, based on analyses of metrical and semantic structure (this example combines features of MaTr and GdM):

θεοὺς γὰρ οὓς σέβει   ἐκεῖνοι διαπτύουσι
 καὶ εἰκόνα   ἣν ἔστησας χρυσῆν·
 τῆς δὲ δεξιᾶς σου   τὸ κῦρος εὐτελίζουσιν
 καὶ τὴν ταύτης   προσδοκῶσι κατάλυσιν,   καθ’
                                                    ἑκάστην εὐχόμενοι·
 |: Τάχυνον, ὁ οἰκτίρμων [. . .]

The modern editors versify the stanzas by a grouping of kola (usually between one and three) into verses or lines. Kola are divided, not by dots, but by an open space within a line or by a line break. Smaller or larger indentations signal smaller or larger continuity with the previous line. I retain the principle introduced by Paul Maas of grouping kola into verses, which has now become a standard, but I have not kept the various indentations. And I have not followed the metrically determined "mis"-accentuation introduced in some places by MaTr and GdM.

Verse divisions sometimes vary slightly between editions; mine mostly align with GdM. For questions of punctuation, more independent choices are made. Where the critical editions differ more substantially regarding words or grammatical forms, choices have been made from case to case, based not so much on independent manuscript studies as on what seems more plausible from a literary perspective. In some cases, I deviate from the solutions of the critical editions, preferring a reading from a manuscript. In these few cases, a note clarifies the choice. For a rich and detailed text-critical apparatus, see the GdM edition.

The refrains constitute a particular challenge, for they frequently undergo minor tweaks from stanza to stanza, in order for them to fit the story; a verbal ending may be modified, or the case of a word may be adjusted. Sometimes the changes will have been inaudible, as when ἡμῖν (us) alternates with ὑμῖν (you). It is fair to assume that the exact wording of a given refrain has been unstable across the lifespan of its kontakion. Scribes did not always bother to write out the full refrain every time it was repeated, and performers probably adapted the refrain as best they could. Modern editors have continued to do the same.

Each kontakion (prelude and stanzas respectively) is written to an existing model stanza (indicated with "πρός" followed by the incipit of the relevant melody or song) or to its own new melody ("ἰδιόμελον"). The model governs both melody and metrical form.

The "titles" of the songs vary from manuscript to manuscript and are secondary; rather than titles they are best understood as short descriptions of the song's topic or festal occasion. I have created English titles based loosely on these descriptions and quoted at least one of the descriptions in the Notes to the Texts. The manuscript headings rarely reflect the fact that women play prominent roles in the stories. The tonal mode (ἦχος) does not reflect a sixth-century practice, but the information is included in the manuscripts; I have included them under the kontakion heading.

I do not highlight or translate the acrostics, which tie each kontakion together, but they appear in the Notes to the Translations.

Notes to the Texts

On Fasting (Adam and Eve)

title Τῇ δ' τῆς β' ἑβδομάδος τῶν νηστειῶν· κοντάκιον κατανυκτι-
κόν P
The text of this song is preserved in P.

Prel. παρὰ σοῦ, μόνε ἀγαθέ ... ἄφεσιν καί: *Trypanis suggests that this is
a later addition (see MaTr). Generally,* ἄφεσιν *is inserted before*
ζωήν *in certain stanzas, but this is clearly a late addition (GdM, vol.
1, p. 85n3)*

6 ζωὴν GdM, MaTr: τὴν ἄφεσιν καὶ ζωὴν P

7 ζωὴν GdM, MaTr: τὴν ἄφεσιν καὶ ζωὴν P

9 φρόνιμος *Ephrem Lash, "On Adam and Eve" n.p.: the kolon lacks
three syllables; other suggestions are* κακοῦργος *MaTr or* δόλιος
GdM

10 ἄνευ ταύτης τήν *MaTr: the manuscript version is five syllables short
here*

13 τὴν τούτου μετάληψιν *GdM:* τὴν τούτων μετάληψιν P *MaTr*

15 εὐάρεστον *MaTr:* ἐνάρετον *GdM*

17 ἐπέχω τὴν ζωήν: ἀπέχω τοῦ ξύλου P. *Most editors have taken this
to be a scribal error. For* ἀπέχω *I follow Johannes Koder, "Konjekturvorschläge zu Hymnen des Romanos Melodos" Jahrbuch der Österreichischen Byzantinistik 54 (2004): 97–99*

18 σὺ ἐθρήνεις με *Nicholaos V. Tomadakis,* Ῥωμανοῦ τοῦ Μελῳδοῦ
ὕμνοι ἐκδιδόμενοι ἐκ πατμιακῶν κωδίκων, *vol. 4 (Athens, 1961),
492:* συνεθρήνεις με *GdM, MaTr*

19 ὀφιοπλήκτους: *a hapax legomenon in Greek literature*

21 ἀφαιροῦσα δὲ ζωὴν τὴν αἰώνιον *GdM*: καὶ ἀφαιροῦσα τὴν ζωὴν
τὴν αἰώνιον *MaTr; the two last kola are missing in the manuscript*

24 τοὺς πάντας ῥυόμενον *GdM*: τὸν ῥυόμενον <ἅπαντας> *MaTr;
the kolon is too short in* P

On Abraham's Sacrifice

title κοντάκιον ᾀδόμενον εἰς τὴν θυσίαν Ἀβραάμ P
The text of this song is preserved in P.

6 ἡμῶν *MaTr*: ἐμῶν *GdM, but "my souls" seems unlikely*

10 <ἄκαιρον> τόκον *MaTr for metrical reasons:* τόκον <ἐν γήρᾳ>
*GdM. The poor manuscript condition for this stanza accounts for
some uncertainties (GdM, vol. 1, p. 149n1)*

14 νῦν αὐχήσω *GdM, MaTr*: νῦν αὔχει σῶσαι P

16 ἐτίθετο ὁ παῖς: ἐτέθετο ὅπως *MaTr*; ἐτίθεντο ὁ παῖς *GdM*

20 τὴν πίστιν σου . . . τῶν αἰώνων *must be corrupt, for the lines are
metrically incorrect*

21 ἢ δόλος ἐν τῷ στόματί μου *GdM*; ἢ<ν> δόλος . . . μου *MaTr: this
kolon has too many syllables*

On the Blessing of Jacob

title κοντάκιον κατανυκτικὸν ᾀδόμενον εἰς τὸν Ἰσαὰκ ὅτε εὐλόγησε τὸν Ἰακώβ P
The text of this song is preserved in P.

5 ὁ πατὴρ *GdM*: ἡ μήτηρ P *MaTr*

6 παράσχου <ἡμῖν> *GdM, MaTr*: παράσχου P

7 παράσχου μοι: παράσχου ἡμῖν P *GdM; I follow Maas, who also
assumed it should be amended (see MaTr, 333)*

9 παρέσχεν *MaTr*: παρέσχ P. *GdM plausibly suggests a subjunctive
for the missing ending, although the Lord has just given his blessing in
the previous line.*

12 τὴν γῆν ἐπεῖδεν *GdM*: <ἡμᾶς> ἐπεῖδεν *MaTr*; τὴν ἐπεῖδεν P.
MaTr and other editions supply ἡμᾶς, *although the word is used in
the previous line.*

On Joseph and Potiphar's Wife

title   ἕτερον κοντάκιον εἰς τὸν πειρασμὸν τοῦ Ἰωσήφ P
The text of this song is preserved in P.

2   παθῶν *GdM*: παθών *MaTr*

5   φάρμακα *GdM*, *MaTr*: τραύματα Δ, *which has the advantage of maintaining a consistent set of injury images, rather than introducing potions, but requires repetition of a word from the next line*

16   τὸ συνειδός μου *GdM*: τοῦ συνειδότος P *MaTr*

On the Prophet Elijah

title   Μηνὶ τῷ αὐτῷ εἰς τὴν κ΄, τοῦ ἁγίου προφήτου Ἠλίου, κον-δάκιον ἰδιόμελον A
The text of this song is preserved in AP, *but* A *does not include stanza 31, and* P *lacks stanzas 22–27, 29–30; there are truncated versions in most other manuscripts.*

9   χορηγοῦντα *GdM*, *MaTr*: *regarding the incongruence, see GdM, vol. 1, p. 317n2*

16   ἐλῶ: ἴδω *GdM*, *MaTr*. *I follow Herbert Hunger's conjecture in his review of* Sancti Romani Melodi cantica, *vol. 1*, Cantica genuina, *ed. Paul Maas and Constantine A. Trypanis*, Byzantinische Zeitschrift *57 (1964): 437–43 (at 442)*

17   σκοπὸν *GdM*, *MaTr*: κόπον P

20   δυνάμεως *GdM*, *MaTr*: παρρησίας A
μὴ θρέψῃ με νομίζων A *GdM*: *lacking in* P; μὴ θρέψῃς με κο-μίζων *MaTr*
τὸν μόνον φιλάνθρωπον Tōmadakis, Ῥωμανοῦ τοῦ Μελῳδοῦ ὕμνοι, *vol. 4, p. 445*: ὁ μόνος φιλάνθρωπος *MaTr*; γενέσθαι φιλάνθρωπος *GdM*

21   ὑπερτίμια *GdM*. *Five syllables are missing here, according to the metrical pattern.*

23   παντοδύναμε *MaTr*: παντοδυνάμῳ *GdM for metrical reasons, in which case it is not part of Elijah's speech*

25   ὑπάρχω φιλάνθρωπος *GdM, MaTr: the refrain variation does not seem necessary here, but it is the manuscripts' reading*

29   ἡ γῆ A *MaTr:* Ἡλίας *GdM*

32   χωρία γηθόμενος A: τῶν φίλων μου P *GdM, MaTr*

On the Beheading of the Forerunner

title   εἰς ἀποτομὴν τοῦ Προδρόμου CM
        The full text of this song is preserved in AC but not P. M and T have abbreviated versions. A has a different text for the final stanza, for which see apparatus in MaTr. The kontakion was not edited by GdM, and there are numerous text-critical issues.

3   ἔφριξεν *MaTr:* ἔβρυξεν AT

5   δέσποινά *MaTr:* μήτηρ A, *which might make more sense, but is used in the first line*

6   πληροῖς *following Riccardo Maisano, Cantici di Romano il Melodo, vol. 2 (Turin, 2002), 128:* πλήρις *MaTr*

11   Ὑπεβλήθη *following* A: Ὑπεκλίθη C *MaTr*

13   νῦν τελεῖται ὅπερ ἤθελον, καὶ φονεύεται ὁ λέγων μοιχάδα ἐμέ *MaTr:* οὐδεὶς ἔστιν ὁ κωλύων οὐδὲ γὰρ [τινὰ] τῶν ἔνδον νήφοντα ὁρῶ C

On the Ten Virgins

title   Ἕτερον κοντάκιον εἰς τὰς ιʹ παρθένους P
        The full text of this song is preserved in C, V (shorter recension), and P (longer recension); several other manuscripts contain parts of it. For a study of recensions and variants and a critical apparatus, see GdM, vol. 3, pp. 303–65.

Prel. 6   στυγνάσωμεν *GdM, MaTr:* νυστάξωμεν *Pitra, Analecta sacra spicilegio solesmensi parata, vol. 1 (Paris, 1876), 471*

2   νυμφῶνος *MaTr:* ἐλπίδος ΔΜ *GdM*

5   βαστασάσας . . . τελέσασας P: τελέσας M; βαστάσαντας . . . τελέσαντας *GdM, MaTr*

7   πάντας *GdM, MaTr:* πάντα P

8   Ἴσμεν γὰρ . . . μένοντας Χριστόν *GdM, MaTr:* Ἀνάστασιν μέντοι ποιεῖν (*Pitra, Analecta sacra 1, corrects to* ποιεῖ) ἔγερσιν

νεκρῶν σάλπιγξ ἠχοῦσα δι' ἀγγέλου· ὑμνοῦσι γὰρ νῦν πάντες
καὶ ἀναμένουσι Χριστὸν T

12 Δ *has a different version of this stanza, which there is numbered 11 (not
12). For editions, see MaTr, 400, and GdM, vol. 3, p. 342.*

22 καὶ μὴ ἐκ πάντων νηστεύειν τῶν βλαπτόντων *GdM, MaTr: this
line is unsatisfactory in P, the only manuscript; a marginal note is interpreted by MaTr to say* κρίνειν ἀδελφὰς μεγάλη γὰρ βλάβη
ἔστι

30 *In the short recension, this stanza precedes 29.*

31 εἰς τὴν βασιλείαν *GdM, MaTr: ΔT include the additional kolon*
πρεσβείαις τῆς Θεοτόκου, *added as a marginal note in* P
πᾶσιν παρέχων P T: ἵνα καὶ σχῶμεν *GdM, MaTr*

ON THE HARLOT

title κοντάκιον εἰς τὴν πόρνην CPV
The full text of this song is preserved in CPV.

Prel. 2 τοῖς νεύμασιν CV *GdM:* τῷ βλέμματι P *MaTr. GdM points to the
parallel use of* νεῦμα *in Isaiah 3:16, where the daughters of Zion
carry themselves inappropriately (*ἐν νεύμασιν ὀφθαλμῶν*)*

3 Ὑπέκνισεν *GdM:* Ὑπέπνευσεν P *MaTr*

7 ἰλύος *MaTr:* ὕλης *GdM*

9 μέλη *MaTr:* πάντα CV *GdM*

10 ἐπέθελξε *MaTr:* ἐπύρωσε *GdM*

12 εἱρμὸν *GdM:* ὁρμὴν P *MaTr*
ἡ σεμνὴ τὸ τερπνὸν μύρον *GdM:* ἡ τερπνὴ τὸ καλὸν μύρον P
MaTr

ON THE WOMEN AT THE TOMB

title Κοντάκιον εἰς τὴν τριήμερον καὶ ζωοποιὸν καὶ ὑπέρλαμπρον
ἀνάστασιν τοῦ Κυρίου καὶ Θεοῦ καὶ Σωτῆρος ἡμῶν Ἰησοῦ
Χριστοῦ P *and similar in others*
The full text of this song is preserved in ABJMPTΔ.

2 πλήρης: *on the form, see GdM, vol. 4, p. 383n3*
προεῖπεν *GdM:* προὔλεγεν *MaTr*

5 οἶκος *MaTr:* θρόνος *in alternative readings and GdM*

473

10   ἀγγέλων *following a minority of manuscripts:* δικαίων *GdM, MaTr,*
        also the reading of many manuscripts
        σαφῶς γὰρ . . . ἐμός, ἔστιν: *the manuscripts feature a great variety,*
        for which see GdM, vol. 4, pp. 396–99
15   μᾶλλον *Tomadakis,* Ῥωμανοῦ τοῦ Μελῳδοῦ ὕμνοι, *vol. 4, p. 403:*
        μόνον *GdM, MaTr*
17   ἄφθαρτος *AJP:* ἄχραντος *GdM;* ἄφραστος *MaTr*
19   θεόπνευστοι *GdM:* φιλόθεοι *MaTr, following some manuscripts*
24   παρίδῃς *GdM:* καταλείπῃς *MaTr*

On the Samaritan Woman

title   κοντάκιον εἰς τὴν Σαμαρείτιδα P
        The full text of this song is preserved in P.
1   χρῆμα *GdM:* κρῖμα P *MaTr. GdM suggests the present reading,*
        which is almost a homophone, makes better sense on a semantic level,
        and fits Romanos's penchant for playing with word forms.
2   τοῖς αἰτοῦσιν <μεταδοῦναι> *GdM:* <διανέμειν> τοῖς αἰτοῦσι
        MaTr
3   ἄρτι: *something is missing here according to MaTr. Other editors, in-*
        cluding GdM, have added some words to fill the lacuna, but I have
        left it open.
4   πηγὴν *GdM:* πνοήν *MaTr*
7   ἐκκλησίας καὶ Μαρίας *MaTr:* ἐκκλησίας καὶ Σαμαρείας P;
        ἐκκλησίας, Σαμαρείας *GdM*
13   ἀμείνην, ὅ: ἀκάνθην, ἢ *Koder,* "Konjekturvorschläge," *102–5*

On the Bleeding Woman

title   κοντάκιον εἰς τὴν αἱμόρρουν P
        The full text of this song is preserved in P.

On the Nativity of the Theotokos

title   κοντάκιον εἰς τὴν γέννησιν τῆς ὑπεραγίας Θεοτόκου *quoted*
        from Maisano, Cantici, vol. 2, p. 86; a manuscript source is lacking
        The full text of this song is preserved in AGJbp.
1   ἡ δὲ ἐν τῷ παραδείσῳ *AGJbp:* ἡ δ' ἐπὶ τῷ παραδόξῳ *MaTr. Like*

474

> *Maisano, Cantici, vol. 2, pp. 86–87, I think the manuscript reading makes more sense, as the line echoes Protevangelium 2, where Anna walks around in her garden (εἰς τὸν παράδεισον αὐτῆς).*

10 ἐλπίδα *GdM, MaTr*: ἀντίληψιν b

On the Annunciation

title Ἕτερον κοντάκιον εἰς τὸν εὐαγγελισμὸν τῆς ὑπεραγίας Θεοτόκου P
The full text of this song is preserved in P.

18 παραδειγματίσαι σε *GdM, MaTr*: παραδειγματίσαι με P
ἀθῳώσαί σε *MaTr*: ἀθῳώσαί με P *GdM*

On the Virgin

title Κοντάκιον μεθεόρτιον τῆς Χριστοῦ γεννήσεως DP
The full text of this song is preserved in P. Manuscript D has the pre-lude and the first three stanzas.

2 καὶ γίνεται παγὶς τῷ παμπανούργῳ μορφὴν ἡμετέραν λαβὼν ὁ
πρὸ αἰώνων P *GdM*: καὶ γίνεται τὸ πᾶν παγὶς τῷ παντουργῷ ἡ
τοῦ φύσει κρύπτουσα βασίλεια D. *The text seems corrupt here;
neither reading is entirely satisfactory (P does not follow the meter);
see GdM, vol. 2, p. 121n2.*

4 *Lines 4–6 are corrupt, with a lacuna in line 6; I follow GdM's restitu-
tion.*

On the Nativity (Mary and the Magi)

title κοντάκιον τῆς τοῦ Χριστοῦ γεννήσεως J *and similar in others*
The full text of this song is preserved in ABCDJMPTw; V *is damaged
and lacks six stanzas in the middle.*

3 οὐρανοῦ *GdM, MaTr: some manuscripts have* οὐρανῶν; *see GdM,
vol. 2, p. 52*

16 φησί . . . ἔφησε: *the repetition of the verb* φησί . . . ἔφησε *is odd, as
GdM points out; none of the manuscripts offer a better alternative,
however*

21 ἐξ CV: δι' *GdM, MaTr; a variation of prepositions seems more in line
with Romanos's style*

22 ἀγγέλους BD: ποιμένας *GdM, MaTr. I follow manuscripts BD, as the stanza focuses on what is glorious and shining, and because the hymn associates the star and the angels as radiant beings.*

On the Nativity (Mary with Adam and Eve)

title Ἕτερον κονδάκιον τῇ ἐπαύριον τῆς Χριστοῦ γεννήσεως, ἤτοι τῆς ὑπεραγίας Θεοτόκου A *and similar in others*
The full text of this song is preserved in AP.

Prel. ἄφραστον *MaTr*: ἄσπορον *some manuscripts and GdM*

6 καὶ τῶν ἀχράντων αὐτῆς ποδῶν ἅψαι σὺν ἐμοὶ νῦν *MaTr*: καὶ αὐτῆς πρὸ τῶν ποδῶν ἐρριμένους θεωροῦσα A *GdM*

11 χαρᾶς γὰρ παραίτιος *GdM, MaTr*: ὑετὸς εὑρέθη μοι A

13 τὰ ἐσχάτως P *GdM*: τὰ γραφέντα A *MaTr*

14 Ἂν δὲ καὶ τὸ ἕτερον . . . τὸ γενόμενον *GdM*: ἂν δὲ καὶ σταυ-ροῦσθαι με μάθῃς, σεμνή, νεκροῦσθαι δὲ δι' αὐτούς, μετὰ πάντων τῶν στοιχείων δονηθήσῃ καὶ θρηνήσεις P *MaTr*

On the Wedding at Cana

title κοντάκιον εἰς τὸν ἐν Κανᾷ γάμον P
The full text of this song is preserved in P. *Since only one manuscript version exists, there are no variant readings, but GdM has marked several readings as uncertain due to poor manuscript quality.*

19 μεταχώνευσις *GdM, MaTr; a hapax legomenon. GdM, vol. 2, p. 319n2, suggests that it may be a corruption of* μεταχώρησις. *There are various uncertain readings in this stanza; the reconstructed form goes back to Paul Maas.*

20 ἀπολαύομεν *MaTr*: ἀνακλίνομεν *GdM*

On the Way to Golgotha

title Κοντάκιον ἕτερον τῇ μεγάλῃ παρασκευῇ εἰς τὸ πάθος τοῦ Κυρίου καὶ εἰς τὸν θρῆνον τῆς Θεοτόκου P *and similar in others*
The full text of this song is preserved in ABMPTΔ.

8 υἱέ μου . . . ὑγιαίνει *MaTr*: πῶς οὖν λέγεις· 'Εἰ μὴ πάθω, εἰ μὴ θάνω, ὁ ταλαίπωρος Ἀδὰμ οὐχ ὑγιαίνει;' *GdM*

Notes to the Translations

On Fasting (Adam and Eve)

The first letters of each stanza of this song (MaTr, no. 51; GdM, no. 1) form the acrostic: τοῦ ταπεινοῦ Ῥωμανοῦ ὁ ὕμνος, "hymn by the lowly Romanos." According to the manuscript, the song is intended for the Wednesday of the second week of Lent. Drawing partly on the biblical story in Genesis 2–4 and on John Chrysostom's *Homily 5 on Repentance* (PG 49:305–14), the poet uses the first humans' transgression to argue for fasting. The refrain is split; only the very last word is repeated in each stanza and thus sung by the congregation.

Prel.   *to its own melody*: For a discussion, see GdM, vol. 1, p. 70n1.

1   *to: The infirmary of repentance*: According to manuscript P, this hymn follows the metrical pattern of the anonymous hymn *On Nineveh and Repentance* (MaTr, no. 52; GdM, unnumbered appendix in vol. 1, pp. 405–27). It does not, however, follow it slavishly. The refrain (or the only repeated word) in that hymn is similarly τὴν μετάνοιαν (the repentance).

    Through this . . . inscription in life: The lines may echo the Jewish liturgical formula "Inscribe us in the Book of Life."

2   *We know that Moses . . . drew near to him*: The stanza is influenced by John Chrysostom, *Homily 5 on Repentance* 2 (PG 49:307–8).

    converse face-to-face: Deuteronomy 5:4. Compare here Luke 9:30.

3   *The race of demons . . . by fasting and prayer*: See Matthew 17:21; Mark 9:29.

4   *She gushes with wisdom*: The Greek word φιλοσοφίαν may also be translated "philosophy," which in late antiquity often has the

477

implication of a virtuous lifestyle (see *On Joseph and Potiphar's Wife* 1).

6   *The Most High . . . impervious to decay*: The stanza is influenced by
     John Chrysostom, *Homily 5 on Repentance* 2 (PG 49:307–8).
     put him in paradise, as it is written: See Genesis 2:8–17.

7   *The tree's actual being . . . your being a partaker*: Romanos ventures
     into the weighty theological terminology of "nature" and "be-
     ing/essence," and he contrasts the being/essence (οὐσία) of the
     tree with Adam's "being-with" (μετουσία), meaning "commu-
     nion" or "participation." Similar Eucharistic allusions appear
     in several stanzas, with the word "participation" (μετάληψις),
     for instance; thus the hymn indirectly portrays this fruit as an
     anti-Communion.

8   *bounty of the others*: I take "the others" to mean the other trees.
     with the image: According to Christian anthropology, the human
     being was created in God's image; see Genesis 1:26.

9   *crafty*: The kolon lacks three syllables and I follow Ephrem Lash's
     suggestion in supplying φρόνιμος (crafty) from Genesis 3:1;
     Lash, "On Adam and Eve," Internet Archive Wayback Ma-
     chine, version from August 12, 2007, https://web.archive.org
     /web/20070812183943/http://www.anastasis.org.uk/On%20Adam
     %20and%20Eve-51. Maas (in MaTr, 441) suggests κακοῦργος
     (evildoing), and GdM, vol. 1, p. 80, δόλιος (deceitful).
     a stumbling branch: The word πρόσκομμα (stumbling) is often
     used with λίθος (stone, or block), but Sirach 31:7 speaks of
     ξύλον προσκόμματος (a wooden stumbling block). It seems
     that Romanos is playing with the ideas of wood or a tree and of
     stumbling here.

11   *the knowledge of the good and the bad*: While Genesis 2 and 3, in the
     transmitted Septuagint form, speak of knowledge of "good and
     evil" (καλὸν καὶ πονηρόν) in the singular, Romanos repeatedly
     employs the plural phrase "of the good [things] and the bad
     [things]" (τῶν καλῶν καὶ τῶν φαύλων).

14   *God made the whole creation good*: Compare Genesis 1:31.
     it possesses life: Understanding the form ἔχοντα (possessing) as a
     neuter singular referring to φυτόν (the "plant" or "tree"); see
     GdM, vol. 1, p. 84n2.

15   *is breathtaking*: The verb μαραίνω might be translated "wither," implying that, like a dying plant, she will waste away, but I think the main point here is the irony, which I have attempted to convey by the word "breathtaking." The tree is amazing but eventually also lethal.

17   *hold on to life*: The manuscript has here ἀπέχω τοῦ ξύλου (and I receive from [the fruits of] the tree).

21   *the enticements . . . the charm*: The word μαγγανεία (enticements) ambivalently connotes both refinement (in relation to cuisine) and trickery. The word χάρις (charm) in the next line comes with a similar ambivalence; although most usually in the Christian context it refers to "grace," it may also refer to a love charm.

22   *the Hebrews offered . . . tithes from their goods*: Leviticus 27:30–33.

23   *the night and day of the Passion's saving Saturday*: Holy Saturday, or Easter Eve.

       thirty-six days and a half, a tenth of the year: Romanos's calculation of the Lenten days is interesting: he does not emphasize the number forty, and he indicates that early Byzantines did not fast on Saturdays and Sundays. The "half" in "thirty-six and a half" is not really explained in Romanos's counting, but his contemporary, Dorotheos of Gaza, has an almost identical calculation, where he counts Holy Saturday (one day) and half the night (*Teachings* 15.159); see L. Regnault and J. de Préville, *Dorothée de Gaza: Oeuvres spirituelles,* Sources Chrétiennes 92, (Paris, 1963), 446–49.

ON ABRAHAM'S SACRIFICE

The first letters of each stanza of this song (MaTr, no. 41; GdM, no. 3) form the acrostic: εἰς τὸν Ἀβραὰμ Ῥωμανοῦ ὕμνος, "a hymn on Abraham by Romanos." The occasion given in the manuscript is Sunday of the fourth week of Lent. The refrain appears in two distinct variants, the first in the prelude and stanzas 20–24, the second in stanzas 1–19; the second seems to allude to Matthew 19:17. But as with other split refrains, its last kolon is repeated almost verbatim throughout. In this poem Sarah opposes the particular economy of gift giving where the giver (God) requests the re-

479

turn of his gift (her son Isaac). Approximating the traditional typological connection between Isaac and Christ, the poet lets Sarah's words to her son resemble those that Mary speaks to her own son regarding his death, particularly in *On the Nativity (Mary with Adam and Eve)*. The biblical version of the Isaac story is found in Genesis 18:1–15, 21:1–7, and 22:1–19. While Romanos must have known this and other early versions, his account is both free and creative. The last half especially, where Sarah plays a crucial role, seems to rely on Ephrem and other earlier Syriac sources; see Sebastian Brock, "From Ephrem to Romanos," *Studia Patristica* 20 (1987): 139–51. But one may also hear echoes of ancient dramas like Euripides's *Medea* and the title character's qualms over the killing of her children.

1 *the one who was calling him*: God is described in this song as "the one who called" Abraham (compare Hebrews 11:8 and Genesis 22:11, 22:15).

    for but one is good: The refrain in stanzas 1–19 is introduced in Greek by the word ὅτι, which has a wide range of meanings. Rather than trying to fit all these meanings into one English term, I shift between "for," "that," and "since."

2 *old man's heart*: The word σπλάγχνα (here, "heart") is difficult to render in English—especially in this song. In Greek it refers primarily to the inward parts of the body and may thus allude to animal sacrifice (innards to be eaten), but it also often connotes the seat of compassion and parental emotions and is thus used to evoke the emotional bonds between parents and their children. Here it also relates to God's words to Abraham about Isaac being ἐκ τῶν σῶν λαγόνων, "from your loins."

6 *your customary calves*: Psalms 50:21(51:19), where the Greek has "calves" (μόσχους) rather than "bulls."

    I've welcomed everyone out of compassion: See Genesis 18:1–8.

7 *through an angel once signaled his birth*: See Genesis 16:11. The three persons to whom Abraham gave hospitality in Genesis 18 are also traditionally taken to be angels; compare Hebrews 13:2.

10 *the dark cluster*: The Greek participle περκάζων has the sense of darkening with age, as here with ripening grapes, or with the face of a young man when a beard starts to appear; but the lan-

guage of ripeness is also that of foreboding (compare Revelation 14:18).

12   *Wife, you should not anger God*: At this point the dialogue turns seamlessly from what Abraham imagines Sarah to say into an actual conversation with her.

    your bosom: The Greek term κόλπος means "bosom," "lap," or "womb," and not least in the plural it often has the latter meaning; Henry George Liddell, Robert Scott, and Henry Stuart James, *A Greek-English Lexicon* (Oxford, 1940), under "κόλπος," I.2. Romanos always uses the plural—whether of a father or a mother—despite the biblical precedence for the singular. Here, and even in the previous stanza, the Greek term κόλποις might possibly be translated as "womb"; see also note to *On the Blessing of Jacob* 11.

    so show your resolve: The word πρόθεσιν, translated here as "resolve," may also connote offering or sacrifice.

13   *You're the boy's sower . . . slayer*: I follow the manuscript in making this question Sarah's, but MaTr has amended the verbal forms to make the line part of Abraham's speech: "I'm the boy's sower; I'll be his slayer." As an interjection spoken by Sarah it does appear abruptly, but it makes more sense as an ironic comment. Abraham's vocative "wife" in the next line also supports this reading.

14   *When she had heard . . . cannot be a murderer*: It is difficult to make exact sense of Sarah's (reluctant?) irony in the stanza, but at least it seems clear that the lines portray the moment when she agrees to let Isaac go.

18   *glimpse, as in a mirror*: As GdM, vol. 1, p. 157n2, points out, catoptromancy, or mirror divination, remained popular in late antiquity.

    an unwilling victim: Many commentators highlight Isaac's willingness to be sacrificed, which makes Abraham's act less cruel and more holy; for Christians it also strengthens the typological connection to Christ as the willing victim.

20   *I've found your faith . . . in the final ages*: See Romans 4.

22   *in you I can sketch . . . bear my imprint*: In current theological

terminology, this is called "typology," the play between types and antitypes, whereby older phenomena can foreshadow or serve as examples for future ones; compare Romans 5:14; Hebrews 8:5.

23   *the ram in a tree*: The biblical expression in Genesis 22:13 is ἐν φυτῷ σαβεκ, "in the thicket plant." While the Genesis story imagines the ram to be caught in the thicket, Romanos seems to envision a ram tied to a tree by the horns. In this stanza he repeatedly uses the term ξύλον, which can mean both "wood" and "tree," and thus the "tree" of the cross.

24   *He who's shown . . . take my spirit*: According to a Jewish legend, Sarah died immediately after Isaac came back; see, Riccardo Maisano, *Cantici di Romano il Melodo* (Turin, 2002), vol. 2, p. 194n54.

      do not slay . . . to benefit us: These two lines are corrupt, but I take "father" here to refer to Abraham, the father of faith (Galatians 3:7), and understand that the singer asks for his intercession.

On the Blessing of Jacob

The first letters of each stanza of this song (MaTr, no. 42; GdM, no. 4) form the acrostic: τοῦ ταπεινοῦ Ῥωμανοῦ, "by the lowly Romanos." The hymn is written to the melody of Romanos's own *On the Women at the Tomb*. The occasion given in the manuscript is Sunday of the fifth week of Lent. This hymn is relatively close to a rewriting of the biblical text (Genesis 27) in verse. Rebecca is instrumental in securing Isaac's blessing for Jacob instead of Esau and in securing peace by separating the brothers afterward. The plotting mother is often an unsympathetic character in ancient literature, but Romanos makes Rebecca into a type of the Christian Church and thus ultimately the heroine of his narrative. She is the mother of both Esau (the Jews) and Jacob (the Christians).

Prel.   *prodigal*: Esau traded his birthright for some stew when he was hungry (Genesis 25:29–34) and caused his parents grief by marrying two Hittite women (Genesis 26:34–35).

1   *never tilled*: Agricultural language for human procreation is not

482

uncommon in ancient Greek; Christians use it frequently when
describing the Virgin Mary, who without husbandry became a
fertile field.

2   *goodwill . . . craving*: The wordplay with προθυμίαν (here, "goodwill") and ἐπιθυμίαν (here, "craving") is difficult to convey.

5   *favor*: The poet engages the word χάρις in all its breadth, as "favor," "gift," and "[divine] grace" throughout this song; it is difficult to translate consistently without overtheologizing.

6   *as the Bible teaches*: Actually, Genesis 27:15 makes Rebecca more
instrumental, while Romanos lets Jacob act on his own initia-
tive in this stanza.

8   *What is this race*: Here and in the next stanza, Isaac's inner monologue turns into speech. I have marked thoughts and speech
with separate sets of quotation marks.

11   *the bosom of the Father*: On the Greek term κόλπος, see *On Abraham's Sacrifice* 12, above. The Christian terminology of κόλπος/
κόλποι τοῦ Πατρός, "bosom of the Father," is connected to
John 1:18, where the Son is described as being εἰς τὸν κόλπον τοῦ πατρός, "in the bosom of the Father." Early Syriac Bible translations render the Greek word κόλπον as *'ubba*, preserving the complex meaning (including "womb") in John 1:18,
and Ephrem used this same Syrian term when contrasting the
womb of the Father with the womb of Christ's mother; see
Sebastian P. Brock, "The Holy Spirit as Feminine in Early Syriac Literature," in *After Eve: Women, Theology and the Christian
Tradition,* ed. Janet M. Soskice (London, 1990), 73–88, at 83.
Since Romanos does nothing to undermine the vagueness or
ambiguity of this word, other possible renderings here might
be "lap of the Father" or "womb of the Father."

14   *was shaken with great agitation*: The peculiar word choice in the
Greek (ἐξέστη . . . ἔκστασιν) is drawn from the biblical text,
Genesis 27:33.

15   *Truly and rightly . . . was he called Jacob*: See Genesis 27:36; compare 25:26. The Hebrew name is supposedly derived from the
word for "heel," and it was given to Jacob since he grasped the
older twin Esau's heel at birth. The term is also related to an

idiomatic expression, implying the deceptive overtaking and supplanting of the other.

He divested me once of my birthright: See Genesis 25:29–34.

17   *blessed Esau with these words*: What might be read as more of a curse in Genesis 27:39–40, Romanos turns into a blessing.

ON JOSEPH AND POTIPHAR'S WIFE

The first letters of each stanza of this song (MaTr, no. 44; GdM, no. 6) form the acrostic: εἰς τὸν Ἰωσὴφ Ῥωμανοῦ ἔπος, "Romanos's poem on Joseph." The manuscript tradition assigns it to Holy Monday, the day after Palm Sunday. The metrical form (melody) is based on that of the anonymous *Akathistos to the Mother of God* (unless we assume that it is the other way around). The hymn dramatizes the sexual battle between Joseph and Potiphar's wife in terms of both rhetorical and physical wrestling. The biblical version of Joseph and Potiphar's wife can be found in Genesis 39, but the story was popular in late antiquity, and both Jewish and Christian authors narrated it freely. It eventually appears in the Qur'an (Surah Yusuf 22–35).

Prel. 1   *Alarmed by the fig . . . sweetness*: See Matthew 21:18–19; Mark 11:13–14. The idea is that ripening involves drying up in people as well as in plants.

Prel. 3   *the righteous Joseph*: "The righteous" is a traditional epithet for Joseph, and Romanos highlights throughout this song all the unrighteous or unfair things Joseph must endure. It is difficult to render the recurring wordplay faithfully, however, without the English becoming strained, since the Greek (ἀ)δικ- covers a broader semantic range.

1   *prudence . . . righteousness*: The four cardinal virtues mentioned here emerge from a philosophical tradition that goes back to Plato's *Republic* 4.426–35.

    crowned: That is, crowned with a wreath, like a victorious athlete.

2   *He who was sold . . . envy*: See Genesis 37:11–28.

    wise master: The Greek term αὐτοκράτωρ, here "master," can mean both someone who is his or her own master and someone who is the sole master or ruler of others, as an emperor. In this context it primarily connotes the master-slave dynamic that runs through the song; a master should be in charge not only of others but also of his own passions.

noble Joseph: As a son of Jacob and Rachel, Joseph was a highborn boy, whom his father had given "a coat of many colors" (Genesis 37:3), before he became a slave in Egypt. Romanos therefore insists on calling him noble or highborn, which also relates to the nobility of his character.

3   *appeared as a king in a dream*: See Genesis 37:5–11.

4   *everyone who sins is a slave to Sin*: John 8:34.

7   *as from a hidden viper*: While this may be read as a subtle allusion to Genesis 3:1, the term ἔχιδνα (viper) is often used of treacherous women.

11   *Two coaches entered together*: While the Greek term βραβευτής usually refers to an arbiter, umpire, or referee, the two characters who enter here act as coaches, cheering on Joseph and the Egyptian woman.

14   *mindless animal*: The Greek word ἄλογον means "speechless" or "irrational," but came to signify animals, and more particularly pack animals. The stanza engages the image of straying pack animals and their lack of sense and direction to describe someone who does not control his or her own passions.

15   *So do not fear . . . no cause for fear*: This passage is influenced by Sirach 23:18–19.

16   *my conscience*: Manuscript P has here instead τοῦ συνειδότος, "he who knows," that is, God, implying that God is both accuser and judge. This is not an impossible reading, since the text focuses more on the external gaze watching over all than on internal self-knowledge.

17   *the examiner of minds and hearts*: The Greek term νεφροὺς literally means "kidneys." Romanos is fond of this biblical expression, which is usually taken to signify human beings' innermost or secret parts; newer biblical translations render it "minds and hearts." See Psalms 7:10(9); Revelation 2:23.

18   *She grasps his tunic*: That the Egyptian woman grabbed Joseph's

garment is mentioned in Genesis 39:12–18, but for Romanos it arguably serves a different purpose. The scene may also be read as a perverse version of the pious woman who touched Christ's robe to be healed.

have sex with me: The Greek verb συνομιλέω means both "to converse with" and "to engage in sexual intercourse with."

19   *Defending his love for her*: That is, for Self-Control.

as a wily fox . . . nothing but leaves: The allusion is to the story of the fox and the grapes, which goes back to Aesop's Fables; see number 15 in Ben Edwin Perry's index, *Aesopica: A Series of Texts Relating to Aesop or Ascribed to Him or Closely Connected with the Literary Tradition that Bears His Name,* vol. 1, *Greek and Latin Texts* (Urbana, IL, 1952).

20   *trampled on the furnace . . . fire's voracious power*: These lines may allude to the three youths in the fiery furnace; see, not least, Daniel 3:50.

pankration: *Pankration* was an ultimate form of mixed martial art in the ancient Olympic Games and in the Roman Empire. The Greek term is retained to complete the wordplay with "panegyric" in the following line.

21   *Previously his kindred . . . sovereignty*: See Genesis 37.

22   *she pulls me*: The pronoun "she" may refer here both to the woman and to Sin, thus conflating the two.

On the Prophet Elijah

The first letters of each stanza of this song (MaTr, no. 45; GdM, no. 7) form the acrostic: τὸν προφήτην Ἠλίαν ὁ Ῥωμανὸς ἀνευφημεῖ, "Romanos lauds the prophet Elijah" in manuscript A; but τὸν προφήτην Ἠλίαν ὁ Ῥωμανὸς ὑμνῶ, "I, Romanos, praise the prophet Elijah," in manuscript P. The refrain is identical to that of Romanos's Candlemas hymn, *On the Presentation of Christ in the Temple,* although the present one introduces some variation in a few stanzas. The manuscript tradition assigns it for July 20, which is later celebrated as a commemoration of Elijah's heavenly ascent; this kontakion refers to his unusual passing only at the very end. The hymn dramatizes the somewhat surprising conflict between God's benevolence or love of humanity *(philanthropia)* and the prophet's stern and rigorous sense of justice, described as hatred of humanity. The biblical story is found in 3 (1) Kings 17–18. Parts of the song draw on Basil of Seleucia's homily on the prophet Elijah (PG 85:148–57). A pseudo-John Chrysostom homily on the topic (PG 56:583–86) is probably a later composition. An earlier fragmentary and anonymous kontakion on Elijah is published in Constantine A. Trypanis, *Fourteen Early Byzantine Cantica* (Vienna, 1968), 101–4. For a study of Romanos's version, see L. William Countryman, "A Sixth-Century Plea against Religious Violence: Romanos on Elijah," in *Reading Religions in the Ancient World: Essays Presented to Robert McQueen Grant on His 90th Birthday,* ed. David E. Aune and Robin Darling Young (Leiden, 2007), 289–305.

Prel.   *benevolent*: The Greek term φιλάνθρωπος literally means "friend or lover of humans," but it usually signifies someone who is benevolent or humane. In certain stanzas one may argue that φιλανθρωπία takes on a thicker meaning as Romanos plays with the word, but the dominant imagery is that of mercy toward lawbreakers.

4   *As the Lord lives . . . except by my word*: This oath closely follows the wording of 3 (1) Kings 17:1. Oaths were a serious matter in Byzantium; they were used to express loyalty and in connection with lawsuits.

7   *the Tishbite*: "Tishbite" is Elijah's demonymic epithet. According to the Septuagint it is derived from Tishbe, in the region of Gilead; 3 (1) Kings 17:1.

9   *The ravens' race . . . fed from above*: Romanos relies on ancient popular ideas. See, for example, Pliny the Elder, *Natural History* 10.15; Job 38:41; Psalms 146(147):9; Luke 12:24.

13   *caring for children*: The Masoretic text (1 Kings 17:12) mentions only one child, but the Septuagint (where the same passage is numbered 3 Kings 17:12) has "children" in the plural.

17   *The jar will . . . flow with oil for you*: This line follows 3 (1) Kings 17:14 almost verbatim, but in the biblical text it is God, quoted by Elijah, who speaks the blessing.

   it says: Romanos may be referring to 3 (1) Kings 17:13–16, but this is not exactly what the text says.

23   *the one who is benevolent*: It is unclear whether the refrain is part

of God's (imagined) words to Elijah or an apposition to the implied σύ (you), in which case it is not part of God's words.

25   *humans all hold . . . their life instead*: Perhaps Romanos is thinking of the statements attributed to God in Ezekiel 18:23, 18:32, and 33:11. As here, Romanos's poetry is rich in document and writing imagery; see Derek Krueger, *Writing and Holiness: The Practice of Authorship in the Early Christian East* (Philadelphia, 2004), 159–88.

28   *plenteous in mercy and patient*: See Psalms 85(86):15.

32   *and be happy*: This is the reading of manuscript A; manuscript P has τῶν φίλων μου, "of my friends."

33   *the Tishbite was lifted in a chariot of fire*: See 4 (2) Kings 2:11–12.
    Christ was lifted in clouds: See Acts 1:9.
    sent Elisha a mantle: See 4 (2) Kings 2:13.

On the Beheading of the Forerunner

The first letters of each stanza of this song (MaTr, no. 38; [GdM no. 59]) form the acrostic: τοῦ ταπεινοῦ Ῥωμανοῦ, "by the lowly Romanos." The manuscript tradition assigns it for August 29, the day of the commemoration of John the Baptist's beheading, and the text seems to be composed for such a commemoration. The Beheading is known to have been observed in Jerusalem since the fifth century, but not in Constantinople this early. The second prelude and the first stanza are still part of the liturgical celebration. The hymn has a dramatic plot typical of the Romanos corpus. The text is, however, less refined in terms of style and narrative coherence than some of his better-known pieces. Herodias, who is Herod Antipas's wife, is not portrayed as a royal person, but rather as a harlot (like Prokopios's Theodora), and her daughter is not named as Salome. The underlying gospel story is found in Matthew 14:1–12 and Mark 6:14–29. The kontakion has a split refrain.

title   *Forerunner*: The standard epithet for John the Baptist in the Byzantine tradition, since he is believed to have prepared the way for Christ and the gospel.

1   *It says that he grieved*: Probably a reference to Mark 6:26; Matthew 14:9.

2 *The adulteress*: According to Matthew 14:3–4 and Mark 6:17–18, John was put in jail for condemning the relationship between Herod and Herodias, who was married to Herod's brother.

 the fruit of the barren one: John the Baptist, as the child of Elizabeth; see Luke 1:7–24, 1:36, 1:57–63.

3 *she trembled*: Manuscripts A and T have an alternative reading, ἔβρυξεν, "gnashed her teeth."

5 *just as Jezebel . . . destruction instead*: See, for example 3 (1) Kings 21:17–29; 4 (2) Kings 9:30–37.

 The Tishbite . . . was not raining on him: 3 (1) Kings 17:1; "the Tishbite" is the prophet Elijah. For this episode, see above, *On the Prophet Elijah.*

6 *when you've grasped . . . missing now*: The Greek text for this line is uncertain, and the translation is somewhat free.

7 *Zechariah was slain*: In the Old Testament, Zechariah ben Jehoiada was stoned (2 Chronicles 24:20–22), but it is more likely that the reference here is to John's father Zechariah, who according to *Protevangelium of James* 23 was murdered by Herod because he refused to reveal where John was; compare Matthew 23:35; Luke 11:50–51.

11 *That day shall be darkness, not light*: The poet combines Job 3:2–4 and Zechariah 14:6 in the Septuagint reading.

 the Light of those in darkness: That is, Christ; see John 1:4–8.

12 *his birthday . . . everyone together*: See Mark 6:21.

13 *My wish . . . will be killed*: Manuscript C has an entirely different reading for this line: οὐδεὶς ἔστιν ὁ κωλύων οὐδὲ γὰρ [τινὰ] τῶν ἔνδον νήφοντα ὁρῶ, "none is holding me back, nor do I see anyone sober among those inside."

 a twisted bow: The meaning of this simile is not clear, and the text is corrupt, but the words echo Psalms 77(78):57 and allude, perhaps, to Eros's bow.

14 *she's smeared for us*: The double meaning suggests both that she put makeup on her daughter and that she stained her with dishonor.

15 *Wisdom . . . perish in the end*: See Wisdom 3:16.

17 *honor the beheading*: That is, honor the memory of the beheading

or commemorate it through the observance of the Beheading on August 29.

18   *Son of a true priest ... and prophetess*: John's father, Zechariah, was a priest, and his mother, Elizabeth, was sterile, according to Luke 1:5–7. While Luke 1:67 describes Zechariah as prophesying, the kontakion text calls his wife a prophetess.

nursling of the desert ... that we may fast: Following Luke 7:33, Byzantine tradition imagines John as a typical ascetic. The commemoration of his beheading, on August 29, is traditionally a day of fasting.

According to Paul ... for food: 1 Corinthians 6:13.

On the Ten Virgins

This song is entitled the *First on the Ten Virgins* (MaTr, no. 47) or the *Second on the Ten Virgins* (GdM, no. 31). There are, in other words, two Romanos hymns on this topic, but the other lacks a focus on the virgins themselves. The one translated here exists in two recensions. In the longer recension (P), the first letters of each stanza form the acrostic: τοῦ ταπεινοῦ Ῥωμανοῦ τοῦτο τὸ ποίημα, "this poetical work is by the lowly Romanos." The acrostic of the shorter recension (CV) reads: τοῦ ταπεινοῦ Ῥωμανοῦ ᾠδή A, "a first[?] song by the lowly Romanos." Stanzas 8, 11, 20, 22–23, and 25–28 are not found in CV; some of these and some of the preludes presumably postdate Romanos. The various preludes, found in different manuscripts, and the miscellaneous ways of organizing the stanzas attest to the creative flexibility of the tradition and highlight the impossibility of knowing precisely which words go back to the historical Romanos himself. Preludes 3–6 are found only in manuscripts with drastically truncated versions of the kontakion, and each is attested only in one or two manuscripts. Prelude 4 has a deviating refrain. Previous editions also do not agree on the order of the preludes, but this would not have mattered to those who sang them, since they probably performed only one; I follow the GdM numbering for them, as MaTr includes only preludes 1, 2, and 6. For a study of recensions and variants and a critical apparatus, see GdM, vol. 3, pp. 303–65. The manuscript tradition assigns this kontakion to Tuesday of Holy Week, and the first prelude is still part of the so-called Bridegroom Service in the Byzantine rite (Tuesday Matins).

The gospel parable of the ten virgins is told in Matthew 25:1–13. Romanos uses the parable to argue that asceticism is fruitless without charity and mercy. Certain parts of the song draw heavily on John Chrysostom's *Homily 3 on Repentance (On Almsgiving and the Ten Virgins)*, PG 49:291–300.

Prel. 1   *to: You who were lifted up on the cross*: This seems to refer to the melody of the anonymous hymn *On the Elevation of the Cross* (whose prelude is still in ecclesiastical use today), but it is unclear whether the latter predates Romanos, so it is possible that Romanos's prelude melody is instead the model for that anonymous hymn; see GdM, vol. 3, pp. 314–21.

brothers and sisters: I take the masculine ἀδελφοί to be gender inclusive here.

virgins: Some English Bibles translate the Greek word παρθένος as "bridesmaid," which may make sense in the context of the parable, but Romanos activates a broad virginal register. As he lets these women enter the bridechamber (νυμφών), a more nuptial and intimate relationship with Christ is implied. For a study of such language, see Elizabeth A. Clark, "The Celibate Bridegroom and His Virginal Brides: Metaphor and the Marriage of Jesus in Early Christian Ascetic Exegesis," *Church History* 77, no. 1 (2008), 1–25.

the imperishable wreath: The refrain may echo 1 Corinthians 9:24–25: "Do you not know that in a race the runners all compete, but only one receives the prize? Run in such a way that you may win it. Athletes exercise self-control in all things; they do it to receive a perishable wreath (φθαρτὸν στέφανον), but we an imperishable one (ἄφθαρτον)." The term στέφανος means "a crown" or "a wreath worn as a crown." Such wreaths or crowns evoked a wide field of connotations in the ancient world, being used to celebrate victory and authority, or joy and festivity. They were part of wedding celebrations (as they continue to be in the modern-day Byzantine rite), and to Christians they also, as in the epistle, symbolized resurrection and eternal life. The wreath of the refrain, then, is a foliage crown that (literally or metaphorically) never withers.

Prel. 4   *to: Today you have appeared*: This is the incipit of the prelude to

Romanos's hymn *On the Epiphany;* these preludes share the same melody and meter.

Prel. 6   *without gloom*: Jean-Baptiste Pitra's alternative suggestion, in *Analecta sacra spicilegio solesmensi parata,* vol. 1 (Paris, 1876): 471, is μὴ νυστάξωμεν, "let us not be drowsy." It is very attractive, since it gives a better rhyming effect with the next line, and because the meaning is more obviously connected to the story of the Ten Virgins, but it lacks manuscript support.

1   *to: In Galilee of the nations*: Romanos's *On the Epiphany.*

2   *the path*: The Greek τὴν ὁδὸν here conveys both the New Testament meaning of the Christian "way," or manner of living (see Acts 9:2, for example), and the concrete meaning of a "path" leading to a place.

5   *Mercy*: I take mercy or mercifulness (ἡ ἐλεημοσύνη) to be a female personification of the virtue. She is merely mentioned here but reappears in stanza 9.

    clearly: It is tempting to see the Greek adverb σαφῶς here as a corruption or misreading of σοφῶς (prudently); indeed, GdM translates the word into French as *prudemment.*

7   *flaming fire*: This phrase has rich biblical connotations of Christ's kingship and judgment, as in 2 Thessalonians 1:8 and Hebrews 1:7, and in Revelation it is particularly connected to his gaze (1:14, 2:18, 19:12).

8   *The call . . . for ages awaited*: Lines 1 and 2 in this stanza are different in manuscript T. There, they translate as "Indeed the sound of the trumpet, ringing from an angel, initiates resurrection and awakening from the dead; everyone now praises and awaits Christ."

    as we know: See 1 Corinthians 15:52 and Matthew 24:31.

9   *Mercy vanquishes . . . imperishable wreath*: With its lofty imagery, this entire stanza seems influenced by John Chrysostom's *Homily 3 on Repentance* 1 (PG 49:293).

10   *faces dazed*: The line may allude to Genesis 4:5, where Cain's "countenance fell" when his offering to God was not accepted, and thus Romanos creates an indirect connection to Cain and Abel.

11   *the oil of his mercy*: This is only one word in Greek, but it contains an important wordplay: ἔλεον means "mercy," while ἔλαιον means "oil." Romanos plays with the homophone words, so when God gives "mercy" it may sound in Greek like "oil."

14   *Judge most just . . . imperishable wreath*: GdM finds the foolish virgins' words in this stanza to resonate with a pseudo–John Chrysostom homily on the same parable (PG 59:530).

15   *But after these virtues . . . imperishable wreath*: See John Chrysostom, *Homily 3 on Repentance* 2 (PG 49:293).

16   *Savior, open your door*: The wording is reminiscent of *On the Nativity (Mary and the Magi)* 7, where Christ is asked to give a signal for the Magi to enter.

        do not turn away your face: The foolish virgins are quoting Psalms 26(27):9.

18   *I was truly hungry*: The poet connects the parable with the judgment scene in the latter part of Matthew 25 (especially 25:35–36).

20   *no stranger . . . under your roof*: The poet develops the broader biblical theme of hospitality to strangers; the word προσήλυτος is used in the sense of "foreign sojourner" in Leviticus 19:33–34.

21   *look down on*: The Greek of this stanza is saturated with the word or prefix κατὰ in various forms, its basic meaning, "down(ward)," here serving to highlight the condescending attitude of the foolish virgins. Unfortunately, this has been difficult to convey in the same way in English.

23   *Pity adorns her . . . enriches her*: It is the other personified virtues who furnish Fasting and her house with greatness.

25   *The harlot . . . forgiveness*: Luke 7:47–48; compare also Romanos, *On the Harlot.*

        The publican . . . inside him: Luke 18:10–14.

        I took pity on Peter . . . tears: Matthew 26:75.

27   *Oh, for the confidence . . . great glory*: Compare John Chrysostom, *Homily 3 on Repentance* 3 (PG 49:295).

28   *If we wish to obtain it . . . neglectful*: Compare John Chrysostom, *Homily 3 on Repentance* 2 (PG 49:294).

        For two small coins: Compare Mark 12:41–44; Luke 21:1–4.

29   *Do you only have two obols*: Compare John Chrysostom's *Homily 3 on Repentance* 2 (PG 49:294). An obol is a Greek coin of little value (one-sixth of a *drachma* in ancient Athens), and the διωβελία was a daily allowance of two obols to the disabled or needy. Like Romanos here, early Christian authors often use the obol to explicate the poor widow's gift of "two small copper coins (λεπτὰ δύο), which are worth a penny" in Mark 12:42, so it conveys the sense of giving what little you have. The two obols may also allude to the practice of placing "Charon's obols" on a deceased person's eyes when he or she was buried; the two coins were the corpse's only property.

cup of cold water to the one in need: Matthew 10:42.

his cup of thanksgiving: The English attempts to capture the double meaning in the Greek: "with gratitude" or "with [the] Eucharist."

ON THE HARLOT

The first letters of each stanza of this song (MaTr, no. 10; GdM, no. 21) form the acrostic: τοῦ ταπεινοῦ Ῥωμανοῦ, "by the lowly Romanos." The kontakaria assign it to Wednesday of Holy Week. The hymn writes itself into a broad tradition in early Christianity of dramatizing and negotiating the pious sexuality of the repenting "sinful woman," who in Romanos becomes a lustful harlot, "an experienced woman who understands and articulates the attendant surge of her emotions"; R. J. Schork, *Sacred Song from the Byzantine Pulpit: Romanos the Melodist* (Gainesville, FL, 1995), 30. See also Kevin Kallish, *She Who Loved Much: The Sinful Woman in Saint Ephrem the Syrian and the Orthodox Tradition* (Jordanville, NY, 2022); for a comparison with Paul the Silentiary's unrepentant harlot poem, see Steven D. Smith, *Greek Epigram and Byzantine Culture: Gender, Desire, and Denial in the Age of Justinian* (Cambridge, 2019), 7–11; and for a general study, see J. H. Barkhuizen, "Romanos Melodos, Kontakion 10 (Oxf.): 'On the Sinful Woman,'" *Acta Classica* 33 (1990): 33–52. Romanos stays closest to Luke 7:36–50, but see also Mark 14:3–9 and Matthew 26:6–13. The harlot is not named Mary in those gospels, as in the similar story in John 12:1–9, nor identified with Mary Magdalene, as in some later Christian traditions.

Prel. 1 *You called a harlot "daughter"*: In the gospels, Jesus refers only to the woman with a hemorrhage as "daughter" (Mark 5:34; Luke 8:48; Matthew 9:22).

from the filth of my deeds: Βόρβορος (filth, mud, mire) works as a metaphor for sin, both here and in other hymns; compare also 2 Peter 2:22. It means both something smelly and disgusting that can make you filthy, and a pool of filth or something you can drown in; compare *Life of Saint Nicholas of Sion* 22, in Ihor Ševčenko and Nancy Patterson Ševčenko, *The Life of Saint Nicholas of Sion* (Brookline, MA, 1984). The harlot appears to be wading in her own filth.

Prel. 2 *perfume*: The word μύρον is difficult to translate. It means "aromatic oil," suggesting on one hand sweet scent and what in modern English would be called perfume or fragrance (thus see Luke 7:37), which might have strong erotic connotations as well as the practical function of hiding or neutralizing a foul smell. On the other hand, there is the more palpable aspect of rubbing or massaging with the oil. In Christian context, μύρον may also suggest kingly anointing and the sacrament of chrismation (or baptismal anointment). A confusion with myrrh (σμύρνα/σμύρνον or μύρρα) seems to be ancient as well, but it is not developed in Romanos. Given the breadth of connotations, consistency in the English translation is difficult, if desirable at all.

1 *like fragrance sprinkling everywhere*: Compare 2 Corinthians 2:14–16.

fornicators: Πόρνος (translated here as "fornicator") is the masculine form of πόρνη, which also means a woman who fornicates or, more specifically, a harlot.

2 *horrors I will see in that place*: That is, in Gehenna or some hellish place of punishment.

3 *the straying woman . . . a dog*: The imagery is confusingly rich; the Greek term ἄσωτον, here, "straying," might also be translated "prodigal," making the line an allusion to the Prodigal Son. "Dog" (κύνα) might also be translated more literally as "bitch."

the Canaanite woman: Compare Matthew 15:21–28.

5   *blow on the filth*: Here and in stanza 17, Romanos apparently alludes to the moment in the baptismal service of the Byzantine rite when the catechumen renounces Satan by exsufflation. For a fuller description see Lash, *On the Life of Christ: Kontakia* (San Francisco, 1995), 245.

6   *Let me come to him . . . not be put to shame*: Psalms 33:6(34:5); compare James 4:8.

      make the Pharisee's house one of enlightenment: A "house of enlightenment" is an allusion to a baptistery.

7   *Rahab once received spies*: Before the Israelite troops entered the Promised Land, Joshua sent two male spies to Jericho. The prostitute Rahab hosted them and thus became an important servant of the divine plan (Joshua 2:1–24; Hebrews 11:31). According to the Babylonian Talmudic tradition, Rahab was exceptionally attractive: "Rahab aroused impure thoughts by her name, i.e., the mere mention of her name would inspire lust for her. . . . Anyone who says Rahab, Rahab, immediately experiences a seminal emission due to the arousal of desire caused by Rahab's great beauty"; Babylonian Talmud, Megillah 15a, trans. Adin Even-Israel Steinsaltz, *The William Davidson Talmud,* accessed June 6, 2023, https://www.sefaria.org/Megillah.

      bore the honorable name of my Jesus: "Jesus" and "Joshua" are originally the same name and are both rendered Ἰησοῦς in Greek; Romanos sees a parallel between the prostitute Rahab and the prostituted heroine of his story, but also a parallel between Joshua, who indirectly initiated the encounter with Rahab, and Jesus, whom the harlot encounters.

      the overseer of all, not a spy of the land: The Greek text contrasts ἐπίσκοπος (one who oversees or keeps watch over, but also a bishop) and κατάσκοπος (a scout or spy). The wordplay between the two -σκοπος nouns is difficult to recreate in English.

8   *Anna in her barrenness . . . Samuel for the one without a child*: The biblical Hannah (rendered as Anna in Greek) was unable to become pregnant, and one day when she prayed to become a mother, her intense and deeply troubled prayer, which was silent although her lips moved, led the priest Eli to think that

she was drunk. After that she gave birth to her only son, whom she called Samuel (1 Kings [1 Samuel] 1). I have transliterated her name as "Anna" throughout, since Romanos occasionally compares or blurs the distinction between the two barren women, the Old Testament Hannah and Mary's mother.

my one and only soul: The word μονογενής may also be used for "only begotten" children (such as Hannah's and the Virgin Mary's sons), so there is a play with words where she compares her only soul to others' only offspring.

the unmarried one by you, Emmanuel: Emmanuel is Jesus, whose mother conceived without a man's participation.

9   *kindled my limbs, my guts, and my heart*: On the expression νε-φροὺς καὶ . . . καρδίαν, see above, *Joseph and Potiphar's Wife* 17. Eschewing the archaic "reins" of the King James Bible, or the "minds" of the earlier passage, I use "guts" here to keep the Greek focus on body organs in the stanza. A similar attention to bodily expressions is found in *On the Samaritan Woman* 20.

11   *Michal loved David . . . That woman fled*: King Saul's younger daughter Michal was given to David in marriage, since she loved him (1 Kings [1 Samuel] 18:20–28). David is not yet a king, but merely a shepherd who has killed Goliath.

12   *the flow of words*: The Greek term εἱρμός, here, "flow," is also used for the pattern stanza of a kontakion. Following manuscript P, MaTr has instead ὁρμὴν, which would give a meaning here of "her desire for words."

her delightful perfume: The alternative reading of manuscript P, followed by MaTr, would give a translation here of "The delightful one grabbed her fine perfume."

anoint at the meal: This might also be translated "anoint the best one (τὸ[ν] ἄριστον)."

13   *scepter of righteousness*: The ῥάβδος εὐθύτητος is a biblical notion; see Psalms 44(45):7; Hebrews 1:8.

18   *The promissory note . . . sign another*: Compare Colossians 2:14.

the capital . . . my flesh: Since κεφάλαιον (capital) has to do with κεφαλὴ (head), and τόκος (interest) can also mean "parturition or offspring," there is an odd corporeal wordplay in this line, so

497

that it might also be translated "the head of my soul, the child of my flesh." Precisely what this would signify is unclear to me, but it is hardly a coincidence.

On the Women at the Tomb

The first letters of each stanza of this song (MaTr, no. 29; GdM, no. 40) form the acrostic: τοῦ ταπεινοῦ Ῥωμανοῦ ψαλμός, "a psalm by the lowly Romanos." The song, often called *On the Resurrection,* is a song for Easter Sunday. Prelude 1 and the first stanza are still in liturgical use, in the solemn Paschal Matins. The complete song has been transmitted in almost all the kontakion manuscripts, making this the most attested of Romanos's six resurrection kontakia. In this song the Byzantine Easter greeting "Christ has risen," resembling the one with which the angel greeted the women in Matthew 28:6–7, is put in the mouth of Mary Magdalene and the women, thus displaying her as the "apostle of the apostles," as she is called in Byzantine tradition. The gospel stories about the women at the tomb can be found in Matthew 28:1–15, Mark 16:1–11, Luke 24:1–12, and John 20:1–18. Romanos follows not least the gospel of John, which focuses on Mary Magdalene, but amalgamates his own version.

Prel. 1   *women with perfumes*: In the Byzantine rite, these women, who prepared "spices and perfumes or ointments" (ἀρώματα καὶ μύρα, Luke 23:56) to anoint the body of Christ, are called μυροφόροι. This term is often rendered as "myrrhbearers," translating μύρον (perfumed oil) as myrrh. I have avoided this slightly obscuring term. Admittedly, in stanza 1 Romanos himself compares these women and their gifts of perfume to the gift-bringing Magi, but he makes no attempt to connect μύρον and σμύρναν linguistically. Both the English terminology and Romanos's comparison reflect a theological desire to connect the beginning with the end.
    Rejoice: Matthew 28:9.
Prel. 2   *undefiled body*: The Greek word ἄχραντον, here, "undefiled," might also gesture toward "untouched" or even "unanointed," as the verb χραίνω means "to touch lightly" or "to smear."
    bleeding and faithful woman robbed of a cure: See *On the Bleeding*

Woman. I have supplied "and faithful" here for metrical reasons.

1   *The maidens*: The Greek word κόρη usually indicates an unmarried woman, maiden, or daughter. Here, as elsewhere, Romanos seems to use it as a synonym for γυνή (woman); compare stanza 9, as well as *On the Bleeding Woman* 4. Whether it should be taken to signal a relatively young age or unmarried status is hard to say, but in the first line of stanza 15 he also uses the word νεάνιδες, "young women" or "maidens," for these women, clearly indicating youthfulness. Kassia, in *Tetraodion for Holy Saturday* 1.1, later calls the same women "maidens" (αἱ νεάνιδες), perhaps influenced by the Song of Songs 1:3; see Antonia Tripolitis, *Kassia: The Legend, the Woman, and Her Work* (New York, 1992), 80–81.

dawn: The word ὄρθρος, here, "dawn," is also the Greek word for the morning service in church, corresponding to Matins in the Latin rite.

seeking the day . . . before the sun: These two lines are later echoed in John of Damascus's *Easter Kanon*, ode 5 *(heirmos)* attributed to John of Damascus and included in the Byzantine rite *Pentekostarion;* for an English translation by Ephrem Lash, see his *The Services for the Holy and Great Sunday of Pascha* (Manchester, 2000), 5–16.

3   *as also the Theologian says*: The evangelist John is called John the Theologian in Byzantine tradition. See John 20:1.

Disciples: The "disciples" may refer to the other women, but also to Peter and John, introduced in the next stanza; see John 20:2.

4   *Kephas . . . Zebedee's son*: That is, Peter, the leader of the disciples, and John, the beloved disciple.

Peter . . . tend my lambs: John 21:15–17.

Blessed are you, Simon . . . the Kingdom: Matthew 16:19.

For Peter . . . he had walked: Compare Matthew 14:28–29.

5   *We have been . . . house of God*: GdM follows the manuscripts that have "throne" (θρόνος) here, but Romanos compares the tomb with the temple, where God may dwell, and where Jesus before his crucifixion went and "looked around" (περιβλεψάμενος)

according to Mark 11:11. The Holy of Holies was a space too sacred for people to enter (except the high priest, see Leviticus 16), and with the crucifixion (Mark 15:38) its curtain was torn in two and visually opened. Although Mary Magdalene stood "outside the tomb . . . [and] bent over [to look] into the tomb" (John 20:11), the male disciples are not able to control themselves.

6   *grace of his own 'Rejoice!'*: According to Matthew 28:9, Jesus gave them the greeting χαίρετε. This is the plural form of the χαῖρε with which Gabriel greeted the Virgin in Luke 1:28, and which engendered a whole form (χαιρετισμοί) in Marian poetry, exemplified by Romanos in *On the Annunciation* 1. This common greeting actually means "rejoice!" or "be glad!" and has been translated as "hail," or simply "greetings." The joyful aspect is particularly important here, as it contrasts with the mournful mood of the women.

7   *the six winged and many eyed*: That is, the seraphim (Isaiah 6:2–3; Revelation 4:8).

       As the Forerunner . . . baptize me: That is, John the Baptist; see above, *On the Beheading of the Forerunner*. At Matthew 3:14 he suggests that Jesus should have baptized him instead.

8   *After four . . . graveclothes*: John 11:38–44.

       like the harlot . . . body and tomb: Compare above, *On the Harlot*.

       you resurrected the widow's son: Luke 7:12–15.

       You brought Jairus's girl to life: Mark 5:22–43.

10   *the other ninety-nine lambs*: Matthew 18:12; Luke 15:4. For the parable of the Good Shepherd, see Matthew 18:12–14, Luke 15:3–7, and John 10:2–4 and 10:14.

12   *Arouse them all . . . light their torches*: Romanos may be alluding indirectly to an Easter procession with torches in the streets of Constantinople; compare GdM, vol. 4, p. 401n1.

14   *I'm shining like Moses*: As here, the Greek text of Exodus 34:29–35 uses the term δεδόξασται to describe how the skin of Moses's face shone when he returned from the mountain where he had met God. A more literal rendering is "was filled with splendor"

or "was glorified," but I have chosen to retain the radiant aspect more explicit in English bibles.

like an olive twig: According to Genesis 8:11, the dove returned to
Noah after the flood with "an olive leaf, a twig (κάρφος)."

15 *Is it true what you said?*: My version deviates slightly from the
MaTr and GdM editions here in rendering this as a question.
They take this to be an affirmation, but it makes little sense
that the people, who have not been witnesses, confirm what
Mary has actually seen and experienced.

this life force: My rendering is slightly free here. The Greek text
does not give the masculine pronoun until the end of the
stanza but presupposes the subject "Life" (which in Greek is
grammatically feminine, although it ultimately denotes Christ),
while playing with the tension between life and death. I have
thus attempted not to introduce a "he" too early. It is difficult to
translate this faithfully in English without strained phrasing.

once freed his servant from the sea monster: Jonah 1–2.

16 *one of our limbs ... come to enjoy*: The language here is reminiscent
of 1 Corinthians 12:26–27, but alludes also to the Christian
rite of Communion, in which the members of the community
share a common cup and take part in the body of Christ.

17 *the tomb ... the womb, uncorrupted*: That the tomb is like a womb
is an ancient idea; here there are clearly Marian undertones as
well. I have translated τόπος as "tomb" instead of the more literal "place" in order to preserve the word similarity, which is
crucial to the original wordplay.

19 *the God-inspired*: Some manuscripts and MaTr read here αἱ φιλόθεοι, "the friends of God," or "the God-loving women."

22 *Lift up your hearts*: The women's words resemble the liturgical
sursum corda spoken by the priest in the Anaphora, the part of
the liturgical celebration when the gifts are offered and conse-
crated on the altar.

23 *as we leap*: Compare Psalms 113(114):4.

You trampled Death: Here and elsewhere, the Easter *troparion* of
the Byzantine rite rings in the background: "Christ is risen

from the dead, trampling down death by death, and on those in the tombs bestowing life!"

24   *Merciful one . . . yours is the power*: This passage is woven with language from the Lord's Prayer and Psalm 50(51).

ON THE SAMARITAN WOMAN

The first letters of each stanza of this song (MaTr, no. 9; GdM, no. 19) form the acrostic: τοῦ ταπεινοῦ Ῥωμανοῦ αἶνος, "a song by the lowly Romanos." Manuscript P assigns this kontakion to the fourth Sunday of Easter, but there is nothing in the text itself to connect it to that particular day. Romanos's narrative reflects the version of the episode in John 4:4–26. The Samaritan woman is not named Photine as in some later traditions.

Prel.   *the streams of the font*: The song repeatedly alludes to the Christian initiation rite of baptism, seeing the image of a baptismal font in the well outside Sychar.

1   *do not hide the talent you were granted*: Compare Matthew 25:13–30.

5   *gone out from . . . and coming*: The poet plays with the words for "exit, departure, leaving" and "entrance, arrival, coming in" in this stanza, alluding to Psalms 120(121):8, "The Lord will keep your going out (ἔξοδόν) and your coming in (εἴσοδον)," and Deuteronomy 28:6, "Blessed shall you be when you come in, and blessed shall you be when you go out."

      one from the nations: That is, "a gentile." While Samaritans may not be gentiles (compare Matthew 10:5) or pagans, Romanos does treat the Samaritan woman as an image of the "gentile" (ἐξ ἐθνῶν) Church.

6   *in surprise*: The adverb εἰλημμένως is a hapax legomenon. GdM, vol. 2, p. 335n2, and Lash, *Life of Christ*, 65, take it to mean "reproachfully." This seems unlikely in the context, for Romanos is portraying the Samaritan woman as a model, and models her in turn on the Theotokos. Johannes Koder takes it to mean "withheld" or "reserved" *(zurückhaltend);* see Koder, *Die Hymnen* (Stuttgart, 2005–2006), vol. 2, p. 659, which makes more

sense here. In the same vein, I interpret it as "taken unawares or with wonder," and so, "in surprise."

how can you, a Jew, ask me: Christians assumed that Samaritans and Jews were not supposed to interact; Romanos portrays the Samaritans as outside the Law.

7   *of the Church and of Mary*: The wording of the Greek text is debatable here. The sole manuscript reads Ἐκκλησίας καὶ Σαμαρείας, "of the Church and Samaria." MaTr suggested the alternative reading Ἐκκλησίας καὶ Μαρίας, which fits the meter and is adopted here. GdM suggests Ἐκκλησίας, Σαμαρείας, which is closer to the manuscript reading while still adhering to the meter; it is, however, difficult to know what the meaning of this would be. A possible interpretation is that the woman is both filthy as the "nations" and purified as the Church (compare stanza 5, line 6). However, Romanos has drawn a connection between the Samaritan woman and the Virgin Mary in the previous stanzas, and this resonates with the tradition (going back to the *Protevangelium of James*) that Mary received the annunciation from Gabriel at a well.

I'll receive you as a like-minded man: The meeting at the well comes with nuptial allusions, like Jacob's encounter with Rachel at a well, which led to marriage (Genesis 29). This explains the language of receiving and taking (in marriage), and perhaps even the conversation about the woman's husbands.

11   *I won't mimic your attitude*: Christ seems to refer to her comment in stanza 6, line 4: "how can you, a Jew, ask me?" While she was reluctant to give him water, he willingly gives to her.

13   *its lavishness*: The meaning of the Greek word ἀμείνην is uncertain since it is unattested elsewhere. GdM offers several suggestions after noting a comparable term, ἀμοινῆς, as found in a hymn of Basil of Caesarea. He wonders if it could be a rendering of the Hebrew for "faith," or πίστις: *'emunah* (GdM, vol. 1, pp. 342–43). GdM also notes a similar sounding word in Latin: *amoena,* meaning "lovely" or "attractive." Marjorie Carpenter, *Kontakia of Romanos, Byzantine Melodist* (Columbia, MO, 1970–

1973), vol. 1, p. 92, connects the word to ἀμείνων (better), which may seem plausible, but renders the meaning of the line obscure. The sense of the passage suggests that the word should be an antonym for bitter—which also resonates well with Romanos's use of sweet versus bitter in root and grafting metaphors elsewhere (see, for example, *On the Victory of the Cross* 12–15). Koder, *Die Hymnen,* vol. 2, p. 781n21, notes biblical passages resonant with the notion of a "bitter root," such as Deuteronomy 29:18 and Hebrews 12:15, and a similar image within the genuine works of Ephrem from the *Hymns on Faith.* My translation "lavishness" reflects the five forms, or horns, mentioned in the strophe and the "extravagance" of having five husbands.

They sacrificed . . . to the demons: Psalms 105(106):37–38.

14   *The betrothed from the nations*: That is, the (gentile) Church.

15   *Is he whom I see . . . from earth*: The woman's words resemble those of the Virgin in *On the Annunciation* 6.

18   *I am he, the one you see*: "I am" (ἐγώ εἰμι) functions as a Christological expression here, as in John 4:26, reflecting the divine self-identification in Exodus 3:14, "I am who I am" (ἐγώ εἰμι ὁ ὤν).

19   *a desolate pit*: The phrase echoes Psalms 39(40):2.

20   *the one who examines . . . and hearts*: See above, *On Joseph and Potiphar's Wife* 17 and *On the Harlot* 9.

21   *the heralds of the Savior*: His disciples, who according to John 4:8 have gone into town to buy food, now return.

   in the earthly household: God's οἰκονομία is God's salvational "household" for the created realm (as opposed to the divine realm), often rendered as the "divine dispensation." My version aims to be less technical.

22   *I will dwell and walk*: Romanos here takes up the Old Testament language quoted at 2 Corinthians 6:16 and combines it with the encouragement of Matthew 19:29, Mark 29–30, and Luke 18:29 to abandon family and possessions. The houses here are a metaphor for the believers, developing Paul's language of believers being temples in which God dwells. The manuscript is dam-

aged, however, and this stanza is barely legible. There is a lacuna at the beginning of line 5, so the reading "in . . . houses" is
a reconstruction, in line with previous verses.

On the Bleeding Woman

The first letters of each stanza of this song (MaTr, no. 12; GdM, no. 23)
form the acrostic: ψαλμὸς τοῦ Κυροῦ Ῥωμανοῦ, "a psalm by Master Romanos." The manuscript assigns it to Wednesday of the sixth week of Easter. Romanos's narrative reflects the three synoptic accounts of the episode, especially those of Mark 5:25–34 and Luke 8:43–48; the third is
Matthew 9:20–22. The hymn makes the ailing woman the protagonist,
foregrounding, through her bold argument with Christ's male disciples,
the blame they cast on her and her just "theft" of Christ's healing. For a
study, see Erin Galgay Walsh, "The Gendered Body in Verse: Jacob of
Serugh and Romanos Melodos on the Woman with a Flow of Blood," *Journal of the Bible and Its Reception* 9 (2022): 1–26.

Prel.   *Healer, heal me*: The terms Σῶτερ and σώζω are more habitually
        translated "Savior" and "save" in Christian texts. This hymn,
        however, embraces the whole spectrum of meanings for the
        verb ("save," "heal," "preserve," "rescue") and clearly empha-
        sizes the healing—which may be understood medically, spiritu-
        ally, or soteriologically. This is also in line with how the verb
        σώζω in this gospel pericope is translated in newer Bible ver-
        sions; see, for example, Matthew 9:22.

1   *to: Those who testify in the whole world*: The melody is based on
        the one for Romanos's *On All Martyrs*.

4   *learned of her healing*: The pronoun "her" here translates the
        Greek term κόρη, on which see above, *On the Women at the
        Tomb* 1.

5   *probably also said to herself*: An inner monologue starts here and
        runs to stanza 11. In it an imagined dispute between the woman
        and Jesus's male followers is played out. It is not entirely clear
        whether it gradually develops into a real dialogue or conflict
        with them remains in her imagination, but I have treated it
        here as a continuous interior drama.

10   *Come to me . . . I'll give you rest*: Matthew 11:28.

11   *Why have I let . . . He is not alone*: There are issues with the manuscript text and the meter here; some phrases are hard to make sense of.

12   *stealthily*: The expression ἐν κλοπῇ has a double meaning. The idiomatic meaning is "secretly," but the literal meaning, "in theft," plays with the theme of stealing.

14   *grabbed my robe like a request*: This is an attempt to convey the Greek wordplay contained in the phrase κρατοῦσα στολὴν ὥσπερ ἐπιστολήν. Here στολήν, "robe," is compared to an ἐπιστολήν, a written "message," "letter," or "order." If the latter is taken as being received *from* Jesus, then it perhaps has the sense of a "prescription," but if it relates to the speechless crying of the previous line and it is passing from the woman *to* Jesus, then it might be taken as the passing of a "note" as opposed to a verbal communication.

15   *Why do you tell me . . . surround me*: Luke 8:45.

On the Nativity of the Theotokos

The first letters of each stanza of this song (MaTr, no. 35) form the acrostic: ἡ ᾠδή Ῥωμανοῦ, "ode by Romanos." The hymn is notably not in manuscript P, where the whole month of September is missing due to a lacuna; nor is it edited in GdM, since that edition is incomplete, although Grosdidier de Matons planned to include it, as no. 57. The manuscript tradition assigns this kontakion to September 8, the feast of Mary's birth, and the prelude and the first stanza are currently part of the liturgical celebration of the feast in the Byzantine rite. If the song was indeed written by Romanos for this day, it is the earliest evidence of the feast's celebration in Constantinople. Grosdidier de Matons suggests, in his "Liturgie et hymnographie: Kontakion et canon," *Dumbarton Oaks Papers* 34/35 (1980): 31–43 (at 39), that the hymn was written by Romanos, not for a feast, but for the inauguration of a church dedicated to Saint Anna in the Deuteron quarter of Constantinople. If so, the prelude addressing the Virgin, "your people . . . are celebrating [your birth] too" (αὐτὴν ἑορτάζει καὶ ὁ λαός σου), would have to be a later addition. Although MaTr and GdM regarded this song as

a genuine work of Romanos's, both the relatively unrefined poetic style
(including the weak integration of the refrain) and the festal theme (there
is otherwise no evidence for the celebration of this feast in Romanos's lifetime) may point to a later poet. The narrative relies on *Protevangelium of
James* 1–8. "Theotokos" is a Byzantine Greek term for the Mother of God.

Prel. *The barren one bears . . . nurse of our life*: The refrain echoes the
       Prayer of Hannah, one of the Biblical odes. The once childless
       mother of Samuel is called "Hannah" in Hebrew, but in Greek
       her name is "Anna," the same as Mary's mother; see above, *On
       the Harlot* 8. In the Prayer, Anna's Old Testament namesake
       says of herself that "the barren has borne" (1 Kings [1 Samuel]
       2:5).

1   *was acceptable*: Since the couple was infertile, their offerings in
       the temple had not been acceptable, according to *Protevange-
       lium of James* 1; see stanza 3 below.

       in the garden: The Greek word παράδεισος may also be trans-
       lated as "paradise," but these lines refer to the story known
       from *Protevangelium of James* 1–2, where Joachim goes out into
       the desert (rather than to a mountain) to pray for a child, while
       Anna remains in the garden. Eventually her garden came to be
       imagined as a paradise, as in Theodore Hyrtakenos's *Descrip-
       tion of the Garden of Saint Anna.* See Mary-Lyon Dolezal and Ma-
       ria Mavroudi, "Theodore Hyrtakenos' Description of the Gar-
       den of St. Anna and the Ekphrasis of Gardens," in *Byzantine
       Garden Culture,* ed. Antony Littlewood, Henry Maguire, and
       Joachim Wolschke-Bulmahn (Washington, DC, 2002), 105–58.
       Here, Anna's "disgrace" is her childlessness.

4   *hosted a party . . . with splendor*: In *Protevangelium of James* 6, this
       party is for Mary's first birthday.

5   *nurtured in holy places*: According to *Protevangelium of James* 7–8,
       Mary spent her childhood years in the temple, fed by an angel;
       chaste daughters of the Hebrews attended with their lamps as
       she entered.

       holy among the holy: The phrase may allude to the temple (the
       Holy of Holies), but also to the liturgical phrase τὰ ἅγια τοῖς

ἁγίοις (the holy [gifts] for the holy ones), which the priest exclaims regarding the Eucharistic gifts in the Byzantine rite.

6 *Oh, mystical accomplishment on earth*: It is unclear whether this line is exclaimed by Anna or the narrator.

Anna whom Eli accused of drunkenness: See 1 Kings (1 Samuel) 1, especially 1:14; the stanza refers to Samuel's mother, Hannah/Anna, as does (indirectly) the refrain.

7 *It is great for me*: Anna's words echo the Magnificat (especially Luke 1:49), but also Mary's articulation of the same in Romanos's *On the Nativity (Mary and the Magi)* 6, and these two lines also echo that kontakion's refrain.

8 *barren Sarah . . . Isaac was born*: The stanza alludes to Genesis 16:1–2 and Genesis 18:9–14.

9 *revealed in a rod*: According to *Protevangelium of James* 8–9, Joseph was chosen to be engaged to Mary through a miraculous sign: a dove flew out of his rod and landed on his head.

10 *she whom each Christian has as protection*: The idea that Mary is the προστασία (protection) of Christians is otherwise not prevalent in Romanos, but very much so in the anonymous kontakion on the Virgin Ὡς ὑετὸς ἐν πόκῳ (As rain in fleece), ed. Trypanis, *Fourteen Cantica*, 159–64.

11 *guard the faithful rulers, with the shepherd*: Grosdidier de Matons, "Liturgie et hymnographie," 39, takes this to refer to the imperial couple and the patriarch of Constantinople, in which case the kontakion must have been composed before Empress Theodora died in 548. (Holy) Wisdom and (Holy) Peace were two of the most central churches in the capital. However, Wisdom (Σοφία) is also a biblical person who participated in the creation of the world (see, for instance, Proverbs 8:22–31), as did the Word (Λόγος). The references are probably meant to be vague and open to various interpretations.

On the Annunciation

The first letters of each stanza of this song (MaTr, no. 36; GdM, no. 9) form the acrostic: τοῦ ταπεινοῦ Ῥωμανοῦ, "of the lowly Romanos." The text lacks a concluding stanza (which often comes in the form of a prayer), so one or more stanzas may be missing. This is probably the earliest preserved hymn composed for the March 25 celebration of the Annunciation, a festival instigated during Romanos's lifetime. The Melodist makes the encounter between the Virgin and the angel in a male form ambiguously sexual. Mary transforms into a self-confident debater and, subsequently, a living mystery. The story reflects Luke 1:26–38 and Matthew 1:18–25, but poetic dialogues between Mary and Gabriel or Mary and Joseph were a particularly developed genre in Syriac poetry, on which see, for example, Sebastian P. Brock, *Mary and Joseph, and Other Dialogue Poems on Mary* (Piscataway, NJ, 2011). An earlier version of this translation was published in Thomas Arentzen, *The Virgin in Song: Mary and the Poetry of Romanos the Melodist* (Philadelphia, 2017), 181–87.

Prel.   *Hail, unwedded bride*: The refrain, which alludes to Gabriel's greeting in Luke 1:28, appears in the famous late antique hymn *Akathistos to the Mother of God.* This hymn is still in ecclesiastical use and is sometimes erroneously attributed to Romanos, but it is unclear when and by whom it was composed. If we assume that it predates Romanos, the Melodist echoes the famous hymn, both in the refrain and in the first stanza. In the *Akathistos,* however, the refrain operates within a different framework, allowing for a different set of connotations; see Thomas Arentzen, "The *Chora* of God: Approaching the Outskirts of Mariology in the *Akathistos,*" *Journal of Orthodox Christian Studies* 4, no. 2 (2021): 127–49. The refrain is notoriously difficult to translate. "Hail" is replaced by "Greetings" in most Bible translations, but the former is still in devotional use, despite its archaic ring. An alternative rendering of νύμφη ἀνύμφευτε might be "bride unbridled," which would capture less of the semantic contrast but more of the phonetic affinity. It would also convey the sense of the wild woman who is not tamed by a man in marriage, but it introduces the image of a bridle, which creates a field of equestrian connotations.

1   *the general to greet the empress*: Following the common Byzantine identification of archangels as ἀρχιστράτηγοι, "archgenerals,"

Gabriel is imagined here, and in the following stanza, as a military leader saluting the empress (Mary).

all peoples call blessed: Compare Luke 1:48. Although the Lucan text πᾶσαι αἱ γενεαί is usually translated "all generations," Romanos is employing political imagery, and "all peoples" seems more appropriate in the context.

2   *benevolence signal*: The Greek word σύνθημα is apparently used here by Romanos in its sense of a "coded military signal or order."

4   *These were the matters . . . like leaves*: The Greek word ὕλη means "stuff," "matter," "brushwood," or "wood." Romanos's line thus contains a wordplay where her confusing "brushwood of thoughts" is burned up like leaves.

5   *I am sealed*: Language of sealing is commonly used in Romanos and other early Christian hymnographers to describe (among other things) the "sealed" or untouched body of a virgin.

6   *with freedom to speak*: The Virgin speaks with παρρησία (boldness, frankness, or openness), an important concept in the Byzantine world for indicating access to those in authority. This is a recurring theme in Romanos, and this stanza, rich in verbs for speaking, represents the turning point where Mary goes from quiet to outspoken.

7   *I am not believed here either*: The background story for this and the next stanza is Gabriel's annunciation to the priest Zachariah and his barren wife Elizabeth, described in Luke 1:5–25.

8   *as he once threw . . . down to Hades*: See, for example, 2 Peter 2:4.

     give my questioner her answer: Gabriel's inner monologue ends here, and he now starts to address Mary openly.

9   *the prophet split apart with his rod . . . nothing going in*: The Virgin uses the story of Moses dividing the Red Sea with his staff in his hand (Exodus 14:16) as an image of sexual intercourse.

10   *He who was entrusted . . . offspring*: Ἀσπασμός means both "greeting" (as in the "hail!" of the refrain) and "embrace." The line plays with the double meaning and what it leads to, a child. Gabriel is not the father, although he is involved in the embrace.

truth is making you shine: While Mary's radiance connotes her new beauty, it may also allude to Moses's radiant face when he had encountered God (Exodus 34:29–35). Compare above, *On the Women at the Tomb* 14.

11 *straightened out all that was tangled*: Both the metrics and the logic are slightly flawed in this line. Perhaps σκολιά (twisted, tangled) is somehow a misreading for σκοτεινά (dark), and the sentence originally meant that, as a being of light, Gabriel corrected or illuminated darkness—but this remains a speculation, as the verb would also need to be changed.

explain: The imperative Greek verb form seems uncalled for here, since Gabriel has already spoken about these things and Mary's command implies that she already knows. The next stanza does not serve to explain these matters either. It is possible that she asks him to declare God's wishes, and that "when he had spoken in due measure" implies that he continues to speak. "You have explained" would have made more sense, but is not attested in the sole extant manuscript.

12 *When he had spoken in due measure*: This could also mean that the angel had spoken in metrical rhythm, as they both have in the song.

How did you not guard my virginity: Compare *Protevangelium of James* 13.

14 *Both great and humble . . . praise your beauty*: The first two lines of this stanza are a typical example of an ambiguity relatively common in Romanos, where it is unclear whether the speaker is still the character (here, Joseph) or the first-person narrator.

Until it was time . . . but not thereafter: This is a short mediation on Matthew 1:25: "And he did not know her [that is, he had no marital relations with her] until she had given birth to a son." Romanos plays with the openness of the word γιγνώσκω, "to know," but also "to know sexually," in order to suggest that Joseph was never intimate with Mary, as she was both a virgin and a mother.

15 *like Moses of old . . . undo my sandals*: The stanza alludes to Exodus 3:1–5, where Moses encounters a bush that is burning with di-

vine presence but not consumed. God orders him to remove his sandals, for "the place on which you are standing is holy ground."

16   *Come near . . . what you see*: Compare Exodus 3:14 and stanza 14, line 5 above.

     saying to me tenderly: The literal meaning of the word δροσινός is "dewy." It suggests moistness and freshness, so there is a play between fire and moisture here, and perhaps even more subtle innuendos.

17   *That greeting*: As above in stanza 10, ἀσπασμός might mean both the greeting of the refrain and the embrace with the angel.

18   *you know that already*: This may refer to 1 Kings (1 Samuel) 2:12, where the sons of Eli are described in a similar way when accused of exploiting those making sacrifices, and the same adjective combination of "sick and wicked" is used in 1 Kings (1 Samuel) 30:22.

     part from you quietly: Compare Matthew 1:19 where Joseph wishes to "dismiss her quietly." In the *Protevangelium of James,* the pregnant Mary hides from the "sons of Israel" (12) and Joseph also wants to hide her from them (14).

On the Virgin

The first letters of each stanza of this song (MaTr, no. 37; GdM, no. 12) form the acrostic: ὁ ὕμνος Ῥωμανοῦ, "hymn of Romanos." The manuscript tradition assigns this kontakion for the Afterfeast of the Nativity, December 26. MaTr calls it *On the Annunciation II,* presumably due to its content, which resembles that of *On the Annunciation.* It may have been written when the annunciation event was commemorated as part of the December celebrations, before the Annunciation was established as a separate Christian feast, on March 25, in the middle of the sixth century; GdM, vol. 2, pp. 113–19, especially pp. 113–14.

The song shares several features with the *Akathistos to the Mother of God* and the anonymous kontakion on the Virgin Ὡς ὑετὸς ἐν πόκῳ (As rain in fleece), ed. Trypanis, *Fourteen Cantica,* 159–64. The latter has a refrain similar to the present one. If these anonymous hymns predate Romanos, as many scholars assume, he must have known them, and they may all have been written for the same "Virginal festival" or "Commemoration of Mary," whether this feast was celebrated on December 26, as in the present-day Byzantine rite, or earlier in December. For an overview of scholarly approaches to the feast, see Mary B. Cunningham, *Wider Than Heaven: Eighth-Century Homilies on the Mother of God* (Yonkers, NY, 2008), 19–20; compare Paul F. Bradshaw and Maxwell E. Johnson, *The Origins of Feasts, Fasts, and Seasons in Early Christianity* (Collegeville, MN, 2011), 205–6. Romanos's prelude is still in liturgical use during Sunday Matins in the Byzantine rite. From stanza 7, the song reflects the narrative in Luke 1:26–38, whereas the earlier stanzas engage various Old Testament images.

There are some textual problems concerning the order of the stanzas and the narrative progress. It is tempting to propose that the first six stanzas have been misplaced at the beginning, and that the acrostic should be Ῥωμανοῦ ὁ ὕμνος. This would recover the usual order of events as known, for instance, from Romanos's *On the Annunciation* and from Matthew 1:18–21: first Gabriel visits, and then Joseph ponders the pregnancy. With this reordering, the song would conclude with "so all may say, 'A virgin gives birth. . . .'" Neither of the manuscripts supports such a rearrangement, however, and it would not explain why Joseph is never properly introduced.

Prel.   *called to mind*: The Greek phrase ἐλάμβανεν εἰς νοῦν might also be translated "absorbed into his mind." Romanos is deliberately juxtaposing the two processes of mental and physical absorption. In fact, the whole stanza is filled with an overwhelming language of being filled or taking up — so that Joseph's mind becomes impregnated and Mary is a burning rod. The hearer is not supposed to understand, but to be amazed by this paradoxical wonder.

          the rain upon fleece: According to Judges 6:37, Gideon placed a fleece on a threshing floor to catch dew, when testing God's purpose for Israel in the struggle with the Midianites. The words about the king in Psalms 71(72):6 conjure a similar image: Καταβήσεται ὡς ὑετὸς ἐπὶ πόκον, "He will descend like rain upon fleece." While Christians used this image Christologically very early, Proclus of Constantinople employs it explicitly for Mary in his *Homily 1 on the Holy Virgin* 1, included with the decrees from the Ephesus Council, as does the kontakion Ὡς ὑετὸς ἐν πόκῳ, mentioned above; see Nicholas Constas, *Proclus of Constantinople and the Cult of the Virgin in Late Antiquity: Homilies 1–5, Texts and Translations* (Leiden, 2003), 136–56.

a bush unburned in flames: Compare Exodus 3:2–3.

the budding rod of Aaron: The primary reference is to Aaron's rod, which budded in the tabernacle of witness in the episode recorded in Numbers 17:1–11, but these lines also allude to *Protevangelium of James* 9, where Joseph is chosen as the Virgin's betrothed through a similar rod election.

your betrothed . . . to the priests: See *Protevangelium of James* 16, where Joseph testifies to Mary's innocence before the high priest.

A virgin . . . a virgin still: The refrain conveys the idea, sanctioned by the Second Council of Constantinople in 553, that Mary is Ever-Virgin. But while the later doctrine came to name three aspects of her perpetual virginity (*ante partum, in partu,* and *post partum,* that is, before, during, and after the birth), Romanos eschews the middle one, generating a cloud of unknowability around her childbirth, typically imagining her virginity as the unopened gate through which only God passes. Compare *Protevangelium of James* 18–20 and Ezekiel 44:2.

1   *to: Joachim and Anna's prayer . . . groaning*: That is, Romanos's *On the Nativity of the Theotokos,* for which, see above. The metrical forms of the two kontakia's preludes also resemble each other.

What I observe, I cannot comprehend: It is possible to read stanzas 1–6 either as Joseph's speech or as the voice of the poetic "I." One might also interpret it as an instance of blurred overlapping, so that Joseph's words become the words of those who sing. I have not marked this speech with quotation marks, for it is not necessary to understand it as the monologue of a particular character.

2   *and becomes a trap for the cunning deceiver*: Manuscript D reads καὶ γίνεται τὸ πᾶν παγὶς τῷ Παντουργῷ ἡ τοῦ φύσει κρύπτουσα

βασίλεια, which may perhaps be rendered, "and she becomes altogether a net for the Maker of all, which by its nature conceals the king" (reading rather τὸν βασιλέαν in place of the final word) or "and she becomes altogether a net for the Maker of all, which conceals with his royal nature" (reading βασιλείᾳ).

3   *An ark . . . writes Moses*: Exodus 16:33–34; compare Hebrews 9:4. To read the Old Testament ark as a Mariological type was common in Romanos's day; see, for instance, section 10 of the anonymous kontakion on the Virgin Ὡς ὑετὸς ἐν πόκῳ. In line 4, Romanos also draws on word resemblances between the golden jar (ἡ στάμνος ἡ χρυσῆ) and the body of Christ (Χριστοῦ τὸ σῶμα) to highlight the interpretive link.

4   *Aaron's rod . . . watered*: See the note on "the budding rod of Aaron" in the prelude, above.

      as Amoz's son Isaiah wrote for me: Isaiah 1:1.

      a rod shall come from Jesse . . . a flower: Isaiah 11:1.

5   *without consuming its thorns*: Thorns do not refer only to the burning bush but also to human nature in Romanos's anthropology; see note to stanza 11, below.

7   *As Gabriel uttered a greeting of joy*: The abrupt change to the encounter between Gabriel and Mary here may indicate that stanzas are missing or in the wrong order, but it may also be an example of Romanos's creative narration.

8   *A woman once . . . from a virgin*: It is possible to translate these verbal forms with more focus on physical motion, but I wanted to highlight the Greek's entanglement of female and divine agency, where God "lifts up" (ἀνέλαβε) the one whom Eve "cast down" (κατέβαλε), and Mary "raises up" (ἀνιστᾷ) the one whom God planned to awaken. The phrase ἐκ παρθένου παρθένος, "a virgin from a virgin," is mostly used for Christ, but here it also refers to Eve, who was born in a "virgin birth" from Adam.

10   *another heaven*: The Greek term πόλος basically means "pole," including the celestial poles, and thus by extension can include the "sky" or "heaven." Romanos seems to imagine a heavenly vault; compare below, stanza 13.

11   *my thorny nature*: Here and elsewhere, Romanos uses the Greek

adjective ἀκανθώδης (thorny) to refer to the carnal or mortal nature of human beings. This also explains the obvious connection he sees with the Burning Bush; Mary's "thorny nature" is flammable but is not consumed. See also note to *On the Nativity (Mary and the Magi)* 11.

12   *as rain . . . upon the fleece*: Psalms 71(72):6; and see the note on "the rain upon fleece" in the prelude, above.

13   *So, Mary, praise the Christ . . . virgin still*: GdM interprets the last stanza as the singer's words and not as Gabriel's.

    dwells in the heavenly vault: Compare Psalms 17:12(18:11).

ON THE NATIVITY (MARY AND THE MAGI)

The first letters of each stanza of this song (MaTr, no. 1; GdM, no. 10) form the acrostic: τοῦ ταπεινοῦ Ῥωμανοῦ [ὁ] ὕμνος, "hymn by the lowly Romanos." The manuscript tradition assigns this kontakion to December 25. The prelude and the first stanza are still part of the liturgical celebration of the Christmas feast in the Byzantine rite. The adoration of the Magi, first told in Matthew 1:1–14, is here imagined as a dialogue between this (unnumbered) group and the Theotokos at the birth cave outside Bethlehem. As Romanos's most famous composition, the hymn is included in the legend about his inspiration: see the section on versifying around *ta Kyrou* in the Introduction.

Prel.   *Magi journey with a star*: In this kontakion, as in other early Christian writings, the star is not a static phenomenon in the sky but a dynamic light-being that runs ahead of the Magi, guiding them; for another example, see the *Arabic Infancy Gospel* 7.

    a little child, God before the ages: The refrain echoes the words of the Niceno-Constantinopolitan Creed: "begotten of the Father before all ages" (τὸν ἐκ τοῦ Πατρὸς γεννηθέντα πρὸ πάντων τῶν αἰώνων).

1   *We've found hidden delight*: The Garden of Eden is called the Garden of Delight (τοῦ Παραδείσου τῆς Τρυφῆς) in Genesis 3:23. The word τρυφή, "delight," thus functioned almost as a syn-

onym for Eden in early Christian writing; in Romanos's stanza it contributes to a parallelism between the two first verses.

there an undug well . . . David yearned to drink: See 2 Kings (2 Samuel) 23:15–16 and 1 Chronicles 11:17–18.

2   *I find my virginity still sealed*: See note to *On the Annunciation* 5, above.

3   *not even a fox hole*: Compare Matthew 8:20; Luke 9:58.

5   *Balaam . . . said that a star was going to rise*: Numbers 24:17.

    a star to extinguish all the . . . auguries: Compare Numbers 23:23.

    From Jacob shall rise: Numbers 24:17.

6   *You've done great things . . . my poverty, child*: There is an allusion here to the wording of the Magnificat, Luke 1:49.

    seeking your face . . . are begging: Compare Psalms 44:13(45:12).

7   *come under your roof*: Compare Matthew 8:8.

8   *Ministering to me . . . fulfilling its service*: The words used in these two lines allude to liturgical ministry.

9   *the unopened gate*: Ezekiel 44:2.

    she opened a door, giving birth to a door: Jesus says "I am the door" in John 10:7–9.

10   *without genealogy*: The rare term ἀγενεαλόγητος appears once in Hebrews 7:3, in reference to Melchizedek.

11   *to the anxious man*: As elsewhere, Romanos uses the Greek adjective ἀκανθώδης to refer to humans or earthly beings as "thorny" or "prickly." William Petersen, *The Diatessaron and Ephrem Syrus as Sources of Romanos the Melodist,* Corpus Scriptorum Christianorum Orientalium 475 (Louvain, 1985), 192–94, traces this usage to Ephrem's Syrian poetry, and it may also refer to the Burning Bush in Exodus 3:2–4. Here, however, it is clearly intended to describe Joseph's tormented mood: G. W. H. Lampe, *A Patristic Lexicon* (Oxford, 1961), under "ἀκανθώδης," thus gives the sense of "anxious" that is used here, likely following the same metaphorical line as being "antsy" or "on tenterhooks" in English.

12   *how those of fire . . . went before you*: Romanos emphasizes how the fiery celestial beings (angels and stars) mingled with the earthly beings of "clay."

13	*The God of gods is Lord*: Compare Deuteronomy 10:17.
14	*Vanity of vanities, all is vanity*: Ecclesiastes 1:2.
	your birth-giving: An alternative translation for the Greek phrase τῷ τόκῳ σου would be "offspring."
15	*this lamp*: That is, the lamp of the star.
	fulfilled the words of the prophecy: Zephaniah 1:12.
	its ark: That is, the Ark of the Covenant.
	The old things . . . renewed all things: Compare 2 Corinthians 5:17.
16	*that prophet-killing city*: See Luke 13:34.
18	*desert that you once crossed*: If stanza 19 is not included (see below), the Magi's reported reply to the Pharisees ends here; if it is included, since it continues to address the Magi in the second person, their speech must continue.
	fiery pillar: See Exodus 13:21.
19	*All the way the star . . . before the ages*: This entire stanza, which extends the Magi's speech, has weak support in the manuscript tradition and is probably a late addition; see GdM, vol. 2, pp. 44–45. The style is slightly different, and the content appears out of place.
20	*Habakkuk came . . . without being tired*: Daniel 14:34–36.
21	*balm of balms*: For the word μύρον, here "balm," see the note, above, to prelude 2 of *On the Harlot*.
	the thrice-holy hymn: That is, the "Trisagion" of the Byzantine rite. The hymn, based on the seraphim's "holy, holy, holy" in Isaiah 6:3, played an important role in the liturgical life as well as in doctrinal debates.
	Do not reject it . . . like Abel's offering: See Genesis 4:4–5.
22	*for the air . . . into harmony through me*: The Virgin's words resonate with the Litany of Peace in the Byzantine rite, which in its current form has the petition "For favorable weather, for an abundance of the fruits of the earth, and for peaceful times, let us pray to the Lord" (Ὑπὲρ εὐκρασίας ἀέρων, εὐφορίας τῶν καρπῶν τῆς γῆς καὶ καιρῶν εἰρηνικῶν τοῦ Κυρίου δεηθῶμεν). See also, for example, Nicholas Cabasilas, *Commentary on the Liturgy* 12.13. I have chosen to retain a more literal rendering

than "favorable weather," not least since εὐκρασίας (pleasant or favorable) is not included here.

On the Nativity (Mary with Adam and Eve)

The first letters of each stanza of this song (MaTr, no. 2; GdM, no. 11) form the acrostic: τοῦ ταπεινοῦ Ῥωμανοῦ, "by the lowly Romanos." Most of the manuscript tradition assigns this kontakion for the second day of Christmas (December 26), which at least later came to be a day for the celebration of the Mother of God in the Byzantine rite, while T, which included four stanzas, assigned it for the Sunday after the Nativity. The prelude and the first stanza are currently part of Matins on December 26.

This chthonic song, where the Theotokos in the birth cave at Bethlehem engages in a subterranean conversation with Eve and her husband, who are kept in Hades, does not base its plot on a particular biblical story, but resonates with several scriptural and nonscriptural motifs, including Genesis 3 and, perhaps, the eleventh book of the Odyssey, where the hero meets his mother in Hades.

Prel.   *Born before the Morning Star*: See Psalms 109(110):3.

most favored one: The refrain stems from Gabriel's greeting to Mary in Luke 1:28, "(highly) favored one" or "full of grace." Romanos returns a few times in this song to the word χάρις, from which the term here, ἡ κεχαριτωμένη, is derived; it can mean "grace," "favor," and even "attractiveness." While all these meanings clearly lurk in the background here, I have chosen "favor," since the focus, both in the refrain and elsewhere, is that by choosing her, God has set Mary apart, made her unique, and empowered her.

1   *The Vine . . . cluster of grapes*: The (feminine) vine here is Mary, and Jesus is the (masculine) cluster of grapes.

delivers from corruption: Romanos shares the idea, widespread in Late Antiquity, that there is a link between the "corruption" (φθορά) of virginity and the postlapsarian corruption of the flesh experienced as aging and ultimately death.

3   *Eve . . . birth to children*: Genesis 3:16.

the son of Amoz ... rod of Jesse: The prophet Isaiah was the son of Amoz (Isaiah 1:1); he mentions a rod or shoot emerging from Jesse and a branch growing from it (Isaiah 11:1).

4 *You heard the swallow ... at dawn*: The idea that spring is announced by a swallow at dawn can be found already in Hesiod's *Works and Days* 568–69 (compare also Sappho, fragment 135), and, in Homer's *Odyssey*, Odysseus's bow sings with the voice of a swallow (21.410–11) before Athena appears in the guise of a swallow (22.239–40). The word ὄρθρος, "dawn," here, is also the Greek word for morning service in church, corresponding to Matins in the Latin rite.

quivered with joy: The Greek verb σκιρτάω is translated as "leap" in Luke 1:41, when the fetus of John the Baptist moves in Elizabeth's womb at the pregnant Mary's arrival. By using the word here, it is possible that Romanos wants to allude to this episode, but in modern Greek the word has come to connote smaller movements and contractions, and this seems more apt for a snake, wriggling with excitement rather than leaping.

5 *words his spouse had woven*: From the first line, with the weaving wife, this stanza alludes to Odysseus, specifically to his encounter with the Sirens, who (like the swallow Mary) may be birds or women, and to the clogging of his ears. With delight (τερπόμενος) Odysseus can eventually hear the Sirens' voice (Homer, *Odyssey* 12.52). Romanos uses the same word "φθόγγος" for voice here, as does Homer for the Sirens' voice (12.41, 12.159, and 12.198). The *Odyssey* 12.40 also uses the same word "enchant" (θέλγω) for the Sirens as Romanos does for the effect of the female voice; the Sirens will enchant with their clear song (λιγυρῇ θέλγουσιν ἀοιδῇ, 12.44), and their clear song (λιγυρὴν ... ἀοιδήν) is mentioned again in 12.183.

clear tone: In Byzantine church music (also in kontakia), the word ἦχος (here, "tone") denotes musical mode.

6 *and touch ... her immaculate feet*: Manuscript A (which GdM follows here) has καὶ αὐτῆς πρὸ τῶν ποδῶν ἐρριμένους θεωροῦσα, "and when she sees us fall down before her feet."

7 *the Tree of Life ... from touching*: Genesis 3:24.

the life-giving breath: This might also be translated "the breath of her who gives life," but the same phrase is used for the breath of God in Genesis 2:7, to which this and the following line allude.

9   *my heart is melting . . . Adam's weeping*: There may be an echo here of Euripides, *Children of Heracles* 642–45, where Iolaus addresses the old Alcmene as "the mother of a noble son," who has long been in anguish or travail, "wasting inwardly" or "pining away in the soul" (ψυχὴν ἐτήκου).

recalls the delight: See the note on *On the Nativity (Mary and the Magi)* 1, above.

I wish you had never . . . into these depths: See Genesis 2:18–21.

11 *Although he is fire . . . my humble self*: Mary compares herself to the Burning Bush of Exodus 3:2. For the word ἀκανθώδης, used of earthly beings in Romanos, see the note to *On the Nativity (Mary and the Magi)* 11.

as David prophesied: Psalms 102(103):13.

be your intercessor: The Greek term μεσῖτις is usually translated as "mediator," but in this case Mary is expected to be a spokesperson for the couple's cause, which makes her more of an interceder.

13 *and agreed*: The Greek word ὑπέγραφεν actually means "signed" or "underwrote." The same idea appears in stanza 15.

14 *I'm perfect . . . develop like a baby*: The Greek phrase ὁ ἐκ τελείου τέλειος is impossible to render directly into English, but it is used to capture the idea that Christ is fully grown or complete ("perfect") as God. Paradoxically, he nevertheless grows and develops as a human child. This paradox is at the heart of Byzantine orthodox Christology. There is also an elaborate use of the Greek verb τελέω in this entire song. This word has a large range of potential meaning, including "completion, accomplishment, fulfillment, bringing to an end, perfection, and consecration." It is used in this hymn for those things that Christ must accomplish or carry out. I have not translated it consistently, as the intricate play with fulfillment and completeness is difficult to render in a meaningful way in translation.

those who long ago wore coats of skin: See Genesis 3:21.

If you learned . . . all the elements: Following manuscript P, MaTr has, for lines 9–10: Ἂν δὲ καὶ σταυροῦσθαί με μάθῃς, σεμνή, νεκροῦσθαι δὲ δι' αὐτούς, μετὰ πάντων τῶν στοιχείων δονηθήσῃ καὶ θρηνήσεις, "If you learn, noble one, that I must be crucified and killed for them, you will be shaken and lament along with all the elements."

15   *I'll speak freely . . . as your mother*: Here, as elsewhere (especially in *On the Way to Golgotha*), Romanos emphasizes Mary's unique παρρησία, her "freedom to speak openly" to God. On the term, see above, the note to *On the Annunciation 6*.

16   *you will see in a little while*: The text here (μικρόν, "in a little while") echoes John 16:16–24, whose language of pain and grief (λύπη) turning to joy (χαρά) after parturition permeates this whole song; compare also *On the Way to Golgotha 13*.

the one you called life: Jesus says in John 16:4, "I am the way, and the truth, and the life," but Romanos seems to associate the very name of Jesus more directly with the meaning "life"; compare *On the Harlot 7.3–4*: "the man who sent them was a figure of life; he bore the honorable name of my Jesus." Although the name Jesus is generally taken to mean "God saves," a close connection between "saving" and "life-giving" in Syriac thought may perhaps explain Romanos's interpretation; see further A. Klijn, "The Term 'Life' in Syriac Theology," *Scottish Journal of Theology* 5, no. 4 (1952): 390–97.

ON THE WEDDING AT CANA

The first letters of each stanza of this song (MaTr, no. 7; GdM, no. 18) form the acrostic: τὸ ἔπος Ῥωμανοῦ ταπεινοῦ, "poem by Romanos the lowly." Manuscript P assigns this kontakion to Wednesday of the second week of Easter, arranged as part of a Paschal series of hymns about Christ's miracles. The underlying gospel story is found in John 2:1–11, but Romanos's rendering is quite free and independent, emphasizing the privileged role of the Theotokos.

Prel.   *the one who has made all in wisdom*: The refrain is an echo of Psalms 103(104):24.

1   *to: On the blinded Adam*: That is, Romanos's second hymn on the Epiphany.

3   *the great Paul wrote . . . bed is undefiled*: Hebrews 13:4. The epistle was traditionally attributed to Paul.

4   *nature of water . . . a ten-plague wrath*: See Exodus 7–12.

       offered the Hebrews . . . like dry land: See Exodus 14:21–31.

       waterless place . . . from the rock: See Exodus 17:1–7.

6   *hadn't worked wonders before . . . wrote*: At John 2:11 the evangelist calls the miracle in Cana Christ's first sign, but here (in stanza 7) Romanos has Mary point out that as Jesus's mother she experienced signs before John came to know Christ. This idea that Mary had access to secret knowledge also appears in some later Marian homilies; see Mary B. Cunningham, *The Virgin Mary in Byzantium, c. 400–1000 CE: Hymns, Homilies and Hagiography* (Cambridge, 2021), 121. An alternative translation for the adjective θεσπέσιος (normally, as here, "Divine," when used as an epithet of John) could be "sublime"; it is used in that way for voices (starting with the Sirens in Homer's *Odyssey* 12.158), signifying something extraordinary, beautiful, divine, or mysterious.

9   *After I'd conceived . . . Anna lauded me*: Mary recounts events described in Luke 1–2.

       Magi from Persia . . . the birth: Matthew 2:1–12.

       With angels . . . their rejoicing: Luke 2:13–15.

11   *hold the hours in check . . . with their intervals*: The word μέτρον means "measures," and the expression seems to presuppose the idea that God measures and organizes the hours, as suggested in the next lines. But μέτρον may also mean "(poetic) meter," and thus God, like a composer of songs, measures out the hours like words. The compositional metaphor is picked up in the next lines with the "intervals" (διαστήματα), which may also be a musical term. On top of this, μέτροις χαλινῶν may possibly mean "bridling (a horse) with bits."

14   *embraced the form of a poor slave*: Compare Philippians 2:7.

18   *As scripture teaches . . . stored in the house*: See John 2:6.

21   *mix your most holy wine with water*: Mixing hot water (called *zeon*) into the wine in the Eucharistic chalice is actually a feature of

the Byzantine liturgical rite, but how old this practice is remains unknown. It eventually became a point of contention
between the Byzantines and the Armenians, who did not pour
any water into their chalice. Since Romanos is not Armenian,
and since it is unlikely that he is attacking his own Church, it is
possible that this comment reflects a historical pre-*zeon* phase,
and that his polemics are directed toward other liturgical traditions—or that the comment should be read as purely metaphorical.

   the fire of Gehenna: The "Gehenna of fire" or "fire of Gehenna" is
a recurring image in the New Testament, where it connotes the
destruction of evil; see, for example, Matthew 5:22 and Mark
9:43. While many later Christian traditions came to merge no-
tions of Gehenna and Hades (the realm of the dead) into a
penal afterlife in hell, this process is not yet completed in Romanos, and thus I have also preserved the distinction in the
translation.

On the Way to Golgotha

The first letters of each stanza of this song (MaTr, no. 19; GdM, no. 35)
form the acrostic: τοῦ ταπ[ε]ινοῦ Ῥωμανοῦ, "by the lowly Romanos." The
composition has often been called *On Mary at the Cross* in modern publications—aligning it indirectly (and anachronistically) with the *Stabat Ma-
ter* and John 19:25—or *On the Lament of the Mother of God,* based on the
manuscript rubrics. But the scene takes place before the crucifixion, and
Christ's message is that his mother should refrain from lamenting. It is a
song for Good Friday. The prelude and the first stanza are still part of the
liturgical commemoration on that day in the Byzantine rite. The hymn is
often counted among Romanos's masterpieces, and it remains one of the
earliest attested meditations on Mary's grief *en route* to the crucifixion.
The poet does not rely on a gospel account, but the drama seems to
emerge from the story about the wailing women who followed him toward
the cross (Luke 23:26–30). Romanos foregrounds the Theotokos and pro-
jects the lamenting "other women" into the background as a quiet choir.

Prel.   *my son and my God*: The refrain echoes the apostle Thomas's words to the risen Christ: "my Lord and my God!" (ὁ Κύριός μου καὶ ὁ Θεός μου) in John 20:28.

1   *lamb being dragged to the slaughter*: The language of the lamb dragged away to the slaughter, and of silence below, is reminiscent of Isaiah 53:7.

    wedding in Cana . . . into wine: See John 2:1–11. Mary's words in this stanza appear almost verbatim in the *Christos Paschon* 454–60, making Romanos a direct source for the drama; see Gerhard Swart, "The *Christus patiens* and Romanos the Melodist: Some Considerations on Dependence and Dating," *Acta Classica* 33 (1990): 53–64.

2   *Filled with palms . . . people's rich praises*: For the triumphal entry into Jerusalem, see Matthew 21:8–11.

3   *I will never deny you . . . must die*: See Matthew 26:35.

    Thomas has left . . . all die with him: See John 11:16.

    your kinsmen and friends . . . who will judge: GdM follows the manuscripts that read οἱ οἰκεῖοι καὶ υἱοὶ οἱ μέλλοντες κρίνειν, "your kinsmen and sons, those who will judge."

    but one for all of them you die: Echoing 2 Corinthians 5:14, "we judge that one has died for all; therefore all have died." Romanos creates a striking critique of Christ's twelve disciples, who will judge the twelve tribes of Israel (Luke 22:30; Matthew 19:27–28). Those who have followed him (Matthew 19:28) are not there, but only Mary, and, by implication, those who follow her.

    you've pleased them all: See 1 Corinthians 10:33.

4   *the other women*: See Luke 23:27.

5   *like the foolish ones*: The Greek refers only to "the foolish (female) ones" (ταῖς ἀσυνέτοις). This might apply to the other women who follow Christ, but "bridal chamber" (νυμφῶνος) in the next line suggests that it also alludes to the foolish virgins, who, in contrast to the wise ones, are excluded from the wedding party in Matthew 25:1–3. See, above, Romanos's *On the Ten Virgins*.

6   *came down from heaven . . . Mount Sinai*: See Exodus 16, where manna is described as food that God provides from heaven for

his people as they are journeying from Elim to Sinai. It is said to taste like wafers made with honey; Exodus 16:31.

the curdled mountain: Romanos assumes an idea about conception and the forming of the fetus that appears in Galen and goes back to Aristotle (see *Generation of Animals* 1.20): the male "rennet" (semen) makes the female liquid curdle into solid flesh. The poet cleverly discovers this gynecological insight in the language of Psalms 67:16(68:15): ὄρος τοῦ θεοῦ ὄρος πῖον ὄρος τετυρωμένον ὄρος πῖον, "O mountain of God, fertile mountain, O curdled mountain, fertile mountain." See Ephrem Lash, "Mary in Eastern Church Literature," in *Mary in Doctrine and Devotion: Papers of the Liverpool Congress, 1989, of the Ecumenical Society of the Blessed Virgin Mary,* ed. Alberic Stacpoole, (Dublin, 1990), 58–80 (especially 70–71); Thomas Arentzen, "Struggling with Romanos's 'Dagger of Taste,'" in *Knowing Bodies, Passionate Souls: Sense Perceptions in Byzantium,* ed. Susan Ashbrook Harvey and Margaret Mullett (Washington, DC, 2017), 169–82 (especially 178–79).

6*   *With the following ... my God*: Since this stanza is included in only four manuscripts, previous editors have judged it spurious. That would make the acrostic's ταπεινοῦ (lowly) lack an ε, but since ει and ι would have been pronounced the same way, it is not impossible for Romanos to have spelled it "ταπινοῦ"; see GdM, vol. 4, pp. 151–55. It is not unlikely that the stanza is a later addition, but the content does not seem entirely out of place, and I have thus retained it.

7   *You cleansed a leper ... only a wish*: See Matthew 8:2–4; Mark 1:40–43; Luke 5:12–14.

    you gave strength to a paralytic: See Matthew 9:2–7; Mark 2:2–12; Luke 5:18–26.

8   *he'll stand up at once and carry his bed*: See Matthew 9:6–7.

    as you did Lazarus: See John 11:43–44.

10   *the depths of Hades*: The same expression for "depths" is used in the Apostles' Creed: Christ descended into the "lowest parts" (κατελθόντα εἰς τὰ κατώτατα). Compare Ephesians 4:9.

12   *the first to see me*: Romanos is here transmitting an ancient tradi-

tion about the resurrection that confuses Mary the Mother of God with Mary Magdalene, so that the Theotokos meets the risen one. See further, Lash, "Mary in Eastern Church Literature," 66–67; GdM, vol. 4, p. 177n2; and more broadly, Robert Murray, *Symbols of Church and Kingdom: A Study in Early Syriac Tradition* (London, 2006), 329–35. Romanos's hymn *On the Women at the Tomb*, however, suggests that Mary Magdalene is the first one to greet the risen Christ.

with how much toil: The editions have πόσων πόνων, "from how many toils/afflictions"; I follow the minority of manuscripts that read πόσοις πόνοις "with how much toil" or "with how many toils," for although Adam's toil is mentioned in stanza 10, what Christ is about to show Mary and his friends with his pierced hands is his own suffering.

displaying the proof in my hands: See John 20:20.

13   *Be patient a little longer*: The language of Mary waiting "a little while" or "a little longer" echoes *On the Nativity (Mary with Adam and Eve)* 16.

like a doctor, undress: Byzantine doctors would undress before they performed surgery; see further, GdM, vol. 4, pp. 178–79n1.

treat their wounds . . . the robe: Throughout these lines there are allusions to elements of the crucifixion. The lance evokes the lance that pierced Jesus's side (John 19:34); the vinegar, used commonly to cleanse wounds in ancient medicine, alludes to the vinegar Christ was given at the cross (Matthew 27:48); the nails refer to those which nailed him to the cross; and the robe (χλαῖνα) makes reference to the scarlet robe that was put on Christ before his crucifixion, at Matthew 27:28.

examining the incision with the probe of the nails: For this line, the manuscripts offer various readings, none of them entirely satisfactory, and editors' and translators' interpretations thus vary. The relatively rare medical term μήλη (probe) has the variant σμίλη (lancet), τόμην (incision or dissection) has the variant νομήν (ulcer or abscess), and the participle ἐρευνήσας (examining) has the variant ἀνευρύνας (dilating). An alternative translation might thus be "opening the abscess with the lancet of the nails." For further discussion, see GdM, vol. 4, p. 179n2.

medicine chest: The Greek term νάρθηξ may also mean "a splint" (for a broken limb); while it would match the shape of the cross better, it makes less sense in the context, since Christ is hardly healing a fracture.

15 *You are going to see life on a tree*: This seems to be intended as a quote, but the words are not in the Bible, and it is unclear what Romanos is citing. GdM suggests that it refers to Numbers 21:8, "And the Lord said to Moses, 'Make a poisonous serpent, and set it on a pole; and everyone who is bitten shall look at it and live.'" Although this passage has been read typologically, the connection to Romanos's argument is not obvious.

16 *elements shake . . . graves emptying*: The stanza reflects a rich register of biblical, apocalyptic language. The lines echo not least Matthew 27:45–54.

temple will rend its garment: While this is a reference to the tearing of the temple curtain (Matthew 27:51), it may also be read as an ironic mimicking of the high priest who tore his clothes in response to what he saw as Jesus's blasphemy (Matthew 26:65).

cry out . . . my son and my God: In Matthew, Christ cried on the cross, "My God, my God, why hast thou forsaken me?" while here Mary is crying, "Spare me, my son and my God!"

Bibliography

EDITIONS AND TRANSLATIONS

Aerts, Willem J., Hero Hokwerda, and Henk Schoonhoven, eds. *Vier Byzantijnse hymnen en de Akáthistoshymne.* Groningen, 1990.

Alexiou, Margaret, trans. *After Antiquity: Greek Language, Myth, and Metaphor.* Ithaca, NY, 2001, 417–29.

Barkhuizen, J. H., trans. "Romanos the Melodist: 'On Adam and Eve and the Nativity': Introduction with Annotated Translation." *Acta Patristica et Byzantina* 19 (2008): 1–22.

——. *Romanos the Melodist: Poet and Preacher.* Somerset West, 2012.

Cammelli, Giuseppe, ed. *Inni.* Florence, 1930.

Carpenter, Marjorie, trans. *Kontakia of Romanos, Byzantine Melodist.* 2 vols. Colombia, MO, 1970–1973.

Grosdidier de Matons, José, ed. *Hymnes.* 5 vols. Sources Chrétiennes 99, 110, 114, 128, 283. Paris, 1964–1981.

Krumbacher, Karl. *Die Akrostichis in der griechischen Kirchenpoesie.* Munich, 1904.

——. *Umarbeitungen bei Romanos: Mit einem Anhang über das Zeitalter des Romanos.* Munich, 1899.

Lash, Ephrem, trans. "On Adam and Eve." Internet Archive Wayback Machine, version from August 12, 2007, https://web.archive.org/web/2007 0812183832/http://www.anastasis.org.uk/kontakion_51.htm.

——. *On the Life of Christ: Kontakia.* San Francisco, 1995.

Maas, Paul, and Constantine A. Trypanis, eds. *Sancti Romani Melodi cantica.* Vol. 1, *Cantica genuina.* Oxford, 1963.

Maisano, Riccardo, ed. *Cantici di Romano il Melodo.* 2 vols. Turin, 2002.

Mellas, Andrew, trans. *Hymns of Repentance: Saint Romanos the Melodist*. Yonkers, NY, 2020.

Mioni, Elpidio, ed. "Romano il Melode: Due inni sul S. Natale." *Bollettino della Badia Greca di Grottaferrata*, n.s., 12 (1958): 5–12.

———. *Romano il Melode: Saggio critico e dieci inni inediti*. Turin, 1937.

Moskhos, Mikhalis, trans. "Romanos' Hymn on the Sacrifice of Abraham: A Discussion of the Sources and a Translation." *Byzantion* 44, no. 2 (1974): 310–28.

Papagiannis, Grigorios, ed. "Romanos the Melodist, Kontakion 'On the Samaritan Woman': New Critical Edition with Commentary." *Byzantina* 33 (2013/14): 11–59.

Peden, James, trans. "Romanos's *kontakion on Elijah*." In *Metaphrastes, or, Gained in Translation: Essays and Translations in Honour of Robert H. Jordan*, edited by M. Mullett, 143–56. Belfast, 2004.

Pitra, Jean B., ed. *Analecta sacra spicilegio solesmensi parata*. Vol. 1. Paris, 1876.

Schork, R. J., trans. *Sacred Song from the Byzantine Pulpit: Romanos the Melodist*. Gainesville, FL, 1995.

Tomadakis, Nicholaos V., ed. Ῥωμανοῦ τοῦ Μελῳδοῦ ὕμνοι ἐκδιδόμενοι ἐκ πατμιακῶν κωδίκων. 4 vols. Athens, 1952–1961.

Trempelas, Panagiotis N., ed. Ἐκλογή Ἑλληνικῆς ὀρθοδόξου ὑμνογραφίας. Athens, 1939.

FURTHER READING

Arentzen, Thomas. *The Virgin in Song: Mary and the Poetry of Romanos the Melodist*. Philadelphia, 2017.

Brock, Sebastian. *From Ephrem to Romanos: Interactions between Syriac and Greek in Late Antiquity*. Aldershot, 1999.

Frank, Georgia. "Romanos and the Night Vigil in the Sixth Century." In *Byzantine Christianity*, edited by Derek Krueger, 59–78. Minneapolis, 2006.

Gador-Whyte, Sarah. *Theology and Poetry in Early Byzantium: The Kontakia of Romanos the Melodist*. Cambridge, 2017.

Grosdidier de Matons, José. *Romanos le Mélode et les origines de la poésie religieuse à Byzance*. Paris, 1977.

Harvey, Susan Ashbrook. *Song and Memory: Biblical Women in Syriac Tradition.* Milwaukee, 2010.

Hunger, Herbert. "Romanos Melodos, Dichter, Prediger, Rhetor—und sein Publikum." *Jahrbuch der Österreichischen Byzantinistik* 34 (1984): 15–42.

Kallish, Kevin J. *She Who Loved Much: The Sinful Woman in Saint Ephrem the Syrian and the Orthodox Tradition.* Jordanville, NY, 2022.

Koder, Johannes. "Imperial Propaganda in the Kontakia of Romanos the Melode." *Dumbarton Oaks Papers* 62 (2008): 275–91.

Krueger, Derek. *Liturgical Subjects: Christian Ritual, Biblical Narrative, and the Formation of the Self in Byzantium.* Philadelphia, 2014.

———. *Writing and Holiness: The Practice of Authorship in the Early Christian East.* Philadelphia, 2004.

Lingas, Alexander. "The Liturgical Place of the Kontakion in Constantinople." In *Liturgy, Architecture and Art of the Byzantine World: Papers of the XVIII International Byzantine Congress (Moscow, 8–15 August 1991) and Other Essays Dedicated to the Memory of Fr. John Meyendorff,* edited by C. C. Akentiev, 50–57. Saint Petersburg, 1995.

Walsh, Erin Galgay. "Sanctifying Boldness: New Testament Women in Narsai, Jacob of Serugh, and Romanos Melodos." PhD diss., Duke University, 2019.

Index

Aaron, *Virgin* Prel., 4

Abel, *Nat. Mary Magi* 21

Abraham, *Abr. Sacrifice* Prel.–24

Adam, *Fasting* 4–9, 16–21; *Bless. Jacob* 1; *Joseph* 8; *Forerunner* 18; *Wom. Tomb* 1; *Bleeding Woman* 12; *Nat. Theot.* Prel.; *Virgin* 2, 8; *Nat. Mary Magi* 1; *Nat. Mary Adam Eve* 3–10, 12, 18; *Golgotha* 4, 7–12, 14

Ahab, *Elijah* 28–29; *Forerunner* 5

Amoz (father of Isaiah), *Virgin* 4; *Nat. Mary Adam Eve* 3

Andrew (disciple), *Wedd. Cana* 17

Anna (mother of Mary), *Nat. Theot.* Prel., 1–4, 6–9

Anna (mother of Samuel), *Harlot* 8; *Nat. Theot.* 6

Anna (New Testament prophetess), *Wedd. Cana* 9

Babylon, *Nat. Mary Magi* 13

Balaam, *Nat. Mary Magi* 5

Bethlehem, *Nat. Mary Magi* 1

Bible, *Bless. Jacob* 6; *Elijah* 4; *Wom. Tomb* 22; *Samaritan* 3–4. *See also* scripture

Cain, *Nat. Mary Magi* 21

Cana, *Wedd. Cana* 4, 7; *Golgotha* 1

Canaanite woman (gospel figure), *Harlot* 3

Chaldea, *Nat. Mary Magi* 18

Chaldeans, *Nat. Mary Magi* 13

Cherubim, *Nat. Mary Magi* 7; *Wedd. Cana* 2

Christ, *Fasting* Prel., 1, 3; *Bless. Jacob* Prel.; *Joseph* 1, 22; *Elijah* 33; *Forerunner* 18; *Ten Virgins* Prel. 1–Prel. 4, 2, 7, 13–14, 16–17, 27–29; *Harlot* Prel. 1–Prel. 2, 1–4; *Wom. Tomb* Prel. 1–Prel. 2, 4, 13, 17, 22; *Samaritan* 3–4, 17; *Bleeding Woman* 11–12; *Virgin* 3, 5, 13; *Nat. Mary Magi* 8–10, 21; *Nat. Mary Adam Eve* 6, 10; *Wedd. Cana* Prel., 3, 5, 7, 9, 18, 20. *See also* Jesus; Messiah

Christians, *Fasting* 20; *Bless. Jacob* 19; *Nat. Theot.* 10

533

Daniel, *Nat. Mary Magi* 20

David, *Harlot* 11; *Samaritan* 13; *Virgin* 12; *Nat. Mary Magi* 1; *Nat. Mary Adam Eve* 11; *Golgotha* 6

Devil, *Fasting* 9–15; *Joseph* 6, 18

Eden, *Bleeding Woman* 12; *Nat. Mary Magi* 1. *See also* Paradise

Egypt, *Joseph* Prel. 3, 12–13; *Nat. Mary Magi* 18, 24

Egyptian(s), *Joseph* 5–6, 19, 22; *Wedd. Cana* 4

Eli, *Harlot* 8; *Nat. Theot.* 6

Elijah, *Fasting* 2; *Elijah throughout*; *Forerunner* 5. *See also* Tishbite

Elisha, *Elijah* 33

Elizabeth (aunt of Mary), *Wedd. Cana* 9

Emmanuel (biblical title), *Harlot* 8

Esau, *Bless. Jacob* Prel., 2–4, 6, 8–9, 13–19

Eve, *Fasting* 9–19; *Joseph* 8; *Nat. Theot.* Prel.; *Virgin* 8; *Nat. Mary Adam Eve* 3–4, 9–10, 12, 18; *Golgotha* 9–12

Forerunner. *See* John the Baptist

Gabriel (archangel), *Annunciation* 1–12, 16; *Virgin* 7, 9–10, 12–13; *Wedd. Cana* 8

Gehenna, *Wedd. Cana* 21

Genesis, *Bless. Jacob* 1

Gospel, *Ten Virgins* 1; *Harlot* 4; *Samaritan* 3; *Annunciation* 14; *Wedd. Cana* 8

Habakkuk (biblical prophet), *Nat. Mary Magi* 20

Hades, *Forerunner* Prel. 2; *Wom. Tomb* Prel. 1, 20; *Annunciation* 8; *Nat. Mary Magi* 8; *Golgotha* 4

Hannah (mother of Samuel). *See* Anna

Hebrews, *Fasting* 22; *Samaritan* 9; *Wedd. Cana* 4. *See also* Israelites; Jew(s)

Herod (Antipas, biblical king), *Forerunner* 1–5, 8–17; *Nat. Mary Magi* 16–17

Herodias (wife of Herod Antipas), *Forerunner* Prel. 2, 2–10, 13–14, 16

Holy Spirit, *Nat. Theot.* 9; *Virgin* 6–7; *Wedd. Cana* 15; *Golgotha* 14

Isaac, *Abr. Sacrifice* Prel.–19, 21–24; *Bless. Jacob* 2–18; *Nat. Theot.* 8

Isaiah, *Virgin* 4; *Nat. Mary Adam Eve* 3

Israel, *Nat. Theot.* 4; *Golgotha* 15

Israelites, *Wedd. Cana* 15. *See also* Hebrews; Jew(s)

Jacob, *Bless. Jacob* Prel., 2–7, 9–11, 15, 18–19; *Joseph* Prel. 4; *Samaritan* 8, 10; *Nat. Mary Magi* 5

Jairus (gospel figure), *Wom. Tomb* 8

Jerusalem, *Nat. Mary Magi* 15–16

Jesse, *Virgin* 4; *Nat. Mary Adam Eve* 3

Jesus, *Harlot* 4, 7, 13, 18; *Wom. Tomb* 7; *Samaritan* 8; *Bleeding Woman*

16; *Virgin* 6; *Nat. Mary Magi* 8;
Nat. Mary Adam Eve 6; *Wedd.
Cana* 9. *See also* Christ; Messiah
Jew(s), *Bless. Jacob* 19; *Elijah* 14;
Samaritan 6–7. *See also* Hebrews;
Israelites
Jezebel, *Forerunner* 5
Joachim (father of Mary), *Nat.
Theot.* Prel., 1–4
Job, *Forerunner* 11
John (disciple, evangelist), *Wom.
Tomb* 4–6; *Wedd. Cana* 6–7, 17. *See
also* Theologian
John the Baptist, *Forerunner* Prel.
1–Prel. 2, 1–8, 11–12, 16–18; *Wom.
Tomb* 7
Jonah (father of Peter), *Bleeding
Woman* 15
Joseph (betrothed of Mary), *Nat.
Theot.* 9; *Annunciation* 2, 12–18;
Virgin Prel., 8, 10; *Nat. Mary
Magi* 10–12
Joseph (biblical patriarch), *Joseph*
Prel. 1, Prel. 3–Prel. 4, 2–22

Kephas (disciple), *Wom. Tomb* 4. *See
also* Peter

Lazarus (friend of Jesus), *Wom.
Tomb* 8; *Golgotha* 8
Levites, *Nat. Theot.* 4

Magi, *Wom. Tomb* 1; *Nat. Mary Magi*
Prel., 4–22, 24; *Nat. Mary Adam
Eve* Prel.; *Wedd. Cana* 9
Mary (Mother of Jesus), *Bless. Jacob*

Prel., 2; *Samaritan* 7; *Nat. Theot.*
throughout; *Annunciation* through-
out; *Virgin* throughout; *Nat. Mary
Magi* throughout; *Nat. Mary Adam
Eve* throughout; *Golgotha* through-
out. *See also* Mother of God; The-
otokos; Virgin
Mary Magdalene, *Wom. Tomb* 2–3,
5–16, 23
Matthew (evangelist), *Ten Virgins* 5
Messiah, *Samaritan* 4, 18. *See also*
Christ; Jesus
Michal (biblical princess), *Harlot* 11
Moses, *Fasting* 2; *Wom. Tomb* 14; *An-
nunciation* 9, 15; *Virgin* 3, 5; *Nat.
Mary Magi* 19; *Golgotha* 15
Mother of God, *Fasting* 24; *Joseph*
22; *Nat. Theot.* throughout; *Annun-
ciation* 1; *Wedd. Cana* 7, 9, 21. *See
also* Mary; Theotokos; Virgin

Nazareth, *Annunciation* 2
Noah, *Wom. Tomb* 14

Paradise, *Fasting* 4–6; *Joseph* 16; *Ten
Virgins* 30; *Nat. Mary Magi* 1, 23;
Nat. Mary Adam Eve 7, 14. *See also*
Eden
Paul (apostle), *Forerunner* 18; *Wedd.
Cana* 3
Persia, *Nat. Mary Magi* 13, 19; *Wedd.
Cana* 9
Peter (disciple), *Ten Virgins* 25;
Wom. Tomb 4–6, 13; *Bleeding
Woman* 15; *Wedd. Cana* 17; *Gol-
gotha* 3. *See also* Kephas

Pharisee(s), *Harlot* 2, 4, 6, 12–13, 15; *Nat. Mary Magi* 17. *See also* Simon (biblical Pharisee)

Philip (the Tetrarch, brother of Herod Antipas), *Forerunner* 4, 9

Potiphar's wife (biblical figure), *Joseph* 2–19, 21–22

Rahab (biblical figure), *Harlot* 7

Rebecca, *Bless. Jacob* 2–5, 11–13, 18–19

Salome (daughter of Herodias and Herod Antipas), *Forerunner* 2–9, 13–17

Samaria (biblical region), *Samaritan* Prel., 2, 4, 14, 17, 22

Samuel, *Harlot* 8; *Nat. Theot.* 6

Sarah, *Abr. Sacrifice* 7–15, 24; *Nat. Theot.* 8; *Nat. Mary Magi* 3

scripture, *Annunciation* 11; *Virgin* 6; *Wedd. Cana* 18. *See also* Bible

Simon (biblical Pharisee), *Harlot* 8, 12–17. *See also* Pharisee(s)

Simon (disciple). *See* Peter

Sinai, Mount, *Golgotha* 6

Sychar (biblical location), *Samaritan* 5, 7, 18

Symeon (New Testament figure), *Wedd. Cana* 9

Theologian (epithet for John, disciple and evangelist), *Wom. Tomb* 3. *See also* John

Theotokos, *Nat. Theot.* title; *Virgin* Prel., 8; *Wedd. Cana* Prel. *See also* Mary; Mother of God; Virgin

Tishbite (epithet for Elijah), *Elijah* 7, 33; *Forerunner* 5. *See also* Elijah

Trinity, *Samaritan* 22

Virgin, the, *Nat. Theot.* 3, 5; *Annunciation* 1–2, 7, 9, 12, 15, 18; *Virgin* 5, 7; *Nat. Mary Magi* Prel., 10, 14, 16; *Nat. Mary Adam Eve* 8; *Wedd. Cana* 6, 12–14, 21; *Golgotha* 17. *See also* Mary; Mother of God; Theotokos

Zarephath (biblical location), *Elijah* 13

Zebedee (father of disciples James and John), *Wom. Tomb* 4

Zechariah (biblical prophet), *Forerunner* 11

Zechariah (father of John the Baptist), *Forerunner* 2, 7; *Nat. Theot.* 9; *Annunciation* 7